Communism and the Emergence of Democracy

Before democracy becomes an institutionalised form of political authority, the rupture with authoritarian forms of power causes deep uncertainty about power and outcomes. This book connects the study of democratisation in eastern Europe and Russia to the emergence and crisis of communism. Wydra argues that the communist past is not simply a legacy but needs to be seen as a social organism in gestation, where critical events produce new expectations, memories, and symbols that influence meanings of democracy. By examining a series of pivotal historical events, he shows that democratisation is not just a matter of institutional design, but rather a matter of consciousness and leadership under conditions of extreme and traumatic incivility. Rather than adopting the opposition between non-democratic and democratic, Wydra argues that the communist experience must be central to the study of the emergence and nature of democracy in (post-) communist countries.

HARALD WYDRA teaches Politics at the University of Cambridge and is a fellow in Social and Political Sciences at St Catharine's College. He is the author of *Continuities in Poland's Permanent Transition* (2001).

T0371543

Communism and the Emergence of Democracy

Harald Wydra

CAMBRIDGE
UNIVERSITY PRESS

CAMBRIDGE UNIVERSITY PRESS
Cambridge, New York, Melbourne, Madrid, Cape Town, Singapore,
São Paulo, Delhi, Dubai, Tokyo, Mexico City

Cambridge University Press
The Edinburgh Building, Cambridge CB2 8RU, UK

Published in the United States of America by Cambridge University Press, New York

www.cambridge.org
Information on this title: www.cambridge.org/9780521184137

First published 2007
First paperback edition 2010

A catalogue record for this publication is available from the British Library

ISBN 978-0-521-85169-5 Hardback
ISBN 978-0-521-18413-7 Paperback

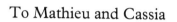To Mathieu and Cassia

Contents

Acknowledgements

This project has been carried through quite a few different stages in my professional life. Its intellectual roots go back to my time at the European University Institute in Florence. The theoretical and methodological shape was conceived when I was a lecturer in the Department of Political Science at the University of Regensburg. Large portions were drafted during a post-doctoral fellowship at the Ecole des Hautes Etudes en Sciences Sociales in Paris, for which the Deutscher Akademischer Austauschdienst and the Maison des Sciences de l'Homme provided me with generous grants. Much of the writing was accomplished at the University of Cambridge, where I have been teaching politics since 2003.

The scope of this book makes clear that I have accumulated huge intellectual and emotional debts to many friends and colleagues who have assisted this project with their scholarly wisdom, friendly advice, and generous criticism. Many of the ideas expounded here have travelled in recent years, gathering stimulating suggestions that substantially improved the argument. The audiences in Montreal, Kraków, Giessen, Warsaw, Halle, Rennes, Lublin, Canterbury, Regensburg, Edinburgh, Granada, and Berlin showed extraordinary intellectual patience with my propositions. At crucial junctures, the moral support and encouragement of some helped me to pursue a project that at times seemed too unwieldy to be mastered. My gratitude goes especially to Michel Dobry for his friendship and intellectual complicity. Arpad Szakolczai and Richard Sakwa have been extremely supportive, showing steadfast belief in this project. Jean-Pierre Dupuy, Leslie Holmes, and Claus Offe gave precious and important advice at the right time. Although the debts incurred in writing this book are too many to be listed, I would like to express my gratitude to Maurice Aymard, Verena Bauer, Daniel Beer, Victoria Bonnell, Hinnerk Bruhns, Patrick Chabal, Elena Chebankova, Marta Craveri, Alex Düben, Jacob Eisler, Marcin Frybes, Jean-François Gossiaux, Vladimir Gradev, Horst-Alfred Heinrich, Oliver Hidalgo, Wolfram Hinzen, Ben Holland, Agnes Horváth, Josef Karl, Basil Kerski, James Krapfl, Paweł Kuglarz, David Lane, Eric Langenbacher,

Chris Layne, Julie Lynch, Ulrich Mählert, Ismael Medesma, Kate Nash, Mark Nowottny, Heino Nyyssönen, Leo Max Pollack, Sergei Prozorov, Robert Pynsent, Glen Rangwala, Jutta Scherrer, Mathias Schmitz, Alan Scott, Ruth Scurr, Kazimierz Sobotka, John Street, Marie Strohe, Tobias Theiler, Vladimir Tismaneanu, Ade Trägler, Elena Trubina, Stephen Welch, Manfred Wilke, Alexander Wöll, Gergana Yankova, and Jürgen Zimmerer. Christian Strobel's work as a research assistant was extremely valuable. John Haslam's sympathy for this project was accompanied by great patience and understanding for various delays in the completion of the typescript. The extraordinarily efficient and thorough work of my copy-editor, Karen Anderson Howes, has considerably improved the typescript's quality.

Here at Cambridge, the intellectual sympathy and generosity of my colleagues in the Department of Politics were vital. John Dunn, Emile Perreau-Saussine, Mary Sarotte, Helen Thompson, and John A. Thompson read and commented on parts of the manuscript. Andreja Zivkovic edited the manuscript and gave me many opportunities to sharpen the argument in engaged discussion. I am particularly grateful to Geoffrey Hawthorn who read and extensively commented on the entire manuscript. Without his perceptive thoughts and generosity far beyond the call of duty, the writing of this book would have been far more of a struggle. While this book leaves many questions unresolved, it tries to cast doubts on established certainties. Needless to say, remaining errors and inaccuracies are entirely my own responsibility.

My gratitude also goes to my college, St Catharine's, which has made me feel at home from the very first day. Last but not least, it has been the students at Cambridge who have been a major source of inspiration, criticism, and challenge. The greatest debt, however, is to my family. My wife Anne put up with countless excuses for too many extensions of office hours and substantial periods of absence during holidays. Her endurance and unfailing care for my soul were decisive in helping me to persevere. As they have been growing up with this book, the spirited nature of my children Mathieu and Cassia has invigorated the argument and given meaning to a book that I dedicate to them.

1 Communism and democracy – a problematisation

> The history of man is older than the material world, which is the work of
> his will, older than life, which rests upon his will.   Thomas Mann

As startling as the sudden and total disintegration of the Soviet Union may
have been, the complete oblivion to which communism has quickly been
consigned has been no less surprising. Political analyses of democratisation
in eastern Europe have all but forgotten the rise of communism in Russia
after 1917 and its enormous influence on the politics of the twentieth
century. This book brings communism back into the study of democracy.
The reason for such a return is not nostalgia for a failed political experiment,
but the conviction that the rash classification of communism as an object of
study for historians overlooks its active role in shaping the post-communist
order. The unexpected collapse of communism indicated that much social
science research was prejudiced with ideas about the immutable and
eternal nature of communist power. Its sudden disappearance not only
prevented corrections of this cognitive failure but also privileged views on
communism as a 'legacy' rather than a social organism in gestation. The
momentous simultaneous transformations in all areas of politics and society
reinforced the pervasive desire in eastern Europe to break with unachieved
modernisation and anti-liberal traditions in the name of democratic development. Democratic transformations were configured as an aggregate body
of rules and norms, which would replace communism's non-democratic
system of government with Western-type models of democracy.

Structural and system-oriented perspectives alike have conceived transformation as particularisation, specification, or differentiation in the institutional framework of a political society. This positivist conception of politics,
which envisages power as an objective force used to control behaviour and
attitudes of people by means of legally enforced systems of rules, conceals
the complexity of the sociogenesis of political order.[1] Not surprisingly,

---

[1] For the distinction between the functional and the genetic inquiries into democracy, see
Dankwart Rustow, 'Transitions to Democracy: Toward a Dynamic Model', *Comparative
Politics*, 2, 3 (1970), 337–63.

much of the theorisation on post-communist political transformations has disconnected the study of a new order from the previous one.[2] Many analysts saw communism not only as preventing democratic development but also as an illusion, which arguably left nothing to posterity.

In a monistic fashion, theories of democratic consolidation have assigned the totality of representation to 'liberal' democracy. They consider democracy not as a socially endogenous process of historical articulation but as based on abstract, logical foundations of democratic individualism, the autonomy of preferences, or the institutionalised rule of law. Such democratic essentialism judges historical evolution by outcomes. Democracy has become a developmental goal, where values such as freedom, equality, and representation are disconnected from historical experience and their contingent articulation. For some, the potentiality of and the obstacles to democratisation are determined not by different points of departure but by a common destination and the imperative of convergence.[3] This presumed universality of liberal democratic arrangements as a developmental goal has obscured the fact that the evolution of democracy – both as a value and as a constitutional form of government – has not been a goal of history, but an 'accident'.[4]

If historical determinants are assumed, they tend to be framed in rather abstract blocs of 'legacies', 'genetic codes', or 'timeless antagonisms' that either obstruct or favour transitional societies' political development into consolidated democracies. Conversely, social, psychological, and symbolic foundations supporting the rise of democracy under conditions of authoritarian dictatorship have received little attention. While politics was reinvented in an environment of uncertainty, political analysis approached 'post-communist' countries with a plethora of certainties and categorisations. Unlike the communist theory about the necessary eventual fall of capitalism, social science in the West had no established theory about the crisis and breakdown of state socialism before it actually occurred. The failure of communism was taken as proof of democracy's superiority and success on a global scale. However, we have largely neglected to inquire into the nature of communist power in the Soviet Union, how it expanded into eastern Europe, and the crisis of communism before its collapse. Viewed from such culturally deterministic perspectives, countries with the 'wrong experiences' lack endogenous sources for democratic politics.

[2] Jon Elster et al., *Institutional Design in Post-Communist Societies* (Cambridge: Cambridge University Press, 1998), 1–2.
[3] Adam Przeworski, *Democracy and the Market: Political and Economic Reforms in Eastern Europe and Latin America* (Cambridge: Cambridge University Press, 1991), xii.
[4] Robert Michels, *Masse, Führer, Intellektuelle. Politisch-soziologische Aufsätze 1906–1933* (Frankfurt and New York: Campus, 1987), 183–5.

In a legitimate attempt to avoid further conceptual confusion and dis-
array about democracy, the study of democratisation processes has usually
focused on the institutionalisation of political authority, separate from
social, economic, or cultural features.[5] Historically, however, the institutional conception of political democracy emerged as a by-product of its
social foundations. Aristotle defined democracy as a regime based upon the
poor freemen, pointing out that poverty, not numerical majority, is the
decisive criterion for distinguishing democracy from oligarchy. Even if
the majority support the rule of the rich, the system remains an oligarchy.
Even if the rule of the poor is based only on a minority, it is still termed a
democracy.[6] Alexis de Tocqueville's philosophical anthropology focused
on psychological universals such as desires, beliefs, and attitudes to explain
human action by subsuming apparently different events under the same
heading.[7] Democracy unites people with a psychological bond according to
which everybody forms his own judgement under the spell of an invisible
authority, public opinion. In such a view, social conditions of equality
produce passions, desires, and beliefs, for which anything can be sacrificed
including love of liberty. Here is where the individual is subordinated
to anonymous powers such as the 'state', the 'people', or 'society'. These
anonymous powers, however, are a precondition rather than a result of
a social equilibrium based on accepted rules and norms. While Tocqueville's
Democracy in America was concerned with relatively predictable outcomes
in a political system of institutions in equilibrium, the central idea in his work
on *The Old Regime and the Revolution* focuses on understanding how the
passage from a state of equilibrium to another state occurs and what it entails.

The collapse of communism demonstrated the inconsistency of deterministic accounts. If totalitarianism was an oppressive force capable of
changing human nature and invading the depths of the human mind, how
could communism implode without any considerable resistance? If political democracy and autonomous civil society were non-existent before
the collapse of communism, on what grounds can one claim that autonomous political elites will adhere to an ethics of responsibility in supporting
democratic transitions and consolidations? If modernisation has been the
underlying force of political development, why is the evolution of democratic development in cases such as post-communist Russia considered to
be problematic at best? If there has been a providential tendency towards

---

[5] This conceptual confusion is reflected in more than 550 'subtypes' of democracy: David
Collier and Steven Levitsky, 'Democracy with Adjectives: Conceptual Innovation in
Comparative Research', *World Politics*, 49, 3 (1997), 430–51.
[6] Aristotle, *Politics*, ed. Stephen Everson (Cambridge: Cambridge University Press, 1988),
Book iv 1290b and Book iii 1280a.
[7] Jon Elster, *Political Psychology* (Cambridge: Cambridge University Press, 1993), 140.

democracy, why has the literature on democratic transformations largely dismissed the experiences, beliefs, values, and psychology of social movements and dissidence before the victory of the principles of liberal political democracy?

A political anthropology of transformative experiences

Western analysts understood democratisation as the set of political processes in the external world of state institutions. They focus mainly on the emergence of democratic elections, voting procedures, party systems, parliaments, governments, economic agencies, and legal institutions that will entail the equilibrium of a constituted political order. Conversely, this book suggests that any inquiry into the emergence of democracy needs to consider the aspirations, expectations, and hopes formulated by people under conditions of oppression and the denial of democratic rights and opportunities. To understand the emergence of democracy, therefore, we need to engage with the experiential basis of communism by examining the potential for the emergence of something new, whose authority in the newly constituted order may be legitimate and durable. Historically, democratic actors challenged monolithic political authority not on the basis of claims that they were endowed with legal guarantees, but under conditions of existential uncertainty, exposed to threats to their own life, and fundamentally aware of the brokenness of political reality. Democracy as a constitutional form has at its root unconstitutional acts beyond the boundaries of existing law. Like all processes of state-formation or changes of regime in the modern world, communism and democracy have been, to an important extent, based on a rupture of elite consciousness from previous orders of representation and political authority. Democratisation has not always involved a meaningful pattern of growth of a new regime after the breakdown of an old one. Contingent upon the conquest of the empty space of power and its own attendant legitimisation, it has been a lengthy, ongoing process of narrative construction and symbolic articulation.

Rather than adapt political reality to institutions, values, and ideologies dominant in other geopolitical contexts, one should try to problematise their emergence. While political science is largely interested in specifying variables and attributes of democracy that distinguish it from non-democracy, the inquiry into foundations of democracy should take the analyst deeper into history than he has commonly been willing to go.[8] Political analysis should delineate its object of study by taking into

---

[8] Rustow, 'Transitions to Democracy'.

account haphazard and contingent historical reality. While many assume a 'causality' of democracy, which would be justified by the 'outcome', or try to measure its adequacy with a predominant 'model', the historical evolution of democracy has not been a predetermined course towards an end goal of development. In Max Weber's terms, if there is any meaningful usage of 'object' at all, it can only be a historical individual that is a complex set of correlations in historical reality that can be connected as culturally meaningful.[9] Whereas the distant analyst can prescribe 'what democracy is', the manifold social foundations of a historically articulated process are not merely reified 'legacies', 'conditions', or variations in 'outcomes', but themselves define the object of study.

This book sets democracy into the dramatic and contingent context of highly disruptive events characteristic of the rise and fall of communism. A number of recent studies have shown how to integrate the communist experience and its practices in the production of new meanings and symbols.[10] Similarly, recent work on democratisation has emphasised the importance of domestic cultural aspects against dominant value-based interpretations of Western-type democracy.[11] The empirical focus of this book is an interpretive understanding of great events such as the October Revolution, the Second World War, the 'small' revolutions in eastern Europe, and the disarticulation of communism. While these events entailed momentous transformations in the political and social world, they were also existential crises entailing significant disruptions not only because political authority was deeply contested but also because acquired meanings dissolved, putting pasts and futures at stake. These crises were, to an important extent, processes of communion among those dependent on a common cause, aspiring to a collective identity, which would be determined against the outside.

---

[9] Max Weber, *Gesammelte Aufsätze zur Religionssoziologie* (Tübingen: Mohr, 1988), 30–1.
[10] Agnes Horváth and Arpád Szakolczai, *The Dissolution of Communist Power: The Case of Hungary* (London: Routledge, 1992); Stephen Kotkin, *Magnetic Mountain: Stalinism as a Civilization* (Berkeley: University of California Press, 1995); Stephen E. Hanson, *Time and Revolution: Marxism and the Design of Soviet Institutions* (Chapel Hill and London: University of North Carolina Press, 1997); Michael Urban et al., *The Rebirth of Politics in Russia* (Cambridge: Cambridge University Press, 1997); Oleg Kharkhordin, *The Collective and the Individual in Russia: A Study of Practices* (Berkeley: University of California Press, 1999).
[11] Nicolai Petro, *The Rebirth of Russian Democracy: An Interpretation of Political Culture* (Cambridge, MA: Harvard University Press, 1995); Jeffrey Isaac, *Democracy in Dark Times* (Ithaca and London: Cornell University Press, 1998); Richard Sakwa, ed., *The Experience of Democratisation* (London: Macmillan, 1999); John Dryzek and Leslie Holmes, *Post-Communist Democratization* (Cambridge: Cambridge University Press, 2002); Laurence Whitehead, *Democratisation: Theory and Experience* (Oxford: Oxford University Press, 2002).

If these events are included in the study of democratisation, it is not because any of these events is 'democratic' in terms of a constitutional form. Rather, these experiences have had a decisive influence on attitudes and practices of individuals, meanings of democracy, and the development of the concept. A political anthropology shifts attention away from positivist or a priori normative models that precede action and towards experiences of historical ruptures. The dual-faceted approach characteristic of the modern episteme either reduces experience to sense perception, as in the case of empiricism and positivism, or assumes experiences are chaotic and unstructured, and therefore conceivable only through the categories of the mind. This book, in contrast, understands transformative experiences in a double sense. Analytically, transformative experiences can be considered as a methodological tool by which to understand the 'rationality' of action in dramatic revolutionary situations characterised by uncertainty and the brokenness of political reality. Substantially, transformative experiences refer to the living through of exceptional circumstances at critical junctures by contemporaries and the emergence of new states of consciousness. A political anthropology of transformative experiences examines how breakdowns of different political orders and their attendant symbolic universes transform consciousness, meanings, and beliefs in individuals.

In other words, the breakdown and the consolidation of a regime need to be set in the context of an irruption in the perceived and symbolically sustained, ordered course of life. In the tradition established by Friedrich Nietzsche and Wilhelm Dilthey, the pioneering studies by Max Weber, Eric Voegelin, Michel Foucault, Norbert Elias, and Claude Lefort have suggested that the constitution of political subjects, collective and individual, occurs through experiences and ensuing fundamental changes in consciousness.[12] The social foundations of politics are crucial because it is the meaning of our experience, and not the ontological structure of the objects such as institutions, states, or systems, that constitutes reality.[13] Linking the study of political order to the historically specific symbolism of its institution suggests that history is not primarily a sequence of well-articulated and stable political orders. It is the brokenness of political

---

[12] This applies, for instance, to Max Weber's study of the spirit of capitalism, Norbert Elias's work on court society and the civilising process, Eric Voegelin's hypothesis of the Gnostic revolt as a source of modernity, or Michel Foucault's disciplinary society. For a recent conceptualisation of 'reflexive historical sociology' as understanding the origins of modernity, see Arpad Szakolczai, *Reflexive Historical Sociology* (London: Routledge, 2000).

[13] Alfred Schütz, *Collected Papers*, vol. I, *The Problem of Social Reality*, ed. and intro. Maurice Natanson (The Hague: Martinus Nijhoff, 1971), 207–59.

reality and the dissolution of order that make up the essence of history. If there is continuity and repetition, it is the repetition of disarticulation, which should inform inquiries into the establishment of political order. This is not because rupture is the rule, but because the exceptional condition of disarticulation of order will influence the articulation of new political authority most profoundly. This is why understanding the emergence of a constitutional form requires recovering the primacy of the historical event (*événementialiser*).[14] It goes along with the need to disentangle the social foundations of underdetermined moments of disorder, to take into account a rupture of evidence or of the taken-for-granted.

An understanding of the political as experience goes beyond a scientific approach in which knowledge finds its self-assurance by defining political reality in terms of a sovereign distance between the subject and the social.[15] The institution of the social order cannot be limited to the comparison of structures and systems as objective forces. Rather, it is simultaneously confronted with the question of its own institution. The historical process of human relations creates meaning and produces markers for distinguishing between true and false, just and unjust, and imaginary and real. It also establishes the horizons of human beings' relations with one another and with the world. In Michel Foucault's terms, 'history becomes "effective" to the degree that it introduces discontinuity into our very being – as it divides our emotions, dramatises our instincts, multiplies our body and sets it against itself'.[16]

A political anthropology of transformative experiences adopts three different but interrelated perspectives on discontinuity in the historical evolution of communism. Initially, the emergence of communism and democracy require understanding the formation of consciousness and dispositions of actors in the authority vacuum of the empty space of power. Revolutionary situations and critical junctures of history are not only chaotic and anarchical but also have their own rationality that produces new states of consciousness. Furthermore, revolutionary events can be approached through the acts of symbolisation that re-establish the equilibrium lost by the dissolution of order, structures, and markers of certainty. Eventually, one needs to acknowledge that such events have had enormous effects on identities as well as on interpretations of pasts and futures. This is why interpretations of meaning need to address the power of memory and the deconstruction of 'second reality' as

[14] Michel Foucault, *Dits et écrits 1976–1988*, vol. IV (Paris: Gallimard, 2001), 23–5.
[15] Claude Lefort, *Democracy and Political Theory* (Cambridge: Polity Press, 1988), 220–1.
[16] Michel Foucault, 'Nietzsche, Genealogy, History', in Paul Rabinow, ed., *The Foucault Reader* (London: Penguin, 1984), 88.

two crucial methods of denouncing the logic of violence characteristic of communism.

Approaching the empty space of power

An important tradition in democratic theory has reduced power to the capacity of an institutionalised set of rules and norms to control the actions, behaviour, and responses of citizens.[17] This way of defining political authority as a complex set of procedures that compel the compliance of the citizenry has focused on the limiting effects of power through accountability and rule of law. Similarly, constitutionalism includes determinants of governmental decisions and prescribed rules that control the behaviour of citizens and influence the legitimate distribution of power among government officials. Historically and logically, however, the constitution of power in a revolution means not the limitation but the foundation and correct distribution of power. In the struggle over the American Constitution, for instance, the main question was not about 'limited' government but about how to establish power.[18] Montesquieu's suggestion that 'power arrests power' is not synonymous with a claim that the power of laws checks the power of man. Laws do not pre-exist their formalisation in the sense of imposed standards, commands, or positivist legality.

In this spirit, a political anthropology of transformative experiences transcends the classificatory category of politics as constituted power. Following Claude Lefort's distinction between *la politique* (politics) and *le politique* (the political), one must differentiate between two realities: on the one hand, a preconstituted domain of politics as delimited within the social order against the non-political fields of society or the economy; on the other, the conditions under which a political order is instituted in social and historical reality with the aim at constituting order on the basis of constitutive principles. The essence of politics is not in the constituted order of norms and rules but is found in the exception, where the power of real life breaks through the crust of a mechanism that has become torpid through repetition.[19] The essence of sovereignty is not in the monopoly of sanction or power but in the monopoly of decision.

---

[17] Robert A. Dahl, *A Preface to Democratic Theory* (Chicago and London: University of Chicago Press, 1956), 13 and 135.
[18] Hannah Arendt, *On Revolution* (London: Faber and Faber, 1963), 146–8.
[19] Carl Schmitt, *The Concept of the Political* (Chicago and London: University of Chicago Press, 1996), 15.

The conditions of institutionalised government conceal that constituent power is logically prior to constitutional arrangements. Historically, the structure of sovereignty is likely to be articulated in exceptional situations of an authority vacuum. Thus, it is reasonable to assume that no political act ever conforms to the standard of being legitimate in terms of a generally accepted sovereign authority.[20] As political acts always lack full legitimacy when enacted, sovereignty occurs with a temporal gap between act and the consent that approves and enables it. The French Revolution not only targeted the absolute power of the monarch, but had to legitimate a newly erected constitutional order whose founders were themselves unconstitutional. Their authority to set down the fundamental law relied on the need to define identities and interests of the people not by means of constitutionally granted political authority but in a legal void. Sieyès's distinction between constituent power and constituted power suggested that the authority of the constituted power could not be guaranteed by the constituent power, as the latter was prior to the constitution itself.[21] The exercise of real power by government had its roots in the nation as the constituent power, which was supposed to be formed solely by natural law and not to be subject to legal prescriptions formulated in positive constitutions. The national will as the origin of all legality, therefore, would always be seen as relying not on a differentiated social order regulated by law, but on a national spirit articulated under exceptional circumstances.

For Rousseau, the founding of a general will as the precondition for sovereignty and democratic participation would be paradoxical. In his view, for an emerging people to follow the fundamental rules of statecraft embodied in the general will, the effect (social spirit) would have to become the cause, and the cause (good laws) would have to become the effect. The problem was how to establish either condition without the previous attainment of the other on which it depends.[22] Seeking practical solutions to this paradox, the French revolutionaries answered with replacing the divine right of kings by what Edgar Quinet called a peo-ple-God (*peuple-Dieu*).[23] They had followed Rousseau's observation that, to establish the validity of manmade laws, one actually would need gods. The task of finding a sound principle of sovereignty for the French nation

---

[20] Paul Ricoeur, 'The Political Paradox', in William E. Connolly, ed., *Legitimacy and the State* (New York: New York University Press, 1984), 254.
[21] Emmanuel Joseph Sieyès, *Political Writings*, ed. Michael Sonenscher (Indianapolis and Cambridge: Hackett, 2003), 136–7.
[22] Jean-Jacques Rousseau, *The Social Contract and Discourses*, trans. and intro. G. D. H. Cole (London: Dent, 1993), 193–5.
[23] Claude Lefort, *Essais sur le politique* (Paris: Seuil, 1986), 176.

in a revolutionary situation required putting the law above man.[24] On the one hand, the people were to become citizens, i.e. subjects who would govern themselves. On the other hand, to substitute a secular principle for the belief in divine right, they would need to inspire an awesome, almost mystical, authority. The radical reorientation of political purpose drew not on pre-existing theoretical principles, but required the mobilisation in people's minds and hearts of a belief, if not of a cult, of the impossible. Yet, the practical business of reconstructing a social order on the basis of powerful, hypothetical futures could not be achieved without destruction, bloodshed, and annihilation of human life, which peaked in the revolutionary terror. Thus, the idealisation of the People-God as the principle of sovereignty came at the expense of sacrificing lives of human beings that made up the 'people'.

Historically, therefore, the exception is not only a theoretical principle. Modern revolutions with their intense collective violence and their lofty, idealised visions of hypothetical futures have deeply ambivalent effects of destructive and formative power. The Janus-like character of revolutions combines the elegant, abstract, humanitarian face that is creative of constitutional norms with the crude, violent, rather nightmarish side where the revolutionary dynamics not only overcomes theoretical principles or concepts, but also destroys human life.[25] As Claude Lefort has suggested, modern democracy is riddled with this ambivalence as it emanates from the dramatic context of the downfall of absolutist monarchy, the revolutionary conflict between antagonistic forces struggling to attain political domination, and the attendant emptiness of the space of power. Democracy's crucial characteristic consists in the dissolution of 'markers of certainty'. Whereas before the nineteenth century political society relied on largely determined relations between corporate parts of society, the 'democratic moment' introduced radical indeterminacy by disentangling the legitimate basis of political power, the sources of moral and legal norms, and the production of knowledge. The modern democratic revolution was about the transformation from power incorporated in two kinds of bodies, the body of the king and the corporate social body.[26] In monarchies, power was incorporated in the body of the king, as the body of the king gave the body to society. Democratic rule, on the other hand, is not entitled to incorporate or appropriate power, as the

---

[24] Arendt, *On Revolution*, 184.
[25] John Dunn, *Modern Revolutions*, 2nd edn (Cambridge: Cambridge University Press, 1989), 4.
[26] Claude Lefort, *The Political Forms of Modern Society: Bureaucracy, Democracy, Totalitarianism* (Cambridge: Polity Press, 1986), 300–5.

exercise of power becomes subject to a periodic competition for this power. Being the rule of the people in their own interest, power in a democracy emanates from the people but it belongs to *nobody*. This empty space of power comes along with the 'dis-incorporation' of individuals who are separated from corporate bodies or 'natural' hierarchies to become the smallest units of the new type of social relations. This double dis-incorporation of the social body and the monolithic political body means that democracy in the modern era must take account of the depth of historical rupture and the profound reversals in meanings, representations, and symbols.

While this idea of constituent power is crucial for modern constitutionalism and the idea of the nation-state, it also intimates that the separation between law and violence is not as clear as constitutional government in modern states would suggest. Although the state as a system of constitutionally based institutions hedges violence by monopolising it, the violent nature of a pre-state community is not removed. Already in Hobbes's *Leviathan* the state of nature survives in the person of the sovereign. The sovereign preserves his *ius naturale contra omnes* and thus is not subject to civil laws.[27] Incorporating the state of nature in society becomes the basis for sovereignty, thus suggesting a lack of distinction between nature and culture, or violence and law. The sovereign conserves the freedom to repeal the laws that trouble him and thus 'he that can bind can release'. In communist regimes, Trotsky's concept of the permanent revolution or Mao's uninterrupted revolution symbolised the continuity of revolutionary constituent power in the constituted power of a 'system'. The autonomy of the communist party and its claim to define law, history, and knowledge coexisted in a parallel fashion with the constituted elements of the state. The authority to decide, in the form of a verdict on life and death for the sake of preserving domestic peace, requires not merely the declaration of an internal enemy but a fight against a real enemy.[28]

As Giorgio Agamben has argued, the fundamental antagonism of modern politics is not the one between friend and enemy but between bare life (*zoē*) and political existence (*bios*).[29] While in ancient Greece *zoē* did not belong to the public realm, modern politics is based on the entry of *zoē* into the sphere of the polis. The constitutional foundation of modern democracy in *habeas corpus* of 1679 did not make the old subject

[27] Thomas Hobbes, *Leviathan*, ed. Richard Tuck (Cambridge: Cambridge University Press, 1991), chap. 26, II.
[28] Schmitt, *The Concept of the Political*, 46–9.
[29] Giorgio Agamben, *Homo Sacer: Sovereign Power and Bare Life* (Stanford: Stanford University Press, 1998).

of feudal relations, the free man, or the future citizen but the body (*corpus*) the new subject of politics. The revolutionary rupture of 1789 put crowd action and bare life on to the stage of politics. The overthrow of feudal order resulted in the constitution of sovereign power, which articulated political society by including the politicisation of bare life with its poten- tially beneficial and destructive effects. The sovereign structure of law derives its peculiar and original force from the state of exception in which fact and law are indistinguishable.[30] If the exception is the structure of sovereignty, then it ceases to be an exclusively political concept or jurid- ical category. The exception is the originary structure in which the crea- tion of law refers to life and includes it in itself by suspending it.

The modern secular state as the holder of the legitimate monopoly of the means of violence hedges violence in the interests of the security of its citizens but it does not make violence disappear. The state brought life into the centre of politics not only in terms of protecting inalienable rights but also in terms of life's politicisation. It came to dispose of life by controlling, disciplining, and, if necessary, annihilating it as a tool for establishing and maintaining power. While the reference to the highest value of the collective body, human life, took the place of a transcendental God, the disruptions of 'normal politics' threatened the body-politic by the dangerous passions of crowds and self-interested factions, but also of public opinion. Similarly, the state's capability of waging war and of disposing of the people's lives implies the double possibility of expecting from its own members the readiness to unhesitatingly kill enemies and to die for the nation.

In this vein, modern democracy has been ambivalent about life as its highest value, an ambivalence that is concealed in the principle of pre- serving human life and dignity in constituted power, but that becomes apparent in the empty space of power. The people are simultaneously the source of power and its victims, due to the granting of control over individuals' lives to the state. While revolutionary violence excludes specific parts of the people (in terms of bare life) by mass violence and terror, it includes the 'people' in terms of articulating the 'nation' or the 'dictatorship of the proletariat' as a representational principle with the capacity of constituent power. If dates such as 1789, 1917, 1956, 1968, 1980/1, or 1989 arouse emotions even today, this is because the constitution of political authority has not exclusively been a matter of political reason or positivist legality, but has been generated through the

---

[30] Agamben, *Homo Sacer*, 27–9.

politicisation of bare life. The revolutionary rupture in 1789 introduced 'democratic politics', with models of popular sovereignty such as 'the nation' and 'republicanism'. Yet, the democratic moment of the revolutionary rupture contained the potential for totalitarian politics. Tocqueville's conceptualisation of social democracy was characterised by the premonition of its reversal, already presaging that old notions such as despotism or tyranny would not be sufficient to make sense of it.[31] The paradox of modern democracy consists in the fact that it wants to put the freedom and happiness of men into play in the very place – bare life – that before had marked their subjugation.[32] The politicisation of people's bodily existence into the rationales of state order has to acknowledge that the democratic moment is not only about representation but also includes the dark sides of democracy. Although democracy's primary value has arguably been the expectation of the happiness of people, it has been incapable of saving *zoē*, as the bare life of the double sovereign cannot be sacrificed yet may, nevertheless, be killed.

Having said this, I would emphasise that introducing the empty space of power as the exception is not intended to adopt an essentialist approach to politics, which would root political order in a foundational principle. Foundationalist political philosophy has postulated, in a monistic fashion, one source or foundation of politics.[33] Whether this foundation is found in self-preservation (Hobbes), freedom (Locke), reason (Rousseau, Kant), history (Hegel, Marx), or conflict (Schmitt), there seems to be a monism of political reality. A similarly foundationalist view is presented by Hannah Arendt's idealisation of the beginning of modern politics in the unique act of foundation of the American Constitution, where political order was established devoid of all secrets, legends, or mythical imaginations.[34] In her view, this act of foundation succeeded in overcoming the historical continuum by postulating a starting point of a new chain of events, and a new consciousness of historical time. Such an idealisation of a 'beginning' rests upon a logical abstraction, which eludes the question of history, where unexpected occurrences can give significance to formerly meaningless patterns and can generate new forms and styles of existence in the tissue of social life. Therefore, while sovereignty articulates in the exception, this exception is not an

---

[31] Alexis de Tocqueville, *Democracy in America: The Complete and Unabridged*, 2 vols., trans. Henry Reeve (New York: Bantam Classic, 2000), 869.
[32] Agamben, *Homo Sacer*, 9–10.
[33] F. R. Ankersmit, *Political Representation* (Stanford: Stanford University Press, 2002), 163–70.
[34] Arendt, *On Revolution*.

abstract theory of chaos preceding order, but it points to the historically concrete situation that comes about once order is suspended. The exception represents the permanently present aspect of politics, as the realisation of the permanent precariousness of life. The irruption of crisis and the dislocation of existing structures is, in anthropological terms, a liminal situation, where the significant upheaval of everyday life introduces a dramatic dimension on a social scale.[35]

As the path-breaking works of Michel Dobry and William Sewell have argued, such 'conjunctural structures' or 'fluid conjunctures' are not simply chaotic but show certain regularities of thought, behaviour, and symbolic 'structures'.[36] Dramatic experiences are not synonymous with anarchy or social void but are in themselves structured and intelligible, and can be analysed on their own terms. A central concern for a new science of politics, as suggested by Tocqueville, Voegelin, or Lefort, was to show that the existence of political societies should not be measured by comparing order and disorder.[37] For these theorists, the history of human arrangements has not been a series of variations in scientifically measurable outcomes but an open-ended process of tensions between order and disorder, between truth and the deformation of reality. History is not a continuous stream of meaningful existence but scattered with significant disruptions, where meaningful existence, truth, and the sense of reality are deformed. 'Existence has the structure of the in-between, of the Platonic *metaxy*, and if anything is constant in the history of mankind it is the language of tension between life and death, immortality and mortality, perfection and imperfection, time and timelessness; between order and disorder, truth and untruth, sense and senselessness of existence.'[38] Social and individual life proceed somewhere between the imaginary extremes of absolute order and chaotic, often anarchic conflict. While there is an endless tension between the two extremes as potential scenarios, there is also remarkable similarity as regards the anthropological basis of such disruptions.

[35] Victor Turner, *On the Edge of the Bush* (Tucson: University of Arizona Press, 1985), 215–21.
[36] Michel Dobry, *Sociologie des crises politiques* (Paris: PUF, 1986); William Sewell, 'Historical Events as Transformations of Structures: Inventing Revolution at the Bastille', *Theory and Society*, 25 (1996), 841–81.
[37] Tocqueville, *Democracy in America*, 8; Eric Voegelin, *The New Science of Politics: An Introduction* (Chicago and London: University of Chicago Press, 1987); Lefort, *Essais sur le politique*, 20.
[38] Eric Voegelin, *The Collected Works*, vol. XII, *Published Essays 1966–1985* (Baton Rouge and London: Louisiana State University Press, 1990), 'Equivalences of Experience and Symbolization in History', 119.

Critical events and their symbolisations

Political transformations hinge on the fluid conjuncture of critical events as they occur through the simultaneous emergence of constitutional order and the concealment of the method of its establishment. Despite their potentially destructive elements, extraordinary revolutionary situations are therefore not only interruptions of peaceful order but they also create internal forces that will eventually sustain a new order. Any authoritative and constitutive act of foundation is bound to reverse cultural representations, legitimate meanings, and the psychology of public opinion. These processes of articulation are relevant for democratisation, as they themselves create symbols, beliefs, and meanings, which become discursive patterns that sustain legitimacy. In many ways, institutions are like medicines. Their success depends not only on their quality or dosage but also on the nature of the body they are applied to. They can succeed in the long term only if the body accepts the cure.

To solve the problem of constitutive foundations, we need to accept that the notion of constitution harbours a double meaning. First, it concerns the results of such constitutive acts, i.e. constitution in the sense of a written document and the rules and laws emanating from it.[39] Second, it can refer to a constitutive act that precedes a regime and constitutes a people as a political community. In the understanding of Thomas Paine, the American Constitution was not the act of a government, but of a people constituting a government. The writers of the American Constitution understood themselves as founders relying upon the authority of their act of foundation. While the main problem of the founders of the United States was not about how to limit power but how to establish it, the French revolutionaries were concerned with dismantling a feudal order. Therefore, constitutional principles such as the Declaration of the Rights of Man and the Citizen postulated rights that did not indicate the limitations of lawful government but were its very foundation. The constitutional process in France between 1789 and 1791 was confronted with the difficulty of how to make intelligible a new constitution for a body-politic that had a natural constitution.[40] Moreover, if the sovereignty of the nation could create a constitution *de novo*, could it not be abolished and replaced on the grounds of the same principle?

---

[39] Arendt, *On Revolution*, 142–5.
[40] Keith Michael Baker, 'Constitution', in François Furet and Mona Ozouf, eds., *Dictionnaire critique de la Révolution Française. Institutions et créations* (Paris: Flammarion, 1992), 179–205.

The nation can be designated as the ultimate source of constituent power only if there is a credible reciprocity between leaders and followers. This cannot be achieved without the diffusion of democratic consciousness into the social realm. Before democracy is institutionalised, the 'people' must acquire a self-consciousness that power emanates from it and is exercised by it (or its representatives) for the good of the whole community. As the idea of popular government rests upon an unconstitutional act, it must be enacted by a specific type of subjectivity. The symbolism by which a collective community accepts representation of its power requires that individuals recognise the Other as a fellow human being.

To my knowledge, the most far-reaching theory that tries to explain the foundation of culture and social order by connecting the modalities of a historically real violent crisis with a generating principle of collective symbolism that is constantly hidden once culture and society are instituted is René Girard's mimetic theory.[41] According to Girard, cultural and social order is built upon the ritualisation of a sacrificial unique victim. Social order emanates from an exceptionally traumatic experience where, in the absence of binding legal relations, the expulsion of bare life and the collective recognition of responsibility for this act provide the generative principle. Mimetic theory is congruous with the central idea of modern political theory that violence and the fear of violence are generative of order. The mimetic hypothesis, however, does not assume man's innately dangerous nature but conjectures that mimetic behaviour is the anthropological constant in human relations. Under conditions of legally guaranteed and culturally sustained order, mimetic relations are unconscious processes of imitation that have a 'positive' capacity for the development of culture, education, and knowledge. Their 'negative' capacity arises from the boundlessness of action, where legal boundaries and hierarchical social differentiations are suspended. The reciprocity of a cycle of vengeance and reprisals is brought to an end by the murder, death, or expulsion of a sacrificial victim upon which the community unanimously unburdens their guilt. The physical annihilation of a victim becomes the guarantee for peace and stability in the community. The expulsion of the scapegoat is not a mere mythological narrative but a concrete murder that becomes a social practice in the ritualised commemoration of this original unanimity.[42]

---

[41] René Girard, *Violence and the Sacred* (Baltimore: Johns Hopkins University Press, 1977), 81; Girard, *Things Hidden Since the Foundation of the World* (Baltimore: Johns Hopkins University Press, 1987), 40.
[42] René Girard, *The Scapegoat* (Baltimore: Johns Hopkins University Press, 1982).

Mimetic theory shares Hobbes's realism about the asocial nature of man and rejects Aristotle's claim about his natural sociability. It is, however, critical of the assumption of a hypothetical state of nature. Although Hobbes's biographical background is the experience of dissolution of order in the English civil war, his theory of politics is not based on historical experience but on a philosophical construction, which conceives of violence as an objective force in a hypothetical state of nature. Mimetic violence, however, refers to the concrete extreme experiences of bloodshed, hatred, and vengeance, with their real effects on bodies, minds, and memories.[43] At the origin of the pacification of society is a 'strategy' to expel violence that emanates from the centre of the community that lived through the act of violence.

The consequences of mimetic rivalry imply that the social foundations of order can be expressed by analogy to Kant's unsocial sociability, according to which the development of human capacities is driven by individual competition for honour, power, or property with the aim of securing status and recognition.[44] The reciprocity of violence between humans, the emotional reactions to such violence, and the unconscious processes of exclusion and integration are all conducive to the production of collective symbolism that sustains order. Much like Girard, Hobbes constructs social order from the perception of the victim, not of the perpetrator. Yet Hobbes's state of nature is not a historical occurrence, which would be chronologically prior to the state, but a principle based on a thought experiment that projects what would happen once this state is dissolved.[45] In a Hobbesian view, the autonomy of individual preferences, as claimed by different versions of democratic individualism, is not affected by emotions, bloodshed, and vengeance. The state of nature is a thought experiment, where the isolation of individuals does not allow for mutual recognition, compassion, or reconciliation. Hobbes's deep insights into the psychology of man, therefore, were achieved at the expense of a bias in his anthropology. In his scathing critique of human passions, Hobbes made human anthropology world-immanent by elevating the disease of self-conceit and pride into the primary characteristic of the individual. While Augustine had distinguished between the *amor Dei* and the *amor sui*, Hobbes's solution focused on the isolated individual who is not oriented towards a common purpose or collective good but

---

[43] For the genealogy of the concept crisis, especially about how Enlightenment thought eclipsed the experiential reality of crisis, see Reinhart Koselleck, *Critique and Crisis: Enlightenment and the Pathogenesis of Modern Society* (Oxford: Berg Publishers, 1988).

[44] Immanuel Kant, 'Idea for a Universal History with a Cosmopolitan Intent', in *Kant, Perpetual Peace and Other Essays*, ed. Ted Humphrey (Indianapolis: Hackett, 1983), 29–40.

[45] Hobbes, *De cive*, ed. H. Warrender (Oxford: Oxford University Press, 1983), 79–80.

motivated only by his passions. In his model, social and political relations are a means for the pursuit of self-preservation by individuals as an absolute end. The idea that individuals not yet involved in social relations originally know their own interests and the consequences of their choices, however, seems to be logically incoherent. This individualistic theory of social order does not explain how self-preservation as the central interest of the individual emerges under conditions in which individuals are fundamentally isolated from each other. For a social order to be possible, individuals must first recognise each other's worth of being preserved. Self-preservation is a relational concept, as we all need to see the worth of our preservation recognised by other human beings.[46]

While in Hobbes's *Leviathan* the sovereign is substantially inclusive, as he incorporates his subject as one person, the overall structure of the social contract works on the basis of exclusion. It leaves the sovereign outside the reciprocal contract of everyone with everyone, making this social contract a unity minus one. In a similar vein, Rousseau's idea of a democracy in a nation requires the presence of an enemy as a precondition for a national unity and indivisibility. Social contract theory, by analogy with classical myths, follows the sacrificial logic whereby a victim is transfigured both for the worse as a scapegoat to be expelled and for the better in terms of bringing peace to the community. In the anthropology provided by mimetic theory, the reciprocity of hatred, vengeance, and murder can be overcome by interpretation. Rather than to ritualise the collectively approved guilt of the victim, individuals may recognise the victim's innocence. In this case the pacifying consequence of ritual is not in the commemoration of the murder, but in the commemoration of the innocence of the victim. According to Girard, the Gospels are the only texts that uncover the mechanisms upon which myths are based. A victim becomes a sacrificial one not due to its physical state but due to the meaning ascribed to this state. This inherent demythologisation is due to the fact that the resurrection of Jesus entailed a dissident movement in the social world. The dissemination of Christian doctrine through the disciples insisted on the innocence of the victim and thus broke the circle of ritual sacrifice as the foundation myth of culture. If it had not been for this dissident movement, the death of Jesus would have become just another mythical account, which would have assembled the perpetrators around the victim who is both sacrificed and divinised.

---

[46] Alessandro Pizzorno, 'On the Individualistic Theory of Social Order', in Pierre Bourdieu and James Coleman, eds., *Social Theory for a Changing Society* (Boulder: Westview Press, 1991), 218–21.

The mimetic cycle of vengeance and violence draws people to follow the collective unconscious drive towards persecution, denunciation, or witch hunting. Yet history provides manifold examples where people not only act in pursuit of their self-interest and self-preservation. They can also act against their self-interest if they are willing to sacrifice their position in society, their prestige, or even their life for the sake of denouncing the sacrificial logic in the name of living in truth. Historically, freedom cannot be assumed as a constituted given protected by sovereignty and the law. As Jan Patočka has suggested, freedom is possible only as a work of consciousness that relies upon experiences of communities of fate.[47] The direct confrontation with the precariousness of life in the front lines of a war or in the persistent humiliation by a totalitarian regime exposes life as unsheltered and unprotected by the guarantees of the rule of law. Freedom cannot be assumed to pre-exist unsheltered life but rather arises from the solidarity of the shaken: that is, from those who have learnt to cope with precarious existential conditions and to stand up against them in a fearless and determined manner. Hence, an interpretive inquiry into democratisation of a given political order should avoid the fatalist temptation of man's subordination to state violence as well as the idealist temptation of seeing liberal democracy as a developmental goal. Rather, it needs to problematise how communities of fate make sense of the unconstitutionality of political existence.

Approaching the emergence of democracy, therefore, requires an engagement with events in which many of the taken-for-granted essentials of democracy such as sovereignty, rule of law, or individual freedom are not only not given but substantially threatened. Communities of fate can potentially give rise to 'traditions' with a fully developed identity, or even to 'movements', which are politically active within history and whose future becomes an explicit concern of its members.[48] The formation of meaning does not depend on timeless and trans-historical symbols with an unchangeable content, but rather emerges as symbolic processes of signification that may either placate or arouse mass publics.[49] In Eric Voegelin's view, symbolisations of experiences are attempts at making sense of the uncertainty of existence by restoring legitimate and meaningful existence. When structural constraints of political authority, social control, legal order, or tradition are weakened, the crisis threatens the basis of human

---

[47] Jan Patočka, *Heretical Essays in the Philosophy of History*, ed. James Dodd (Chicago and La Salle: Open Court, 1996), 38–9 and 134–5.
[48] Stefan Rossbach, *Gnostic Wars: The Cold War in the Context of a History of Western Spirituality* (Edinburgh: Edinburgh University Press, 1999), 15.
[49] Peter Berger and Thomas Luckmann, *The Social Construction of Reality* (London and New York: Penguin Books, 1966), 113.

existence and demands an existential response to it. Therefore, the study of human arrangements with a view to facts, data, and events in the external world is only one important component of 'political reality'. Human arrangements are also a little world, a cosmion, illuminated with meaning from within by the human beings who continuously create and bear it as the mode and condition of their self-realisation.[50] In current usage, symbols evoke an impression of being representative of something real, turning them into a decorative element. The notion of a merely 'symbolic' act, for instance, appears to oppose it to the 'real' effects of material forces. Symbolisations, however, do not pre-exist action but are engendered by historical experiences. Symbolisations stand for, evoke, or bring into being something else, something absent. They denote a kind of relationship whereby certain components exist elsewhere but are connected with others that are present. Originally, the Greek word suggested that a symbol was a token, the present half of a broken coin or medal, which performed its social function by recalling the absent half to which it could have been potentially reconnected. The verb *symballein* meant 'to try an interpretation, to make a conjecture ... to infer from something imprecise, because incomplete, something else that it suggested, evoked, revealed, but did not conventionally say'.[51]

Symbolisation is not about a given meaning that prefigures the experience; it is the search for meaning in existential uncertainty. Taking into account the vagueness, looseness, and partial quality of the reference, symbolising is 'an exact reference to something indefinite'.[52] Symbolisation is a culturally creative act in response to the means-to-end contexts of situational premises, when thinkers, political leaders, or social movements refer to each other in order to clarify their concerns to themselves and to others. Symbolisations are meaningful to contemporaries in a way that often contradicts the observer's view. Conditions of the harshest repression may be associated with freedom, whereas political liberalisation may be experienced as precariousness and uncertainty. The crucial point is not to prescribe the outcomes of revolutions, wars, and transitions. Rather, political inquiry should maintain the open-endedness of coming to terms with critical political events. Political crises produce new symbols in order to make sense of the disruptions of a community's political existence. Every act of symbolisation puts these new symbols at

---

[50] Voegelin, *The New Science of Politics*, 27–41.

[51] Don Handelman, *Models and Mirrors: Towards an Anthropology of Public Events* (Cambridge: Cambridge University Press, 1990), 12–13.

[52] Hanna Pitkin, *The Concept of Representation* (Berkeley: University of California Press, 1967), 67.

risk, inflecting the meanings of such symbols or transforming them by the uncertain consequences of practices.[53]

Democratisation can be seen as a sequence of symbolisations, with a myriad of quests for a new symbolic universe, which both precedes and follows ruptures. Democratic transformations depend on three dimensions of socially mediated dramatic action and the formation of meaning as part of existential representation.[54] First, there is the institutional formalisation (*mise en forme*), which suggests that the dissolutions of political order not only affect law and institutions but also imply the politicisation of bare life, where people's lives, identities, and representations are at stake. Second, there is the articulation of meaningful relations (*mise en sens*), which requires the subordination to authority to be accepted, trusted, and legitimised by the public. Existential representation is the precondition for endowing political power with a meaningful claim to represent society authoritatively. Finally, there is the performative element in the representation of power (*mise en scène*), which suggests that a political society cannot maintain its existence without representing the idea of its institution by a range of symbols and their ritualisation.

Although the October Revolution represents the beginning of modern Russia, its meaning has been the object of considerable historiographical and political contention. Stalin's goal to create a social and economic basis attuned to the ideological claims of Marxism-Leninism entailed a rupture with the myth of the Bolshevik Revolution. For Trotsky, Stalinism was a counter-revolution, as was the Hungarian revolution for the Soviets. Although the system the Bolsheviks established in the name of "the dictatorship of the proletariat" was a repressive one, the use of this symbolic formula implied that a communist society was, instead, democratic. The symbol of the People-as-One – as the carrier of political development, modernisation, and the dream of the realm of freedom from oppression – denied internal divisions. Although the communists appropriated the Great Fatherland War as a symbol for a national revolution, the social experience of the Second World War in the Soviet Union for large parts of the populace came down to a first 'de-Stalinisation', replacing repression with a sense of self-determination. The Cold War divided the world in a Manichaean spirit, supported by two overarching collective symbolisations, which endowed political rule with meaning on the grounds of the myths of totalitarianism and of anti-fascism. While the two types of political systems were antagonistic in their

---

[53] William H. Sewell jnr, 'The Concept of Culture', in Lynn Hunt and Victoria Bonnell, eds., *Beyond the Cultural Turn* (Berkeley: University of California Press, 1999), 51.
[54] Lefort, *Essais sur le politique*, 282–3.

functional set-up and moral foundations, this non-communication was crucial both for the self-fashioning of the liberal democratic model in the West and for the psychological attraction democracy acquired in the East. Although de-Stalinisation in Soviet Russia and the challenges to communist power in the revolutions of 1956, 1968, or 1980 failed to discontinue communist power, they generated a powerful counter-symbolism that was to denounce the sacrificial logic of communist power.

Democracy as a process of meaning-formation

The notion of symbolic articulation refers to nothing less than the historical process by which political societies – the nations, the empires – rise and fall, as well as the evolutions and revolutions between the two terminal points. If existential crisis is the experiential background to the articulation of political society, political transformations require a study of the conditions of representation, where a people authorise representatives to act for them. In order to be authorised to act, a representative needs to rely upon a credible reciprocity with those who conferred this authorisation.[55] An experiential approach to democratisation complements a legalist-positivist understanding of democracy as a constitutional form. In terms of allegiance and legitimacy, therefore, representation requires such a congruity prior to its legally or constitutionally enforced act. In terms of its symbolic power, however, representation goes beyond the constitutional sense. It requires that power must be accepted subjectively as representative in the existential sense of realising the idea of the institution.

This book complements the standard view that conceives democratisation processes as characterised by the revolutionary effects of bureaucratic rationalisation and institutional differentiation.[56] In institutional accounts, the revolutionary force comes from outside, as it rests upon technical means that shape the order of things most profoundly. As a consequence, rational goal-setting modifies and increases the conditions of adaptability of human beings to the external world. Charismatic authority, on the other hand, consists in beliefs of revelation and heroic creativity. Such beliefs revolutionise from inside as they grasp the spirit of human beings before shaping institutional order and the material world. Acts of resistance by individuals or groups may revolutionise, in that they make credible claims for existential representation. The opposition between external and internal spheres is not within the person or the

---

[55] Voegelin, *The New Science of Politics*, 33.
[56] Max Weber, *Wirtschaft und Gesellschaft*, 5th edn (Tübingen: Mohr, 1980), 657–8.

experiences of the creator of ideas or deeds. Rather, the differences are in the modalities of how they are internally appropriated by those who are dominated and led, how they are lived through.

In a masterly discussion of the anthropological forms of the concept of 'power', Heinrich Popitz distilled four fundamental conditions.[57] The first condition is the power of action, by which man inflicts injuries and remains vulnerable to physical attacks. The second type is instrumental power, when the threat of punishment and promise of reward can be used to control behaviour or establish permanent subordination. Yet, the capacity to impose one's will on others by instrumental power has natural limits. Even total or absolute power can be constrained by acts of martyr-dom or tyrannicide. The individual (and sometimes collective) defiance of the pressure to comply with communist rituals, for instance, posed a concrete threat to incumbents of a powerful state. The third condition relies upon the distinction between 'external' and 'internal' power. Internal power does not need the externalisations of legal or military threats, but enforces conformity in situations where actions cannot be controlled. This type of power relies upon the anthropological need for orientation, the need for yardsticks (*Maßstabs-Bedürftigkeit*) or markers of certainty. Even if this type of power has lost its transcendental legitima-tion, the secular state has produced markers of certainty such as the bordered territory, which contains the nation, or democracy, reflecting the equality of human beings. Beyond the political impact of external markers of certainty, 'internal' power also seeks confirmation through recognition. The fourth condition draws on the power of data-setting, systematic control, and the modification of the natural world for human purposes. By changing the natural environment for our purposes, we exercise power over nature but also over humans. Planning and engineer-ing determine conditions of life, spaces of freedom, and constraints on people. Any new technological artefact adds a further reality to human life, influencing people not merely by objects or material constructions, but primarily through the producer's will to exercise power over the conditions of human life. Modern political spirit has been characterised by a powerful merger of the third and fourth conditions with attempts to rationally design entire systemic orders that would replace existing real-ities with better ones.[58] Although the design of modern politics relied heavily on the bureaucratic-scientific data-setting power, this type of power needs symbolic markers of certainty to sustain it.

[57] Heinrich Popitz, *Phänomene der Macht* (Tübingen: Mohr, 1992), 11–39.
[58] Zygmunt Bauman, *Modernity and the Holocaust* (Ithaca: Cornell University Press, 1989).

   A problematisation of communism and democracy hinges on the relationship between the acts of symbolisation that created political authority around the sacrificial logic of communist power and those symbolisations that exposed them as deforming life, truth, and reality. Even if revolutionary challenges failed to produce a democratic 'outcome', they bequeathed a political symbolism, communicative memory, and civic consciousness. If looked at through the lens of a theory of regime consolidation in general, the stability of the Soviet-type regimes seemed to be as precarious as any construction of a political body in the empirical world.[59] Dissidence, for instance, was primarily neither a political philosophy of democratic liberalisation nor an opposition strategy with a distinctive political agenda. It was an existential response to the attack on the basics of human liberty and the powerlessness inflicted on societies by Soviet military intervention and repressive politics. Rejecting the collective logic of shaping the consciousness of the masses by organising them institutionally, it left it up to the individual to develop his subjectivity as an act of moral perfectionism, not of political partisanship.[60] Dissidence lacked a revolutionary utopia and renounced power politics but could draw on social and cultural memory of freedom, solidarity, and popular self-affirmation. In conjunction with the psychological appeal of the West, dissidence promoted the existential alternative of an individual's rejecting the system by his or her life-conduct and the 'care of the soul'.[61]

   Formulated as a long-standing dichotomy in political thought, the symbolic articulation of democracy rests upon a 'realist' standpoint that engages in the substance of the brokenness of political reality, where conflicting views on political existence are not mediated by the certainties of constitutionally guaranteed and predictable political relations. As Machiavelli made clear, realism is not confined to the interplay of forces but requires reflexivity by leaders in their attempt to acquire and maintain power. In such a view, the constitution of democracy is not only a question of violence and necessity but also of consciousness, life-conduct, and spiritual leadership.

   Theoretically, this book suggests that any mirrored opposition between communism and democracy is flawed. Communism was not only an anti-democratic regime based on a military machine, bureaucratic repression,

[59] Stephen Hanson, 'Defining Democratic Consolidation', in Richard Anderson et al., *Postcommunism and the Theory of Democracy* (Princeton: Princeton University Press, 2001), 126–51.
[60] Vaclav Havel, 'The Power of the Powerless', in John Keane, ed., *The Power of the Powerless: Citizens Against the State in Eastern Europe* (London: Hutchinson and Co., 1985), 23–96.
[61] Patočka, *Heretical Essays*, 79–118.

the destruction of meaningful ties and relations between individuals, a
contempt for human beings, and a deterministic view of history. Its
absolute politics also generated a civilisation and a way of life, in which
people had to make sense of their existence with what was there.
Historically, the October Revolution, the emergence of the Cold War,
the rise of dissidence, and the disarticulation of communism are
extremely complex, highly diverse, and contested political phenomena
in their own right. Given the infinitude of existential judgements in an
endless number of events, it would be futile to claim that any event has a
definite final meaning for different groups or societies at different times in
history.[62] Therefore, it would be absurd to argue that the articulation of
Bolshevik power was simply 'undemocratic' or the articulation of dissidence simply 'democratic'. The Cold War not only entailed the division
of a 'totalitarian' East and a 'democratic' West, but also endowed the
concept of democracy with a quasi-magical attraction.

The common classification into 'pre-communist', 'communist', and
'post-communist' pasts reduces legacies to structural constraints that rest
upon obsolete models of political development. Democratisation as
meaning-formation understands the past not as a legacy, which would
precede a new stage of political development. Any study of a legacy not
only risks turning into a moralistic crusade based upon a clear dividing
line between what is good and what is to be condemned, but also studies
contemporary problems of justice, truth, and morality by simply blaming
the 'past'. Although communism annihilated the past by organised forgetting, challenges to communist power remained sources of resistance
and symbolised a quest for truth and meaning as well as aspirations for
freedom. Alternative memories of different 'pasts' were socially and
culturally available and proved influential in articulating the community
of the 'people'. Similarly, communism's institutionalisation of utopia
established the authority of an imaginary 'second' reality. Communism
promoted mythical realities – such as 'enemy', the 'correct line', and the
prospective future transition to an ideal state of full freedom – into
markers of certainty. In order to overcome this imaginary reality of a
future paradise, the individualisation of life-conduct and a symbolism
that would strengthen the civic spirit of the citizenry were required.

Conceptual history (*Begriffsgeschichte*) is capable of clarifying the multiple stratification of meaning descending from chronologically separate
periods. Beyond a strict alternation of diachrony and synchrony it relates to
the simultaneity of the non-contemporaneous. It claims that the historical

---

[62] Max Weber, *On the Methodology of the Social Sciences*, trans. and ed. Edward A. Shils and
Henry A. Finch (Glencoe, IL: Free Press of Glencoe, 1949), 78.

depth of a concept is not identical with the chronological succession of its meanings. Rather, the emergence of democracy – despite numerous influences from 'outside' – has been, to an important extent, a quest for meaning and self-grounding in response to traumatic experiences 'within' communism. Transformative experiences in the evolution of communism modified symbolic worlds by articulating a new form of representation, a new spirit, but also by changing attitudes towards the past and the future. Democratisation has been a process of meaning-formation by which the eradication of enemies through real violence is overwritten through acts that symbolise rather than destroy enemies. While communism relied on heavy coercion and the identification of the enemy, the emergence of democracy relied on acts of denouncing this sacrificial logic of violent reciprocity. For the reciprocity of ritualistic violence and fear, dissidence substituted mutual recognition and the affirmation of the inalienable nature of human life and dignity. The civilising process of democratisation would make the entire people participate not in the exclusion of an enemy but in the symbolisation of communists as the 'Other'. Although it has been historically unique, it has had substantial similarities with the history of democratisation of western Europe. Before becoming the most successful and universally accepted constitutional form of government, the rise of democracy in the Western world provided an urgent hope and a vision of freedom, often in opposition to the dominant political authority of the times.

Methodologically, this book abstains from the positivistic effort to adapt political reality to the classificatory certainty of causes, stages, or sequences of political development. It is insufficient to see democracy as an institutionalised form of government, whose rationally based division of labour relies upon essentialist assumptions and abstract principles such as democratic individualism or the rule of law. Contrary to its recent triumphant advance, democracy throughout the centuries was more an object of philosophical inquiry than a system of political practice. A comparative typology of experiences does not claim to discover the roots or origins of communist or democratic 'identity'. Despite the observer's tendency to assume profound intentions, meanings, and immutable necessities at work in historical processes, the true historical sense confirms our existence among a profusion of entangled events without external landmarks.[63] Contrary to 'historicist' arguments about the uniqueness of every society, every culture, and every epoch, this book provides generalised propositions on the grounds of an analytical

---

[63] Foucault, 'Nietzsche, Genealogy, History', 81–9.

correlation of historically unique and circumstantial cases. From the perspective of a comparative typology of experiences, democratic transformations cannot be about being, essence, or identity. What works for a constituted system of government seems to be insufficient for understanding the emergence of democracy as a historically contingent process. The validity of the propositions cannot be 'tested' objectively but needs to be composed by placing them in the historical field of experiences and their symbolisations, i.e. in the time dimension of the empty space of power and the articulation of political society itself. Thus, the equivalence of critical events is not in the similarity of institutional outcomes, which will be different in any individual case. Rather, the equivalence is in the articulation of new symbols, which respond to and make sense of an existential crisis. Despite each instance's historical uniqueness and dependence on specific circumstances, this search for meaning is nevertheless central to a social scientific inquiry.[64] As work in cultural anthropology has claimed, drawing general propositions from historical detail is the basis of any scientific theory.[65]

Structure of the book

This book is divided into three parts. Part I proposes an interpretive approach to communism and democracy based on the experiential basis of consciousness and meaning-formation. Chapter 2 conceptualises periods of high uncertainty as fluid conjunctures, where the situational logic of action is formative of political consciousness. Chapter 3 argues that communism was a political religion, whose institutionalisation of utopia and mythological constructions of reality failed to set constitutive foundations of political order. Chapter 4 examines democratic transformations with a view to the impact of dramatic events on subjectivity and meaning-formation. It claims that the emergence of democracy occurred 'within' communism, involving individual acts of interpretation and narrative reconstruction that would turn the people into a subject of politics. Part II sets out to give an interpretive account of four critical events of revolutionary scope with a view to their symbolisations. Chapter 5 analyses the rise of Bolshevik power with reference to the symbolism of the dictatorship of the proletariat and the permanent revolution in one country. Chapter 6 conceptualises the Second World War as a social revolution and suggests that this liminal experience was crucial for the division of two worlds in the Cold War. Chapter 7 seeks to understand the

---

[64] Voegelin, *Published Essays 1966–1985*, 121–2.
[65] Clifford Geertz, *The Interpretation of Cultures* (New York: Basic Books, 1973), 51–2.

articulation of dissidence as a quest for meaning in response to the violent overthrow of people's revolutions. Chapter 8 examines the disarticulation of communism with a view to transitional uncertainty and the demise of symbols of democracy. Part III conceptualises democratisation as a process of meaning-formation. Chapter 9 expounds that forms of social memory such as those representing acts of resistance to communism were crucial for the emergence of democratic consciousness. Chapter 10 links the diffusion of democratic consciousness to individual acts of rejection of the second reality that had been established by the political symbolism of communism. Fundamentally, democratic 'identity' relied on the power of individuals to denounce the ritualistic violence by their own life-conduct. Chapter 11 contrasts essentialist assumptions about democratic consolidation with the emergence of democracy as a series of interpretive acts of overcoming violence. Rather than assuming an existing institutional 'model' of civilised, non-violent conflict resolution, it argues that democracy has been a civilising process, where conditions of incivility and violence were overcome by the power of consciousness.

Part I

The experiential basis of communism
and democracy

2 Revolutions, transitions, and uncertainty

One's own free and unfettered volition, one's own caprice, however wild, one's own fancy, inflamed sometimes to the point of madness – that is the one best and greatest good, which is never taken into consideration because it will not fit into any classification, and the omission of which always sends all systems and theories to the devil.

Fyodor Dostoyevsky

The logic of outcome

Revolutions reverse political structures to such an extent that political analysis can hardly escape approaching them as an outcome of a specific historical development. The deep political and social transformations in the wake of revolutions on both the domestic and international level largely eclipsed the situational premises of the French Revolution in 1789 or the Russian Revolution in 1917. The focus on the outcomes of revolutions such as the birth of the nation-state, republicanism, or the consolidation of Soviet communism downplays the importance of turmoil, violence, and uncertainty. Similarly, the revolutions of 1989 in eastern Europe and soon after in the collapsing Soviet Union were almost immediately approached from the developmental perspective of 'transitions to democracy'.

Animated by normative expectations of structure and order, interpretations of radical change in modern political societies have privileged a view on political transformations that was guided by goals of development or political modernisation.[1] In a similar vein, the cataclysmic power of historical revolutions has induced analysts to view their causality as being rooted in something akin to fate: revolutions are not made; they come.[2]

---

[1] Samuel Huntington, *Political Order in Changing Societies* (New Haven and London: Yale University Press, 1968), 1–90.

[2] Theda Skocpol, *States and Social Revolutions: A Comparative Analysis of France, Russia, and China* (Cambridge: Cambridge University Press, 1979), 17.

Structural approaches have likened revolutions to objects of historical development, where the social preconditions of the transitional or revolutionary period are disconnected from desired or expected outcomes. They seem to understand political antagonism in terms of 'objective' forces that oppose each other. Thus, the revolutionary class stands against the bourgeoisie, society competes with the state, and communism and democracy are thought to be at extreme ends of the spectrum. This bifurcation of analytical viewpoints reflects the observer's reluctance to engage in the chaotic historicity of such periods of uncertainty. Revolutionary or transitional uncertainty is the exception, where the substance of historical action is marred by disruptive violence, turmoil, and uncertainty. The transitional uncertainty that seizes hold of a political society is seen as 'abnormality' where 'normal science methodology' does not apply; analysts are keen to make up for this by bridging the gap between one system and another. This chapter argues that uncertainty can be methodologically normalised. Rather than approaching deep uncertainty by considering the dichotomic separation between causes and outcomes, I argue that the substance of the situational premises creates consciousness. Without pretending any complete typology, one can outline three major aspects of outcome-logic that bypass the chaotic substance of the empty space of power.

The logic of causality

A number of authoritative studies have examined the origins of democracy and totalitarianism.[3] Barrington Moore's work on the social origins of democracy and dictatorship was concerned with 'important stages in a prolonged social process which has worked itself out in several countries'.[4] He identified three routes to the modern world, which followed paths towards what would become either the democratic, the fascist, or the communist variant of modernity. In a similar vein, political sociologists intend to retrieve a causality, to explain how and why a specific order had to collapse at the very moment of revolution or political transition.[5] Thus, Charles Tilly's work on revolutionary violence over the past three centuries has differentiated between 'reactive', backward-looking, locally

---

[3] Hannah Arendt, *The Origins of Totalitarianism* (London: George Allen, 1951); J. L. Talmon, *The Origins of Totalitarian Democracy* (London: Secker & Warburg, 1952).
[4] Barrington Moore, *Social Origins of Dictatorship and Democracy: Lord and Peasant in the Making of the Modern World* (Boston: Beacon Press, 1966), ix.
[5] For a critique, see William Sewell jnr, 'Three Temporalities: Toward an Eventful Sociology', in Terrence Mcdonald, ed., *The Historic Turn in the Human Sciences* (Ann Arbor: University of Michigan Press, 1996), 245–80.

oriented violence, and 'proactive', forward-looking, nationally oriented violence.[6] While Tilly's distinction between revolutionary situations and revolutionary outcomes is useful as far as the differentiation between popular contention and the transformation of power is concerned, there is an important risk involved. Following an outcome-logic, the historical result is not only the basis for the explanation of a new condition. It also becomes the starting point for vindicating the origin of a regime, class, or identity. Capitalist development and state centralisation are seen as occurring offstage, as ever-present and ever-rising forces. The revolutionary situations and the violence involved hinge on invisible causes, which make situations largely effects, never causes, of change.

Theda Skocpol's comparative work on social revolutions in France, Russia, and China locates the causes for revolution in a complex set of fiscal crises of the state based on military backwardness as a result of interstate conflict, which is exacerbated by the resistance of recalcitrant landlords.[7] In order to move from political revolutions to social revolutions with a transformation of the country's class structure, mass uprisings of a well-organised and autonomous peasant class are required. These causal factors are conceptualised in this order: factor one induces a political crisis; the addition of factor two turns the political crisis into a political revolution; eventually, factor three turns the political revolution into a social revolution. The causality in this analysis works with separate 'trials' of an experiment, which have to be both equivalent and independent. The principle of equivalence implies that each new trial (in this case, each new revolution) should be a genuine replication of earlier trials, with all relevant variables held constant. The relevant temporality in this logic is purely internal to the trial: the posited causal factors must exist prior to their posited consequence. Consequently, the three great social revolutions become a uniform class of objects governed by identical causal laws, which are seen as causally independent from each other.

Similarly, explanations of the collapse of communism have reproduced assumptions on the equivalence of causal structures, where legacies of the past are not connected to concrete experiences but are supposed to be causally interconnected.[8] In such a view, post-communist states inherit from the past regime material legacies, constraints, sets of habits, and cognitive frames. Furthermore, there is a turbulent configuration of new actors and new opportunities that emerge as the old regime loses its

[6] Charles Tilly, *European Revolutions 1492–1992* (Oxford: Blackwell, 1993), 23.
[7] Skocpol, *States and Social Revolutions*.
[8] Jon Elster et al., *Institutional Design in Post-Communist Societies* (Cambridge: Cambridge University Press, 1998).

repressive grip on society. Finally, a new consolidated institutional order is slowly appearing which is likely to institutionalise agency and provide for a measure of sustainability. Although the power of the past is acknowledged, this framework overemphasises the stability of legacies, taking communism as a consolidated system where the monopolisation of political power all but suspended autonomy of human action. Following the widespread tendency to classify Russian and east European history in developmental stages such as pre-communist, communist, and post-communist pasts, the determinants of the emergence of the new order are seen as independent from the factors that caused the breakdown of the old regime.

Recent research on political transformation has argued that one has to go beyond the linear statement that 'history matters' or 'history strikes back'. Rather, contentious memories and meanings of historical events influence transformative periods of reconstruction.[9] Despite their sensitivity to the multiplicity of pasts and paths, however, even these approaches tend to see 1989 in terms of a causality that explains the victory of capitalist democracy. They postulate the outcome of political economy in a country by tracing back multiple paths from which post-socialist political and economic institutions evolved. The concept of 'recombinant capitalism', for instance, suggests that economic reforms in eastern Europe followed different paths of extrication by recombining different institutional patterns from their communist past. However, such approaches neglect the fact that the underlying conceptual and institutional reality of capitalism with which these approaches operate is the result of altogether different, complex, and in themselves quite haphazard processes of 'path-dependence' in western Europe, i.e. in a completely different historical environment.[10] By trying to explain the outcome of a transition process using a historical sequence, path-dependence assumes a law-like unfolding of historical development. It thus attributes a specific result to the specificity of its path.

The logic of heroism

The almost obsessive need to conceive a given political order as the outcome of a specific causality is complemented by the similarly obsessive idea that the present is the consequence of the intentions and goals

[9] László Bruszt and David Stark, *Post-Socialist Pathways: Transforming Politics and Property in East Central Europe* (Cambridge: Cambridge University Press, 1998).
[10] Michel Dobry, 'Paths, Choices, Outcomes, and Uncertainty', in Dobry, ed., *Democratic and Capitalist Transitions in Eastern Europe* (Dordrecht: Kluwer, 2000), 52.

pursued by exceptional individuals. An important trend in social explanation suggests that an individual leader or collective groups such as an elite or a social class master a situation of anarchy and disorder. This tendency has two important sources in political and social thought. First, it is associated with the Machiavellian idea about the *virtù* of an individual actor as forging a political order according to his liking. The complex processes that ushered in the modern nation-state transferred the principle of power politics from princely sovereignty to the sovereign collectivity of the nation and reinforced the heroism in symbolic attachment to and sacrifice for the nation. Second, there is the influential Marxist approach according to which the continuous struggle for domination between classes will inevitably lead to the victory of the collective class of the proletariat. In line with hero identification as one of the most fundamental mechanisms of coming to terms with a crisis in many myths of humanity, either view justifies outcomes by individual heroic action.[11] This 'heroic illusion'[12] suggests that individual actors or collective groups are endowed with dispositions that provide them with strategically and tactically adequate behaviour during this crisis. While, prior to the Russian Revolution, for instance, Marxist-Leninist analysis had stressed the objective patterns of Russian authoritarianism and economic backwardness, during the revolutionary crisis all of a sudden the subjectivity of Lenin became the guiding force in transforming the objective order. Assumptions of the exceptional quality of uniquely determined leaders such as Lenin were reproduced in the literature on democratic transitions. The individual's autonomous will power and his insight into the appropriateness of action provided for a specific type of subjectivity needed to 'craft democracies'.[13]

The influential subdiscipline of transitology was interested in highly underdetermined moments of uncertainty.[14] As an early work on transitions argued, such transformations would require a theory of abnormality in which the unexpected and the possible are as important as the usual and the probable. When social and political differentiation is low, rules and norms are volatile, and decision processes risk being caught in a constant flux, normal social science methodology seems to be

---

[11] Joseph Campbell, *The Hero with a Thousand Faces* (London: Fontana Press, 1949).

[12] Michel Dobry, *Sociologie des crises politiques* (Paris: Presses de la Fondation Nationale des Sciences Politiques, 1986).

[13] Giuseppe Di Palma, *To Craft Democracies: An Essay on Democratic Transitions* (Berkeley: University of California Press, 1990).

[14] Philippe Schmitter and Terry Karl, 'The Conceptual Travel of Transitologists and Consolidologists: How Far to the East Should They Go?', *Slavic Review*, 53, 1 (1994), 173–85.

inappropriate for grasping such processes analytically.[15] Nevertheless, the concept of transition remained focused on the structural features of 'from' and 'to' phases. This dichotomisation of perspectives on the post-communist period casts a shadow on assessments of the political evolution of communism itself. Since the conceptual tools and methods were attuned to the aftermath of systemic collapse, the problematisation of revolutionary phases of uncertainty prior to the breakdown of communism received less attention. Consequently, the comparative study of post-communist transitions has largely been focused on the prerequisites for the expected regime type (such as a liberal-democratic arrangement), thus excluding conceptual discussions of transition.[16] Thus, transition, by default, has widely remained a negative concept, which tries to express the unstructured period between two potential extremes characterised by systemic stability.

Theorists who portray regime transformations as an irresistible dynamics of individualism tend to exclude the modalities of the emergence of consciousness, beliefs, and attitudes on the grounds of a logical abstraction. A recent study on regime diversity after communism proposed an ontological conception of causal mechanism.[17] In this view, causal mechanisms are processes that convert certain inputs into outputs, bringing about the effects that can be seen as causes of social phenomena. The objective is to shift the level of causal process analysis from that of aggregates and structures to individual action under constraints. This ontological conception relies upon a 'weak methodological individualism', which links the preferences and dispositions of people to the social knowledge they have acquired. Nevertheless, ontological stability suggests that individual action can be predicted to obey specific law-like mechanisms or be appropriate with a given system of norms and values.

The logic of appropriateness

Outcome-logic tends to measure the dispositions and intentions of political actors on the basis of how appropriate their behaviour is with regard

---

[15] Guillermo O'Donnell et al., eds., *Transitions from Authoritarian Rule: Prospects for Democracy*, vol. IV, O'Donnell and Philippe Schmitter, *Tentative Conclusions About Uncertain Democracies* (Baltimore and London: Johns Hopkins University Press, 1991), 2–6.

[16] Gerardo L. Munck, 'The Regime Question: Theory Building in Democracy Studies', *World Politics*, 54 (2001), 124–6.

[17] Herbert Kitschelt, 'Accounting for Postcommunist Regime Diversity: What Counts as a Good Cause?', in Grzegorz Ekiert and Stephen E. Hanson, eds., *Capitalism and Democracy in Central and Eastern Europe* (Cambridge: Cambridge University Press, 2003), 49–86.

to institutionalised logics such as classes, leaders, or political regimes. This logic of appropriateness has permeated dominant interpretations of major revolutions. Theorists tend to read meanings of an event not with regard to the potential of the situation but with regard to the post-revolutionary order. A prominent example is the idea that the abolition of feudalism by the French National Assembly on 4 August 1789 replaced aristocratic inequality with bourgeois inequality. Such a judgement with hindsight neglects that money at this conjuncture was seen as the great equaliser, as the universal tool for destroying aristocratic privilege. In a similar vein, rooting Soviet communism either in the 'inevitability' of a socialist revolution or in Lenin's voluntarism follows a bifurcation of analysis motivated by ex-post justification. Such a bifurcation discon-nects the 'before', i.e. the social forces of revolutionary effervescence, from the 'after', i.e. the heroic achievement of Lenin and the proletariat. It neglects the fact that the objective status of the Bolshevik party as an outsider sect and the party's serious internal disagreements throughout 1917 made a Bolshevik success quite unlikely. The rebirth of civil society under *perestroika* in the late 1980s as a movement from 'below' is dis-connected from state consolidation after 1991, which was conducted by a strong presidency from 'above'. This bifurcation disregards the social effervescence and mass activism of the Gorbachev era. Similarly, it involves imposing a logic of appropriateness on historical reality, if Poland's elite-negotiated 'revolution from above' at the round-table in 1989 is seen as causally independent from Solidarność's 'revolution from below' in 1980.

There has been a noticeable tendency in transition studies towards conceiving political change by measuring the appropriateness of inten-tions with regard to a normatively desirable model of a liberal democratic arrangement of political authority. Whether transitions are defined as the interval between one political regime and another, or as the passage from a non-democratic to a democratic regime, the concept's strong tendency towards a mechanistic two-step movement has been conspicuous. This requires bridging the apparent structural void between two aggregate periods, when stability gives way to flux and uncertainty, when rules and norms are contested and pasts and futures are at stake. Transition studies suggest that some individuals or a class inside the pre-revolutionary system are endowed with a transformative disposition that would be in tune with the institutional logic of the post-revolutionary system. Thus, they tend to exclude the relevance of this historical experience for the sake of the logical coherence of a normative model.

The use of logically different variables suggests a two-step movement, which disconnects political reality from its experiential basis. In practical terms, revolutionary or transitional processes appear as relations between two entities or states of affairs: that existing before, and that existing afterwards. While this bifurcation disconnects experiences 'before' and 'after', it pre-emptively connects them by assuming that the actors' dispositions were guiding the outcome.

The situational logic of action

These different facets of outcome-logic concur in assuming some underlying and invisible structural necessity according to which political evolution occurs. Scholars tend to 'freeze' and 'fracture' history by treating the histories of revolutions or transitions as if they took place in isolation from one another, rather than as a sequence of historically connected events. They either introduce 'causality' as an invisible power that justifies outcomes or they assume that dispositions of individuals are guided by goals of development that are somehow universal or 'trans-historical'. Causal mechanisms, path-dependent trajectories, capitalist development, state centralisation, and liberalisation become the actors of history. In the logic of heroism, the objective trajectory of history is shaped by the rationality of individual or collective preferences, which may be constrained by the situation but nevertheless remain ontologically stable. Analyses based on the assumption of appropriateness constrain the inchoate historical context by 'adjusting' it to a supposedly non-contingent model of systematic arrangement. Subjective dispositions become either adequate or inadequate to meet the criteria of positively postulated institutional arrangements in ordered, law-based, 'normal' routine politics.

Obsessed with goal-seeking and problem-solving, modern social science research tends to forget that people pursue misguided goals, are ignorant of their goals, or simply are deceived by their goals.[18] As I shall argue, models for political evolution are not only derived from objective rationality but also are created in chaotic historicity. If revolutions and wars are the types of events that throughout their duration detach themselves from the conditions of their outbreak, the task of critical understanding is not to arrest such movements by causal laws, models, or developmental goals, but to elucidate how the situational premises shift, develop, and transform from the rupture to the redress of crisis.

---

[18] Thomas C. Schelling, *Micromotives and Macrobehavior* (New York: W. W. Norton, 1978), 18–19.

Given the self-deception of revolutionaries and momentous obstacles for 'democratisers', theorising uncertainty requires linking assumptions on the rationality of actors and necessity in a potentially boundless situation.[19]

Modern usage has established action as a logically coherent movement towards the outcome or goal and thus diverted political analysis from the boundlessness of action.[20] As Hannah Arendt pointed out, Greek and Latin contained two different and yet interrelated words with which to designate the verb 'to act'. 'To act', in its most general sense, means to take an initiative, to begin (as the Greek word *archein*, 'to begin', 'to lead', and eventually 'to rule', indicates), and to pass through, to achieve, to finish (*prattein*). The corresponding words in Latin are the verbs *agere* (to set into motion) and *gerere* (whose original meaning is 'to bear'). *Prattein* and *gerere* became the accepted words for action in general, whereas the words designating the beginning of action became specialised in meaning, at least in political language. *Archein* came to mean chiefly 'to rule' and 'to lead' when it was used, and *agere* came to mean 'to lead' rather than 'to set into motion'.

Revolutionary 'accelerations' are set into motion by the removal of obstacles that are higher during 'normal', structured times than during 'abnormal' periods of underdetermined change. While intentions of actors do not pre-exist action but are conjuncturally shaped in the process of action as setting in motion, revolutions produce consequences quite opposite to the intentions of the revolutionaries. Revolutionary actors often, if not always, fail to attune their 'intentions' to the 'consequences' of their action. Does this imply that their dispositions had no influence on future developments? A structuralist perspective holds that the wealth of unintended and unforeseen outcomes flaws any study of the intentions of classes or groups of actors in revolutionary processes.[21] Outcome-logic links the intentions to the consequences under the assumption that intentions and consequences pertain to the same logic. The failure to foresee the consequences would vindicate disregarding revolutionary intentions. As the consequences play against the interests of the actors involved, it would be futile to decipher the logic of the processes of a social revolution by following the actions of any one class or organisation.

In historical experience, however, there is good reason to assume that critical junctures are formative of consciousness as far as the situation

---

[19] Karl Popper, *The Poverty of Historicism* (London and New York: Routledge, 1957), 138.
[20] Hannah Arendt, *The Human Condition* (Chicago and London: University of Chicago Press, 1958), 189.
[21] Skocpol, *States and Social Revolutions*, 14–18.

is the only reliable basis of judgements and expectations. The term
'unintended consequences' judges the failure of intentions by the certainty of the outcome and thus conflates two different realities. Forming
expectations according to unexpected turns is not irrational, but is
another form of rationality that works according to a logic that is not
conceived from a cognitive distance to the situation. Even if actors in
critical situations have more confidence than is justified in uncertain
conditions, knowledge on which to base predictions of the future is
extremely inadequate. As John Maynard Keynes remarked about the
expectations of an investment's yield, the basis of knowledge for estimat-
ing the yield ten or even five years hence of a railway, a copper mine, an
Atlantic liner, or a building in London amounts to little and sometimes to
nothing.[22] Thus, investments rely upon a convention according to which
the existing market valuation, however arrived at, is uniquely correct in
relation to our existing knowledge of the facts. The formation of long-
term expectations relies upon scanty knowledge, which derives its confidence not from the forecast of the likelihood of the result but by
disproportionately relying upon existing knowledge. This will influence
the yield of the investment and it will change only in proportion to
changes in this knowledge. However, it cannot be uniquely correct,
since our existing knowledge does not provide a sufficient basis as a
calculated mathematical expectation.

While an important task of social and political inquiry consists in
explaining the effects of events with regard to intentions, it is not the
only legitimate one. Intentions may well not be focused on logically
predetermined or normatively prescribed outcomes and still matter.
Dispositions of actors may actually be redirected during critical situations
and become the causes of effects that would have been unthinkable before
they actually occurred. Any critical event includes a variety of social
actions, ad hoc decision-making, and acts of signification, entailing
many contested meanings and existential judgements. Recent research
in political sociology and social theory has conceptualised revolutions and
political crises as 'conjunctural structures' or 'fluid conjunctures'.[23] The
recently growing branches of contentious politics and crisis theory provided sophisticated in-depth studies of critical events, great events,

[22] John Maynard Keynes, *The General Theory of Employment, Interest and Money* (London: Macmillan, 1961), 148–52.
[23] Dobry, *Sociologie des crises politiques*; William Sewell jnr, 'Historical Events as Transformations of Structures: Inventing Revolution at the Bastille', *Theory and Society*, 25 (1996), 841–81.

events-in-history, and cultural aspects of power struggles.[24] These studies carefully dissect the processes of political mobilisation, the constitution and maintenance of social movements, the cognitive status of the guiding ideas, the composition of actors and strategies, and the circumstances of the demobilisation of such movements.

The boundlessness of action is both constrained by and productive of the dispositions of revolutionary actors. Experiences in revolutionary situations matter as far as the dispositions of actors are logically different from ideological premises such as the 'historical inevitability' of revolution or the classificatory logic of 'class'.[25] At the systematic level, the dislocations of structures not only constrain individual dispositions, but fundamentally reverse them as intentions can become contaminated with fear, hatred, or violence. Such extraordinary and socially dramatic situations with their accelerated rhythms, intensified emotions, and bodily participation create an ontological openness in human beings that can profoundly reshape cognitive frames. Disruptive sequences of violence or civil unrest generate responses in communicative processes, thus shaping social knowledge and moral values but also expectations. The central point is that the subjectivity of experiences of social effervescence or collective violence breaches the objective logic of classes, regimes, or systems. Moreover, individual actors and collective groups that repeatedly undergo traumatic experiences may be caught in double binds, i.e. a self-perception of being a potential victim and the desire to overcome this. Finally, although uncertainty in revolutionary situations will draw to an end, the situational premises not only are a circumstantial hazard, but have a modelling power for politics. Individuals do not act according to the logic of self-interest defined by an outside observer but are tied to a means-to-ends context depending on the subjectively assessed meaning and desirability of an anticipated future. If the brokenness of political reality remains a permanent aspect of politics, as Machiavelli suggested, then the empty space of power and its attendant breakdown of authority, loss of meaning, and social drama challenge assumptions about the ontological stability of rationality and individual preferences. While violence works according to the reciprocity of giving and taking and thus nurtures cycles of vengeance, this reciprocity can be overcome by agreeing to give without expecting anything in exchange.

---

[24] Doug McAdam et al., *Dynamics of Contention* (Cambridge: Cambridge University Press, 2001), 22–4; Grzegorz Ekiert, *The State Against Society: Political Crises and Their Aftermath in East Central Europe* (Princeton: Princeton University Press, 1996).
[25] Arpad Szakolczai, 'Experiential Sociology', *Theoria* (April 2004), 59–87.

The fluidity of critical events

Revolutionary politics is characterised by action as setting in motion. A credible challenge to political authority involves the levelling of status roles and differences, the intensification of emotions, and radical social polarisation. Contentious politics in the empty space of power is the concrete event of a perpetual dialectical relationship over time between order and its dissolution.[26] Going beyond the structuralist tradition, social interactions in dramatic events are active sites of cultural creativity, where spatial arrangements and the mastery of time regimes play a crucial role. Similarly, interpersonal communication and the negotiation of identities figure centrally in the dynamics of contention. Essentially, these approaches concur in examining fluid conjunctures with a view to how socially thick contexts of contention frame the perceptions of actors, codes of communication, language, and identities. In this view, political order not only is instituted on the grounds of normative-legal-constitutional acts but also is appropriated through an experiential basis in emotionally intensive and symbolically significant events that bring about internal transformations of man.

As Michel Dobry has suggested, such critical events are characterised by an intensification of social emotions, by simplifications of the social space, by the undifferentiation of social relationships, and by a tendency towards one-dimensionality of personal identity. Mobilisations simultaneously affect several sectors or social fields and weaken the influence of sectional logics on the calculations of actors.[27] This dissolution of several differentiated social spheres corresponds to a sudden breakdown of sectional boundaries. Critical events may affect other fields such as literature or art by aligning the temporalities in these fields with rhythms in the central event. Beyond the harmonisation of rhythms, the acceleration of events can bring about simultaneous and unexpected discontinuities to routine behaviour patterns for a very short period of time. The confrontation as such may be productive of an axis of action that seizes hold of actors, whether they like it or not.[28]

It would be inaccurate, however, to understand critical events along the lines of 'volcanic' theories of revolution, which assume that misery and deprivation suddenly lead to an explosion of discontent.[29] Critical events

[26] Victor Turner, *The Ritual Process: Structure and Anti-Structure* (New York: de Gruyter, 1969), 112.
[27] Dobry, *Sociologie des crises politiques.*   [28] Dobry, *Sociologie des crises politiques*, 166.
[29] For a critique, see Rod Aya, *Rethinking Revolutions and Collective Violence* (Amsterdam: Het Spinhuis, 1990).

are no *tabula rasa* situation, where power is absent. The fluidity of critical junctures is not always opposed to previously existing structures, which would intimate a spontaneous march of societies towards a social void or towards the overall disappearance of all structure. Revolutions or transitions are not situations where disorder interrupts periods of order. Rather, disorder is creative of order, as norms, rules, and the law are established through active and often costly intervention of social actors – often more costly than the activities of restoration or maintenance of structures. Even several days of crowd gathering linked with the temporary disappearance of authority structures, or the annihilation of state structures through war or foreign occupation, will not leave large parts of society in a complete void. Even when repressive occupation regimes deny any right or possibility of societal self-organisation, 'underground states' – such as Poland during the Second World War or Kosovo in the late 1980s and early 1990s – can build up functioning and effective structures of civic education as well as of moral and political authority.

The crucial point is to recognise that structure and order are pregnant with disorder. This is because disorder is not brought from outside but because orderly structures bear inside themselves the potentiality of dissolution of order. The limitations of the law are never entirely reliable safeguards against criminal acts, just as the boundaries of the territory are never entirely reliable safeguards against foreign invasion. This boundlessness of action is only the other side of the tremendously productive capacity of power.[30] Regardless of the outcomes, in revolutionary situations legitimate authority is up for grabs, is highly and credibly contested or subject to double or multiple sovereignties.[31] The dual-power scenarios of the February Revolution in 1917 or the factual dual power in Germany in the post-First World War turmoil displayed the potential of the authority vacuum. Right after the Second World War, dual-power structures continued to exist in the Soviet Union, as important resistance movements operated in the Baltic countries and in western Ukraine. The Hungarian revolution in October 1956 and the Solidarność revolution in Poland in summer 1980 were clear instances of dual sovereignty. The Lithuanian and Russian declarations of sovereignty in spring 1990 set off a wave of such declarations by former Soviet union republics, autonomous republics, and provinces provoking a 'parade of sovereignties'. Such situations of dual power (*dvoevlastie*) not only blurred the distinction between authorities and lower-level institutions but also pointed to the underlying similarities between revolution and nationalist secession.

---

[30] Arendt, *The Human Condition*, 190–1.
[31] Charles Tilly, *From Mobilization to Revolution* (Englewood Cliffs: Prentice-Hall, 1978).

Thus, the consolidation of political order after revolutions is not only a matter of normatively inspired and constitutionally guaranteed doctrines but needs to take into account the fluidity of the conjuncture, which builds up as a process of disorder, violence, and social effervescence. As William Sewell has argued, the French Revolution was not only the birthplace of democratic politics and constitutionalism. The conjuncture between the new concept of revolution and the idea of sovereignty of the people was produced in the significant upheaval of everyday life and social communication associated with crowd violence. The legally sanctioned structural transformation of popular sovereignty occurred in the haphazard configuration of crowd action.[32] Memorable events such as the attack on the Bastille, after which the National Assembly forced the king to consent to popular sovereignty, were not primarily based on the intentional consciousness of heroic individuals. Rather they should be understood as a set of transformations of meaning in the contingent social context. The Great Fear as the most astonishing mass panic in recorded history was decisive for the legislative act of abolishing feudalism and privilege by replacing them with equality before the law. The mass panic of the Great Fear interrupted the National Assembly negotiations on the constitution and the declaration of rights because of the pressing situation of how to deal with increasing disorder in the provinces. Similarly, insurrectionary peasant violence had a positive effect on emancipation and democracy.[33]

The modelling power of critical events

Regime theory assumes that communist regimes belonged to different classes from democratic regimes. Common sense has it that Bolsheviks hated the bourgeoisie and, consequently, imposed class struggle as the driving force of the revolution. Common sense has it also that counter-revolutionary forces and the capitalist West hated the Bolsheviks and therefore inflicted internal and external conflicts upon them. The self-proclaimed nature of Bolshevik communism as the dictatorship of the proletariat and the functional-descriptive antagonism between democratic and totalitarian regimes reinforced such classificatory schemes. Standard institutional accounts draw a dividing line between constitutional forms because they classify them according to their institutional practices, their modes of organisation of power, and their modes of communication.

[32] Sewell, 'Historical Events as Transformations of Structures', 871–4.
[33] John Markoff, 'Violence, Emancipation, and Democracy', in Gary Kates, ed., *The French Revolution* (London and New York: Routledge, 1998), 236–78.

As Gregory Bateson has suggested, any real communication between people in the substance of lived experiences in the social world is at a different level from how it is perceived and interpreted by concepts, typologies, or ideas.[34] In the heat of a military battle or of revolutionary crowd action, leaders and participants often cannot distinguish winners from losers, let alone formulate a new moral purpose or goal of development. New concepts, ideas, and 'models' of political order arise only as a consequence of such material action, by means of deliberation, linguistic differentiation, and making sense of what occurred with regard to existing cultural patterns. This dimension of formalisation, communication, and discourse invokes no things, forces, or impacts but only differences, images, ideas, and theories.[35]

Based on work in anthropology, communications analysis, and psychotherapy, Bateson's double-bind theory aims to understand why there is a discontinuity between a class and its members. Drawing on the theory of logical types, the class cannot be a member of itself nor can one of the members be the class, since the term used for the class is of a different level of abstraction – a different logical type – from terms used for members.[36] In historical experience and communicative practice, the continuity between a class and its members is continually and inevitably breached as people, governments, and individuals undergo internal transformations. Double binds can be described as patterns of communication that emanate from repeated experiences of being a victim. They refer to situations of dependence of at least two subjects in which one may potentially become a victim, and victimisation can become habitual expectation. The intense relationship of absolute dependence on a superior being or structure requires the victim to accurately discriminate what sort of message is being communicated in order to respond appropriately. In a second possibility, victimisation is not a necessary outcome of this relationship but can be avoided by shifting to become a different sort of person. Here, the individual is caught in a situation in which the other person in the relationship is expressing two orders of message and one of these contradicts the other. Finally, the individual cannot comment on the message; he cannot make a meta-communicative statement. In this third possibility, the subject neither becomes a victim nor is he able to shift to become somebody else. In this case, identity is formed

---

[34] Gregory Bateson, *Steps to an Ecology of the Mind: Collected Essays in Anthropology, Psychiatry, Evolution, and Epistemology* (Chicago and London: University of Chicago Press, 2000), 478.
[35] Bateson, *Steps to an Ecology of the Mind*, 271–2.
[36] Bateson, *Steps to an Ecology of the Mind*, 202–10.

through a double constraint that cannot be entirely resolved. One of these keeps being directed towards the role of the victim, while the second aims to affirm a personal identity independent from and often opposing the first.

While double-bind theory was developed for understanding the behaviour of individuals, the specific history of state-formation in Russia and eastern Europe strongly suggests its applicability for the social world. Russia's self-perception as a 'backward' or 'underdeveloped' country originated in the borrowings of advanced technology in the sixteenth and seventeenth centuries, as an emergent state beat its way out of subordination to neighbouring powers. This sense of backwardness reinforced invidious comparisons and a drive to correct social inadequacy by imitating 'the West' and overcoming it.[37] At the root of the contest between Russia and the West are not two entirely different civilisations, but Russia's psychological desire for supremacy over the European model. The split can be found in the different way in which patterns of absolutism and power legitimisation developed in western Europe and in Russia prior to the second half of the nineteenth century.[38] The Russian nation was forged by an extension of the imperial Russian framework into every aspect of political and social life.[39] While Western absolutism declared the legitimacy of power, Eastern absolutism declared the mystic 'truth' of power, forcing its subjects to accept this framework. In order to compete with the economically expanding West, Russian absolutism had to give up its separate 'world economy' and open up a window to Europe, a process mainly initiated by Peter I. The Russian state never assumed an existence independent from the person of the monarch as it did in France or Britain. However, the process of Europeanisation associated the emperor's divine right of legitimacy with the secular state, thus linking the traditional Russian pattern of development to 'European qualities' such as economic and technological progress, and the expansion and strengthening of the state.[40]

As mimetic theory suggests, cycles of vengeance and violence produce double binds between people who are unconsciously contaminated by the reciprocity of desires. When contagion with emotions suspends individual judgement, action ceases to be individually motivated or structurally

---

[37] David Joravsky, 'Communism in Historical Perspective', *American Historical Review*, 99, 3 (1994), 854.

[38] Jeno Szücs, 'Three Historical Regions of Europe', in John Keane, ed., *Civil Society and the State* (London: Verso, 1988), 315–22.

[39] Richard Pipes, *Russia Under the Old Regime*, 2nd edn (London: Penguin Books, 1995).

[40] Richard Wortman, *Scenarios of Power: Myth and Ceremony in Russian Monarchy*, vol. II (Princeton: Princeton University Press, 2000), 7.

constrained but is guided by 'inter-dividuality'.[41] Violence arises as the object of contention loses importance, while the rivals are caught up in a double bind, where the closer the imitator gets to the model, the more the model becomes an obstacle. Bolshevik propaganda radicalised peasants in an atmosphere of growing social polarisation. This 'trench Bolshevism' identified the enemies of the Bolsheviks as 'class enemies' and was crucial to the growing popularity of Bolshevism among peasant-soldiers. The streamlining of identity in the Russian Civil War radically simplified pre-crisis social hierarchies, swept aside estate, class, and ethnos, and left a stark confrontation between Whites and Reds, thus making neutrality impossible.[42] Later, during Stalin's Great Terror, mass denunciations could spread like a contagious disease, passing on 'the infection of inevitable arrest by a handshake, by a breath, by a chance meeting on the street'.[43] The emergence of revolutionary communism under conditions of external and civil war prompted many analysts to apply the psychopathological category of schizophrenia to Russians in order to express the conditions of everyday life under real socialism.[44] The 'self-sacrifice' of practically all those accused in Stalin's show trials threw many communist party activists, especially abroad, into a double bind in which they would, by a focus on the victims of fascism, vindicate the fact that they themselves imitated the defendants in the trials by trying to justify their adherence to the party.[45] Conversely, in the disintegrating Yugoslavia of the late 1980s, nationality as the single attribute of collective identification suddenly eliminated Yugoslav identity and became contagious and rampant.[46]

A similar dichotomy based on outcome-logic guides thinking about wars, which are mainly approached as interruptions of peaceful order. The underlying assumption about war's influence on politics sees the destructiveness of war in opposition to lofty aspirations to secure life, property, and security. In other words, the dark sides of war are only destructive and have not only little influence on peace, but are diametrically

---

[41] René Girard, *Things Hidden Since the Foundation of the World* (Baltimore: Johns Hopkins University Press, 1987), 35.
[42] Geoffrey Hosking, *Russia: People and Empire 1552–1917* (London: Fontana Press, 1997), 453.
[43] Alexander Solzhenitsyn, *The Gulag Archipelago: An Experiment in Literary Investigation*, vols. I and II, trans. from the Russian by Thomas P. Whitney (Boulder: Westview Press, 1998), 75.
[44] Czesław Miłosz, *The Captive Mind* (New York: Alfred A. Knopf, 1953).
[45] Manès Sperber, *Die Zeit der Tyrannis und andere Essays*, ed. Janka Sperber (Munich: DTV, 1987), 14.
[46] Slavenka Drakulić, *The Balkan Express: Fragments from the Other Side of the War* (New York and London: W. W. Norton, 1993), 50–1.

opposed to it.[47] From such a perspective, political history appears to be a continuum where individuals incessantly move towards a better life interrupted only by necessary ruptures of mass killing in wars. Yet war is the continuity of politics by other means.[48] War is a chameleon with an ever-changing nature. It combines the substance of boundless violence with the play of probabilities about interests and strategies. Similarly, war can be a political tool in the hands of rationally minded politicians. While wars are in essence unpredictable, the 'total wars' of the twentieth century were even more so. The very unfolding of wars turns upside down the situations that lay at their origins and makes new rationales of political conduct appear that would have been unthinkable even in the last moments of war action. The limitless potential of world wars thwarted rational calculations about arms control before the Second World War and about political alliances after its end. It is the battle itself and not the origin of the conflict or a peace treaty that is the most important issue and develops the most far-reaching consequences.[49]

Calculations about war as a strategy or a policy are at a different logical level from the substance of war. A message about war or a policy of warfare is not part of the experiential basis of war. The negotiations for a peace treaty are not within the same ethical system as the deceptions and tricks of battle. Men have felt for centuries that treachery in a truce is worse than trickery in battle. Values such as the nation or the homeland quickly vanish as the spiritual life energy of the population in dramatic situations focuses on the acquisition of basic food or the 'egoistic' aim of saving one's own life. Despite the risks and dangers of a strenuous struggle for national survival in a war, vital energy, resources, and mass volition can be directed at unleashing a revolution against the very pillars of legitimacy and power of its state. The outbreak of the February Revolution of 1917, for instance, was met by sheer incredulity by Westerners shocked at people giving priority to a domestic political revolution at the expense of fighting the German enemy.[50] Even failures by elites to provide security of borders and the survival of a nation may inspire a moral purpose in the population. Despite the failure of state-building or state defence, the short-term independent statehood or restored statehood in east European countries such as Poland, Czechoslovakia, and the Baltic countries during the

---

[47] Jan Patočka, *Heretical Essays in the Philosophy of History*, ed. James Dodd (Chicago and La Salle: Open Court, 1996), 119–38.
[48] Carl von Clausewitz, *On War*, ed. and trans. Michael Howard and Peter Paret (London: D. Campbell, 1993), book 1, chap. 1, no. 28.
[49] Raymond Aron, *Les guerres en chaîne*, 12th edn (Paris: Gallimard, 1951), 22.
[50] George F. Kennan, *Russia and the West Under Lenin and Stalin* (Boston and Toronto: Little, Brown and Company, 1961), 6.

interwar period and the national struggle for survival in the Second World War acquired an enormous moral value, which nurtured expectations of national liberation.[51] Rather than being caused by a specific class, the revolutions in Hungary in 1956 or in Poland in 1980 dissolved social hierarchies by producing a spiritual community that became representative of the nation. Members of the Polish Solidarność movement framed their demands for free and independent trade unions in terms of romantic national tradition, an ethical civil society, and universal democracy. This was met by profound disbelief in circles of the Western left, as the revolution was not carried out by a working class in the classical socialist conception but in the name of the Polish nation and under the aegis of religious symbols.

In critical events, people adopt a rationality or consciousness that emerges in the situation, and is not representative of a rationality or logic external to that situation. Anthropological research distinguished 'events-that-model' from 'events that present the lived-in world' or 'events that re-present the lived-in world'.[52] Ritualised events such as the great celebrations of statehood in the Soviet Union or eastern Europe were events of presentation that held up a mirror to social order. Such ritualised events do not follow a logic of situational uncertainty but rather selectively substantiate or affirm versions of symbolic meanings of modelling events that are largely known. Events-that-model, on the contrary, are culturally creative as they open up dynamic potentiality but also define limits of empowerment within social orders. Contingency and uncertainty guide their logic, as they are embedded into the presumed stability of the phenomenon that is to undergo this radical transmutation. Revolutions are such events-that-model, where action has a certain teleological leaning as it unfolds in a means-to-end context in which they are embedded and from which their symbolic potential unfolds. People engaged in the teleological means-to-end context of dramatic situations assign meaning and purpose to their actions differently from how theorists of modernisation, development, and state centralisation would have it.

Even though periods of intense violence are followed by peace, identity-formation in aggregate entities such as states, nations, and regimes is characterised by tensions and conflicts on two fronts.[53] Norbert Elias's concept of dual-front strata overcomes a static conception of class by

---

[51] Joseph Rothschild, *Return to Diversity: A Political History of East Central Europe Since World War II*, 2nd edn (New York and Oxford: Oxford University Press, 1993).
[52] Don Handelman, *Models and Mirrors: Towards an Anthropology of Public Events* (Cambridge: Cambridge University Press, 1990), 22–57.
[53] Norbert Elias, *Die höfische Gesellschaft: Untersuchungen zur Soziologie des Königtums und der höfischen Aristokratie*, 8th edn (Frankfurt am Main: Suhrkamp, 1997), 387–90.

focusing on the tension between a stratum above and a stratum below. Russian elites, for instance, based their leadership aspirations on the movements between two fronts. The first movement was inspired by the desire to share professed similarity with the prestige of distant Europe to ensure the legitimacy of power. Russian rulers conscientiously cared about the symbolic staging of sacrality and embodiment of heroic history, as derived from distant historical or geographical sources.[54] A second movement concerned the dual fronts in domestic politics. In many respects, the educated classes and the Russian intelligentsia remained distant from the common people, born to remain in between a higher civilisation and the lower stratum of the people for whose liberation they fought.

The formation of consciousness

How can critical situations effect internal transformations at the level of consciousness? My intuition is that beyond material factors any possible analytical criteria need to pay at least equal attention to how experiences affect spirit, mind, belief, and emotions. Experiences themselves, in the way they are 'lived through' by human beings, have a structure of their own, and therefore do not require the external categories of the transcendental mind for intelligibility. Social anthropology has suggested that the dramatic set-up of liminal experiences can be structured. In Victor Turner's classification, a social drama consists of four phases.[55] It takes off with the breach of regular social relations or the radical challenge of the rules normally binding members of a community, either in a premeditated manner or caused by an unplanned event. A second phase consists of the crisis in which the sudden acceleration of events takes on a life of its own. At this critical juncture, relevant spheres of society are characterised by haphazard coalition-building around burning issues, which polarise the community into rival and conflicting groups. The third phase is the redress, which refers to attempts at arresting the process of disintegration and at restoring social order by a legitimacy-creating political consensus. Finally, after the 'deployment of legal or ritual mechanisms of redress', there is either a return to phase two through another crisis, or a return to normal order, in a phase of reintegration.

The crucial point is that in the fluidity of the conjuncture reality ceases to be perceived as a rationally testable 'objective force'. Rather, it can

---

[54] Wortman, *Scenarios of Power*, 6.
[55] Victor Turner, *On the Edge of the Bush* (Tucson: University of Arizona Press, 1985), 215–21.

become horizontally felt as immediate participation in the dramatic action of social effervescence of a collective body. In revolutionary dramas, the two main aspects of experience coincide in the 'objective' character of a major and sudden event, and the 'subjective' perspective of how this event was lived through by the individuals undergoing the changes. In these cases, individuals go through their 'initiation rites' during major socio-political transformations, making the impact of the social particularly strong. Thus, social dramas make two distinct structures of consciousness appear.[56] Commonly, consciousness is associated with some degree of intentionality of human beings who focus on external objects or things outside themselves. In times of peace or relatively stable social relations, the intentional consciousness of political actors is generally characterised by well-articulated goals and purposes implying the predictability of policy strategies, and the pursuit of sectional or class interests. It is at the con-juncture of crisis situations where the density of social relations generates another, second 'dimension' of consciousness.

In this second type, consciousness belongs not to man in his bodily existence, but to the comprehending reality in which man participates with other partners in the community of being. In such participatory events, human consciousness, as it were, flows between man's bodily existence and intentional reality directed at objects. This second, con-cretely located and experienced consciousness is also real, although it appears to be emotional and unconscious through participation in a social community.[57] War, for instance, has always been unmatched in inspiring solidarity and community, combined with devotion and an unconditional sense of sacrifice for the nation.[58] The appeal of war thus overpowers pacifist discourse as its appeal to sacrifice one's life to the cause of the nation becomes an overwhelming moral purpose. This 'spiritual force' of war makes it difficult to find a 'moral equivalent of war'.[59] The German invasion of the Soviet Union in 1941 provoked the revival of national emotions, conjuring up Russian traditions of heroic resistance and national community in the past.[60] Thus, war itself has an explanatory value as an event of meaning-formation where the solidarity of the shaken forms a unity, strictly divided in the effort of antagonistic

[56] Eric Voegelin, *Order and History*, vol. V, *In Search of Order* (Baton Rouge and London: Louisiana State University Press, 1985), 15–16.
[57] Voegelin, *In Search of Order*, 15.
[58] Max Weber, *Gesammelte Aufsätze zur Religionssoziologie* (Tübingen: Mohr, 1988), 548.
[59] William James, *The Writings of William James: A Comprehensive Edition*, ed. and intro. John J. McDermott (Chicago and London: University of Chicago Press, 1978), 666.
[60] Nina Tumarkin, *The Living and the Dead: The Rise and Fall of the Cult of World War II in Russia* (New York: Basic Books, 1994), 63.

forces at the front but united in the mobilisation of a moral purpose for the community.[61]

Moreover, shifts of consciousness need not be limited to 'great events' of higher publicity. Minor occurrences may be crucial for the formation of consciousness of future leaders or may reverse or alter strong trends, as small causes may produce big effects. Lenin's single most important experience of initiation in the revolutionary fight against tsarism was reportedly the execution of his brother Alexander in 1887, in the wake of a conspiracy against Tsar Alexander III.[62] This event was significant both sociopolitically and individually, setting Lenin on the path of a devoted intellectual and political fighter for revolution. The Polish dissident Adam Michnik declared that he owed everything to the communists who arrested him 1965 at the age of nineteen and who thus decided his further trajectory as an eminent dissident.[63] Similarly, structures can be open to doubt or scepticism far before any event challenges them openly. Important events of defiance against communist rule were in gestation long before the final disruption. The Prague spring did not arise as a spontaneous happening; it was the result of a gradual awakening, a sort of creeping opening of the hidden sphere of society.[64] Prior to 1968 there was no necessity for independent dissident initiatives because power structures themselves had not yet attained the static, impenetrable, and stable forms that they had in the wake of 1968.

Although this second sphere of consciousness is as real as the first one, the experiential reality inside a critical situation is logically different from the certainties and constraints under constituted power systems. A seminal contribution to the rationality of collective action argued that differences in the position of a group in the class structure lead not only to differences in power but also to differences in the associational practices and the types of collective action.[65] The difference of class, however, is also a matter of experience, language, and discourse. Historically, the constitution of class but also of states and regimes is more likely to be a result of action rather than a given based on vested interests. Although the

---

[61] Patočka, *Heretical Essays*.

[62] See Leonard Schapiro, *Russian Studies*, ed. Ellen Dahrendorf (New York: Viking, 1987), 190.

[63] Adam Michnik, *Diabeł naszego czasu* (Warsaw: Niezależna Oficyna Wydawnictwa, 1995), 398.

[64] Vaclav Havel, 'The Power of the Powerless', in John Keane, ed., *The Power of the Powerless: Citizens Against the State in Eastern Europe* (London: Hutchinson and Co., 1985), 43.

[65] Claus Offe and Helmut Wiesenthal, 'Two Logics of Collective Action: Theoretical Notes on Social Class and Organizational Form', *Political Power and Social Theory*, 1 (1980), 67–115.

writers of the American Constitution were intensely conscious of their role as founders and stressed the importance of their acts for 'generations yet unborn' or 'posterity', their dispositions were not equivalent to liberal democracy as a type of government.[66] Rather than grounding constitutionalism in an absolute principle, they combined the imitation of the Roman example with republicanism in the Machiavellian tradition. Their consciousness was not in tune with a determinate model of political organisation but became transformed through the very act of founding a new system of political authority, which postulated a 'beginning of time' through a return to the past.[67]

As all political actors in critical events, the French revolutionaries did not have a choice between an imaginary and a potentially viable political project but between alternative imaginative constructions of the social and political world.[68] Initially, the aim of the French revolutionaries was not the reversal of the *ancien régime* but its reconstitution.[69] The period 1789–90 was not a radical precursor to the Terror, but was dominated by moderates who were keen to avoid counter-revolution and who pursued the establishment of constitutional government. In the context of the French Revolution, not only did the representatives of the third estate not have socially homogeneous backgrounds but they also lacked a revolutionary disposition, even as an ideological standpoint.[70] Whereas the early revolutionaries proclaimed a rupture with the *ancien régime*, the radical Jacobin phase paved the way to bureaucratic centralisation.

Neither the end of tsarism in February 1917 nor the Bolshevik Revolution and its maintenance in civil war and war communism was inevitable.[71] Leninism was not a coherent ideology that was inevitably to lead to the dictatorship of the proletariat. At the moment of realising the *coup d'état* in Petrograd on 24 October 1917, Lenin turned upside down the theory of representative government of the soviets. Rather than being representative of a major social group, the Bolsheviks followed a zigzag path with haphazard coalitions and attuned their strategies, often due to chance events. The growing class antagonism in the Russian army and in

---

[66] Cecilia M. Kenyon, 'Constitutionalism in Revolutionary America', in J. Roland Pennock and John W. Chapman, eds., *Constitutionalism* (New York: New York University Press, 1979), 84–121.
[67] Hannah Arendt, *On Revolution* (London: Faber and Faber, 1962), 204–5.
[68] William Sewell jnr, 'A Rhetoric of Bourgeois Revolution', in Kates, *The French Revolution*, 143–56.
[69] Alexis de Tocqueville, *L'ancien régime et la révolution* (Paris: Flammarion, 1988).
[70] Timothy Tackett, *Becoming a Revolutionary: The Deputies of the French National Assembly and the Emergence of a Revolutionary Culture (1789–1790)* (Princeton: Princeton University Press, 1996).
[71] Richard Pipes, *Three Whys of the Russian Revolution* (London: Pimlico, 1998), 11–19.

the major cities in the aftermath of the February Revolution was reminiscent of the two 'societies' in Russia, the people (*narod*) and enlightened civil society (*obshchestvennost*). However, it was by no means prefigured before 1917 but was rather a result of the failed political project of the dual-power set-up. The construction of the term *burzhua* (bourgeois) as the class enemy was primarily defined by its fluidity, vagueness, and makeshift character. In the crowd violence of 1917, the aroused masses vented their anger not against an abstract 'bourgeoisie' or a social class but against real people they met in face-to-face relationships on the streets, unable to clearly identify a potential enemy in class terms.[72]

The revolutions in Hungary in 1956, in Czechoslovakia in 1968, and in Poland in 1980/1 were objective crises in communist political societies but modified attitudes of power incumbents and of individuals as they subjectively tried to make sense of such major sociopolitical transformations. The Soviet intervention on 21 August 1968 in Czechoslovakia produced two realities.[73] Although it failed to achieve its political objectives, the military occupation by Soviet forces was consolidated within a few days and became a reality in Czechoslovak life. Simultaneously, and quite unexpectedly, the overwhelming majority of the country's population challenged the Soviet occupation force by means of spontaneous collective solidarity and non-violent resistance, symbolising the unity of the Czechoslovak people. The Soviet Army's utter surprise about the population's reaction manifested the profound misinterpretation of the situation by the Soviet authorities.

The experience of resistance to communism reflects the insights of social theorists that the logic of warfare and reciprocal vengeance is not an anthropological constant. As anthropologists such as Marshall Sahlins have argued, the exchange of goods in primitive forms of economy was not based on the pursuit of private self-interest but was driven by the need to establish a social bond. Exchanging goods, therefore, was tantamount to a kind of social contract which prevented violence from breaking out.[74] The rich and controversial literature in the wake of Marcel Mauss's seminal essay on 'The Gift' has been intrigued with the force by which a gift induces somebody to reciprocate it. Explaining the logic of the counter-gift, Claude Lefort argued that giving back a gift implies that

---

[72] Orlando Figes and Boris Kolonitskii, *Interpreting the Russian Revolution: The Language and Symbols of 1917* (New Haven and London: Yale University Press, 1999), 177–8.

[73] Fred H. Eidlin, *The Logic of 'Normalization': The Soviet Intervention in Czechoslovakia of 21 August 1968 and the Czechoslovak Response* (New York: Columbia University Press, 1980), 156.

[74] Marshall Sahlins, *Stone Age Economics* (Chicago: Aldine, 1972), 172–4.

the other is like me who ought to act like me.[75] This gesture is supposed to confirm the truth of my own gesture, which is my subjectivity. As Luc Boltanski argued for the specific act of *agape*, conditions of peace are possible, which renounce common notions of self-interested reciprocity, justice, or expectations of receiving back as a result of giving.[76]

The focus on democratisation as starting after the end of communist power has concealed the formative power of situational premises. Both revolutionary violence and conditions of peaceful *communitas* have been formative for dispositions of individuals and collective groups. Democratic transitions after communism do not depend only on predetermined dispositions appropriate for liberal democracy but should include the utopian possibilities of democracy, which subscribed to ethical individualism, images of full freedom, or anti-political attitudes of 'living in truth'. In the context of fluid conjunctures, actors are concerned not just with violence and vengeance; their consciousness is also formed by mutual recognition and the desire for community. Solidarity with fellow citizens and other human beings who suffer from oppression or humiliation may become a major concern for people during spontaneous mobilisation, even prompting the disobeying of orders by the government or the police force. The different logic of behaviour requires approaching the situation as a microcosm where objective events and subjective attitudes are mutually dependent on each other. Mutual recognition is the precondition for the constitution of conditions of peace.[77]

In Czechoslovakia, individual experiences of having signed Charter 77 evoked sudden and powerful feelings of genuine community among people who were all but strangers before. Although the challenge to the Polish communist party-state by the trade union movement Solidarność in 1980 was enormous – due to both the numbers of followers and the moral purpose for an independent nation – the action of Solidarity precluded the seizure of power. Similarly, neither party reformers nor opposition forces on the eve of the round-table negotiations in early 1989 had a transformative interest. The central objective of the Solidarność opposition in Poland associated with the round-table negotiations followed the sectional logic of a relegalisation of the trade union. Former enemies converged in an unprecedented *communitas*, with Solidarność representatives and party negotiators united in mutual forgiveness and heartfelt personal sympathy. Throughout the two months of negotiations, the gap

---

[75] Claude Lefort, *Les formes de l'histoire. Essai d'anthropologie politique* (Paris: Gallimard, 1978).
[76] Luc Boltanski, *L'amour et la justice comme compétences* (Paris: Métaillé, 1990).
[77] Paul Ricoeur, *Parcours de la reconnaissance* (Paris: Stock, 2004), 359–78.

between the opposition and the regime was drastically reduced and top party negotiators came to perceive the apparatchiks as 'them', while including themselves with their partners from the trade union movement in an 'us' category.[78]

Sociologically, revolutionary movements were defined as contentious gatherings of crowds, where specific rhythms of collective action had an impact on the transformation of consciousness. In this view, 'a jagged short-term rhythm' depends heavily on shifts in the relative strategic positions, shared understandings, and resources of connected actors. Conversely, 'a smoother long-term rhythm' characterises incremental transformation processes of social relations such as state-formation, industrialisation, or democratisation.[79] Focused on a number of people that gather in publicly accessible places and make claims that may – if realised – affect the interests of other persons not present, this concept ignores individual forms of resistance as well as the routine operation of institutionalised groups. It is likewise insensitive to the incremental development of collective identities and of consensus mobilisation preceding contention, because public records tell us little about these cultural and socio-psychological processes.[80] Recently, the politics of friendship has been developed as a resource for the civilisation of Russian political life.[81]

The experiential basis of political forms suggests that the 'objectively' verifiable habits, behaviours, and attitudes of revolutionary or transitional leaders are both a precondition for and an effect of 'subjectively' experienced fluidity of conjunctures. As William James argued, mental states, calculations, or dispositions do not follow upon each other consecutively but must take into account the bodily and emotional changes following upon the perception of an exciting fact.[82] In this view, experiencing the changes as they occur *is* the emotion. Thus, the more rational statement is that 'we feel sorry because we cry, angry because we strike, afraid because we tremble, and not that we cry, strike, or tremble, because we are sorry, angry, or fearful, as the case may be'. In Max Weber's terms, the knowledge of cultural events is inconceivable except on the basis of

---

[78] Wiktor Osiatyński, 'The Roundtable Talks in Poland', in Jon Elster, ed., *The Roundtable Talks and the Breakdown of Communism* (Chicago and London: University of Chicago Press, 1996), 59.

[79] Charles Tilly, *Popular Contention in Great Britain* (Cambridge, MA: Harvard University Press, 1995), 23 and 63–5.

[80] Sidney Tarrow, 'The People's Two Rhythms: Charles Tilly and the Study of Contentious Politics. A Review Article', *Comparative Studies in Society and History*, 38 (1996), 593.

[81] Oleg Kharkhordin, *Main Concepts of Russian Politics* (Lanham, MD: University Press of America, 2005), 115–54.

[82] James, *Writings of William James*, 449–50.

the significance that the concrete constellations of reality have for us in certain individual concrete situations.[83] In the means-to-end context of such fluid conjunctures, the intentions of actors are guided by contradictory images of future goals and past dependencies.

The impression of irrationality in revolutionary crisis or transitional situations arises because historians tend to measure action by different variants of outcome-logic.[84] As the designs and options of actors alter incrementally through time, their purpose is not attuned to any objectively conceived political development in stages, periods, or paths. From a perspective of 'situational reality', however, the designs of individuals and groups, but also of classes, states, and nations, are never static, nor are they complete in themselves. It is not enough to suggest that revolutionary action cannot be studied for its own rationality because it produces unintended consequences. What needs to be done is to attune the disposition of actors to the fluidity of the revolutionary conjuncture. Historically, critical situations have a rationality of their own, shaping the consciousness and dispositions of actors. The following two chapters aim to contextualise such transformations of consciousness with regard to the dramatic situations that underlie communist power and democratic transformations. From such an experiential perspective, it will appear that communism and democracy are more related than is usually assumed.

---

[83] Max Weber, *On the Methodology of the Social Sciences*, trans. and ed. Edward A. Shils and Henry A. Finch (Glencoe, IL: Free Press, 1949), 80.

[84] Max Weber, *Gesammelte Aufsätze zur Wissenschaftslehre*, 3rd edn, ed. Johannes Winckelmann (Tübingen: Mohr, 1968), 120.

3   The political symbolism of communism

The death of the spirit is the price of progress.   Eric Voegelin

The political spirituality of Bolshevik power

A variety of causes have been put forward to explain how the Soviet superpower could collapse so suddenly. This chapter complements views that ascribe importance to factors such as imperial overstretch, economic competition, or a legitimacy crisis. I shall argue that the spiritual foundations of Bolshevik power account for the paradoxical nature of communism. Revolutionary consciousness and the modalities of the seizure of power by the Bolsheviks failed to establish constitutive foundations for communist power. The credentials of communism as a political religion were crucial for the mobilisation and legitimisation of an economically disastrous but politically fascinating and temporarily quite successful experiment. Conversely, these very spiritual foundations accounted for the structural weakness of communist power and the failure to achieve constitutive politics. My aim is not to explain what 'caused' the collapse of communism. Important studies have examined the inherent weakness of Soviet-type institutions and have, in a path-dependent manner, looked at paths of extrication for the new order.[1] Rather, I am challenging the notion according to which communism was a constituted system of power.

The focus on transitions to democracy through the related processes of constitution-building, the introduction of election-based party competition, and the pursuit of a capitalist market economy deliberately overlooked the fact that political analysis must conceive of political order by

---

[1] Agnes Horváth and Arpad Szakolczai, *The Dissolution of Communist Power: The Case of Hungary* (London: Routledge, 1992); Valerie Bunce, *Subversive Institutions: The Design and the Destruction of Socialism* (Cambridge: Cambridge University Press, 1999); Oleg Kharkhordin, *The Collective and the Individual in Russia: A Study of Practices* (Berkeley: University of California Press, 1999).

distinguishing at least two levels.[2] It must address an instrumental aspect
that looks at the institutionalisation of political authority, rights, claims,
and conflict. It must also assume, however, that in a functioning system
the nature of man and his volition hinge on the irrationality of political
constitutions and the expressive and symbolic functions of the polity.
Symbols, rites, and myths permeate society not only as analogies. They
are also recognisable reference points in different domains of everyday
life, such as in political discourse, campaigns, and state ideology. The
meanings of values and norms associated with the intentions and behaviour of leadership do not pre-exist action as belief-systems. Rather, they
are often established in liminal experiences where otherwise 'solid' forms
of political authority and social order are disarticulated. In historical
experience, the resulting crises of existential scope demand existential
and, therefore, pre-political responses. Beyond institutions and material
constraints, 'political reality' also consists of meanings and symbolic
markers of certainty that illuminate human beings who continuously
create and bear them as the mode and condition of their self-realisation.[3]

'Political spirituality' suggests that leadership in the form of shaping
and guiding human arrangements in political society does not depend on
the innate qualities of the leader or on legal stipulations, but on the
situational link and the responsiveness between a great number of followers and their spiritual adherence to this leader. Max Weber introduced spiritual power into political science under the notion of charisma
as a type of legitimate authority.[4] Following this 'spiritualist' construction
of the modern capitalist economy as a way of life, the central issue of
political spirituality is the mobilisation of human beings, the raising of
their souls. Notions such as spirituality meet with scepticism as they lie
beyond any straightforward analytical categorisation, often associated
with mysticism or religion. Although current political analysis seems to
have all but forgotten, Weber's paradigmatic example of charismatic
power is not a politician but a prophet. Power comes from the super-
natural, setting a typology of the prophet against the priest and the
magician.[5] The spirit of capitalism as the source of the increase in
power of man over the things of his world springs from the distance
which man puts between himself and the world, that is, from world

[2] Murray Edelman, *The Symbolic Uses of Politics* (Urbana: University of Illinois Press, 1964), 12–20.
[3] Eric Voegelin, *The New Science of Politics: An Introduction* (Chicago and London: University of Chicago Press, 1987), 27–41.
[4] Max Weber, *Economy and Society: An Outline of Interpretive Sociology*, ed. Guenther Roth and Claus Wittich (Berkeley: University of California Press, 1978), 241–54.
[5] Weber, *Economy and Society*, 439–40.

alienation. In Weber's view, the 'economic ethic' of Protestant capitalists derived practical impulses for action from 'internal states', psychological impulses or inducements that were rooted in the pragmatic contexts of religions.[6]

Political spirituality as a source of power is not rooted in the theological belief in transcendence but relies on the bond that is created and becomes effective between social actors and what they believe to be a relevant motive force for action. As the charisma of a leader stems not from rules or norms but from the belief his followers project on to him, charismatic leadership comes close to the performance of a convincing dramatic actor.[7] This dramatisation of power around a moral purpose or spiritual cause reflects the insights of several strands in political and social thought. While Montesquieu's 'spirit of the laws' grounded objectified legislation in the existential basis and mental dispositions of people, Tocqueville argued that, despite a constitutionally and legally guaranteed democratic state, there would be no guarantee for the continuity of freedom and equality without a spiritual alertness and the ability to raise one's soul.[8]

Going beyond the current symbolic separation, one could make a case for the close affinity of spirituality with religion, a relationship that has been distorted due to a split of meaning in the wake of the Reformation and the Enlightenment. Since the Enlightenment at the latest, religious symbols were not seen as being grounded in empirical reality but as having a function. As a result of these changes in interpretation, the modern mind cannot but treat compounds of religion and politics as examples of closed bodies or systems of beliefs, dogmas, 'fundamental-ism', or 'ideology'.[9] The unusual combination of concepts such as politics and religion was at odds with common sense as, in modern times, politics and religion emerged as two entirely distinct realities, the former embod-ied institutionally by the state, the latter by the church. One may attribute the conceptual separation of state and religion to Hegel, who argued that 'the people' is the state as the spirit in its immanent reality and thus as the absolute power on earth. The opinion that state power was original or

[6] Max Weber, 'The Social Psychology of the World Religions', in H. H. Gerth and C. W. Mills, eds., *From Max Weber: Essays in Sociology* (London: Routledge and Kegan Paul, 1970), 267.

[7] Laurence Whitehead, *Democratisation: Theory and Experience* (Oxford: Oxford University Press, 2002), 43.

[8] Charles de Montesquieu, *The Spirit of the Laws*, ed. Anne C. Cohler et al. (Cambridge: Cambridge University Press, 1989); Alexis de Tocqueville, *Democracy in America: The Complete and Unabridged*, 2 vols., trans. Henry Reeve (New York: Bantam Classic, 2000), 672.

[9] Stefan Rossbach, *Gnostic Wars: The Cold War in the Context of a History of Western Spirituality* (Edinburgh: Edinburgh University Press, 1999), 2.

absolute was not based on rational knowledge; it was more the dogma of a believer.[10] This clear-cut distinction emanates from the symbolic uses of language attuned to the outcome of Western state-formation, not the original spirit. It did not maintain the reality of the intimate engagement by which these entities reinforced each other up to the late Middle Ages and early modernity, but has symbolised and vindicated the very contrasts of the struggle.[11]

The decline of religion as a function of the growing separation of church and state and patterns of legal-rational domination should not conceal that both logically and historically modern politics rests upon a theological-political formation and its redeployment in social relations.[12] The indeterminate nature of social relations and of political power in nascent democratic society was based on a rejection of transcendence but, simultaneously, proposed an image of society as homogeneous in principle, as manageable by knowledge and power, and as an image of the people, which would efface social divisions. The disintegration of the body of social institutions, the loss of a defining centre of power and identity, was met by an attempt to sacralise human and secular institutions such as Property, the Family, the State, Authority, the Nation, or Sovereignty.[13]

Political spirituality does not separate religion from the state but suggests that the emergence of the political and the appearance of the modern state did not expunge transcendence and godly ends.[14] At the outset of the modern state, the dissociation was not of religious from state power but of the spiritual from the temporal powers. Before the territorialisation of the state – which allowed for the identification of the 'Other' as not belonging to or as threatening this territory – the church delimited the space between friend and enemy spiritually. The origin of the Western style of power consisted of an absolute project that established spiritual power as a compound of four types of power: the control of organisation of knowledge, the production of norms, the politics of devotion, and the identification of the enemies of society. The democratic age did not fundamentally discontinue the engagement between religion and politics. The French Revolution can be likened to a religious revolution in so far as

---

[10] Eric Voegelin, *Political Religions*, Toronto Studies in Theology, vol. XXIII (Lewiston, NY: Edwin Mellen Press, 1986).
[11] Voegelin, *The New Science of Politics*.
[12] Claude Lefort, *Essais sur le politique* (Paris: Seuil, 1986).
[13] Claude Lefort, *The Political Forms of Modern Society: Bureaucracy, Democracy, Totalitarianism* (Cambridge: Polity, 1986), 293–306.
[14] Alessandro Pizzorno, 'Politics Unbound', in Charles S. Maier, ed., *Changing Boundaries of the Political* (Cambridge: Cambridge University Press, 1987), 43–9.

it affected the citizen in an abstract way, much as religion affects man in an abstract way with regard to transcendence.[15] Human beings were not only constituent parts of the French nation but were considered as representative for other nations and cultures in this immanent world.

This religious inspiration postulated universal, trans-national, and permanent values as the basis of the common good in a republican form of government. The totalitarian version of democracy linked an extreme idea of popular sovereignty to a specific religious type of autocracy, based in an all-embracing and pervasive influence of politics on human existence. Its persistence despite its contradiction to empirical facts was mainly due to the religious appeal it had on the utilitarian philosophers that invented it.[16] Despite the rejection of metaphysics and the anti-religious attitude of its protagonists, the utilitarian creed was a perfect substitute. The classical doctrine of democracy became the political complement for those who were still religious believers. Only the religious interpretation explains the believer's attitude towards criticism. Both democrats and socialists consider fundamental dissent not only as a dangerous threat in terms of a contest for the established power system but also as a sin; dissent therefore elicits not merely logical counter-arguments but also moral indignation.

Communism as political religion

The notion of spirituality may sound inappropriate if one thinks of the destructiveness and coercive nature of communism in post-revolutionary and Stalinist Russia. The impact of terror and violence on society should not, however, conceal the crucial influence of revolutionary messianism. Soviet communism was a project of absolute politics that engineered the human mind and human culture by incorporating the political symbolism of traditional Russian patterns for the self-legitimisation of the new regime.[17] Creating a mythology of power based on the dogma of Marxism-Leninism, the utopian promise of a prospective paradise on earth, the cult of the leader, and Soviet patriotism, Bolshevism was an exercise in political spirituality. The revolutionary Bolshevik regime merged radical currents of Russian nihilism with messianism and the absolutism of modern rational design of an all-encompassing revolutionary

[15] Alexis de Tocqueville, *L'ancien régime et la révolution* (Paris: Flammarion), 105–9.
[16] Joseph A. Schumpeter, *Capitalism, Socialism, and Democracy*, 5th edn (London: George Allen & Unwin, 1976), 265–6.
[17] Stephen Kotkin, *Magnetic Mountain: Stalinism as a Civilization* (Berkeley: University of California Press, 1995), 14.

project. Determined to seize political opportunities and to adapt the 'programme' to Russian reality, Lenin introduced the category of the 'professional revolutionary' whose guidance would make Marx's scientific theory of history politically viable.

This re-emergence of religious principles in modern politics had its origins in Christianity itself, deriving from components that were suppressed as sectarian and heretical by the universal church.[18] As Eric Voegelin has shown, the definite symbolism associated with a redivinisation of politics can be traced back to the person and work of the twelfth-century Cistercian abbot Joachim of Flora, who created the aggregate of symbols that govern the self-interpretation of modern political society up to this day. The first symbol is the conception of history as a sequence of three ages, of which the third age is the final Third Realm. The second symbol is that of the leader. The third symbol, with a certain affinity to the second, is that of the prophet of the new age. The fourth symbol is that of the brotherhood of autonomous persons. The third age of Joachim, by virtue of the arrival of the spirit on earth, will transform men into members of the new realm without sacramental mediation of grace. This Gnostic spirituality has found its secularised equivalent in periodisations of history as claimed by Hegel or Comte. It also underpinned Marx's historical materialism and his utopian idea of a realm of freedom after the withering away of the state. Thus, modern politics has been thoroughly affected by the structure of symbols that came into being in the wake of applying Christian eschatology to an interpretation of an essential meaning of history in the worldly sphere, a doctrine that acquired the highest political impact with Bolshevism and Nazism.

Generated at the crossroads between the crisis of European modernity and the crisis of the tsarist system in pre-revolutionary Russia, Bolshevism was an intellectual current that challenged tsarism from an exogenous ideological tradition, which was Marxism. Although Marxism was a response to the crisis of European modernity, large parts of the Russian intelligentsia became captivated by this 'scientific' solution to the problem of oppression in Russia, which domestic populism, nihilism, or anarchism could not solve. The boundary that divided the Russian intelligentsia from other classes was itself determined not by material but by spiritual facts, for revolutionary thinkers from different social origins such as Bakunin, Kropotkin, and Tolstoy were united by the spell of European civilisation.[19] Attracted by the 'West' and aspiring to be equal, they were

---

[18] Voegelin, *The New Science of Politics*, 112–14.
[19] Franz Borkenau, *World Communism: A History of the Communist International* (Ann Arbor: University of Michigan Press, 1971), 28–9.

at the same time resentful and endowed with a sense of inferiority. The intelligentsia as a 'transformer class' lived in a no-man's land between two extremes: on the one hand, its own backward society, which it aspired to emancipate but from which it had increasingly alienated itself, lacking recognition for its efforts; on the other, the 'model society', from which it derived its expectations but which would never accept it as an equal partner.[20]

Intellectual elites and their hold on the monopoly of legitimate education played a decisive role in the development of modern social order. Emerging in the particular circumstances of nineteenth-century Russia, the term 'intelligentsia' was imported from the West and applied to a specific group of members of the intellectual urban elites of the country with a special interest in 'educating society' and managing processes of modernisation.[21] Unlike their Western counterparts, members of the intelligentsia of backward countries only reluctantly specialised in their careers, as they dedicated much of their energy to achieving a wholesale transformation of their countries.[22]

Why did communist practice make enormous efforts to rewrite national histories in the light of the Marxist-Leninist philosophy of history? Why did the Bolsheviks aim to create new symbolic universes by destroying traditional symbols, deforming language, and manipulating religion and culture? Political messianism established a preordained, perfect scheme of human collective organisation based on the idea of transforming human nature by social engineering and promises of world-immanent redemption.[23] The challenge posed by Marxism to Western modernity was generated primarily from a spiritual movement that rested upon a romantic secularisation of properly religious experiences. Modern revolutionary ideologies were inspired by the symbols and intentions of medieval heresies such as Gnosticism, which based political consciousness on messianic expectations.[24] The revolutionary messianism of Bolshevik communism found fruitful soil in messianic ideas in Russia, where the symbol of the Third Rome was turned into a national

---

[20] Zygmunt Bauman, 'Love in Adversity: On the State and the Intellectuals, and the State of Intellectuals', *Thesis Eleven*, 31 (1992), 81–104.

[21] Richard Pipes, *Russia Under the Old Regime*, 2nd edn (London: Penguin Books, 1995), 251–3.

[22] David Joravsky, 'Communism in Historical Perspective', *American Historical Review*, 99, 3 (1994), 854.

[23] Waldemar Gurian, 'Totalitarianism as Political Religion', in C.J. Friedrich, ed., *Totalitarianism* (Cambridge, MA: Harvard University Press, 1954), 119–29.

[24] Norman Cohn, *The Pursuit of the Millennium: Revolutionary Millenarians and Mystical Anarchists of the Middle Ages*, 3rd edn (London and New York: Oxford University Press, 1970).

programme of salvation. This merger of programmes of salvation largely accounts for why an atheistic ideology became successful in a deeply religious, orthodox country.[25] Lenin's lifelong fascination with the revolutionary messianism of the 1860s democrats such as Chernyshevsky, Pisarev and Tkachev is reflected in his adherence to the Revolutionary Catechism of 1871, which emphasised the true revolutionary's total self-denial, renunciation of worldly attachment and morality, and property.[26] Lenin echoed the catechism when he wrote at the end of 1897 that the life of the revolutionary demanded the highest degree of endurance and self-denial, dedicating all his powers to monotonous, strictly regulated work, often without results. His political messianism instilled into many an extraordinary revolutionary ardour, an intoxicating promise of a new freedom that obscured passions such as hatred and the Bolshevik spirit of civil war.[27]

Revolutionary messianism encountered a Russian state that before the First World War had accelerated economic modernisation in order to catch up technologically and economically with the more advanced Europe. The massive migrations from the countryside to the cities since the early twentieth century were accompanied by half-hearted political reforms and conditions of social unrest. The peasant community's devotion to the tsar declined considerably only after the 1905 revolution and all but collapsed during the First World War. At the conjuncture of this devastating war, Bolshevism captured the minds of many peasant-soldiers through extensive propaganda in the trenches.

Although the social conditions and the political articulation of Nazism in Germany and of Bolshevik communism in the Russian case differed considerably, they displayed crucial similarities. Overall, neither of the two totalitarian ideologies were alien imports from outside suddenly menacing the West. As products of a deep spiritual crisis, they combined tyrannical impulses with the social conditions of mob rule. Throughout the nineteenth century, social, economic, and technological revolutionary processes produced masses uprooted from familiar ways of life in the countryside and bereft of any generally accepted core body of values. The acquisitions of modern technology had penetrated life so much that they

---

[25] Nikolai Berdyaev, *The Russian Revolution* (Ann Arbor: University of Michigan Press, 1961); Peter Duncan, *Russian Messianism: Third Rome, Revolution, Communism and After* (London: Routledge, 2000).

[26] Leonard Schapiro, *Russian Studies*, ed. Ellen Dahrendorf (New York: Viking, 1987), 195–6.

[27] Merle Fainsod, *How Russia Is Ruled*, 2nd enlarged edn (Cambridge, MA: Harvard University Press, 1963), 95.

were taken for granted not as human constructions but as if they were given by nature.[28]

The psychological condition of a vast number of Russians was characterised by what Hannah Arendt has seen as a crucial source of totalitarianism: the fact that loneliness, once a borderline experience usually suffered in certain marginal social conditions such as old age, has become an everyday experience of our century. The merciless process into which totalitarianism drives and organises the masses looks like a suicidal escape from this reality.[29] Bereft of religious awe and of faith in an ultimate authority, people could be attracted by any effort that seemed to promise the salvation they longed for. The recklessness of revolutionary leaders and the corruption of their moral principles were concealed behind a radically dichotomic world-view. Communism divided reality according to archetypical images of good and evil, adhered to logics of Salvationism, and demanded the unconditional devotion of its followers.[30]

Whereas National Socialism was a 'revolt against the West' from within, Bolshevism in Russia was nurtured by the Western heresy of Marxism outside the West.[31] Whereas limited government in the West rested upon the idea of parliament and law in order to check arbitrary power, communism as a political religion rejected the idea of a government by laws by endowing political rule with a 'sacred' duty of creating law and history. Despite its anti-religious ideology and its ruthless crackdown on the Orthodox Church, Soviet communism relied on a religious principle that regarded man as an abstract category that was to undergo physical and spiritual reconstruction. The Bolsheviks blended a teleological vision of progress with the expectation of paradise on earth and the complete transformation of human nature. Inspired by Marx's scientific theory of history, the desire for freedom from state oppression and the longing for salvation came along with a universal and abstract design for humanity, the creation of a new man and a new society. For Marx, the proletariat was not only destined to replace the dominant class of oppression but also possessed central heroic attributes of a collective redeemer class. The battle against institutionalised Orthodox religion was central for the Bolsheviks in their attempt to conquer society by engineering the human soul.[32] The dictatorship of the proletariat as the new symbol of

---

[28] José Ortega y Gasset, La rebelión de las masas (Madrid: Castalia, 1998), 173.

[29] Hannah Arendt, The Origins of Totalitarianism (London: George Allen, 1951), 478.

[30] Raymond Aron, The Dawn of Universal History (New York: Perseus, 2002), 164–242.

[31] Franz Borkenau, The Totalitarian Enemy (London: Faber and Faber, 1940).

[32] Orlando Figes, A People's Tragedy: The Russian Revolution 1891–1924 (London: Jonathan Cape, 1996), 732–51.

communist political authority imposed an absolutist project based on the dogmatism of a secular eschatology that would mark the end of politics.[33] In Trotsky's view, the future task of communism was to produce a new improved version of man. Man was himself the raw material whose nature must be transformed.

In terms of identity politics, Bolshevik communism gave rise to a theocracy of the vanguard party, combined with the dogmatic defence of communist orthodoxy and a civil religion of Marxism-Leninism, which aimed at large-scale social engineering towards a redivinisation of society.[34] Although the Bolsheviks led a merciless battle against religion and the clergy, they used practices that were not only largely inspired by traditional practices of orthodox religion but sometimes even identical to them. Bolshevik techniques of power were permeated by Orthodox Christian practices, techniques of self-fashioning such as self-sacrifice, and the transformation of a *telos* of Christian sainthood into hero worship and hero identification.[35] Supported by new methods of mass propaganda, the Bolsheviks' aim was to prove the inexorable march of history projected by Marxism-Leninism through the cultivation of symbolic imagery of the collective hero of world history, the proletariat.[36] Using symbolism similar to that in religious painting, poster artists represented workers and peasants in conjunction with the colour red as opposed to black as the colour of evil.

The identification of the enemy

The institutionalisation of political authority in post-revolutionary Russia went significantly beyond the recasting of economic relations required by Marxist-Leninist ideology. The Bolshevik Revolution primarily destroyed the old civilisation and improvised a new one.[37] While many portrayed the 'golden twenties' of the New Economic Policy as socialism with a human face, displaying cultural diversity and private enterprise, it contained the foundations of Stalinist rule, which included systematic terror, dismissal of older values, longing for unanimity, and self-abasement.[38]

---

[33] A. J. Polan, *Lenin and the End of Politics* (London: Methuen, 1984).
[34] Kotkin, *Magnetic Mountain*, 286–305.
[35] Kharkhordin, *The Collective and the Individual in Russia*, 263.
[36] Victoria Bonnell, *Iconography of Power: Soviet Political Posters Under Lenin and Stalin* (Berkeley: University of California Press, 1999), 21–41.
[37] Vladimir Brovkin, *Russia After Lenin: Politics, Culture, and Society, 1921–1929* (London and New York: Routledge, 1998), 1–19.
[38] Nadezhda Mandelstam, *Hope Against Hope: A Memoir* (New York: Atheneum, 1970), 168.

As a result, Bolshevism engaged in a struggle for representation that was beyond the materially visible, objectively verifiable external side of political reality. In a politically constituted order, representation is usually exercised through practice and experience, as the people actively participate in producing democratic government.[39] Yet the practice of representation in its dimensions of functional aspects of government control, articulation of voters' demands, and accountability in a constituted system of government must be separated from the conditions of its formalisation. One can distinguish formal representation as the representative's authorisation to act, descriptive representation as the idea of the representative's correspondence or likeness and resemblance to his or her constituents, and symbolic representation as suggesting the role of irrational belief and the importance of pleasing constituents.[40]

History, however, can produce human arrangements in state and society where the elementary rules and norms of institutional reality are at odds with existential symbolic universes. The growing economic and intellectual importance of the Third Estate in late eighteenth-century France preceded the idea of the Nation, which gained enormous symbolic significance by portraying itself as a victim of the absolutist feudal state and its discriminating corporate structure.[41] After the establishment of parliamentary democracy in Weimar Germany, many contemporaries were convinced that the democratisation of mentalities, beliefs, and values would follow. Inspired by ahistorical rationalism, this view sidelined culture and national characteristics. The brotherhood-and-unity formula in post-1945 Yugoslavia could not conceal that the legal-constitutional doctrine of the Titoist state was increasingly at odds with perceptions in the republics, which had assigned the task of existential representation to the ethnic community, not to the federal state. Although the constitution of 1974 conferred quasi-autonomy to the republics of Vojvodina and Kosovo, decentralisation was never really accepted by the Serbs.

Before 1917, Russian political order never came to constitute a legal entity superior to and independent from the will of monarchs. Until the second half of the nineteenth century, the state (*gosudarstvo*) as an independent and autonomously regulated machine of power did not exist in

---

[39] Schumpeter, *Capitalism, Socialism, and Democracy*, 269.
[40] Hanna Pitkin, *The Concept of Representation* (Berkeley: University of California Press, 1967).
[41] William H. Sewell jnr, *A Rhetoric of Bourgeois Revolution: The Abbé Sieyes and 'What Is the Third Estate?'* (Durham and London: Duke University Press, 1994), 41–65.

the perception of the bulk of Russian society.[42] As the primary allegiance of the vast majority of the population, the peasants, was the local community (*mir*), the notion of common good embodied by the fatherland (*otechestvo*) through the state remained highly abstract. The tsars had to rely on autocratic means to hammer this idea of the common good into the heads of their subjects. While keeping them in social misery and under political tutelage, tsarism maintained the myth of social monarchy through the tsar's special concern for the peasantry.[43]

In regarding Soviet communism as a counter-model to the liberal Western democratic state, we neglect the symbolism established by the Bolsheviks in post-revolutionary Russia and later in eastern Europe. Westerners confused constitutionalism in communist countries with Western constitutions, as they did not realise that the revolution did not establish a constitutive act in terms of creating a political community.[44] Communism was devoid of larger popular support and failed to develop full representation in the formal (constitutional) sense. The formalisation of communist political authority did not occur through a constitutive act of a national constitutional assembly. The Bolsheviks remained permanently contested in the descriptive sense and had to rely largely upon radical shifts in symbolic representation. Representation in the constitutional sense in a political society is no insurance against the disintegration of existential representation. When a representative is not in a condition to fulfil his existential task, no constitutional legality of his position will save him; if a creative minority turns into a dominant minority, it is in danger of being replaced by a new creative minority. While Soviet communism failed to provide formal and descriptive representation, however, it produced a principle of representation of its own.

Lenin and the Bolshevik party espoused the symbolism of the dictatorship of the proletariat, which assigned the leading role to the party as a representative of humanity itself. This dictatorship defined itself as anti-liberal, anti-religious, progressive, and determined to uproot traditional values and ideas of social and political organisation for the sake of consolidating the revolution. Given the deep social polarisation in revolutionary

---

[42] Oleg Kharkhordin, *Main Concepts of Russian Politics* (Lanham, MD: University Press of America, 2005), 1–40.

[43] Richard Wortman, *Scenarios of Power: Myth and Ceremony in Russian Monarchy*, 2 vols. (Princeton: Princeton University Press, 2000), vol. II, 525.

[44] According to historian Norman Davies, the American editor of the *Encyclopedia Britannica* insisted despite lengthy altercations that the entry on Poland should begin with a description of the Polish constitution; see Norman Davies, 'Polish National Mythologies', in Geoffrey Hosking and George Schöpflin, eds., *Myths and Nationhood* (London: Hurst, 1997), 156.

Russia, however, the creation of the Bolshevik regime required identification with a collective historical body. Following the Marxist-Leninist vision
of a dictatorship of the proletariat, communism claimed to represent a class
that, once in power, would abolish any existing division in society and
eventually make the state obsolete.[45] The Bolsheviks' projection of the
unifying One claimed the indivisibility of the people in their social reality
from the party as the revelation of historical truth. In Trotsky's words,
'none of us wishes to be or can be right against the party. In the last instance
the party is always right ... One can be right only with the party and
through the party, because History has not created any other way for the
realisation of one's rightness.'[46] The representational doctrine of the
People-as-One included the party, which did not have a specific reality
within society but claimed to be identical with the proletariat. The crucial
point is that the dictatorship of the proletariat as the symbol of the new
power merged a Marxist notion with the situational premises of a radically
polarised contentious revolutionary politics. According to Marx and
Engels, the revolutionary class overcomes oppression from the old class
but develops no class interest of its own, thus being equivalent with the
'people'. Lenin's denial of divisions between state and society and signs of
internal social division went along, however, with the affirmation of a
fundamental division between the People-as-One and the 'Other'. This
Other was projected as representing counter-revolutionary forces such as
the tsarist order, the kulaks, or the bourgeoisie, but increasingly also the
intra-party opposition. The image of the People-as-One needed the imaginary Other in two crucial respects: on the one hand, the definition of the
enemy was constitutive of the identity of the People-as-One but, on the
other, simultaneously threatened its unity permanently.

Not unlike the persecution of religious dissenters in religious wars of
the Middle Ages, the communists' aim was to fight not only actual but
also potential opposition.[47] Communist parties set themselves off from
enemies, be they the bourgeois or social-fascist class enemies in the West,
fifth columns, or independent movements such as human rights activists
or dissidents. The Stalin epoch needed binary opposites in order to
delimit Evil as a clearly definable opposite to Good, i.e. to the building
of Stalinism.[48] Periods of apparent relaxation preceded phases of intensified campaigns against enemies. Whereas in February 1934 Stalin

[45] Lefort, *The Political Forms of Modern Society*, 273–98.
[46] Quoted in Michael Waller, *The End of the Communist Power Monopoly* (Manchester and New York: Manchester University Press, 1993), 58.
[47] Milovan Djilas, *The New Class: An Analysis of the Communist System* (New York and Washington: Praeger, 1964), 26.
[48] Bonnell, *Iconography of Power*, 21–2.

announced that there were no enemies left to fight, only two years later the Great Terror unleashed a kind of mass psychosis that denounced hundreds of thousands. In 1937, Stalin declared that the closer socialism came to communism, the stronger and more dangerous its enemies would become.[49]

This identification of the enemy was not Stalin's invention, as claimed by Khrushchev in 1956, but had been an integral part of the Bolsheviks' strategy long before October 1917. Born in a world war and plunged into a civil war shortly afterwards, the Bolshevik Revolution turned the stigmatisation of the enemy into a representative principle that became a crucial bond, a symbolic 'structure'. As the Bolsheviks could neither fulfil expectations of a steady expansion of the revolution abroad nor build up a functioning economy, their goal was to internalise a feeling of being threatened by networks of conspiracy and enemies of the revolution, thus inducing the population to reciprocal suspicion and the duty of denunciation. 'The enemy, in a potential form, will always be there; the only friend will be the man who accepts the doctrine 100 per cent. If he accepts only 99 per cent, he will necessarily have to be considered a foe, for from that remaining 1 per cent a new church can arise.'[50] 'Enemies of the people' were a kind of social prophylaxis ensuring a group's identity by expelling its waste matter. The accusations against counter-revolutionaries during Stalin's Great Terror not only forced the accused to make rationally induced self-convictions of harmful activities and treason against the party and the revolution, but also persuaded many foreign observers of their authenticity.

The faith in the party went so far as to rationalise the self-confession of crimes never committed in the name of a higher logic of the party. The self-attribution of guilt not only fulfilled the political function of admitting the treason against the party as an objective fact. It also revealed how techniques of communist power had divided the personalities of the defendants. The accused in the show trials between 1936 and 1938 rationally acknowledged that they had perpetrated harmful activities and treason against the party and the revolution.[51] Caught up in a double bind, they vindicated the unjust condemnation with a rational adherence to the right faith. The life of a communist and his attachment to the movement formed a reality of its own to which he was entirely dedicated; if he were to be expelled for treason, sabotage, or hostile acts – for which he did not repent – it would be equivalent to making him lose all his life's

---

[49] Kotkin, *Magnetic Mountain*, 238.
[50] Czesław Miłosz, *The Captive Mind* (New York: Alfred A. Knopf, 1953), 214.
[51] Arthur Koestler, *Darkness at Noon* (London: Vintage Books, 1940).

meaning. Bukharin's decision to testify after three months of silence was based on a reassessment of his past. 'If I ask myself today, "For what am I dying?," I am confronted by absolute nothingness. There is nothing for which one could die, if one died without having repented and unreconciled with the Party and the Movement. Therefore, on the threshold of my last hour, I bend my knees to the country, to the masses, and to the whole people.'[52]

After the Second World War, the fascist enemy came to be of central importance for the self-legitimisation of communist regimes. The construction of enemies by communist ideology pursued the double task of stressing the democratic credentials of the state and of supporting its domestic consolidation. The watchword of the day in people's democracies was state vigilance against possible reversals operated by remnants of pre-1945 state structures. Such a representation of the historical continuity of fascism allowed post-war communist rulers to present themselves as the adversaries of fascism on the grounds of their own anti-fascist past and their commitment to democracy. Fascism was never really defined but essentially symbolised the 'enemy'. In some countries, such as Yugoslavia or Albania, outside enemies meant countries in the socialist camp, such as the Soviet Union or Yugoslavia, respectively. Tito and the communist party leadership, for instance, concealed the enmities underlying the civil war between 1941 and 1945 by emphasising the internationalist brotherhood of the Yugoslav nations.

Mythological constructions of reality

Soviet communism was an unprecedented grand experiment that sought to implement progress by institutionally and spiritually separating expectations from experience. This attempt at politically implementing Marxist revolutionary theory rejected Western modernity by trying to fulfil it. This utopian project of catching up with the West by industrialisation virtually from scratch shifted from pragmatic reason to a political practice that generated closure and exclusivity.[53] However, Bolshevik-type parties transcended the earlier, utopian ideas about the historical necessity of progress in two respects. They linked the centuries-old intellectual project of encasing the world in a single, perfect utopian discourse with the idea of progress, messianism and a worldly eschatology. Furthermore, this discourse became connected to certain 'means' necessary for its

[52] Koestler, *Darkness at Noon*, 199.
[53] Richard Stites, *Revolutionary Dreams: Utopian Vision and Experimental Life in the Russian Revolution* (New York and Oxford: Oxford University Press, 1989), 167–222.

realisation: the formation of a regular apparatus of teachers and soldiers, or, rather, teacher-soldiers.[54] The absolutist project of breaking radically with the past and pronouncing the inevitability of the transition to communism introduced double standards of reality into daily life. The institutionalisation of time-regimes testified to a life in a split existence where day-to-day economic development merged with utopian expectations of the future. Bolshevik time-regimes radically broke with perceptions of 'normal' time.[55] The destruction of daily routines in a revolutionary situation followed by a civil war made it difficult to make sense of time either in terms of abstract rational measurements or through the experience of concrete cycles of repetition. Charismatic revolutionary leaders in times of crisis gather followers around them because they forcefully suggest that they can successfully guide a social world where ordinary time no longer appears to function. Once mundane time ceases to explain or master events, any successful exercise of leadership is likely to appear as nothing short of 'miraculous'. Both the Leninist polity and the Stalinist economy relied upon a synthesis of charisma and rational-legal proceduralism. In this vein, analytic dichotomies between 'utopia' and 'development' in Soviet history seem invalid. The political institutions established after the Bolshevik Revolution and the economic institutions set up during the First Five-Year Plan were built upon the principle that 'utopia' could be realised by building time transcendence into time-bound development itself. Revolutionary messianism promised a radiant future by projecting a future political and social order that was supposed to overcome conditions of political oppression and economic backwardness. Stalin's speech at the First All-Union Conference of Managers of Socialist Industry in 1931 forcefully expressed how the horizon of expectation of progress through industrialisation was pitted against the Russian experience. In his view, longstanding backwardness – military, cultural, political, industrial, and agricultural – was responsible for Russia's humiliation. Catching up in the fastest tempo possible was Stalin's proposal for overcoming Russia's weakness.[56]

The institutionalisation of utopia was accompanied by the communist party's fervent zeal to create law and history by the 'annihilation of the past' and the production of history by the manipulation of memory.

---

[54] Horváth and Szakolczai, *The Dissolution of Communist Power*, 76–7.
[55] Stephen E. Hanson, *Time and Revolution: Marxism and the Design of Soviet Institutions* (Chapel Hill and London: University of North Carolina Press, 1997).
[56] Richard Sakwa, ed., *The Rise and Fall of the Soviet Union 1917–1991* (London and New York: Routledge, 1999), 187–8.

Reference to real events in the present or in the past was prohibited, as it could endanger the doctrine of an irreversible political order. The Soviet ritual system quite explicitly saw itself as inaugurating a time of new beginnings, converting all previous history into 'pre-history'.[57] The history of the construction of socialism became synonymous with national history. To different degrees, it included elements of national traditions or heroic resistance against invaders in order to accommodate communist rule with the traditions and memories of the nation. Setting the goals for the future required transforming meanings of the past. Despite the promise of a transition to communism, the rites and rituals devised for the Soviet people oriented them to the past – to the Great October Revolution, the Great Fatherland War, and, above all else, events in the life of Lenin. While tsarism's ideological complex included the triad of Orthodoxy, absolutism, and nationality, Soviet mythology consisted of Marxism-Leninism, the cult of the leader, and Soviet patriotism.[58]

Disfiguring the past and projecting a utopian future, the present became compressed between two dream worlds. Analytical psychology developed the concept of archetypes by which it referred to primordial images that are inherent to humanity. Archetypes are not equivalent to meanings of definite mythical images or motifs. They are without known origin but they reproduce themselves in any time or in any part of the world. Rather than inheriting variable representations, 'the archetype is a tendency to form such representations of a motif, representations that can vary a great deal in detail without losing their basic pattern'.[59] Archetypes resemble instinctive trends, having their own initiative and their own specific energy. Some analysts located the purest expression of totalitarianism beyond its systemic claim of total control of society in the fictional and symbolic images, in its power as a dream, as a nightmare.[60]

If the history of humanity has generated mythology, theology, philosophy, and science as four stages of legitimatisation, periods of crisis and uncertainty reintroduce the power of apparently obsolete forms.[61] People

[57] James Thrower, *Marxism-Leninism as the Civil Religion of Soviet Society: God's Commissar* (Lewiston: Edwin Mellen Press, 1992), 118.

[58] Michael Urban et al., *The Rebirth of Politics in Russia* (Cambridge: Cambridge University Press, 1997), 18.

[59] Carl G. Jung et al., *Man and His Symbols* (London: Arkana, 1990), 67.

[60] Quoted in Giovanni Sartori, *The Theory of Democracy Revisited* (Chatham, NJ: Chatham House Publishers, 1987), 212 n. 59. With reference to Joyce's remark that history is a nightmare from which one tries to awake, one can define totalitarianism by adding that for some it was a nightmare from which they did not try to awake; see Pierre Hassner, *La violence et la paix* (Paris: Editions Esprit, 1995), 222.

[61] Peter Berger and Thomas Luckmann, *The Social Construction of Reality* (London and New York: Penguin Books, 1991), 128.

believe myths not because the historical evidence is compelling but because they are objectifications of man's social experience. While myth refers to the conceptual side of a historical narrative with a strong appeal to collective emotions, it also grasps the perceptual side of making sense of experiences. Mythology, like interest-based and utility-seeking democratic politics, tries to capture reality. It suggests a high degree of continuity between social and cosmic order, and between all their respective legitimatisations; all reality appears as if made of one cloth. Mythologies have a basis in experience but are flexible in terms of being exploited for ideological programmes or political practice. They are the movement of the matter, something solid and flexible, matter-like and yet not static, but transformable.[62] Myths have a communicative function with the aim of establishing mutual support with others, as they externalise inner impulses and tensions. The important point is not the externalisation of a concrete myth but the political applicability and mobilising force by which the masses can be aroused. They are not based on the factual accuracy of their content but on their usefulness for creating loyalty, unanimity, and belonging. Bringing to mind the motive force and emotive potential of the dramatic succession of associated images, myth depicts the social struggle in the starkest possible terms, accentuating oppositions between the two sides.[63] Myth designates a distinctly temporal 'aspect'; it begins when a genesis, a becoming, a life in time, is attributed to forces, figures, and images.[64] Myth aims to produce action by making history 'falsification-proof' and by projecting an image of the future in order to make it instrumental for the present.[65] Thus, political myths are no mere figments of the imagination but artificial things fabricated by very skilful and cunning artisans. Paradoxically, the great technical age of the twentieth century developed a new technique of manufacturing myths in much the same sense and according to the same methods as any other modern weapon – as machine guns or airplanes.[66] Whereas the world began to worry about Germany's rearmament in 1933, the real rearmament had begun with the rise of the political myths to which the later

[62] Karl Kerényi, *Wege und Weggenossen*, ed. Magda Kerényi (Munich: Langen Müller, 1985), 11–84.
[63] Christopher G. Flood, *Political Myth: A Theoretical Introduction* (New York and London: Garland Publishing, 1996), 48.
[64] Ernst Cassirer, *The Philosophy of Symbolic Forms*, vol. II, *Mythical Thought* (New Haven and London: Yale University Press, 1955), 104.
[65] Georges Sorel, *Reflections on Violence* (New York and London: Collier Books, 1967), 124–5.
[66] Ernst Cassirer, *The Myth of the State* (New Haven: Yale University Press, 1946), 282.

military rearmament was only an accessory and a necessary consequence of the mental rearmament.

The dogmatic canonisation of a cult of Lenin turned the revolutionary leader into an object of religious worship. Similarly, the building of a socialist society was anchored in a wholesale mythology of a Stalin cult that linked up with the cult of Lenin and the mythology of the October Revolution, but actually wanted to do away with the experience of the revolutionary heritage by streamlining one vision of the revolution.[67] Such mythological constructions of reality were not alien to established practices in Russian politics. The identification of the tsar with the Russian state drew on theatrical and ritualised ceremonies of the imperial Russian court, which showed the sources of power, but simultaneously held their subjects spellbound.[68] The animating myth of Russian monarchy from the fifteenth to the late nineteenth century associated the ruler and the elite with foreign images of political power. This internationalist myth of Russian tsarism drew on mythical sources in its self-representation of being profoundly European. Ritualised ceremonies in the Russian monarchy throughout the eighteenth and nineteenth centuries reinforced the legitimisation of power not only by religious sanction and tradition but also by an ongoing dramatisation of the ruler's foreignness. At the same time, the objective of tsarist power was to become a bulwark against the modern Europeanised Russian intelligentsia whose aim was to weaken Russian monarchy.

Mythological constructions of Soviet history also reaffirmed the democratic credentials of the Soviet Union. Portraying the Soviet Union as the highest form of democracy, Stalin argued that in the country there were only two classes, workers and peasants, whose interests – far from being mutually hostile – were, on the contrary, identical. Consistent with Lenin's critique of parliamentary democracy, he despised democracy in capitalist countries as 'democracy for the strong, democracy for the propertied minority. In the USSR, on the contrary, democracy is democracy for the working people, i.e., democracy for all.'[69]

Failure of constitutive politics

Why did communism disappear so suddenly and completely? Among numerous explanations for the collapse of communism, many pointed to the inner contradictions nurtured by dynamics such as competition

---

[67] Geoffrey Hosking, *The First Socialist Society: A History of the Soviet Union from Within* (Cambridge, MA: Harvard University Press, 1990), 217–20.
[68] Wortman, *Scenarios of Power*, vol. II, 5–7.   [69] Fainsod, *How Russia Is Ruled*, 139.

with the West, economic decline, or imperial overstretch.[70] The most comprehensive factor was a profound legitimacy crisis affecting many areas of public belief in authority. This crisis of legitimacy is often attributed to deficiencies in the institutionalised framework that became subversive, causing corruption, economic decline, and inefficiency.[71]

From a perspective of political symbolism, the grave social consequences of the October Revolution failed to make communism politically constitutive. Although communism established repressive political systems based on secret police and military power, its foundations were of mythical character, as it lacked an identifiable systemic structure. Communist political societies crafted their legitimacy on the basis of ideological indoctrination and coercion, which undermined meaningful relations of social trust, accountability, and loyalty. Imposed from above, trust in the social fabric bred a permanent presumption of disloyalty, disobedience, and guilt.[72] If a well-institutionalised social order is one in which the contingent constitutional rules according to which political and distributional conflicts are carried out are relatively immune from becoming themselves the object of such conflict, then under communism order was not institutionalised. From their seizure of power, the Bolsheviks were in a double bind between competing demands. Faithful to Marx's and Lenin's prescriptions, the state as an organisation of the political interests of the dominant capitalist class would be thrown off as a result of the abolition of private property. The necessity of consolidating the revolution, however, required the use and strengthening of pillars of state power such as the army, the police, and the bureaucracy. Despite the temporary effect of the New Economic Policy or the spectacular achievements of Soviet military and space technology, communism did not develop a regular pattern of economic growth or a modernising idea of political development. Similarly, the international expansion in the form of the Comintern witnessed many ups and downs but no steady progress, not a single lasting success.[73]

The Bolsheviks failed to develop representation in the constitutional sense and remained permanently contested in the existential sense. The makeshift character of Bolshevik leadership was tangible in repeated attempts to look for support with different social groups through inflicting havoc upon others. The historical unfolding of Bolshevism as a form of

[70] Leslie Holmes, *Post-Communism* (Durham: Duke University Press, 1997), 23–62.
[71] Bunce, *Subversive Institutions*.
[72] Piotr Sztompka, *Trust: A Sociological Theory* (Cambridge: Cambridge University Press, 2000), 148–9.
[73] Borkenau, *World Communism*, 413.

political domination lacked an axis in time and a climax of development. Soviet communism eschewed the responsiveness of the masses, social structures, and the accountability of power incumbents. Instead, it built upon combativeness, archetypical schemes such as the stylised mythology of the party leader, and hatred for anything non-communist. The 'constitution' of Soviet communism consisted of a sequence of disruptive and violent acts that led to the internalisation of violence.

As Rousseau showed, the truly effective basis of a political order is in establishing a civil religion.[74] The historically concrete figure of the legislator with his facility to gather the community around simple dogmas of a civic religion is the decisive founding figure of the state. However, the government is supposed to control the opinions of its citizens only to the extent that they are of public utility. The sovereign steers the profession of the citizens' creed not so much as a religious dogma but as a sentiment of sociability. Thus, civic religions are responses in the social world to spiritual necessities of collective groups, or nations. Although the American Constitution lacked overt reference to a deity, symbols fraught with religious import readily became part of national life. The reference to the United States as a *novus ordo seculorum* (new order of the ages) mirrored the spirit of mission and destiny, represented in the Fourth of July as a quasi-religious holiday.[75]

The political symbolism of communism reflected the communists' incapacity to achieve an existentially sustained symbolic universe among its citizens. The latent civil war against the population led to radical shifts in symbolic representation and the establishment of constitutional myths.[76] Communists aimed to uproot people by systematically attacking the very foundations of interpersonal links, cultural reference-points, and sociability. They aimed to transform human nature by rendering people 'alone on earth'.[77] The latent civil war between the government and the people seemed to be the only way an underground sect of outsiders could stay in power. Aware of the significant disproportion between the boundless character of revolutionary promises and the poor means available, a central trait of the psychology of Bolshevik leaders led them to deliberately keep society in a permanent state of confusion. This ongoing confusion is probably best captured in

---

[74] Jean-Jacques Rousseau, *The Social Contract and Discourses*, trans. and intro. G. D. H. Cole (London: Dent, 1993), 298–308.
[75] Charles Lippy, 'Religion', in Mary Kupiec Cayton et al., eds., *Encyclopedia of American Social History*, 3 vols. (New York: Charles Scribner's Sons, 1993), vol. I, 513–29.
[76] Fainsod, *How Russia Is Ruled*, 363.
[77] Irena Talaban, *Terreur communiste et résistance culturelle. Les arracheurs de masques* (Paris: PUF, 1999), 188–9.

Trotsky's theory of the permanent revolution, which suggested that the revolutionaries intended to keep society unconsolidated and in continual movement.[78]

Perhaps the most outstanding mental trait of a Bolshevik was combativeness, not in terms of a hysterical aggressive but rather as a socialisation in terms of a military soldier. The radicalisation of the party promoted the most extreme elements into key positions. Bolshevik rule was not the monolithic rule of a bureaucratic state but rather relied upon a relatively small, mobile, strictly hierarchical, and tightly controlled quasi-military machine.[79] It relied on an extreme volatility in allegiances, identities, and representations, a fact that entailed important consequences for the relationship between leadership and its followers. Commonly, communist elites were seen in their hierarchical position in a constituted system of government and not in their cultural and historical embeddedness. As classical elite theory has suggested, the composition of political elites draws on certain excellent traits in their credible pursuit of a moral principle that is followed by large segments of society.[80] Conversely, the isolation of Soviet rulers behind their Kremlin walls meant that for 'most people they are only names, and names with a slightly mythical quality at that'.[81] Communism was not a myth because of an inherent mythical content in its ideology or an endemic irrationality. Rather, it was overtly rational in its autocratic high modernism, its systematic repression, and the indoctrination of individual minds. Nevertheless, it relied on absurdity in two ways. It was absurd as it attempted to solve problems such as the federal organisation of nationalities, poverty, or economic backwardness by old methods of the absolutist state. It was all the more absurd because it claimed that this old and obsolete technique of rule represented the future.[82]

To a considerable extent, communist power produced an elite-less society, as there was no broad societal consensus through which leaders could pursue a generally accepted political project in a calm and creative fashion.[83] Communist rulers in Soviet Russia and elsewhere in eastern Europe had to modify their own rules according to the circumstances.

---

[78] Leon Trotsky, *Permanent Revolution and Results and Prospects*, 3rd edn (New York: Pathfinder, 1969), 132–3.
[79] Zevedei Barbu, *Democracy and Dictatorship: Their Psychology and Patterns of Life* (London: Routledge & Kegan Paul, 1956) 184–94.
[80] Gaetano Mosca, *The Ruling Class*, ed. and rev. Arthur Livingston (New York: McGraw-Hill, 1939), 71.
[81] George F. Kennan, *Sketches from a Life* (New York: Pantheon Books, 1989), 154.
[82] Horváth and Szakolczai, *The Dissolution of Communist Power*, 210.
[83] Arpad Szakolczai, 'In a Permanent State of Transition: Theorizing the East European Condition', http://limen.mi2.hr/limen1-2001/arpad_szakolczai.html.

From the very outset, the Bolsheviks changed fundamental assumptions about the spread of their revolution abroad, about the bureaucratisation of the party, and about the economic strategy to follow. The communist party was not the backbone of the country but rather a source of nearly continuous turmoil. Making techniques of disruption and latent civil war a central strategy of communist power was consistent with the party's revolutionary origins, and with the need to endow the party with a role parallel to state institutions.[84] Local party life was characterised not by orderly processes of administration but by an all-pervading atmosphere of urgency, tension, and emergency measures in order to cope with tremendous pressure to realise seemingly impossible objectives.

Although communism was a most powerful system in the external world, it seems quite misleading to classify communism as featuring an 'extraordinarily powerful party-state and a weak and dependent society'.[85] The communist state was not simply a bureaucratic party-state but was characterised by a latent civil war between the government and the people. The modalities of its political articulation shed some light on the paradoxical effect of a political system that ruled half of the globe and a military giant that suddenly collapsed without leaving much to posterity in terms of ideas, institutions, leaders, or symbols. Given the quasi-religious fervour to identify enemies and dilute politics in mythological constructions of reality, the constant uprooting of social relations was a perfectly rational technique of power.

Communism adopted this uprooting of social relations. The sacrificial logic of Marxist-Leninist ideology and the absolute politics of communism not only exuded falseness and artificiality, but also made the localisation of power all but impossible. Under communism, power seemed to be everywhere but could also be totally absent.[86] Although communism is often associated with a charismatic type of leadership, empirical evidence about communist leaders requires a completion of the Weberian categorisation. While the ideological claim of Bolshevik leadership was the promise of a paradise on earth, its experiential basis was civil war, violent repression, and self-victimisation. This twilight existence between the proclaimed knowledge of the historical mission and the fear of encirclement by enemies kept Bolsheviks in a double bind. While they proclaimed the unity of the people expressed in the identification with the party, their techniques of power thwarted sociability, prevented the accountability of public officials, and undermined existential representation. Communist leadership displayed striking analogies with the archetypical figure of the

[84] Kotkin, *Magnetic Mountain*, 291–2.   [85] Bunce, *Subversive Institutions*, 130.
[86] Claude Lefort, *La complication. Retour sur le communisme* (Paris: Fayard, 1999), 11–12.

trickster. In Maxim Gorky's memorable words of 1917, Lenin as the self-proclaimed leader of the proletariat was 'not an omnipotent magician but a cold-blooded trickster who spares neither the honour nor the life of the proletariat'.[87] As a study of the speeches of the Hungarian communist party leader Mátyás Rákosi argued, the conditions of disruption, hatred, and permanent liminality produced communist societies in which the leaders and the members of society lived double lives.[88] Communist leadership embodied a continuous shift between realities, thus connecting the initial charismatic appeal of mobilising society with an inherent impotence and self-victimisation.

Thus, communist power seemed to be characterised by diametrically opposed movements. On the one hand, it appeared totally political in terms of permeating every aspect of public or private life. On the other hand, it seemed totally apolitical as it postulated the outcome of history and life.[89] In Foucault's adaptation of Bentham's design of the Panopticon as the central metaphor of modern power, the move from the visibility and performative dramaturgy of monarchical power to the invisibility of the manager's power is crucial. The power of the modern state relies upon the flexibility of state bureaucrats in control of space and time, as opposed to the citizens who are bound to space and controlled without knowing the identity of those controlling them. Whereas much of social science research on Soviet totalitarianism concurred in focusing its attention on the vertical top-down relationship of domination, more recent evidence suggests that Soviet power relied fundamentally on horizontal networks of mutual surveillance and on techniques of dissimulation.[90] In the absence of legal-rational domination, the group is entrusted with the task of controlling itself. Rather than an institutional trick adopted as a last resort, mutual surveillance was the cornerstone of the establishment of Soviet power, and its collapse was synonymous with the collapse of Soviet power.

Unbound by legal regulations, communist leaders were not bureaucrats but ruled a political society, founded on violence, by a militaristic type of rule. Communist rule was not equivalent to an excess of state power; it was, rather, defined by the subjugation of both state and society together under a utopian, non-political claim to exercise rule. The low degree of institutionalisation, the lack of coherent collective identities, the atomisation of individuals, and the often chaotic internal conditions of

---

[87] Maxim Gorky, *Untimely Thoughts: Essays on Revolution, Culture and the Bolsheviks 1917–1918* (New Haven and London: Yale University Press, 1995), 86.
[88] Agnes Horváth, 'Tricking into the Position of the Outcast: A Case Study in the Emergence and Effects of Communist Power', *Political Psychology*, 19, 2 (1998), 331–47.
[89] Lefort, *The Political Forms of Modern Society*, 273–91.
[90] Kharkhordin, *The Collective and the Individual in Russia*, 110.

party rule suggest that communist states were 'overbureaucratic' only in so far as they issued laws and regulations based on ideological doctrine rather than the consideration of social reality. However, these legal and abstract 'socialist' formulas that ruled daily social life were characterised by a high degree of wastefulness of human and economic resources.

From a perspective of political symbolism, communism was not simply a totalitarian regime but a new type of society, a social organism in gestation, where the assault against the basics of human coexistence and the modernising thrust made up a civilisation of its own. Communism was not only a regime relying on total subjugation of society by the party. Within the system, individuals and groups developed spaces of autonomy, strategies of resistance, and a self-consciousness that challenged, by the power of its own symbols, the fragile symbolic frame of communism. The post-Stalinist period, when mass repression and terror subsided, revealed the incapacity to establish a constitutive system of symbolic world main-tenance. De-Stalinisation laid completely bare the truth that a latent civil war against the population comes at the price of a terrifying insecurity that haunts power-holders with the fear of their own annihilation. This fear made the ruling class aware that it was no longer able to claim even to itself that the end justifies the means.[91] The symbolic structure of the People-as-One against enemies was gradually challenged by claims to existential representation sustained by an alternative political symbolism. While the cleavage line between the People-as-One and enemies was crucial for the maintenance of communist power, de-Stalinisation and ensuing chal-lenges to communist power recast the binary oppositions, generating a dividing line between growing dissidence and communist authorities. By destroying any sphere of open conflict and political alternative, commun-ist systems caused the centre of gravity of any potential political threat to shift towards the existential and the pre-political.[92] Political impulses could hardly come from professional politicians that had adopted the political habits and techniques of communist power, but rather need to come from outsiders. Not surprisingly, 'non-politicians', dissidents, and anti-communist resisters were very much aware of the stakes of genuine political reality. The later distinction between 'us' and 'them', so common in communist societies, drew very much on the dichotomy between the People-as-One (the community of dissident society or opposition) against the enemy (the communist party-state).

[91] Djilas, *The New Class*, 147–63.
[92] Vaclav Havel, 'The Power of the Powerless', in John Keane, ed., *The Power of the Powerless: Citizens Against the State in Eastern Europe* (London: Hutchinson and Co., 1985), 44–51.

4   Experiencing democratic transformations

> A democracy is more than a form of government; it is primarily a mode
> of associated living, of conjoint communicated experience.
>
> John Dewey

It is rarely contested that the political process of Soviet-type governments
was not democratic, as it was characterised by a power monopoly, a lack
of accountability, fake constitutionalism, and the absence of meaningful
elections. The normative imperative of establishing political democracy,
however, has made analysts disregard the social foundations of democratisation. The formal distinction between a previous 'non-democratic'
period under communism and an ensuing 'democratic' period after its
demise illustrates the political conflict of the Cold War but explains little
about the emergence of democracy. It would be shortsighted to assume
that democracy 'failed' with the victory of the October Revolution in
1917 and 'won' with the collapse of communism in 1989 and 1991.
Historically, any politically useful conception of democratic transformation requires connecting the meanings, representations, and expectations
of people and elites under communism. Experience is thus not simply
the dead hand of the past but a living and creative process of social
reordering.

This chapter examines the epistemological basis of the mirrored opposition between communism and democracy. The determinism of consolidating liberal democracy has purged the subjectivity of actors and the
formative influence of political symbolism on the emergence of
democracy. Confined to a positivist focus on the functional, procedural,
and legal-normative aspects of political systems, much social inquiry has
pre-empted the political struggle over their foundations.[1] While the socio-
genetic particularities of the communist experience have become reified
as 'legacies', political developments leading away from communism were
seen as 'outcomes'. The renaissance of the paradigm of totalitarianism in

---

[1] Claus Offe, 'Capitalism by Democratic Design? Democratic Theory Facing the Triple
Transition in East Central Europe', *Social Research*, 58, 4 (1991), 865–92.

recent years, for instance, has attributed many of the defects of recent transformations to the systemic legacy of communism. Against this view, however, one can argue that the communist experience has generated forms of consciousness that would sustain meanings of democracy in the absence of political democracy. Democracy before 1989 was more a socially mediated, vague, almost utopian vision cherished in small communities and with little institutional reality. Being ardently desired but out of reach as a governmental practice, democracy in communist eastern Europe was an empire of the mind, tinged with eschatological expectations, and pregnant with hazy images of total freedom.

The roots of democratic determinism

A considerable amount of work on democratisation in Russia and eastern Europe has been tinged with assumptions about a specific ontology of tradition and assumptions of civilisational backwardness. This claim was complemented by the view that Russia and eastern Europe lacked an endogenous democratic tradition, for two main reasons. On the one hand, the historical sequence according to which the modern economy took shape before the modern state seems to be reversed. The state was not the product but the instrument of change, gaining ascendancy over all aspects of social life of the nation. Rather than the gradual development of a capitalist economy or a 'bourgeois society', one could witness a gradual increase in etatism, which produced a society of pariah entrepreneurs, and of political classes competing for the spoils of the state.[2] The traditional pattern of development in Russia – state-induced reform – was sustained by the weakness of civil society, apathetic masses, and strongly authoritarian patterns of leadership. This cultural backwardness was also reflected in how eastern Europe as a concept in political history was invented by Enlightenment thought, which endowed rising nation-states in the West with a mythical 'Other'.[3] Consequently, Western historiography has tended to exclude eastern Europe from the concept of Europe on the grounds of natural, unbridgeable differences, implying that the West is superior and alone deserves the name of Europe.[4]

---

[2] Andrew Janos, *The Politics of Backwardness in Hungary 1825–1945* (Princeton: Princeton University Press, 1982), 314.

[3] Larry Wolff, *Inventing Eastern Europe: The Map of Civilization on the Mind of the Enlightenment* (Stanford: Stanford University Press, 1994).

[4] Norman Davies, *Europe: A History* (Oxford: Oxford University Press, 1996), 16–25.

On the other hand, culture was an enormous factor in east European politics but as regards its politicisation rather than in terms of its flowering. Since many of these countries did not 'exist' in the west European sense of relatively unbroken historical continuity, intellectual elites engineered cultural roots based on linguistic separatism, ethnic distinctiveness, and historical master narratives of a beginning of the nation. As a consequence, ideas of culture in these countries have been strongly influenced by the temptation of determinism.[5] Especially in multi-ethnic contexts, they have been associated with cultural racism, erecting boundaries of exclusion or legitimising violence. Similarly, cultural preconceptions such as Russian authoritarianism, a Balkan mentality, or the fatalistic Orthodox soul are considered as mysterious residual variables, which bar the path to development.

The two major strands of theorisation on communist power reflected such cultural determinism. While modernisation theory saw communism as the developmental carrier for overcoming tradition and backwardness in Russia, the theory of totalitarianism considered communism as a consequence of specific national characteristics and an authoritarian political culture. It denounced the violent and dehumanising character of Soviet-type regimes. Essentially, both approaches concurred in assuming that communism was profoundly anti-democratic. Modernisation theory affirmed the universal reach and developmental potentiality of democracy as a system of government rooted in the Western model of the nation-state, where it had been crafted and from which it had to be diffused. As one of three components of Western-type modernity (besides capitalism and industrialisation), democracy exerted a spell on the communist version of modernity. Accordingly, modernisation theory acclaimed the collapse of communism as a decisive, if not the final, step forward in political development. Whereas the collapse of the Soviet Union had been hailed as a 'vindication of modernisation theory' in the early 1990s, it has become a standard view to attribute the ensuing disenchantment with the development of Russia's democracy to the continuity of its authoritarian culture.[6]

This cultural bias linked up with conceptual determinism. In the political antagonism of the Cold War, the concept 'totalitarian' was established as the polar opposite of 'democratic', as a pejorative term that simultaneously

[5] C. M. Hann, *Postsocialism: Ideals, Ideologies, and Practices in Eurasia* (London: Routledge, 2002), 8.
[6] Stephen Hanson, 'Defining Democratic Consolidation', in Richard D. Anderson et al., *Postcommunism and the Theory of Democracy* (Princeton: Princeton University Press, 2001), 132.

designated and disapproved of one-party states and mass terror.[7] This dichotomisation was partly a result of the shift in meanings with regard to two interpretive strands in the thought on totalitarianism.[8] Ideologically, the earlier conception of totalitarianism followed a phenomenological and philosophical approach highlighting totalitarian rule as the peak of the crisis of the modern nation-state. This approach relied on a concern for the way in which the person stands in a meaningful relation to the world, as it appears to him or her in everyday experience. Especially after Stalin's death, however, the liberal approach came to see totalitarianism as its own antithesis. Totalitarianism came to be considered as a set of ideologically prescribed organisational methods developed and employed for the purpose of the violation of freedom of conscience, the politicisation of all areas of social life, and the destruction of meaningful ties in society.[9]

Methodologically, the liberal view developed a whole range of comparisons of functional-empirical criteria, which established totalitarianism as the mirror image of a Western-type liberal regime. Despite its usefulness in a typology of political regimes, however, totalitarianism was a simplistic notion as far as the sociohistorical foundations of political reality are concerned. One of the best critical discussions of the variety of meanings of totalitarianism in the Western world concluded that totalitarianism is not a political science concept.[10] Even if it is problematic to speak of 'errors' in the evolution of concepts, there is good reason to see some validity in such a claim with regard to the theory of totalitarianism. This 'error' arises when something that cannot be grasped except through its totalising character and that should be understood as a philosophical problem is classified using criteria of empirical social science. Empirical research in American Sovietology was not able to comprehend communism's assault on the basis of human dignity and human coexistence, something that only literary works such as those of Orwell, Solzhenitsyn, Grossmann, Miłosz, Havel, and others could express. Inspired by the antithesis with liberalism and oblivious of social foundations and complexities of concrete life, the concept of totalitarianism also reduced Stalinism and even the post-Stalin period to a mere undertaking

[7] David Joravsky, 'Communism in Historical Perspective', *American Historical Review*, 99, 3 (1994), 849–50.
[8] Michael Halberstam, *Totalitarianism and the Modern Conception of Politics* (New Haven and London: Yale University Press, 1999), 5–6.
[9] Carl Friedrich and Zbigniew Brzezinski, *Totalitarian Dictatorship and Autocracy* (Cambridge, MA: Harvard University Press, 1956), 17.
[10] Pierre Hassner, *Violence and Peace* (Budapest: Central European University Press, 1996), 221–68.

of lies and constraints, where a 'totalitarianism from below' made resistance by *homo sovieticus* meaningless.

The 'error' is somehow reproduced in empirical theories of democracy. The implicit standard by which democratic transformations are measured is arguably linked to the empirical theory of democracy as it was established during and after the Second World War.[11] This vision propagated liberal representative democracy on the basis of functional and descriptive characteristics of governmental practice, based on elections through universal suffrage and the regular competition of elites for power in a consolidated legal framework. A major argument about the empiricism of this approach consisted in the claim that it was realistic, as it reflected the status quo of advanced liberal democracies. However, Joseph A. Schumpeter's seminal book *Capitalism, Socialism, and Democracy* was published in 1943 in the middle of a world war, which constituted an existential threat to political democracy as a constitutional form of government. It has been convincingly suggested that – given the empirical conditions of democracy in much of the Western world, including the war mobilisation in Anglo-Saxon countries – the book was not so much an empirical description of how things really are.[12] Rather it came down to a normative prescription about the only possible way to avoid the evils of totalitarianism, and thus should be seen as an attempt to bring theory into accord with reality. During the Cold War, the empirical model has become, in a monistic fashion, the only way to conceive of democracy as a constitutional form of government.

The cultural determinism of a specific ontology of tradition and the conceptual determinism by which the functional and procedural aspects of communist rule are fundamentally opposed to liberal democracy go along with historical determinism. Consistent with its narrow empirical focus on liberal political democracy, the dominant discourse has disconnected the 'non-democratic' or 'pre-democratic' period from the democratic period, when democracy becomes the 'only game in town' and the temptation of essential players to boycott the game is rendered inoperative.[13] Although the classical formulation of the idea of transitions to democracy was very much interested in the genetic aspects of the concept,

---

[11] Joseph A. Schumpeter, *Capitalism, Socialism, and Democracy*, 5th edn (London: George Allen & Unwin, 1976); Robert Dahl, *A Preface to Democratic Theory* (Chicago: University of Chicago Press, 1956).

[12] Jeffrey C. Isaac, *Democracy in Dark Times* (Ithaca and London: Cornell University Press, 1998), 31–2.

[13] Juan Linz and Alfred Stepan, *Problems of Democratic Transition and Consolidation: Southern Europe, South America and Post-Communist Europe* (Baltimore and London: Johns Hopkins University Press, 1996), 5.

the focus was soon shifted towards assessing criteria for the global convergence of democracy.[14] Identifying the beginning of democratisation with the collapse of communism assumes that what did happen is what had to happen. Comparative studies in democratisation suggested treating post-communism in analogous fashion, at least initially, to the 'wave of democratisation' that began in 1974 in Portugal.[15]

Studies of 'consolidation' suggested the overdetermination of democracy through durable compliance with the rules and procedures of liberal democracy as a system of government. Democratic consolidation has advocated closure and has tended to reduce historical experience to an appendix of an idea generated in completely different contexts. Setting democratisation as a social end and a goal of development, the premises of liberal democratic theory have excluded the meaningfulness of endogenous historical experiences when they claim that in eastern Europe 'the major obstacle to democratisation was Soviet control: once it was removed, the movement to democracy spread rapidly'.[16]

Moreover, the monism of liberal democracy as a developmental goal reproduces the deterministic historicist account of the concept of transition in Marx's philosophy of history. Methodologically, such an approach suggests that a systemic and institutional arrangement becomes non-contingent as a consolidated democracy is characterised by deeply internalised attitudes in social, institutional, and even psychological life. Comparatively, this would imply that the democratisation of the United States, Britain, France, or Germany could not be properly studied before these countries actually met the requirements of mature liberal democracy by introducing fully equal voting rights such as female voting or by abolishing prerogative rights. Theoretically, much of the literature on transitions to democracy has transposed the assumption on the inevitability of communism by 'liberalising' the Marxist paradigm and projecting a teleological outcome-expectation for democracy.[17] While some

---

[14] For a genetic perspective, see Dankwart Rustow, 'Transitions to Democracy: Toward a Dynamic Model', *Comparative Politics*, 2, 3 (1970), 337–63; for a view on democracy aiming at global convergence, see Adam Przeworski, *Democracy and the Market: Political and Economic Reforms in Eastern Europe and Latin America* (Cambridge: Cambridge University Press, 1991).

[15] Philippe Schmitter and Terry Lynn Karl, 'The Conceptual Travel of Transitologists and Consolidologists: How Far to the East Should They Attempt to Go?', *Slavic Review*, 53, 1 (1994), 173–85.

[16] Samuel P. Huntington, 'Democracy's Third Wave', in Larry Diamond and Marc Plattner, eds., *The Global Resurgence of Democracy*, 2nd edn (Baltimore: Johns Hopkins University Press, 1996), 7.

[17] See Nicolas Guilhot, 'The Transition to the Human World of Democracy: Notes for a History of the Concept of Transition, from Early Marxism to 1989', *European Journal of Social Theory*, 5, 2 (2002), 219–43.

authors proclaimed the victory of liberal democracy as the only political ideology, others argued for the relevance of a renaissance of Marxism precisely because the victorious liberal democracy failed in its central promises.[18]

The drama of democratic transformations

Does the absence of a democratic tradition under communist rule vindicate the claim about the absence of a democratic consciousness or even preclude a country's democratic development? How would democracies in the West have come into being without important and influential groups in society that had developed a specific consciousness before the establishment of institutional democracy? The political evolution of communism warrants the choice of a dramatic perspective on democratisation that links the social context to the theatrical, performative, and expressive features of actors.[19] The theatrical analogy not only allows for a defence against the imposition of 'prefabricated' categories, but also is consistent with the dramatic history of democracy, which until the late nineteenth century was virtually a term of abuse.[20] Despite its origins in ancient Greece, it was a particular series of dramatic social and political upheavals at the end of the eighteenth century that made democracy reappear as a viable concept of political organisation. Revolutions in 1789 and 1917 socialised meanings of republic or democracy.

If modern democracy as a constitutional form of government has its roots in the American or the French Revolution, the self-perception of key actors was not that of democrats, let alone 'liberal democrats' in the late-twentieth-century sense. Although Enlightenment thought dynamised classical notions of democracy and republic by coining the term 'republicanism', the American founding fathers mistrusted 'democracy'. In the first age of democratic revolution, there were no 'democrats', while the age of aristocracy, as long as it was unchallenged, heard nothing of 'aristocrats'.[21] The French Revolution popularised democracy by

---

[18] Francis Fukuyama, *The End of History and the Last Man* (New York: Avon, 1993); Alex Callinicos, *The Revenge of History: Marxism and East Europe* (Cambridge: Polity Press, 1991); Jerzy Szacki, *Liberalism After Communism* (Budapest: Central European University Press, 1996).

[19] Laurence Whitehead, *Democratisation: Theory and Experience* (Oxford: Oxford University Press, 2002), 36–64.

[20] John Dunn, 'Conclusion', in Dunn, ed., *Democracy: The Unfinished Journey* (Oxford: Oxford University Press, 1992), 239–66.

[21] R. Palmer, *The Age of the Democratic Revolution*, vol. I (Princeton: Princeton University Press, 1959), 13–21.

weaving the egalitarian Christian notion of the equal value of human beings into the Enlightenment tradition of the emancipation of man.

The massive dislocation of political and social structures at the revolutionary conjuncture mobilised social forces and opened up politics as the realm of uncertainty. The complex and volatile history of the revolution turned into the struggle between aristocratically inspired and elite-based order of egoism and the order of equality. The long shadow of Thermidor initiated the radical egalitarian turn of the French Revolution as the figures of Gracchus Babeuf and Filippo Michele Buonarroti provided democracy with a meaning of a fiercely divisive political category as opposed to the victory of the order of egoism in the United States.[22] A lasting effect of the French Revolution was that democracy lost its fixation on the constitutional realm and became a socially relevant but also ideologically manipulative term. In the wake of the French Revolution, democracy became a possible form of domination, a central historical movement that was to draw more and more attention from the crowd.[23]

Although the institutional origins of American democracy are to be found in the American Revolution, its evolution was not predetermined. A victory by the Southern states in the American Civil War might have led to the establishment of the Southern plantation system, entailing a scenario in which the United States could have been in the position of some modernising countries today, with a *latifundia* economy, a dominant anti-democratic aristocracy, and a weak and dependent commercial and industrial class, unable and unwilling to push forward towards political democracy.[24] The Emancipation Proclamation, issued by Abraham Lincoln in 1863, did not free a single slave. It was in the contingent struggle of force during the last two years of the civil war that the Republican Party adopted the Emancipation Proclamation as a policy to be pursued without knowing its merits and meaning.[25]

Historically, democracy does not rely upon one essential source or foundation. It consists of a sequence of dramatic contexts that entail a host of interpretive traditions, which remain, in one way or another, influential on generations of political actors to come. Assumptions of elite-initiated democratisation need to be qualified with a view to the cultural, historical, and

---

[22] John Dunn, *Setting the People Free: The Story of Democracy* (London: Atlantic Books, 2005), 119–47.

[23] François Furet, 'The French Revolution Revisited', in Gary Kates, ed., *The French Revolution* (London and New York: Routledge, 1998), 71–90.

[24] Barrington Moore, *Social Origins of Dictatorship and Democracy: Lord and Peasant in the Making of the Modern World* (Boston: Beacon Press, 1966), 112–15.

[25] Michael Vorenberg, *Final Freedom: The Civil War, the Abolition of Slavery, and the Thirteenth Amendment* (Cambridge: Cambridge University Press, 1997).

social tissue of which civil society is made.[26] In terms of a country's or a region's history, such a context-dependent view needs to consider communist political societies as social organisms in gestation. The involvement of the masses in the initiation of regime change is not only a function of the disposition of the ruling elites. Their capacity for action and influence is dependent upon the historically defined location that they occupied in society.[27]

Concepts such as people's democracy, revolutionary democracy, or totalitarian democracy enjoy only faint support among political scientists, because they are not considered to be viable options for constitutional government. Historically, however, the emergence of democracy and that of absolutism were tightly related, suggesting that democracy as a constitutional form is much more of an authoritative type of government than is usually acknowledged. In antiquity, the establishment of the Athenian polis or of the Roman republic followed upon monarchical rule. Athens's victory against the Persian empire, its rise to the status of a sea power, and the need for protection of its Asian colonies obliged the democratic polis to build an empire over large parts of Greece.[28] Similarly, the rise and the decline of the Roman republic portray the intrinsic elements of imperialist democracy. Democracy in modernity originated from revolutions (the English, the French, and the Russian) that marked the culmination of the development of the three major ideological movements of the modern age: Protestantism, the Enlightenment, and socialism.

The beginning of 'democratic politics' in the French Revolution opened up the potential of totalitarian democracy.[29] In Jacob Talmon's view, two currents of democracy, one liberal and the other totalitarian, have existed side by side ever since the eighteenth century. Before 1917, totalitarian democracy was an ideological current, not a coherent pattern. It emerged in the French Revolution and asserted itself through revolutionary outbursts such as in the Paris Commune in 1871. In the October Revolution of 1917, totalitarian democracy became a political force inspired by ideological currents and further radicalised through historical action. Totalitarian democracy, with its tendencies to tyranny, hypocrisy, and self-deception, was the result of attempting to reconcile the

---

[26] Graeme Gill, *The Dynamics of Democratisation* (Basingstoke: Macmillan, 2000), 192–212.

[27] Michel Dobry, ed., *Democratic and Capitalist Transitions in Eastern Europe* (Dordrecht: Kluwer, 2000); Dirk Berg-Schlosser and Jeremy Mitchell, eds., *Conditions of Democracy in Europe, 1919–1939* (Basingstoke: Macmillan, 2000).

[28] Christian Meier, *Athen. Ein Neubeginn der Weltgeschichte* (Berlin: Siedler Verlag, 1996), 592–3.

[29] Jacob Talmon, *The Origins of Totalitarian Democracy* (London: Secker & Warburg, 1952).

incompatible nature of an all-embracing creed of salvation with the political realisation of liberty.

While the emergence of the term 'totalitarian' is associated with the classical notions of tyranny, totalitarianism in the twentieth century has its sources also in the democratic conditions of incipient mass society with its relativity of norms and values. In a very specific way, the emergence of totalitarian rule in Russia and later in Nazi Germany confirmed earlier insights about the contagion of regime types, as the tyrannical autocracy of Bolshevik communism and Nazism seemed to be the only viable end to mob rule.[30] The politically relevant appearance of democratic mass society in the early twentieth century was crucial for connecting mob rule as a social force with the lawlessness of tyrannical power. Historically, this is shown by the fact that 'totalitarian' as a notion arose in Italy in the early 1920s to designate the Fascists' breach of election procedures when they refused to accept the majority–minority principle, instead favouring a 'total' solution.[31]

Against the historically deterministic assumption about the opposition of two types of democracy, one liberal and the other totalitarian, political systems draw on a complex merger of authoritarian and democratic elements. In the dramatic context of the empty space of power, the close connection between liberalism and democracy is not evident. The conceptual determinism of the Cold War period obfuscated the insight that democratic culture inherently bears within itself the germs of a dictatorial type of domination menacing the self-expression and humanity of man. Liberalism was born in the struggle against the tyranny of absolute kings and is primarily concerned with the limitation of power of the state over the individual. Conversely, a fully fledged democracy would be a regime where the majority, through their representatives, could carry through their will against any minority. As the basic principle of modern democracy, the idea of majority rule permeates public opinion, the legislature, the executive, and the judiciary. As a consequence, a person wronged may have trouble finding adequate securities against this 'tyranny of the majority'.[32] In extreme situations, 'democrats' may be forced to opt for authoritarian or totalitarian solutions in order to safeguard democracy. Democracies are not tolerant, and there is hardly any more determined entity than a democracy at war. Embattled democracy puts

[30] Franz Borkenau, *The Totalitarian Enemy* (London: Faber and Faber, 1940), 150–2.
[31] See Abbot Gleason, *Totalitarianism: The Inner History of the Cold War* (Oxford: Oxford University Press, 1995), 14.
[32] Alexis de Tocqueville, *Democracy in America: The Complete and Unabridged*, 2 vols., trans. Henry Reeve (New York: Bantam, 2000), 299–302.

all its life energy in fighting the enemy, who becomes the embodiment of evil, which has to be crushed by the forces of democracy as the centre of all virtue.[33] If Carl Schmitt claimed that, 'in particular, a dictatorship cannot come into being by other than democratic means',[34] this was not to blur any distinction between democratic and non-democratic as forms of political organisation but to recognise the inherent ambivalence of constituent power. In this vein, the foundation of post-fascist democracies in Germany, Italy, or Japan was achieved by a temporary constitutional dictatorship.

Communist leaders claimed to embody true democracy not because of their substantial contribution to political democracy but because this claim was part of the existential struggle for legitimising power domestically and for achieving international recognition. Communism relied upon the crucial institution of absolutist power that was the early-modern police, not only developing a bureaucracy but also essentially creating a new class of owners and exploiters.[35] In terms of political communication, however, communism developed a democratic terminology based on techniques that stressed the centralising element, which is expressed in notions such as people's democracy or democratic centralism. Originally introduced for the purpose of curbing the power of the Central Committee of the Communist Party of the Soviet Union, it became a hierarchically top-to-bottom principle of strict inner party discipline after 1934.[36]

The emergence of the 'people'

Democracy in the modern world has largely shown a tendency to achieve ever-higher levels of equality in spheres of existence that had been far more exclusive beforehand. Thus, social equality in the moment of the political is not only enshrined politically in the constitutional claim of popular sovereignty of the people as put forward by the classical doctrine of democracy. Historically, it also becomes socially productive as an expression of insurrectionary crowds, contentious politics, and collective violence.[37] Popular sovereignty has not only been a matter of normatively

---

[33] George F. Kennan, *Russia and the West Under Lenin and Stalin* (Boston and Toronto: Little, Brown and Company, 1961), 5.
[34] Carl Schmitt, *Verfassungslehre* (Munich: Duncker & Humblodt, 1928), 237.
[35] Milovan Djilas, *The New Class* (New York: Praeger, 1964), 37–69.
[36] Stephen Kotkin, *Magnetic Mountain: Stalinism as a Civilization* (Berkeley: University of California Press, 1995), 546 n. 50.
[37] John Markoff, 'Violence, Emancipation, and Democracy', in Kates, *The French Revolution*, 236–78.

inspired and constitutionally guaranteed doctrines. Before constitutive acts are established, democratic action requires a self-consciousness of individuals as acting on behalf of the people as a political subject.

The modern conception of representation includes the symbol 'people' in two meanings, both as legitimising the government and as being represented.[38] Abraham Lincoln's classical formulation of democracy as 'the government of the people, by the people, and for the people' indicates that the notion of the people absorbs three dimensions whose simultaneity, however, should not be taken for granted. It designates the articulated political society, its representatives, and the membership that is bound by the acts of the representative. This set of different dimensions has not been a timeless constant but has developed as a result of several crises. Lincoln's Gettysburg address of 1863 gives the classical synthesis of democracy as an act of honouring the dead in the civil war who gave the last full measure of devotion to the community. Lincoln resolved that present and future generations should be firmly convinced that these dead had not died in vain but had bequeathed the nation a new birth of freedom.

By contrast, in medieval language it was common sense to distinguish the 'people' into two different categories, the 'realm' and the 'subjects'. One cause for exalting the central notion of equality in processes of democratisation is intimated in the strong egalitarian element of Christianity. The essential spiritual motif for democratisation in the West was formulated by the English reformers of the fourteenth to the eighteenth century, when they took the life of the Christian community and of the community-constitution as a model for the existence of citizens in a national society also in secular matters.[39] Lincoln's definition of democracy must be set into the broader historical context of the emergence of the spiritual source of this appeal. This is to be found in the prologue to John Wycliffe's 1384 translation of the Bible: 'This Bible is for the government of the people, by the people, and for the people.' Constitutional democracy, especially in the Anglo-Saxon countries, has been a form of civil theology, inherent to the prophetic and messianic monotheism of the Judaeo-Christian tradition, concerned with the unity of universal history, and characterised by an eschatological tension that takes the constitutional form as an article of faith and projects a 'finality' to it.[40] If one central heritage of Christianity and specifically Protestantism

---

[38] Eric Voegelin, *The New Science of Politics: An Introduction* (London and Chicago: University of Chicago Press, 1987), 38–41.

[39] Eric Voegelin, *The Collected Works*, vol. XI, *Published Essays 1953–1965* (Columbia and London: University of Missouri Press, 2000), 'Democracy in the New Europe', 61.

[40] Voegelin, *Published Essays 1953–1965*, 183.

was the generation of a civil society ruled by law, it was reinforced by spiritual sanction on an individual basis and a self-restraint that forms the essence of liberal democracy.[41]

The almost providential tendency towards democratic equality has not been a law of social development. Transformations of consciousness in individuals are often responses to unexpected and dramatic experiences. Modern political thought and democratic theory have interpreted such transformations as based on the power of will, choice, and action. In the political moment, individual leadership is supposed to be ontologically stable and not constrained by cultural and historical tradition. This democratic individualism has been central to democratic theory and its focus on individual autonomy.[42] Whereas New Right thinkers have in general tied the goals of liberty and equality to individualist political, economic, and ethical doctrines, New Left thinkers have defended the desirability of certain social or collective means and goals. Yet, 'legal' and 'participatory' theorists have a set of propositions in common. They are connected through concepts of 'autonomy' or 'independence' that link these aspirations together and help explain why they have been shared so widely. Autonomy connotes the capacity of human beings to reason self-consciously, to be self-determining in different situations upon deliberation, judgement, and choice to act.

Revolutions and periods of deep uncertainty are at odds with such essentialist assumptions regarding human autonomy. Human power in terms of the potential capacity to form political arrangements is boundless. In the boundlessness of action, however, the actor is never merely a 'doer' but always and at the same time a 'sufferer'.[43] In revolutionary conditions, equality can be likened to what Marcel Mauss termed 'total equality'.[44] An anthropologically informed view suggests that democratisation is not only based on the autonomous choice of an appropriate model exogenous to the situation but needs to integrate the situational premises of experiences of total equality. As a total social phenomenon, it comprises political, economic, juridical, moral, aesthetic, and psychological realities. Revolutions are liminal experiences where the equality of conditions blurs hierarchies of political agency, establishes multiple sovereignties and structures of dual power, dissolves identities and social

[41] David Apter, 'Political Religion in the New Nations', in Clifford Geertz, ed., *Old Societies and New States: The Quest for Modernity in Asia and Africa* (New York: Free Press, 1963), 76.
[42] David Held, *Models of Democracy* (Stanford: Stanford University Press, 1987), 268–70.
[43] Hannah Arendt, *The Human Condition* (Chicago and London: University of Chicago Press, 1958), 190–1.
[44] Marcel Mauss, *Sociologie et anthropologie*, 9th edn (Paris: PUF, 2001), xxv–xxx.

roles, and enhances the reciprocity of desires. Popular sovereignty has not only been a matter of normatively inspired and constitutionally guaranteed doctrines; it has also been politically articulated through socially dramatic events. In the boundless potential of the empty space of power, the principle of inequality is the driving force at the bottom, as revolutionaries either pursue the consolidation or the destruction of social inequality.[45] Even in the greatest anarchy, self-perceptions of bodily existence, of the flow of historical time, and of some notion of one's own past, as well as the awareness of one's existence in space, will provide for certainties. Thus, equality of conditions refers not only to a legal prescription laid down in democratic constitutions that would guarantee equal treatment and equal respect for every man. When politics are unbounded, the equality of conditions takes on a meaning beyond equality of estimation, which would imply legally enforceable equal treatment and equal respect for everybody. Therefore, equality not only is the object of a belief or the principle of social hierarchies and political rights but also provides human relationships with meaning as far as it becomes irreversible on the level of thought, even though in reality many inequalities persist.

The democratisation of social conditions in the contentious politics of a revolution acquires an autonomy of its own, articulating new meanings of political concepts, which subsequently become politically constitutive. While the representational principle of 'the king in parliament' preserved the differences of rank, in itself it symbolised the relationship of head and member in a single body-politic. Earlier, such as in the aftermath of the Magna Carta, the 'people' originally meant only a rank in society without any possibility of articulating – or aspiration to articulate – representation. The attack at the Bastille in July 1789 endowed the concept 'people' with a new meaning. An act of violence conducted by the people as a social entity was interpreted by the representative body of the National Assembly as an authoritative expression of popular sovereignty and legitimacy, thus converting an act of popular mass violence into the constitutive act of the people as a political subject.[46]

After the February Revolution of 1917, the political project of turning an autocracy into a constitutional regime was thwarted by the social polarisation among the Russian people (*narod*) in a society out of joint. In the confusion of dual power, the solution for filling the empty space of power provided by communism was not only to declare but also to

---

[45] Tocqueville, *Democracy in America*, 796.
[46] William H. Sewell jnr, 'Historical Events as Transformations of Structures: Inventing Revolution at the Bastille', *Theory and Society*, 25 (1996), 841–81.

monopolise the interpretation of values, law, history, and knowledge.[47] The Bolsheviks appropriated the symbolism of revolutionary equality in the dictatorship of the proletariat. In the doctrine of the permanent revolution, the communist party claimed to exercise sovereignty through the non-political ideal of embodying the social spirit, the consciousness, and the source of laws. Lenin used the slogan 'All Power to the Soviets' in order to highlight the specifically social meaning of the 'people' in opposition to the Western liberal concept of political representation. Supported by longstanding revolutionary desires and earlier uprisings such as in the Revolution of 1905, the Russian Revolution of 1917 with its two peaks in February and October deepened social polarisation and transformed meanings of democracy. Concepts of liberal rights, individual responsibility, and limited government were not wholly alien to traditions of 'good governance' before the revolution.[48] Yet the initially liberal project for a constitutional democracy was crowded out by socialised meanings of democracy in the dramatic and violent context of a deeply divided society. Through the deep social polarisation between February and October 1917, the initial liberal-constitutional notion of democracy acquired a quasi-dictatorial meaning whereby the socially disadvantaged aimed to expel the 'bourgeois elements' in the state as enemies.[49]

Although some consider that Lenin rejected democracy as the rule of the majority, in Lenin's view the Soviet regime was majority rule. He did not question the majoritarian principle of democracy but adapted the situational premises of social polarisation to the conceptual meaning of socialist democracy. In his view, the Western conception as one where the liberal principle (based on individual autonomy and dignity) of majority rule is part of the institutional apparatus of the state (parliament, pluralism, etc.) neglected the sociological element of the people as potentially participating in the work of government. Faithful to the Marxian idea that the revolutionary class of the proletariat has no class interest, under the dictatorship of the proletariat the people would no longer be separated by societal divisions, and the division between society and state would also be removed. For Lenin, majority was therefore not associated with the struggle for representation and votes in a parliamentary system; rather, it rested on the identity of the vanguard party and the proletarian people

[47] Claude Lefort, *The Political Forms of Modern Society: Bureaucracy, Democracy, Totalitarianism* (Cambridge: Polity, 1986), 301–3.
[48] Richard Sakwa, 'Subjectivity, Politics and Order in Russian Political Evolution', *Slavic Review*, 54, 4 (1995), 943–64.
[49] Orlando Figes and Boris Kolonitskii, *Interpreting the Russian Revolution: The Language and Symbols of 1917* (New Haven and London: Yale University Press, 1999), 122–4.

upon which the new state was based. Thus, the new power as the dictatorship of the overwhelming majority could and did maintain itself only by
winning the confidence of the great masses, only by drawing, in the freest,
broadest, and most energetic manner, all the masses into the work of
government.[50]

While the Bolshevik Revolution is commonly seen as 'anti-democratic',
the situational premises warrant its strongly 'democratic' appeal as rule of
the people, by the people, and for the people – that is, elements of democracy that reproduce Lincoln's classical synthesis of democracy. It has been
argued that this phrase derives its democratic credentials not from
any essence of democracy but only from Lincoln himself. It defies exact
analysis and does not suffice to define democracy because Stalin might
have used it first and he might have found plausible arguments to justify
it.[51] The liberal critique of the inexactitude of Lincoln's formula and its
possible abuse by Stalin, however, misses the point because it conceives of
democracy as a set of political institutions that safeguard liberal values as an
end in themselves.

The need for contextualisation is also important for the democratic
credentials of dissidence in eastern Europe. From a liberal perspective,
the intentions of dissidence in eastern Europe as a pursuit of 'truth' were
seen as largely inadequate for the institutionalisation of a new political
order or for conducting public policy.[52] If the ethics of anti-politics are
discarded as a viable alternative to democratic action, however, two
logically opposed standards of autonomy are applied. Essentially, democratic theory would not see the manifestation of autonomy in the context
of a communist dictatorship as equivalent to the autonomy of civil society
necessary for a consolidated democracy. The autonomy demanded by
theories informed by democratic individualism differs contextually and
culturally from the very social conditions under which resistance against
communist rule was articulated historically. In such usage, autonomy
remains 'outside' concrete experience and is posited as an essence that
necessarily pre-exists the consolidation of a regime-type. Such a double
standard suggests that democratic preferences, sustained by individual
choice and self-interest, remain stable despite the boundlessness of action
and the dissolution of legal boundaries in the empty space of power.

[50] V. I. Lenin, *Selected Works*, 12 vols. (London: Lawrence & Wishart, 1939), vol. VII, 252.
[51] Giovanni Sartori, *The Theory of Democracy Revisited* (Chatham, NJ: Chatham House
Publishers, 1987), 35.
[52] Claus Offe, *Varieties of Transition: The East European and East German Experience*
(Cambridge, MA: MIT Press, 1997), 187.

Yet, presupposing a constituted system of power as the 'final' political outcome of what democracy essentially *is* may not be congruous with the production of meanings of democracy in the experiential basis of history. In the dissolution of autocratic power, everything depends on how the new type of power is symbolised in accordance with the social fabric. In a twentieth-century version of Rousseau's paradox of sovereignty, C. B. Macpherson argued that there would be no further growth in democratic participation without prior changes in social inequality and in consciousness. Thus, changes in social inequality and consciousness could not be achieved without a prior increase in democratic participation.[53] The historical evolution of communism has seen revolutionary outbreaks, when democratic participation occurred not as acts of voting under constitutional guarantees but as appropriating the empty space of power by public opinion and emotional solidarity among citizens.

Can autonomy be refused to the Hungarian revolutionaries of 1956, the initiators of the Prague spring, or to the Polish Solidarność movement? Does the absence of volition to enforce institutional reform and to press for realistic change vindicate the failure of the democratising effort of dissidence? If autonomous sectors in society were a *sine qua non* for the establishment of democratic institutions such as constitutionalism, political pluralism, or the rule of law, existing Western states could never have established themselves as democracies. Although anti-politics in eastern Europe was dismissed by many due to its manifest denial of reforming the political system of communist government, it revealed the emptiness of the space of power as it credibly established an 'anti-political' spiritual movement based on the project of building a 'hidden' sphere, where citizens would be liberated from the constraints imposed by the institutionalised logic of official politics. The symbolism of these revolutionary ruptures and popular memory associated with them was crucial for the development of a participatory spirit of belonging to a nation. Moral codes of ethical individualism and moral perfectionism did not emanate from the pursuit of individual self-interest in a system of institutions but from a positive affirmation of freedom and dignity against the socially oppressive non-political logic of post-totalitarian rule. Its share of democracy can be found in the determination of many individuals to distance themselves spiritually from the contagious overall influence of communist bureaucracy and the totalitarian lie.[54] They also emanated from the concrete

---

[53] C. B. Macpherson, *The Life and Times of Liberal Democracy* (New York: Oxford University Press, 1977), 100.

[54] György Konrád, *Antipolitics: An Essay*, trans. from the Hungarian by Richard E. Allen (San Diego/New York/London: Harcourt Brace Jovanovich, 1984), 231.

events of living through community experiences. As Tadeusz Mazowiecki formulated it for the Polish case: 'To defend [him]self from totalitarianism, man need not return to individualism ... Only responsibility for the society, for forming its organisations and institutions, so that the social community will strengthen the development and the respect for human personality ... can restore equilibrium and sanity to the society and proper conditions for the individual development of the human being.'[55] Under communism, political impulses can hardly come from 'professional politicians' who have adopted the political habits and techniques of communist power; they need to come from outsiders. Although it refrained from active political reform, anti-communist dissidence was aware of the stakes of genuine political reality. While citizens in former communist countries have much to learn about the workings of liberal democracy as an institutionalised system, Westerners have much to learn from them about the practice of democratic citizenship.[56]

Meanings of democracy

While deterministic accounts see democracy as an outcome in terms of political arrangements and their efficient control of behaviour through power, an inquiry into democratisation requires including the symbolisation of dramatic experiences for the formation of meanings of democracy. Visions of equality and cultural representations of democracy are appropriated through social memory and popular consciousness, which in turn sustain meanings of and prospects for freedom and emancipation. As products and objects of political struggles and social crises, meanings of democracy enter cultural memory, they reinforce or challenge traditions, and they are culturally reshaped.[57]

Historically dated meanings of democracy, therefore, are not only episodes without real impact on the future development of the concept. As a crucial concept in political theory, the notion of democracy in the West was characterised by important shifts in meaning, which can roughly be classified in three groups.[58] Traditional concepts such as Aristotelian

---

[55] Cited in Adam Przeworski, 'Economic Reforms, Public Opinion, and Political Institutions: Poland in the Eastern European Perspective', in Bresser Pereira et al., eds., *Economic Reforms in New Democracies* (Cambridge: Cambridge University Press, 1993), 187.

[56] Isaac, *Democracy in Dark Times*, 178.

[57] John Markoff, *Waves of Democracy: Social Movements and Political Change* (Thousand Oaks, CA: Pine Forge Press, 1996).

[58] Reinhart Koselleck, *Futures Past: On the Semantics of Historical Time* (Cambridge, MA: MIT Press, 1985), 82.

constitutional thought retain an empirical validity even under modern conditions. Other concepts such as the terms 'history' (*Geschichte*) or 'class' have kept the same word as a shell, but the meanings have changed radically and can be recovered only historically. Finally, there are recurrently emerging neologisms such as 'communism' or 'fascism' that react to specific social or political circumstances. Despite endless transitions and superimpositions in the course of time, democracy can be considered to be a traditional as well as a constantly changing or a recent concept. Many definitions, procedures, and regularities of the ancient democracy of the polis as a potential constitutional form are still present in modern democracies. Following its modernisation in the eighteenth century, the concept became equivalent to a new organisational form typical of the large modern state and its social consequences. Introducing the rule of law and the principle of equality modified old meanings. In the wake of social transformations in the nineteenth century, democracy became increasingly associated with a state of expectation which, within a historico-philosophical perspective – be it legislative or revolutionary – claimed to satisfy newly constituted needs so that its meaning might be validated. In the twentieth century, 'democracy' became a general concept replacing 'republic' (*politeia*) that consigned to illegality all other constitutional types as forms of rule. Due to this global universality, democratic theory essentially produced a whole myriad of qualifying attributes as perhaps the only manner by which democracy as a system of government could retain any functional efficiency.

From an experiential perspective, however, autonomy goes beyond the methodological individualism of autonomous subjects in a democratically constituted system. The lived experiences in exceptional revolutionary situations acquire autonomy of their own. Few people would deny that the Russian Revolution of February 1917 in the contextual meaning of the time started off as a genuinely democratic revolution when the overthrow of the tsar introduced 'equality' as a social driving force. Not unlike Russia's victory over Napoleon's armies more than a century earlier, the Second World War in Russia not only inflicted unprecedented suffering, despair, and destruction on society, but also stimulated free thought and autonomy that accompanied the activities of masses of people together risking or sacrificing their lives in defence of their country and its state.[59] After Stalin's death, de-Stalinisation brought about a transformation in the communicative context, which – although vague, limited, and contradictory – was mediated by the focus on socialist

---

[59] Michael Urban et al., *The Rebirth of Politics in Russia* (Cambridge: Cambridge University Press, 1997), 30.

legality and in a not insignificant way revived the category of 'democracy' in Soviet society. Under the conditions of the non-political claim to rule by a monopolistic party, where civil liberties, the rule of law, and an effective political pluralism were suspended, the 'small' revolutions in Hungary in 1956, Czechoslovakia in 1968, or Poland in 1980 were open manifestations of autonomy and constitution of subjectivity. Such popular resistance created an empty space of power, which not only challenged political structures of domination but also bequeathed a communicative memory of ethical individual choice and the value of self-sacrifice upon society.

At yet another stage, the Soviet dissident movement took up the intellectual thrust of democracy in its letter to the Soviet leaders of 19 March 1970, which prefigured what was to become the language of Gorbachev's *perestroika* and *glasnost*.[60] The democratic renaissance in the Soviet Union at the end of the 1980s was primarily interested in strengthening the accountability of party officials by reviving the soviets in the republics as representative organs. Giving back genuine accountability to 'the people' was consistent with Gorbachev's early statements according to which *perestroika* prioritised cultural change with a focus on attitudes, psychology, and consciousness. It thus included the educated masses as a source of wisdom and information. It required not only the formal accountability of officials but also the 'pluralism of opinions' and systemic criticism, which realised an equalisation of status between officials and the masses.[61]

Democracy as an urgent hope has been contingent upon the cultural context in society and the personal credentials of political leaders. For instance, the Polish Solidarność movement adopted the tradition of the democracy of the gentry – the only form of democracy to have taken strong root in Poland – that was endowed by an ideal of unanimity and a corresponding image of a unitary and single national will. Moreover, it represented the legacy of national romanticism that valued Polish messianism and the loyalty to the national idea more than the responsibility for current national affairs. Thus, the concern for an idealised past became a structuring principle for Solidarność that was based more on myth than on reality.[62] In Poland's self-limiting revolution in 1980 and 1981, the combined effort of intellectuals, workers, and the Catholic

---

[60] Urban et al., *The Rebirth of Politics in Russia*, p. 62.
[61] George W. Breslauer, *Gorbachev and Yeltsin as Leaders* (Cambridge: Cambridge University Press, 2002), 67.
[62] Andrzej Walicki, *The Three Traditions in Polish Patriotism and Their Contemporary Relevance* (Bloomington: Polish Studies Center, 1988), 10–13.

Church merged romanticism and religious spirituality with the action of the working class that propagated a democratic utopianism in the concept of Solidarność.

Democracy in communist Europe has been shaping up across multiple changes of meanings, as a context-laden and historically generated concept. Civil resistance was an attempt to transform society by processes of subjectivisation. Political opportunities become available only when subjectivity is culturally empowered through symbols and memories that sustain political imagination. Subjectivity is not synonymous with the self-interest of ruling elites assumed by democratic individualism. Rather, it refers to the recognition of the people as the source of political authority and the need to represent this common destiny by symbolic acts and the bestowal of political meaning. Not only objective causes but also conjunctural factors affected the timing of the breakthrough in eastern Europe.[63] These include the formation of autonomous political groups, the role of individual political leaders and their choices, the diffusion of democratic ideas, and the influence of external forces, such as the liberalisation process in the Soviet Union and the attraction of the Western political and economic model.

Thus, even failures to produce 'democratic outcomes' in terms of regime change may be influential in providing models, beliefs, and the spirit for overcoming autocratic rule. More broadly, national memories or even myths of a democratic past may facilitate popular acceptance of democratic political structures.[64] Despite its openly anti-liberal systemic features such as a negation of the rule of law, civil liberties, and constitutional rights, the political evolution of communism contained shifts in subjectivity and the development of new meanings of democracy.[65]

The tension between the emotional urgency and the intrinsic haziness of democracy was characteristic of parts of central and east European and Russian political culture. The diversity of meanings of democracy in the political discourse of various post-communist countries intimates the connection with historical experience and representations of democracy before the collapse of communism. A closer examination of meanings of democracy in post-communist countries such as in Russia, for instance, suggests at least four roads to democratisation: the liberal, the republican,

[63] Geoffrey Pridham and Tatu Vanhanen, eds., *Democratization in Eastern Europe: Domestic and International Perspectives* (London and New York: Routledge, 1994), 255–62.
[64] Attila Agh, *Emerging Democracies in East Central Europe and the Balkans* (Cheltenham and Northampton: Edward Elgar, 1998), 20.
[65] Sakwa, 'Subjectivity'.

the participatory, and the statist.[66] Despite the hegemonic discourse of a nascent Western identity and liberal democracy, post-communist societies are characterised by a confusing array of multiplicity of symbols and meanings. While the democratic revolution of 1989 and 1991 brought about the victory of liberal democracy and human rights, it is also associated with an unprecedented wave of war, ethnic cleansing, exclusion, and discrimination.[67]

The rise of Bolshevik power in Russia, of people's democracies in eastern Europe, and the small revolutions in 1956, 1968, and 1980 constituted not only outcomes in the domestic evolution of communism, but also fundamentally transformed meanings of democracy in the West. Originally a constitutional form of government with the concomitant system of institutions, democracy became a normative aggregate, standing for an alternative civilisational truth and source of authority. In its wake, democracy in the West did not remain confined to a constitutional form, but became tinged with a strongly positive moral leaning. Democracy became equivalent to a good society in operation, the antithesis of the evil and dehumanising empire of communist dictatorship.[68] Furthermore, Western democracies drew much of their own legitimacy as the 'good society' from a pervasive fear of contagion with communism and its ensuing stigmatisation as the 'empire of evil'. Paradoxically, this fear of contagion rested upon the fact that the systemic antagonism between democracy and Soviet totalitarianism lacked the empirical reality of open military conflict or an inherited hostile tradition. Following the Second World War, Germany as the military enemy was replaced by the totalitarian paradigm, which equated the Soviet Union with the total externalisation of evil, thus promoting democracy, in a binary fashion, as the morally good opposite.

Democratisation has been a process of movement towards an outcome that is neither fully stable nor entirely predetermined. It might be objected that working with such a hazy and by definition uncertain variable would flaw any analytical value of such a procedure. As the broad literatures on the European Union or on the global market economy suggest, these research topics are confronted with unpredictable outcomes, unspecified sequences of development, and uncertain time frames. Still, even if the European Union falls apart or the trends towards

[66] John Dryzek and Leslie Holmes, *Post-Communist Democratization: Political Discourses Across Thirteen Countries* (Cambridge: Cambridge University Press, 2002), 268–73.
[67] Michael Mann, *The Dark Side of Democracy: Explaining Ethnic Cleansing* (Cambridge: Cambridge University Press, 2004).
[68] Seymour Martin Lipset, *Political Man: The Social Bases of Politics* (London: Heinemann, 1960), 403.

a global marketisation are reversed, this kind of value-oriented social inquiry will be important for our understanding of such processes.[69] The diversity of meanings of democracy in the post-communist world reflects rather than contradicts democratisation patterns in the Western world. Despite the lack of institutionalisation and minimal procedural guarantees under communist regimes, these visions of democracy must not be considered as a mendacious version of reality. It is safe to assume that democracy in the Western hemisphere has gained acceptance not despite but *because of* its utopian bent. Whereas the Greeks coined the term 'democracy' to describe their already existing form of government, modernity has revived a term that prescribes an impossible form, making 'democracy' first and foremost a normative word: it does not *describe* a thing, it *prescribes* an ideal.[70] The linkage between original Athenian democracy and modern democracy is anchored precisely in the idealisation of the former, driven by a diffuse and urgent hope that human life in the settings in which it takes place may come to be more a matter of committed personal choice and less a matter of enforced compliance with impersonal and external (and unwelcome) demands.[71]

A critic might well argue at this point that considering democratic transformation as a drama is relativist and risks depriving democracy of its specific character as a constitutional form of government. However, the focus on global contingency and the potential decay of any manmade order is anything but original. Rather, it reflects the tenuous success of democracy before the second half of the twentieth century.[72] The driving forces of a society may undermine the very system once social conditions have changed. Starting from Aristotle, political thought acknowledged that democratic government is not autonomous from social conditions such as war or mob rule, and therefore is one part in a sequence of other forms of political domination.[73] In Machiavelli's view, the disunion and strife among patricians and plebeians were the cause of liberty, stability, and power in the Roman republic.[74] Although man's task is to provide for the best and most durable constitution of a body-politic, as Rousseau argued, a durable regime must not be confused with an eternal one. The

[69] Whitehead, *Democratisation*, 33.
[70] Giovanni Sartori, 'Democracy', *International Encyclopedia of the Social Sciences*, ed. David L. Sills, vol. IV (New York: Macmillan and Free Press, 1968), 115–16.
[71] Dunn, 'Conclusion', 256.
[72] Robert A. Dahl, *On Democracy* (New Haven and London: Yale University Press, 1998), 1.
[73] Aristotle, *Politics*, ed. Stephen Everson (Cambridge: Cambridge University Press, 1988), Book V, 1314a, 34–1314a1.
[74] Niccolò Machiavelli, *Discourses on Livy*, ed. and trans. Harvey Mansfield and Nathan Tarcov (Chicago: University of Chicago Press, 1998), Book I, chaps. 4–5.

body-politic, as much as the human body, starts dying from the moment of its birth and carries within it the causes of its destruction.[75] Rather than identifying democracy with a specific doctrinal source, it is reasonable to claim that it has been a by-product of the entire development of Western civilisation.[76]

Any claim about the inevitability of establishing liberal democratic regimes in the contemporary meaning in, say, France or the United States would not be intellectually acceptable. Similarly, any claim about political societies that are immune to extremism or that are particularly sensitive to totalitarian menaces would be utterly ahistorical.[77] What appears as the fundamental antagonism between two systems, two worlds of values, or 'two souls' is likely to be flawed in historical reality. It is impossible, for instance, to distinguish between a 'good' and an 'evil' Germany, because one was inherently linked with the other. According to Thomas Mann, 'the evil was simultaneously the good, the good errant and in decay'.[78] To argue that Russia is Europe's double and therefore ineluctably set on a path of political and economic convergence with the West is to overlook how the conjuncture of many Russias, often in deep rivalry with the West, was influential in the pre-revolutionary and post-revolutionary political evolution.[79] It is impossible to scientifically decide between different systems of values such as, for instance, between French or German culture. This comes down to an eternal quarrel between different Gods. Engaged in an irresolvable reciprocal struggle, the permanent contention of representational truths has been rationalised in comparison to the mythical fights in old Greece, but this fight keeps on being ruled by destiny, not by science.[80]

In Russia, for instance, the road to communism and to a totalitarian system was not predetermined, as Russian society did not meet the 'objective' requirements of a revolutionary situation according to Marxist requirements, characterised by a class struggle between a strong industrial proletariat and a well-developed bourgeoisie. The determinist claim about its 'undemocratic' nature has neglected the social foundations of meanings

---

[75] Jean-Jacques Rousseau, *The Social Contract and Discourses*, trans. and intro. G. D. H. Cole (London: Dent, 1993), 260–1.
[76] Sartori, 'Democracy', 112.
[77] Michel Dobry, 'France: An Ambiguous Survival', in Berg-Schlosser and Mitchell, *Conditions of Democracy in Europe*, 157–83.
[78] Quoted in Aleida Assmann and Ute Frevert, *Geschichtsvergessenheit, Geschichtsversessenheit. Vom Umgang mit deutschen Vergangenheiten nach 1945* (Stuttgart: DVA, 1999), 121.
[79] Martin Malia, *Russia Under Western Eyes* (Cambridge, MA: Harvard University Press, 1999).
[80] Max Weber, *Wissenschaft als Beruf*, ed. Wolfgang J. Mommsen and Wolfgang Schluchter (Tübingen: Mohr, 1992), 99–100.

of democracy. Rather than being a utopian and impractical view of revers-
ing a system of political domination, practices of resistance to oppression
took shape in the hidden sphere through individual acts of written or
spoken defiance before they merged with the public sphere.[81] It has been
a distinctive part of the communist experience that democracy has been a
civilising force that relied upon emotional bonds with the West but also was
grounded in experiences of freedom in the solidarity of the shaken, living in
dignity, or living in truth.[82]

---

[81] James Scott, *Domination and the Arts of Resistance: Hidden Transcripts* (New Haven and
   London: Yale University Press, 1990).
[82] Harald Wydra, 'Democracy in Eastern Europe as a Civilizing Process', in Dennis Smith
   and Sue Wright, eds., *Whose Europe? The Turn Towards Democracy* (Oxford: Blackwell,
   1999), 288–310.

Part II

Critical events and their symbolisations

5   The rise of Bolshevik power

In a real revolution the best characters do not come to the front . . . They are its victims: the victims of disgust, of disenchantment – often of remorse. Hopes grotesquely betrayed, ideals caricatured – that is the definition of the revolutionary success.   Joseph Conrad

Russia unbound

The October Revolution is usually considered to be the beginning of an anti-democratic and non-constitutional totalitarian type of regime. One can point to the most obvious consequences such as the monopolisation of all means of power in the hands of a revolutionary party, the seizure of control of all economic, state administrative, juridical, and cultural institutions, and the institutionalisation of revolutionary terror through the Cheka, the secret police established by the Bolshevik regime in December 1917. While this has been an accepted view in political history and comparative politics, its judgement is based on outcome-logic, which has dominated the two major interpretations of the October Revolution. On the one hand, the focus was on the chain of unpredictable and rather situational factors that made this unique constellation of power seizure through the Bolsheviks possible.[1] Critical of the social foundations of the Bolshevik Revolution, such a view claimed that the Soviet totalitarian state was not a society but an ideocratic regime that could not have emerged without Lenin's personal will power. Conversely, there has been the central assumption about a causality according to which the revolution was the inevitable result of the class struggle between the underprivileged classes (workers and peasants) and the bourgeoisie. By means of a turn towards social history, the so-called revisionist school replaced the manifestly

---

[1] Richard Pipes, *The Russian Revolution* (New York and Toronto: Vintage/Random House, 1991).

flawed totalitarian thesis with Leon Trotsky's perspective of Stalin's rule as a counter-revolution.[2]

This chapter argues that the October Revolution not only institutionalised a new type of political regime, but also gave rise to an entirely new form of political society. The experiential basis of the revolutionary rupture and its symbolisation as a permanent revolution cast doubt on dichotomic accounts of the October Revolution. The Russian Revolution[3] as the most important event in modern Russian history requires adopting an experiential and cultural dimension.[4] Following upon the tortuous development since the emancipation of the serfs and the conflict-ridden evolution of social, psychological, and political identities, 'the Russia that underwent the revolution of 1917 was a society out of joint, and the severe convulsions that beset it under the stresses of the civil war were, at least in part, but a demonstration of this fact'.[5] The February Revolution was not only a prelude to October, characterised by a failed political experiment in 'constitutional' government. It also produced a massive change in the symbolic universe of Russian society as it replaced the tsarist monarchy with a secular and anti-religious movement.[6] Absolute monarchy was followed by an ill-fated attempt to establish a constitutional government based on a parliamentary assembly and a soviet (council) system. Unlike modern revolutions in America or in France, the Russian Revolution – although neither the direct nor the inevitable consequence of the war – would have been utterly unthinkable without the conditions of the First World War. The February Revolution further radicalised the erosion of political authority structures that had begun with the Revolution of 1905 at the latest and had accelerated during the war.

Burdened from the beginning by its duality, the dual power consisted of the Provisional Government (relying upon the Constitutional Democratic Party (known as the Cadets), leading members of the Progressive bloc,

[2] Stephen Kotkin, *Magnetic Mountain: Stalinism as a Civilization* (Berkeley: University of California Press, 1995), 6.
[3] The Soviet usage eschewed the term Russian Revolution and referred to the 'October Revolution' or 'October'. The favoured post-Soviet term seems to be the 'Bolshevik Revolution' or the 'Bolshevik putsch'; see Sheila Fitzpatrick, *The Russian Revolution*, 2nd edn (Oxford: Oxford University Press, 2001), 173 n. 1.
[4] Kotkin, *Magnetic Mountain*, 14.
[5] Leopold Haimson, 'The Problem of Social Identities in Early Twentieth-Century Russia', *Slavic Review*, 47, 1 (1988), 1.
[6] Alexander Solzhenitsyn's attempt to study the February Revolution as the central event of modern Russian history gradually made him aware that he needed to explain how tsarism and society had developed by that time; see David Remnick, *Resurrection: The Struggle for a New Russia* (New York: Random House, 1997), 149.

and the radical Socialist Revolutionary Alexander Kerensky) and the Petrograd Soviet that was established on 28 February 1917. This dual-power arrangement is less important for its failure to establish durable forms of authority than for the very uncertainty of authority in a configuration of multiple sovereignties. The coherence of the Provisional Government did not emanate from a political philosophy with a clear-cut objective, but from an intellectual tradition that was inspired by a 'negative' impulse, the liberation from the old regime. Heirs of the Russian intelligentsia, the members of the Provisional Government were alienated from all institutions of the old regime and were passionate about a liberty that they embraced with almost religious faith. They hated the old order, but they also feared the revolution. Thus, the First Provisional Government was characterised by a situation in which 'the blind ... led the halt along to the final drama of October'.[7] In the dual-power regime after February 1917, the unresolved question about what to do with the war exhausted the short-lived Provisional Government and considerably contributed to the initially improbable seizure of power by a conspiratorial minority.

The unexpected turns of the First World War gave a further twist to political developments between February and October. Arguably, no other issue was as disruptive in the relations between the soviets and the Provisional Government as the question of whether to continue the war effort. Not only did the First World War constitute an important precondition for the outbreak of the February Revolution and for maintaining the revolutionary efforts of the Bolsheviks throughout the summer and autumn of 1917, but the high degree of mobilisation, indiscriminate crowd action, and the combative spirit of an ongoing war also provided the background conditions for the rise of the Bolsheviks. After Brest-Litovsk, it was not peace that loomed large; open warfare against the population became the single most important activity pursued by the Bolsheviks, eclipsing even the defeat of the White armies. Playing on the antagonisms between resentful and dislocated Russians, the political articulation of communist power occurred in a wartime spirit of violence and repression and of 'siege psychosis'.[8]

The war effort triggered the autocracy's unexpected and total collapse. Although the weakness of the tsar's political authority had been evident prior to the outbreak of the February Revolution, the war abruptly

---

[7] Leonard Schapiro, *Russian Studies*, ed. Ellen Dahrendorf (New York: Viking, 1987), 115.
[8] Marcel Mauss, 'A Sociological Assessment of Bolshevism' in Mike Gane, ed., *The Radical Sociology of Durkheim and Mauss* (London and New York: Routledge, 1992), 183; Peter Holquist, *Making War, Forging Revolution: Russia's Continuum of Crisis, 1914–1921* (Cambridge, MA: Harvard University Press, 2002), 204.

discontinued the positive effects of state-led industrialisation, economic expansion, and demographic increase.[9] This adverse development was reinforced by the split of command structures between Grand Duke Nikolai Nikolaevich as the supreme commander of the army in western Russia and the tsar in Petrograd.[10] This arrangement for directing warfare established a *de facto* dual power, without much co-ordination between the two. After Tsar Nicholas II took up supreme command in August 1915 to face the German offensive, an atmosphere of panic, chaos, and moral defeat became rampant in the army. Approximately one million soldiers surrendered during the retreat, preferring the prospect of becoming prisoners of war to fighting a seemingly lost cause against a superior army. Rather than raising their spirits, the tsar's decision to take up supreme command had a catastrophic effect on the morale of the troops. At the same time, his absence from the capital weakened his authority in the hinterland, giving way to the development of a 'bureaucratic anarchy'.

The situation in 1917, therefore, was considerably different from 1905, when the workers' belief and hope in the tsar was quite crucial for the unfolding of events. The tsar had lost any moral purpose, which would have legitimated his remaining in office. Quite disinterested in how matters evolved in February 1917 in Petrograd, he was not considered by the populace to be the interlocutor. Such reciprocal distrust was reinforced by the endemic weakness of tsarism. This waning authority was not simply due to the personality of Tsar Nicholas II, but owed much to the bureaucratisation of tsarist autocracy long prior to the First World War.[11] As the Russian state had not emerged from below but had been imposed from above, it was characterised by the absence of a solid network of intermediate elites between the top of the state and the populace. At the outbreak of the First World War, not only had tsarism lost faith in its own leadership capacity; the masses had also lost faith and awe in the tsar's person as embodying the monarchy.

For all its endemic weakness, however, tsarism was not doomed to fall.[12] Tsarism had survived several onslaughts such as the Revolution of

---

[9] The demographic leap from 100 million inhabitants in 1890 (including Poland and Finland, but excluding Siberia, Central Asia, and the Caucasus) to approximately 150 million at the outbreak of the war was even greater proportionally than the population growth in Germany; see John Maynard Keynes, *The Collected Writings of J. M. Keynes*, vol. II, *The Economic Consequences of the Peace* (Basingstoke: Macmillan, 1971), 8.

[10] Orlando Figes, *A People's Tragedy: The Russian Revolution 1891–1924* (London: Jonathan Cape, 1996), 249–69.

[11] Max Weber, *Zur Russischen Revolution von 1905*, 23 vols., vol. X, *Schriften und Reden 1905–1912*, ed. Wolfgang J. Mommsen and Dittmar Dahlmann (Tübingen: J. C. B. Mohr, 1989), 401–13.

[12] Richard Pipes, *Three Whys of the Russian Revolution* (London: Pimlico, 1998), 11–19.

1905, and it could also be reassured by the relative calm of the Russian village, which made up approximately 85 per cent of the empire's population. There was no cogent transformative interest, as the people and foreign observers seemed to believe that tsarism would survive for a long time to come. This is reflected in the way the tsar's unexpected abdication was met with utter confusion and bewilderment of all parties.

Despite the decisive influence of the First World War, it would misrepresent the perceptions of most contemporaries if the war were taken to be the single most important factor leading to revolution. Nourished by long-standing revolutionary desires, many individual Russians accorded the First World War nothing like the same significance as the revolution. The crucial point is not the chronological sequence in which the war is followed by the internal crisis of a revolution, but the simultaneous breach of the established relations of power, social existence, and continuing war-like conditions. As the catalyst of social polarisation and an ongoing crisis of authority, the war changed values and allegiances drastically. Few army officers refused to take the oath to the Provisional Government in March 1917. Conversely, many peasant soldiers did not perceive the dual-power regime as a new power structure, but remained confused about the representations of authorities, enemies, and friends. 'These peasant soldiers' notion of soviet power – even though most of them now probably viewed this power as their very own, rather than as a superordinate authority, however benevolent, hovering over them – did not encompass any conception of the relationships between themselves, their village communities, or even the peasant estate as a whole, and other social groups – let alone any generalised view of the Russian body politic as a whole.'[13] The volatility of the labels – the terms *burzhua* (bourgeois) and *pomeshchik* (landlord) were interchangeably applied to representatives of the old regime and the crumbling power structure – reflected how the war radicalised peasant-soldiers against officers and introduced the sharply radicalised social polarisation into an otherwise apathetic peasantry. This 'trench bolshevism' was echoed in the Bolsheviks' formula 'Peace, Land, and Bread'.

The dictatorship of the proletariat

The success of Bolshevism would have been unlikely without the revolutionary conjuncture. At the outset of the February Revolution, the Bolshevik party was a marginalised and sectarian movement with little

---

[13] Haimson, 'The Problem of Social Identities', 13.

influence, and without a policy or plan for the future.[14] Although its membership increased constantly from an estimated 24,000 in February 1917 to a total of some 350,000 in October 1917, only slightly more than 5 per cent of Russia's industrial workers belonged to it at the beginning of this period, and this in a country in which industrial workers made up only 1 or 1.5 per cent of the population.[15] Already in the April theses, written approximately two months prior to *State and Revolution*, Lenin called for the withdrawal of all support for the 'imperialist' Provisional Government. He admitted that his party was in a minority, and in the current moment in a weak minority, in most of the soviets of workers' deputies, compared to the bloc of all the opportunist petty-bourgeois elements.

The revolutionary conjuncture produced moral confusion and social polarisation, which matched the psychological outlook of the leaders of the Bolshevik party. The Bolshevisation of Russia was, to an important extent, historically rooted in the material, spiritual, and cultural heritage of the Russian revolutionary tradition. On the one hand, the enforced Westernisation of nineteenth-century Russia and the conflict between native and Western ways of life produced an important layer of 'outcasts'. These outcasts comprised a social category among which different groups of the intelligentsia, such as the Westerners, the Slavophiles, or fanatic revolutionaries, became most important in trying to negate Western values. The tormented biographies of many of the Bolshevik revolutionaries were predictive of their behaviour in the aftermath of the October Revolution. The people who came to power in Russia in October 1917 had grown up under the regime of 'Extraordinary' and 'Temporary Laws'; this was the only Russian constitution that they had ever known.[16] On the other hand, Bolshevisation radicalised the party by promoting the most extreme elements into key positions.

In the turmoil of the first months after the *coup d'état* of October, the relationships between social groups, political contenders, and military opponents were decisively reshaped. Therefore, the modalities of the monopolisation of power and the evolution of Bolshevism were not only a matter of the institutionalisation of an ideology. They also had an impact on the formation of political consciousness through powerful symbols and attitudes, new forms of speech and language, and new

[14] Leonard Schapiro, *The Origin of the Communist Autocracy* (London: G. Bell and Sons, 1955), 25.
[15] Fitzpatrick, *The Russian Revolution*, 52.
[16] Richard Pipes, *Russia Under the Bolshevik Regime 1919–1924* (London: Harvill, 1994), 317.

ways of behaving in public and private. The revolution was an ongoing experience through which it was possible to imagine and strive to bring about communism as a 'new civilisation'.[17] In this vein, the civil war and war communism were the decisive elements in the stabilisation of Bolshevik power.

The antagonists in the civil war were not ideological camps but concrete social groups, political actors, and military contingents. With the mobilisation of more than twelve million peasants as soldiers in the First World War, the formerly closed universe of the peasant community opened up to the accelerated logic of warfare. In forging their 'alliance' with the peasantry, the Bolsheviks instrumentalised the deep social conflicts between the countryside and the town for their immediate goal of stabilising power. In desperate need of human resources for the purpose of bureaucratic control, the membership structure of Bolshevik party was soon substantially transformed.[18] The promotion of many peasants into middle-range positions of the party as well as internal party purges turned the peasants into the most numerous group in the rank and file. The programme of state nationalisation of the means of production had swollen the state bureaucracy up to six million employees precisely at a point when the proletariat undertook a mass exodus from the cities due to famine and disease. These profound transformations not only threatened the character of a 'proletarian' revolution but also reversed the trend to massive migration from the countryside into the towns.[19] In the wake of 1917, traditional conflicts such as the deeply rooted tensions between the town and the countryside developed into a social war, confronting the 'two societies' of the Russian nation. For peasants in revolt, there was no distinction between a soldier, a bandit, or a state spy.[20] More than a year after the civil war and the military confrontation between the Red and the White armies, a second 'civil war' developed at several focal points of local and regional resistance against Bolshevik power, reaching its climax in the rebellion of the marines in Kronstadt in early 1921.

Lenin's theory and practice of the dictatorship of the proletariat need to be understood in connection with the party's 'outcast' position and its low level of representativeness. Lacking a pre-existing nationwide consensus, the Bolshevik spirit had been forged through experiences of persecution and victimhood under tsarism. Unlike the Jacobins in

---

[17] Kotkin, *Magnetic Mountain*, 14.
[18] According to the census of 1922, only 2.7 per cent of the 376,000 members had joined before 1917, but they were in charge of key positions; see Pipes, *Russia Under the Bolshevik Regime 1919–1924*, 482.
[19] Isaac Deutscher, *The Unfinished Revolution* (Oxford: Oxford University Press, 1969).
[20] Marc Ferro, *La révolution de 1917* (Paris: Albin Michel, 1967), 682.

France, they were not the product of revolutionary events but one of several sectarian revolutionary parties, organised militarily, ready to fight for power, and aiming to transform man and society. In search of a broader institution to make their claim for representation viable, they targeted the soviets as the representative bodies of the factories and – during the war – of the regiments. Although the Bolsheviks gained the majority in the Moscow and Petrograd Soviets during the late summer of 1917, the preliminaries to the secret *coup d'état* on 24 October 1917 indicate that they did not have the masses behind them.[21] The seizure of power in October 1917 did not have many immediate repercussions on a national scale, and the population offered relatively little resistance precisely because it believed that the Bolshevik regime could not last.[22]

An assessment of relations as complex as those between professional revolutionaries and the masses requires great care. For my purposes, only some general lines should be sketched out. As a skilful manipulator of crowd psychology, Lenin knew that it was not enough to ascertain the will of the majority. Despite his contempt for the masses, he needed to connect his bid for power to the psychology of the crowds for the sake of propaganda and mass mobilisation. Rumours and haphazard alerts about an imminent attack by the revolutionary troops could arouse spontaneous solidarity between soldiers and the crowds, especially after the latter invaded the barracks. Lenin's own attempt to seize power by instigating the masses reflects his awareness that the only real chance of success lay in taking advantage of heightened emotions and social flux. Three times, in April, June, and July 1917, he tried to take advantage of the Provisional Government's weakness by means of street riots.[23] After the failed *coup d'état* in July 1917, Lenin became an outcast again and had to pass three and a half critical months in constant hiding.

Aware of the party's weakness, Lenin insisted that it focus on 'patiently, systematically, and unyieldingly explaining to the masses the errors of the tactics practiced by the soviets'.[24] Together with the uncertain division of powers and the lack of reliable authority structures, this mobilisation of crowds instigated the masses with the aim of toppling the Provisional Government. The makeshift character of Bolshevik leadership was tangible in its repeated attempts to elicit support from different social groups

[21] In Trotsky's account, approximately 25,000 to 30,000 people took part in the events of October in Petrograd (in a city of 2 million and a country of some 150 million); see Pipes, *Three Whys*, 32.
[22] Pipes, *Three Whys*, 60–1.
[23] Maxim Gorky, *Untimely Thoughts: Essays on Revolution, Culture and the Bolsheviks 1917–1918* (New Haven and London: Yale University Press, 1995).
[24] Ferro, *La révolution de 1917*.

by inflicting havoc upon others. A typical account of the days of the February Revolution in Petrograd demonstrates how crowds manifested their discontent without a clear-cut strategy, devoid of mass volition or concrete programmes in political groups.[25] The Bolsheviks created a 'service for spiritual aid' that was destined to keep control of crowds that assembled suddenly in the streets and could become a danger for public order. Their key idea was to act upon the mass from the inside. Whenever there was open aggression in the streets, their agents mingled with the masses in order to agitate from inside, to destroy the crowd's coherence, and to become its centre. The scenes of crowd panic and mass hysteria that were sparked off by the Bolsheviks on 4 July 1917 conveyed a picture of hopelessness and national disaster.[26] The failure of the major military offensive in July 1917, initiated by the Kerensky government, entailed the 'conspiracy' of General Kornilov against the government that had appointed him. It not only caused considerable chaos in the army but also discredited the Cadets and Kerensky personally. To a considerable extent, this failure reinforced Lenin's determination to repeat the attempt of a *coup d'état*.

Although Lenin gave a theoretical justification of the democratic nature of the soviets and their relationship to the dictatorship of the proletariat, he was profoundly sceptical of them. It is the irony of history that the one achievement that Lenin had regarded as essential, the soviet regime, never came into being. From the first day of the Bolshevik Revolution, the soviets lost power to the dictatorship of the party. They lost any practical importance when all parties but the Bolsheviks themselves were driven underground and the soviets, instead of expressing anybody's opinion, became mere administrators.[27] In the immediate aftermath of the seizure of the Winter Palace, Lenin was not at all interested in sharing power with the Petrograd Soviet. Through the creation of the Military Revolutionary Committee, Lenin seized exclusive power in the aftermath of 25 October 1917. Ostensibly created to defend Petrograd against the Germans, this Bolshevik-dominated body used the cover of soviet legitimacy to seize power in the capital. In reality, the new power structure did not emanate from the previously institutionalised organ, which was the Petrograd Soviet, but from a conjunctural entity that had been created during the insurrectionary process itself.

---

[25] Serge Tchakhotine, *Le viol des foules par la propagande politique* (Paris: Gallimard, 1952), 155–8.

[26] Gorky, *Untimely Thoughts*, 72–5.

[27] Franz Borkenau, *World Communism: A History of the Communist International* (Ann Arbor: University of Michigan Press, 1971), 55–6.

It has been suggested that the Bolsheviks united the oppressed classes such as the peasants and the proletariat in their hatred of the bourgeoisie. In the first article of the theses on the peace, Lenin portrayed the success of the revolution as a result of the joining of the working and the peasant masses.[28] Moreover, the peasant revolts between the spring and autumn of 1917 – parallel to the mutiny of the Russian army – constituted a second great social revolutionary movement.[29] Did the revolutionary situation create a socially integrative movement of class action? Evidence suggests that the perception of a socioeconomic class of 'bourgeoisie' as the enemy representing liberalism did not pre-exist the October Revolution, but that this enemy was a construction of the revolutionary process itself. In the Russian Revolution, the masses had no perception of a 'bourgeoisie' as an abstract social class, but instead were acting against real, living people whom they called *burzhua* (bourgeois), *barzhua* (bargeowners: from *barzhui*), and *birzhua* (stockbrokers: from *birzhye*). They vented their anger not against some imaginary class called the 'bourgeoisie', but against real people they met on the streets, in trams, and in trains.[30] The violence during 1917 hit almost every layer of society including officers, great landowners, kulaks, and civil urban authorities, as well as political antagonists both at the bottom and at the top, in a quasi-random fashion.[31]

Moreover, the coalition between the Bolsheviks and the peasantry was volatile and fragile at best. Most of the peasants refrained from adhering to any political current such as the Bolsheviks or even the Social Revolutionaries. They appeared to be either disoriented or to be defending their own path with the major objective of claiming land and freedom.[32] By and large, the peasants' mentality was characterised by a twofold tendency. On the one hand, there was a local particularism that reflected a continuity stemming from the very beginning of the Russian state and that eroded only gradually before being definitely reversed by Stalin's collectivisation and the destruction of the *mir*, the traditional peasant community. On the other hand, the refusal to defer to any superordinate authority constituted a definite change in the peasantry's attitude, although it had been prefigured by the behaviour of their deputies in the soviets and in the Second State Duma. This self-sufficiency of the

[28] Victor Serge, *L'an I de la révolution russe. Les débuts de la dictature du prolétariat (1917–1918)* (Paris: La Découverte, 1997), 186.
[29] Theda Skocpol, *Social Revolutions in the Modern World* (Cambridge: Cambridge University Press, 1994), 151.
[30] Orlando Figes and Boris Kolonitskii, *Interpreting the Russian Revolution: The Language and Symbols of 1917* (New Haven and London: Yale University Press, 1999), 177–8.
[31] Ferro, *La révolution de 1917*, 878.   [32] Haimson, 'The Problem of Social Identities', 16.

peasantry emanated, to a large extent, from the long-term aim of tsarist power to achieve a special relationship with the peasantry at the expense of the Europeanised, modernist, revolutionary intelligentsia.[33]

Furthermore, the Bolsheviks' traditional ideological attitude exhibits its profound contempt for the peasantry. After the extinction of the populist Narodnaia Volia, the Russian revolutionary movement sought coalition with the masses. Potentially the most effective coalition of the revolutionary intelligentsia with the peasants had failed repeatedly, as the peasantry remained apathetically traditionalist. While the *narodniki* had opted for the populist solution, Marxist social democrats (and later on the Bolsheviks) attempted a coalition with the working class. The identity of this 'working class' remained quite murky, as it came to be constituted in considerable out-migration from the countryside only in the late 1890s. Uprooted from their traditional milieu and shaken by economic convulsions and the industrial revolution, members of the labour movement did not constitute a self-conscious class with defined interests, but remained an object of the revolutionary ideas of the intelligentsia.[34]

It can safely be assumed that the broad masses of the peasantry did not support the Bolsheviks at the time of their seizure of power. If there was something such as a 'peasant rationality' in the Russian Revolution, then it can be most generally qualified as the desire to be left alone.[35] Such a conjecture is also confirmed by the traditional relationship between town and countryside, which had been one of reciprocal fear and enmity.[36] As the conflict between the countryside and the governmental authorities in the cities predated the revolution, it was one of the sources rather than the consequences of the revolution. Moreover, as the big upsurges such as the Antonov revolt (Antonovshchina) and other peasant rebellions showed during the last moments of the civil war, and after its official ending, the peasantry fought the Bolsheviks quite fiercely. As late as 1920–1 the Bolsheviks still seemed to be in opposition to the majority of the social groups in the country. Eventually, the peasants became a most important target for Bolshevik cynicism, an indicator of which are the large-scale famines that wiped out millions of peasants: the Bolsheviks did not do a great deal to prevent these, but instead exploited them for political purposes. In the famine of 1933 alone an estimated 6.7 million

---

[33] Richard Wortman, *Scenarios of Power: Myth and Ceremony in Russian Monarchy*, 2 vols. (Princeton: Princeton University Press, 1995), vol. I, 406.
[34] Borkenau, *World Communism*, 34–5.
[35] Haimson, 'The Problem of Social Identities', 19.
[36] Ferro, *La révolution de 1917*, 673–85.

people died.[37] The Bolsheviks' problem of not representing any particular group in Russian society existentially was to be resolved neither by a 'natural' social alliance nor by Lenin's voluntarism. Lenin's renunciation of a war of national liberation reflected the extreme ideological fragility of the regime, the indifference of the people, and the small likelihood of surviving such an enterprise.

Permanent revolution in one country

The transformation from tsarist authoritarianism to the dictatorship of the proletariat was a series of cataclysmic events in which Bolshevik success was not a foregone conclusion. The February Revolution produced a fierce struggle for political authority, which remained unresolved due to dual-power structures. The *coup d'état* of October entailed the progressive eradication of a multiplicity of independent centres of social, political, and cultural activity. Against this background, the Bolshevik idea of the withering away of the state into a classless society seemed to be little more than demagoguery.

When he published his treatise *State and Revolution* belatedly in spring 1918, Lenin himself criticised the prediction of the withering away of the state as being a violation of historical perspective.[38] Lenin acknowledged that the material conditions for socialism in Russia were lacking, and supported a radical turn away from past experience by promising the creation of a new humanity, a new man, and a bright future.[39] Constant mobilisation of society became the central feature of Bolshevik power. Leninism was a political technique of modernisation in the name of political development and was based on the absolute supremacy of the revolutionary party, which made the Bolsheviks capable not only of centralising power but also of expanding it.[40] Faced with the immediate challenge of civil war and the daunting task of adjusting ideological demands to social realities, mobilisation was a central means of maintaining power as Soviet communism relied upon a low degree of formal institutionalisation.

State and Revolution was written in the summer of 1917, in a period of deep disorientation and with a view to providing a theoretical basis for

[37] Krzysztof Pomian, 'Anatoli Vichnevski. La faucille et le rouble', *Le Débat*, 107 (1999), 59.
[38] Schapiro, *The Origin of the Communist Autocracy*, 351.
[39] See Richard Sakwa, *The Rise and Fall of the Soviet Union 1917–1991* (London and New York: Routledge, 1999), 152–3.
[40] Samuel P. Huntington, *Political Order in Changing Societies* (New Haven and London: Yale University Press, 1968), 334–43.

solving the practical problem of representation. Although his practical political action turned Marx on his head, Lenin's writing attempted to retain Marx's central point about the destruction of vast inequalities of power. Lenin adumbrated the Marxist claim about the withering away of oppressive power and the state, promoting the post-revolutionary society as politically egalitarian. Yet, how could a down-to-earth and shrewd politician like Lenin believe in the feasibility of ruling large illiterate masses through a direct democracy and workers' control? Indeed, the treatise is marked by the conspicuous incompatibility of a dictatorial regime and its seemingly democratic tenor. There seems to have been a paradox in Lenin's writings due to his hypnotic faith in ultimate harmony, which was the root of the claim that dictatorship was only a transitional phase.

Marx's theoretical assumptions about a classless society and Lenin's ideas about a dictatorship of the proletariat were at odds with the nature of social relations. Their messianism made them blind to the fact that the sources of oppression suffered by workers arose not from men, nor from institutions, but from the very mechanism of social relations. Marx's contradiction consisted in assuming that the factors of oppression, so closely bound up with the actual mechanism of social relations, would suddenly disappear in the course of revolution.[41] How could the workers in conditions of exploitation of manual labour, sacrificed to lifeless machinery and to the overall objective of production, be more than mere cogs? How could they become the 'ruling class'? This can only make sense if one accepts the messianic vision of a vanguard party as the expression of the true will of the people and acting as an instrument of history. In this view, the 'messianic vision was not an afterthought and an excuse. It was the point of departure.'[42]

Revolutionary terror

Bolshevism as a millenarian movement promised redemption in a terrestrial and collective dimension. The most outstanding feature of salvation, however, is the fact that it is not attained by rationally appropriate means, but is bestowed in a redemptive catastrophe. Nascent Soviet society was recurrently uprooted by disasters such as the civil war, demographic losses, the terror against political enemies and the church, and famines. Political repression and terror not only entailed a huge, albeit

---

[41] Simone Weil, *Oppression and Liberty* (London: Routledge, 2001), 138–46.
[42] Jacob L. Talmon, *The Origins of Totalitarian Democracy* (London: Secker & Warburg, 1952), 424.

undetermined, number of human deaths, but also brought about a deep recrudescence in terms of torture and absolute contempt for human life.[43] Hatred and terror became fundamental to communist state-formation, as communist techniques of social control and power maintenance entailed an internalisation of violence.[44] An important object of contention in the historiography of Soviet communism concerns the roots of the Terror.[45] There is good reason to assume that the Great Terror of the mid-1930s was a crucial component of Stalin's 'revolution from above', which disrupted a Soviet Union that appeared to be successful and society that was considered to be calm and stabilised.[46] The lawlessness in Soviet Russia, however, did not start with the show trials between 1936 and 1938, but can be traced back at least to the trials against the church and the Socialist Revolutionaries in the early 1920s.[47] From 1917 onwards, the Russian state was progressively subordinated to an expanding violent party regime that performed a systematic assault on history, law, and human dignity. As the personal and ideological heritage of the revolutionary experience remained a serious threat, Stalin's 'revolution from above' was not an accident but a necessary step in order to blame somebody for the obvious defects of socialism.

The Red Terror was not a reluctant response but a prophylactic measure designed to drown any thought of resistance to the dictatorship. This 'prophylactic' destruction of opposition forces was also at the heart of the large-scale enterprise of collectivisation between 1928 and 1932. By means of a ruthless attack against potential peasant leaders such as the kulaks, by breaking lateral ties between and inside villages, and by successfully disrupting the peasants' repertoire of contention, the Bolshevik party prevented any kind of a large-scale rebellion such as in 1921 to occur.[48] With the notion of 'kulak', a social stratum that had disappeared during the revolution was turned into a symbolic marker of an enemy.[49] Before 1917 'kulaks' referred to those relatively few, miserly, and

---

[43] Nicolas Werth, 'A State Against Its People', in Stéphane Courtois et al., eds., *The Black Book of Communism* (Cambridge, MA: Harvard University Press, 1998), 33–268.

[44] Arno Mayer, *The Furies: Violence and Terror in the French and Russian Revolutions* (Princeton: Princeton University Press, 2000).

[45] According to Roy Medvedev (*Let History Judge* (New York: Vintage Books, 1973)), mechanisms of terror such as torture were introduced by Stalin. Against such a view, see Alexander Solzhenitsyn, *The Gulag Archipelago: An Experiment in Literary Investigation*, vols. I and II, trans. from the Russian by Thomas P. Whitney (Boulder: Westview Press, 1998).

[46] Robert Conquest, *The Great Terror* (London: Macmillan, 1969), 277.

[47] Solzhenitsyn, *The Gulag Archipelago*, 334–67.

[48] J. C. Sharman, *Repression and Resistance in Communist Europe* (London and New York: RoutledgeCurzon, 2003), 42–67.

[49] Solzhenitsyn, *The Gulag Archipelago*, 55.

dishonest rural traders who enriched themselves through usury rather than through their own labour. After 1917, not only had the revolution totally destroyed the basis of their activities, but also, by a transfer of meaning, the name 'kulak' had begun to be applied to all those who in any way hired workers, even if it was only when they were temporarily short of working hands in their own families. The big campaigns of collectivisation and industrialisation met with broad consent in society because Stalin's prestige had been forged through a carefully prepared cult of personality, which achieved a 'subjugation of the spirit' and mobilised support for Stalin's measures far beyond the bureaucratic caste.[50] Collectivisation was preceded by the elevation of his personality to supreme guide on the occasion of the twelfth anniversary of the October Revolution.[51]

Searching for enemies developed from a method of purification and screening inside the party towards the overall purge in the Great Terror.[52] Marxists have argued for the irrationality of Stalin's purges, which perverted the revolution by exposing anybody in society to unexpected arrest or execution as a traitor. Yet this purging was the central mechanism that ensured the Bolshevisation of society and kept the vanguard party in power. This psychology of revolutionary terror turned the 'permanent purge' into a 'complex and dynamic instrument of power', an inherent technique of government specific to Soviet totalitarianism.[53] The realist aspect of violent destruction in the logic of continuous warfare promoted the sacrificial logic of the identification of the enemy. In his novel *Life and Fate*, Vasily Grossmann described how communist regimes prepared populations for mass murder through frenzied campaigns 'to stir up feelings of real hatred and repulsion'. As a consequence, 'the violence of a totalitarian state is so great as to be no longer a means to an end. It becomes an object of mystical worship and adoration.'[54] In such a view, the purges assume an expansive tendency, keeping party members and leaders alike in a condition of fear of annihilation.

For a long time historians and social scientists have favoured a binary view, which saw the establishment of the Cheka either as a primacy of political will or as a consequence of social pressure. Rather than assuming

[50] Claude Lefort, *La complication. Retour sur le communisme* (Paris: Fayard, 1999), 156–8.
[51] Geoffrey Hosking, *The First Socialist Society: A History of the Soviet Union from Within* (Cambridge, MA: Harvard University Press, 1990), 219–20.
[52] Kotkin, *Magnetic Mountain*, 298–332.
[53] Zbigniew Brzezinski, *The Permanent Purge: Politics in Soviet Totalitarianism* (Cambridge, MA: Harvard University Press, 1956), 9–12.
[54] Quoted in Abbot Gleason, *Totalitarianism: The Inner History of the Cold War* (Oxford: Oxford University Press, 1995), 212.

that the Cheka terror was directed 'from above', however, it seems that it was extremely decentralised in its early phase. The terror had a double basis in social violence and in the Bolsheviks' struggle for consolidation of power. It seems quite plausible that the Bolsheviks – although they actively promoted the terror – were considerably influenced by the agitated masses. Haphazard coalition-making between the Bolsheviks and important social groups such as the peasantry or the workers reflected the contradictions between the Marxist-Leninist doctrine and the practical consequences of a *coup d'état*. Aware of their status as a sectarian movement, the Bolsheviks used techniques of inciting the masses but were, simultaneously, also influenced by the crowd psychology of incipient mass politics. In many ways, the leaders of the party were pushed by the same agitated crowds, which they clumsily and desperately tried to keep down.[55] Moreover, the atmosphere of the civil war justified the terror, which was accepted by the different factions such as Left communists, the Democratic Centralists, and the workers' opposition as essential for their survival.[56] Following the assault on the villages, the Bolsheviks turned against the church in order to seize its wealth to meet political and economic needs of the regime.[57] According to Feliks Dzerzhinsky, the Cheka terror only channelled and structured the hatred accumulated against its oppressors by the revolutionary proletarian classes throughout centuries.[58]

As recent work on the French and the Russian Revolutions has argued, revolutionary violence is inherently linked to the challenges of counter-revolution.[59] In Russia, however, there is evidence that the Red Terror was established in December 1917 not so much as a reaction against counter-revolutionary activities, since at that point there was no serious organised resistance. Rather, revolutionary violence can be seen as the consequence of the awareness that a minority group could not do otherwise if they were to stay in power. Terror was not the essence of or the *sine qua non* for the establishment of communism but rather was necessary to make the unreal and absurd real. It was necessary to hide away the essence of Bolshevism; rather than aiming at creative power for the purpose of peaceful reconstruction of society, it used force for the sake of blinding people to its actual intentions of transforming human

---

[55] Tchakhotine, *Le viol des foules*, 332.
[56] Schapiro, *The Origin of Communist Autocracy*, 351.
[57] Boleslaw Szczesniak, ed., *The Russian Revolution and Religion* (Notre Dame: University of Notre Dame Press, 1959).
[58] Figes, *A People's Tragedy*, 535.   [59] Mayer, *The Furies*.

relations according to a utopian and fanatic belief and to avert possible dissidence from it.

The social upheavals in the 1920s and 1930s left a remarkable and durable impact on demography, industry, urban life, and agriculture. Stalin's 'revolution from above' transformed a rural country, where on the eve of the First World War between 80 and 85 per cent of the Russian population lived in the countryside, into a country of urban centres where, in 1990, 66 per cent of the population lived. The Soviet industrial revolution resulted in a 'car pulled by a horse', while the urban revolution led to 'cities without citizens'.[60] The rapid social engineering brought about the ruralisation of the cities. A view on the *longue durée* of social burdens in post-revolutionary Russia suggests for the period between 1917 and 1922 alone approximately 12.7 million premature deaths due to the civil war, famines, and epidemics.[61] In addition, at least 7.5 million (9.8 million according to most recent estimates) people died as a cause of the famine and of terror between 1926 and 1938. For the period between 1939 and 1953, 22.5 to 26.5 million dead are estimated.[62] These numbers are all the more significant if one relates this demographic collapse to the population growth in the years immediately preceding the First World War, when the excess of births over deaths in Russia as a whole was at the prodigious rate of 2 million per annum.[63] Furthermore, these figures tell only half of the story, since under normal conditions the population would have increased.[64]

In short, post-revolutionary social and demographic conditions might be grasped in two metaphors that express the liminal condition between past and present, between the modernising project and the pains to leave the past behind. The violent social and economic restructuring of the late 1920s and the early 1930s differed from the waves of social upheaval in the twentieth century only in kind, not in principle. The important mass protests of workers in 1890, between 1904 and 1907, in 1912, 1917 and 1919, in 1926 and 1928, and in 1932 and 1941 allow the relativisation of the absolute rupture of 1917. March 1921 was not equivalent to the restoration of civil peace, and dekulakisation was not limited to 1929 and 1930, whereas the famines of 1932 and 1934 were, for the masses, much more

---

[60] Pomian, 'Anatoli Vichnevski', 54–60.
[61] Pipes, *Russia Under the Bolshevik Regime 1919–1924*, 508–9.
[62] Quoted in Pomian, 'Anatoli Vichnevski', 59–60.
[63] Keynes, *The Economic Consequences of the Peace*, 8.
[64] Projections by Russian statisticians indicate that in 1922 the population should have numbered more than 160 million rather than 135 million; see Pipes, *Russia Under the Bolshevik Regime 1919–1924*, 508–9.

terrible than the peak of the Great Terror in 1937.[65] Far from being consolidated up to late 1930, the regime's survival through the anxious period of the early 1930s was seen by many communists as victory, perhaps even a miracle.[66] This persistent uncertainty partly explains why the periodisation of the revolution has remained quite contested, making it possible to extend the revolutionary period up to the late 1930s.[67] Yet, the big upheavals of industrialisation and collectivisation are not enough evidence to allow us to consider Soviet society as a highly mobilised society. If compared to the exuberance of social life in Western societies, its institutions rather suggest the existence of a blocked society with any movement dependent on control by and permission from the party.

Situational reality and 'unintended consequences'

Rather than dismissing serious policy failures of the post-1917 period as 'unintended consequences', the profound misapprehensions of Bolshevik leadership with regard to the initial revolutionary goals laid bare the initial spirituality of a political religion. Revolutionary messianism and permanent revolution are complementary, not at odds with each other. Most importantly, the permanent revolution in terms of the extension of Soviet power all over the world, which was considered as indispensable to maintain power in Russia, did not occur. Furthermore, the party organisation became heavily bureaucratised, a process that appalled Lenin. Finally, the economic development in the first couple of years after the revolution was disastrous. In all three areas, Lenin's misjudgements were not simply personal errors but reflected how the confusion of the revolutionary conjuncture became a model for the party's governmental practice.[68] Lenin's sudden and unforeseen changes in policy bewildered his followers. Not only did he suddenly, in April 1917, abandon the idea of two orthodox phases of revolution. He also jettisoned the promise of revolutionary war in favour of an immediate peace on any terms in March 1918, thus introducing the idea of 'socialism in one country' long before Stalin. Aware of the increasing threat of a civil war, Lenin opted for this premature peace with Germany at Brest-Litovsk at the expense of the loss of sensitive territories.[69] Similarly, Bolshevik power

---

[65] See Werth, 'A State Against its People'.   [66] Fitzpatrick, *The Russian Revolution*, 153.
[67] Fitzpatrick, *The Russian Revolution*, 3–4.
[68] Schapiro, *The Origin of Communist Autocracy*, 349.
[69] Beyond territorial losses of Poland, the Baltic countries, and Ukraine, Russia lost approximately 34 per cent of its population, 32 per cent of its arable land, 54 per cent of its industrial plants, and 89 of its coal mines; see J. Wheeler-Bennett, *Brest-Litovsk: The Forgotten Peace* (New York: W. W. Norton, 1938), 269.

did not achieve democratic legitimacy by means of elections in workers' councils and the soviets; finally, the sudden switch from war communism to the New Economic Policy came unexpectedly to many.

Convinced of the revolutionary potential of the working classes in other countries, the Bolsheviks regarded the export of their revolution as a *sine qua non* for the continuity of their power.[70] With the temporary exception of Hungary, however, the history of the Communist International was a complete failure.[71] The incapacity of Bolshevik leadership to sense true social relationships and their misrecognition of cultural and psychological factors such as national identity, for instance, became apparent in the Polish–Russian war of 1920–1. Although the Poles started the war by invading Soviet Ukraine at the end of April 1920, recent evidence indicates that the Soviets might have anticipated them.[72] The lack of realism within the Bolshevik leadership was demonstrated by their use of Poland as a launchpad for a general assault on western Europe. As bold as this proposition seemed to be, its failure only confirmed the insufficient capacity of Bolshevik leadership to attract foreign masses for the revolutionary cause. In the aftermath of the defeat in autumn 1920 and the humiliating peace treaty of Riga in March 1921, when Soviet Russia had to surrender territories lying well to the east of the Curzon Line, including Vilnius and Lviv, Lenin's plan for world revolution by means of military intervention was shattered.

Furthermore, Lenin underestimated the momentous consequences of his decision to maintain the unity of the party even at the risk of both the overbureaucratisation of the party's leading apparatus and its estrangement from the rank and file. Whereas in *State and Revolution* Lenin had predicted that under communism there would be no bureaucracy at all, he had to acknowledge by January 1919 that the apparatus had already become too large for any one person to run. In the only relatively open and fair elections to the Constituent Assembly in January 1918, the Bolshevik party gained a mere 24 per cent of the vote, being outnumbered by the Socialist Revolutionaries. Their lack of popularity and the practical need to consolidate their power on a vast territory and against foreseeable resistance in the countryside forced the small gang of professional revolutionaries to seek a rapid increase in party membership. Accordingly, the total membership of the Bolshevik

[70] George F. Kennan, *Russia and the West Under Lenin and Stalin* (Boston and Toronto: Little, Brown and Company, 1961), 66.
[71] See Borkenau, 'World Communism', 95–133.
[72] Pipes, *Russia Under the Bolshevik Regime 1919–1924*, 179–93.

party would soar to more than 600,000 by 1920. This steep rise in absolute numbers was aptly characterised as the 'quick evaporation of original Bolsheviks'.[73] More significant than the increase in numbers is the comparison between those original members who stayed on in the Bolshevik party after October 1917. Compared to the original party membership of 24,000 in February 1917, the number of original members was reduced by half (to 12,000) in 1922 and dropped even further, to 8,000, in 1927.

While there was a political aspect to inner party purges, there was also a social one: they aimed to quickly and disproportionately promote neo-Bolsheviks of rural origin. In substance, however, the bureaucratisation of the party and the state was also related to a loss in quality. The members' educational level was exceedingly low and not commensurate with their responsibilities and authority. Dismayed with this fatal development, at the end of his life Lenin called Russia a workers' state with bureaucratic distortions, acknowledging that the bureaucratic machine was directing the communist party.[74]

The transformation of political and economic structures – such as the experiments of war communism, the nationalisation of the means of production, the abolition of private trade, the elimination of money, and the introduction of forced labour – left Russia's economy in a shambles. Compared to 1913, large-scale industrial production in 1920 and 1921 had fallen by 82 per cent, whereas worker productivity had decreased by 74 per cent and the production of cereals by 40 per cent. The demographic loss from urban centres due to food shortages was enormous, as Petrograd lost 70 per cent of its population and Moscow over 50 per cent. Workers' real wages declined to one-third of the level of 1913–14.[75] The unfulfilled expectations were most evident in the failure to restructure the economy. Rather than an economic programme, war communism justified the disastrous consequences of economic experimentation by the alleged exigencies of the civil war and foreign intervention. War communism, therefore, can be considered not just as a response to the civil war but must also be seen as a particular means of constructing communist society by making and continuing civil war.[76]

[73] Ferro, *La révolution de 1917*, 877–8.
[74] Vladimir I. Lenin, 'Political Report of the Central Committee of the Russian Communist Party', in *Collected Works*, 45 vols., vol. XXXIII (Moscow: Progress Publishers, 1965), 237–42.
[75] Pipes, *Russia Under the Bolshevik Regime 1919–1924*, 71.
[76] Figes, *A People's Tragedy*, 612–15.

In 1925, Trotsky emphasised that the decisive aspect about moving towards socialism was speed.[77] Only if the speed of development of state industry and trade in comparison to private capital was high enough could a positive relationship in favour of socialist forces be ensured. Yet the most important factor was the relationship between the speed of the development of Soviet economy and that of the world economy. According to Trotsky, it would be an extraordinary success if the Soviet economy not only quantitatively but also qualitatively attained the pre-war level. Most significantly, he argued that this success would be the starting point from which to launch the economic competition with world capital.

The disaster of Brest-Litovsk is usually seen as the end of the 'permanent revolution', which prompted Lenin to focus on the consolidation of power, on socialism in one country. The power struggle between Stalin and Trotsky was symbolised as the antagonism between socialism in one country and permanent revolution as ideological formulas for the development of communism. Yet the significant disproportion between boundless revolutionary promises and the poor means available would make constant uprooting of social and economic life the rule in the 1920s and 1930s. The psychology of Bolshevik leaders led them to deliberately keep society in a permanent state of confusion. This is probably best captured in Trotsky's theory of the permanent revolution, which revealed that the revolutionaries intended to keep society unconsolidated and in permanent upheaval.[78] The first pillar consisted in claiming that the way towards democracy was prepared by the dictatorship of the proletariat. The second aspect of this theory concerned the socialist revolution in its consequences for human relations. It puts forward the need to reshape all social relations through continuous struggle. Through political conflict, i.e. clashes between different groups of the transforming society, outbreaks of civil and external wars would alternate with periods of peaceful reforms. The essential point of the permanence of socialist revolution was that constant reversals of any field of human existence would prevent society from achieving equilibrium. The third element postulated the internationalist character of the revolution, claiming that a proletarian revolution in one country could only be provisional and would inevitably be threatened with failure due to growing internal contradictions unless carried abroad, preferably to more advanced countries.

---

[77] Leon Trotsky, *Denkzettel. Politische Erfahrungen im Zeitalter der permanenten Revolution*, ed. Isaac Deutscher, George Novack and Helmut Dahmer (Frankfurt am Main: Suhrkamp, 1981), 153.

[78] Leon Trotsky, *Permanent Revolution and Results and Prospects*, 3rd edn (New York: Pathfinder, 1969), 132–3.

The articulation of Bolshevik power essentially reinforced mechanisms of social oppression by those institutions that were perpetuated without any greater change from the tsarist regime; the bureaucracy, the police, and the army. The rise of 'Soviet democracy' and a 'proletarian dictatorship' keen on building socialism turned out to be neither democratic nor soviet, but rather a state of a totalitarian bureaucracy intent on keeping the country in permanent revolution. Far beyond an illusion or an ideocratic regime based on the hatred of the bourgeoisie, the permanent revolution shaped a new 'civilisation' with new practices and values. Although Soviet communism relied upon contempt for personal dignity and freedom and inflicted a large number of catastrophes on the population, it was also a huge enterprise in social engineering and meaning-formation.

Totalitarian democracy

Given Lenin's contempt for parliamentary democracy and the monopolistic rule of the Bolshevik party, it has been widely agreed that the dictatorship of the proletariat suppressed any kind of meaningful democracy as a constitutional form of government.[79] Such a viewpoint underemphasises the affinity between socialism and democracy prior to the abolition of tsarism. It would hardly have occurred to any observers in late 1916 to dispute the socialists' claim to belong to the 'democratic club'.[80] Although the social conditions of the Russian Revolution excluded the advent of a liberal form of democracy, revolutionary Bolshevism claimed to be the highest form of democracy. It did this on the grounds of presenting communism as a classless society based on the rule of an all-embracing majority, the entire society.[81]

The revolutionary conjuncture deeply affected the viability of democracy as a political concept, as meanings of the word in Russian political discourse underwent a profound transformation. While the term *demokratiia* in early 1917 was associated with a universal political concept, it soon became an exclusive social term, which reflected the growing domination of the idiom of class in 1917. The crucial point is that, at the revolutionary conjuncture, the social understanding of the word 'democracy' was not just dominant but dictatorial. 'Democracy' was almost

[79] Neil Harding, 'The Marxist-Leninist Detour', in John Dunn, ed., *Democracy: The Unfinished Journey* (Oxford: Oxford University Press, 1992), 155–87.
[80] Joseph A. Schumpeter, *Capitalism, Socialism, and Democracy*, 5th edn (London: George Allen & Unwin, 1976), 235.
[81] See Merle Fainsod, *How Russia Is Ruled*, 2nd enlarged edn (Cambridge, MA: Harvard University Press, 1963), 139.

exclusively understood to mean 'the common people' – and its opposite was not 'dictatorship' but the 'bourgeoisie' or indeed the whole of privileged society. This peculiar – one might even say revolutionary – interpretation of the word 'democracy' appears to have stemmed from common usage: *demokratiia* was practically interchangeable with the notions of *narod* (the people) and *trudiashchikhsia* (the workers) in the language of the street.[82] In the understanding of the workers and common people, democracy and social revolution were both directed at the same goal, which was the political rejection of the 'bourgeois' state. The increasing rift between social classes favoured social exclusiveness, thus undermining attempts by Russian democratic leaders to impose the ideals of 1789 on to the realities of 1917. There was no real cultural or social foundation for the liberal conception of democracy in Russia, at least not in the midst of a violent revolution, and the liberals themselves were ambivalent about the need to address their message to the urban masses. This was reinforced by the weak bond of national consciousness in a country where the imperial and state-centred expansion of *Rossiia* (associated with the territory, the multi-national empire, the European great power) came at the expense of *Rus* (associated with humble, homely, sacred, and popular).[83] *Rossiia* uprooted the Russian people, enticed them away from *Rus*, transformed the peasant into a soldier, an organiser. In many ways, *Rossiia* obstructed the flowering of *Rus*, i.e. the building of an empire impeded the formation of a nation.

When the Bolsheviks dissolved the Constituent Assembly in 1918, they renounced any attempt to elaborate a constitution as a written document. In spite of the constitutions of 1918, 1924, and 1936, Soviet power continued the sham constitutionalism of tsarist Russia. It based its power on constitutional myths and the mirage of democratic legitimacy behind the ruling group in the Kremlin.[84] However, it was not in a merely dictatorial fashion that the Bolsheviks passed over the results of the elections to the Constituent Assembly, which showed them to be in a clear minority with regard to the Socialist Revolutionaries.[85] Rather, Lenin looked for arguments to justify this move in terms of democratic

[82] Figes and Kolonitskii, *Interpreting the Russian Revolution*, 122–4.
[83] Geoffrey Hosking, *Russia: People and Empire 1552–1917* (London: Fontana Press, 1998), xix.
[84] Fainsod, *How Russia Is Ruled*, 349–85.
[85] The results of the elections to the Constituent Assembly were: on 30 November, of 520 elected deputies, 161 were Bolsheviks, 267 Socialist Revolutionaries, 41 Ukrainian Socialist Revolutionaries and Mensheviks, 15 Cadets, 3 Mensheviks, and 33 deputies (mostly Socialist Revolutionaries) from national minorities. See Serge, *L'an I de la révolution russe*, 152.

standards of minority–majority relations. In a document written in 1919 with a view to explaining the dissolution of the Constituent Assembly, Lenin acknowledged that the Socialist Revolutionaries and Mensheviks together had taken approximately 62 per cent of the vote, while the Bolsheviks had received only 25 per cent.[86] Everything, however, depended on how these numbers were read. While the countryside voted for the Socialist Revolutionaries, industrial cities voted for the Bolsheviks. According to Lenin, the proletariat thus granted the Bolsheviks the overwhelming share of their vote.[87] The Bolsheviks also attracted the vote of approximately half of the army, including an over-whelming majority among those army members who fought in the front lines close to the two capitals; they were the most informed and thus the most important in Bolshevik eyes.[88] For Lenin, the influence of the modern proletariat in society seemed to be infinitely greater than its actual numerical representation with regard to the total population. He was persuaded that the proletariat could gain the votes of the peasant masses only after having seized power.

Despite the open hostility between the Bolsheviks and the Socialist Revolutionaries, the latter directly and indirectly supported the former.[89] Such shifts in identification and allegiance are also reflected in the policy and strategies performed by the Menshevik party throughout 1918.[90] For the Mensheviks a Constituent Assembly had been a primary demand since the February Revolution. It was synonymous with an antidote to dictatorship and terror after its violent dissolution by the Bolsheviks in January 1918. Yet throughout 1918 a revision of party policy took place mainly under the pressure of shifting allegiances and coalitions. Many party members defected to Bolshevism not only for ideological and careerist reasons. There were growing doubts about the meaning of democracy and about the need for a Constituent Assembly as an imme-diate objective. These doubts were largely evoked by the fact that the existence of a leftist Bolshevik government pushed the position of the

---

[86] Serge, *L'an I de la révolution*, 153–4.

[87] The results in the two capitals (Petrograd and Moscow) were as follows: Cadets 515,000 votes, Socialist Revolutionaries 218,000 votes, and Bolsheviks 837,000 votes.

[88] The vote in the army was distributed as follows: Socialist-Revolutionaries 1,885,000 votes, Cadets 51,000 votes, national minorities 756,000 votes, and Bolsheviks 1,791,000 votes. According to Lenin, the vote among army members in the front lines close to the capital showed a distribution of 1,000,000 votes for the Bolsheviks against only 420,000 votes for the Socialist-Revolutionaries (Serge, *L'an I de la révolution*, 153).

[89] Pipes, *Three Whys*, 59–60.

[90] David Dallin, 'The Outbreak of the Civil War', in Leopold Haimson, ed., *The Mensheviks: From the Revolution of 1917 to the Second World War* (Chicago and London: University of Chicago Press, 1974), 156–90.

Constituent Assembly to the right. Essentially, the Mensheviks gave up their demand for a Constituent Assembly and changed their original concept of revolution, which had relied on a theory of transition in a long evolutionary process. They supported the Bolsheviks on quite a few questions, such as the liberation of Russian territory from foreign occupation.

Against the monolithic thesis of totalitarianism, Soviet society under Lenin and Stalin showed several forms of autonomy. A provisional typology of societal resistance may include four domains.[91] The first refers to temporary, spontaneous, and usually not durable moments of collective action. Active resistance (*soprotivlenie*) comprised, for instance, the organised resistance against collectivisation in the first half of 1930 and especially the resistance against Sovietisation in Ukraine and the Baltic states between 1945 and 1948. The second type of resistance concerned what was usually considered as insubordinate behaviour and deviance (*stikhiinost*). These practices were not so much elaborate strategies aimed at a complete rejection of the system but rather attempts to bypass controls imposed by the regime in various domains of political, economic, and social life. The third type can be characterised as fledgling autonomy of opinion. It particularly affected industrial workers who became progressively disenchanted with the deteriorating conditions of life.[92] The final important aspect of societal resistance can be summarised as the impermeability of cultures. Religious practices and demographic dynamics varied widely in different parts of Soviet society. Throughout the 1930s, self-affirmations of Christian faith and celebrations of religious rites were frequent even in the years of the Great Terror, and they increased when political repression subsided during the war years. Despite the massive impact of mass terror, famines, and extermination, the Soviet regime did not discontinue habits of family life and population growth, for instance, in Central Asia.

For many historians, intellectuals, and large parts of society, the Bolshevik Revolution was perceived as genuinely democratic and kindled enthusiasm inside the country and abroad. The Socialist Revolutionaries and Mensheviks did not oppose it fundamentally, although they could have done, because in comparison to the tsarist regime there seemed to be a progress in democracy. As Prince Lvov remarked in 1923, Russia belonged more than ever to the people, although the Bolsheviks had

---

[91] Nicolas Werth, 'Les formes d'autonomie de la "société socialiste"', in Henry Rousso, ed., *Stalinisme et nazisme* (Paris: Editions Complexes, 1999), 145–84.

[92] Party membership of workers dropped from 8 per cent in 1933 to less than 3 per cent in 1941; see Werth, 'Les formes d'autonomie', 178.

betrayed the people and turned them into slaves. The popular masses supported a Soviet regime that integrated people of their kind into the apparatus, thus giving the impression of being theirs.[93] To the vast majority of those who lived through it, and even to most of its enemies, Stalinism, far from being a partial retreat let alone a throwback to the Russian past, remained forward-looking and progressive.[94] Stalinism exerted a powerful influence over the entire world because what happened in the country during the 1930s seemed to be an outstanding achievement in the forward march of modern history. The Soviet Union assumed the role of anti-fascist bulwark during a time when, elsewhere, reaction or indecisiveness appeared to be the order of the day. Foreign writers, intellectuals, and politicians were under the spell of Lenin and Stalin, of which the widespread approval of the confessions in the show trials in the Great Terror are a conspicuous proof.[95] Until the publication of *The Gulag Archipelago*, public opinion in Western societies was blind to the real nature of Soviet Bolshevism.

[93] Figes, *A People's Tragedy*, 815–16.   [94] Kotkin, *Magnetic Mountain*, 6.
[95] Conquest, *The Great Terror*, 499–502.

6   The emergence of the Cold War

The idea that war itself might be something that can explain, that itself has the power of bestowing meaning, is an idea foreign to all philosophies of history and so also to all the explanations of war we know.

Jan Patočka

The Second World War as a social revolution

The persistent stability of post-war structures accounted for the tendency in comparative politics and in political thought to approach the Second World War from an outcome-perspective. It entailed durable geopolitical changes, of which the most salient were the expansion of Soviet influence into eastern Europe, the division of Germany, and the ensuing split into a bipolar world. The Second World War also marked a modernising turn in a great many domains of domestic and international politics. One of the consequences of the war was the democratisation of an important number of countries, especially the defeated Axis powers Germany, Italy, and Japan. The creation of the United Nations and the promulgation of the Universal Declaration of Human Rights were milestones in the acknowledgement of the priority of law over violence.[1]

While the Second World War as an international military conflict between states was clearly delimited by temporal and spatial boundaries, the rise of communism and fascism in the decades after 1917 allows historians to speak of a 'European civil war' or 'Europe's Second Thirty Years' War' that spans from 1914 to 1945.[2] Not only did the political religions of communism and National Socialism act against liberal values, the individual, and his reason but, in eastern Europe, the interwar period was also characterised by the fragility of fledgling independent

---

[1] Antonio Cassese, *Violence and Law in the Modern Age* (Cambridge: Cambridge University Press, 1998).

[2] Ernst Nolte, *Der europäische Bürgerkrieg 1917–1945. Nationalsozialismus und Bolschewismus*, 6th edn (Munich: Herbig, 2000).

nation-states. Almost every country in the region had to come to terms with a new political order and the attendant problems of the integrity of national borders, ethnic homogeneity, and the security of external ethnic minorities.[3] The collapse of the Habsburg, Ottoman, and Russian empires produced a mix of over- and undersized states.[4] The latter – 'rump states' such as Austria and Hungary – developed an irredentism aimed at claiming back lost territory and bringing national minorities under the rule of the state. Oversized states such as the second Polish republic or the newly founded Czechoslovak state had to cope with the tensions that resulted from their nationalising consciousness and the incomplete political settlements of their multi-ethnic composition. The dominance in state and bureaucracy of the titular nationalities against major minority groups in states such as Poland, Czechoslovakia, or Romania thwarted practices of democratic citizenship and legitimacy. A winner of the First World War, Czechoslovakia needed to define a Czechoslovak citizenship positively by developing a Czechoslovak national consciousness through programmes of civic education by excluding the socially dominant German minority. Such aspirations proved largely utopian, as a fundamental constitutional legal category – the construction of a 'Czechoslovak nationality' – remained a 'ubiquitous fiction'.[5] While Czechoslovakia or the Baltic countries had not existed as independent states prior to 1918, most of the Balkans had just lived through a major war in 1912–13. As a consequence of recurrent wars between the late nineteenth and the late twentieth century, between 7 and 12 million people were forced to migrate within the Balkans. The territorial claims by Soviet communism and German Nazism after the substantial territorial losses in the First World War threatened east European countries whose experiences of state disintegration, loss of territory, forced migration, national humiliation, and mass killings reinforced an already existing collective psychology of fear of annihilation.[6] Hitler's aggressive demands for living space for the German people in the East were based on reclaiming lost territory such as Gdańsk. Deprived of an independent state for more than a century, Poles resisted Russian occupation, Nazi occupation between 1939 and 1945, and the ensuing Soviet domination. Hungary had lost its battle for

[3] Rogers Brubaker, *Nationalism Reframed* (Cambridge: Cambridge University Press, 1996).
[4] Mark R. Thompson, 'Building Nations and Crafting Democracies – Competing Legitimacies in Interwar Eastern Europe', in Dirk Berg-Schlosser and Jeremy Mitchell, eds., *Authoritarianism and Democracy in Europe, 1919–1939* (Basingstoke: Palgrave, 2002), 20–38.
[5] Derek Sayer, *The Coasts of Bohemia: A Czech History* (Princeton: Princeton University Press, 1997), 175.
[6] István Bibò, *Misère des petits états d'Europe de l'Est* (Paris: Albin Michel, 1993).

independence in 1849 and after the First World War was deprived of approximately two-thirds of its territory in the treaty of Trianon, a traumatic experience that has weighed upon Hungarian collective consciousness ever since and was reinforced after 1945.[7] In Czechoslovakia's history, the events of 1938, during the Nazi protectorate, the communist seizure of power in 1948, and 1968 came down to a series of traumatic experiences. In Yugoslavia, in the twentieth century alone a series of civil wars (1912–13, 1941–5, 1991–2, 1992–5, 1998–9) led to mass extinction, forced migration, and contested territorial claims. Bulgaria has been traumatised by the failure to incorporate Macedonia. The trauma of the Baltic countries after the invasion by Soviet troops in 1940 remains very vivid in their collective memory.

While the reconstitution of the Polish republic or the foundation of the Czechoslovak state after 1918 held out prospects of democratic development, the Versailles treaty, the multi-ethnic set-up of new states, and economic grievances meant that the interwar period existed in a genuine in-between condition. The radicalisation of the masses after the First World War brought about an ideological vacuum, a 'disastrous in-between existence, with liberalism and the bourgeois concept of constitutional democracy being caught up between progressivist and crisis thought, between materialist and religious interpretations of the world, between a bureaucratic-socialist strengthening of the state's power and an apolitical individualism or indeed anarchism'.[8] John Maynard Keynes's analysis of the economic consequences of the Treaty of Versailles on eastern Europe grasped that, in countries such as the Soviet Union, Hungary, or Austria, the miseries of life and the disintegration of society signalled how the malady of the body passes over into malady of the mind.[9] Although the outside world would care little as these societies patiently endured their situation, physical efficiency and resistance to disease would slowly diminish, until human endurance reached its limits and counsels of despair and madness stirred the sufferers from lethargy, which preceded the crisis. Stalin's rule caused great waves of collectivisation and industrialisation, which entailed the mass murder of kulaks but also correspondingly great waves of starvation and famine. The consolidation of Stalin's power was accompanied by imminent expectations of war as a defining feature of the social psychology of Soviet citizens throughout

[7] Paul Lendvai, *Die Ungarn. Ein Jahrtausend Sieger in Niederlagen*, 2nd edn (Munich: C. Bertelsmann, 1999), 504.
[8] Karl-Dietrich Bracher, *The Age of Ideologies*, trans. from the German by Ewald Osers (New York: St Martin's Press, 1984), 39–40.
[9] John Maynard Keynes, *The Collected Writings of J. M. Keynes*, vol. II, *The Economic Consequences of the Peace* (London and Basingstoke: Macmillan, 1971), 158.

the late 1920s and 1930s. In the 1920s, the cycle of violence experienced in the post-revolutionary phase and in the civil war generated in the minds of people a hypothetical but constantly evoked war against the imperialist camp.[10] The wave of arrests in June 1927, the widespread apocalyptic visions and rumours of war in the countryside, and the Great Terror constituted three major cycles of a collective 'war psychosis' in the Soviet Union.

The Second World War in eastern Europe radicalised the liminal conditions of crisis. It was a social revolution, as the socialisation of warfare breached normal human relations and uprooted customary life through forced expulsion, mass genocide, civil war, material devastation, and the violation of territorial boundaries.[11] The dissolution of social and political order brought about an unprecedented degree of existential uncertainty, where the life of civilians became a front-line experience, destroying patterns of trust and social consensus, and undermining beliefs in elites and political authority. In this vein, the war entailed important shifts not only in political alliances but also in the symbolic universe of most societies that sent troops or were battlefields. International alliances were not the same in 1947 as they had been in 1945, and these differed substantially from those in 1940 or in 1938. In the absence of a peace treaty, the Second World War lost its original meaning as a struggle between Germany and the Allies and became associated with a sort of bloody prelude to other confrontations such as civil wars in Lithuania or western Ukraine or, later on, the attempts at liberation in 1956, 1968, or 1980.[12] 'Germany' quickly took on a new meaning, turning it from the enemy into an ally against the Soviet Union.

Although the social and political roots of Nazism and Soviet communism differed widely, the wartime conditions were conducive to fusing the defining characteristics of these regimes, making it possible to see their claim to total domination as mirror images. Although the establishment of a planned economy in post-war eastern Europe owed much to Soviet influence, many of the post-war economic structures were prefigured by the political economy of the war years. The economic exploitation of east European countries pursued by German occupation forces fostered the etatisation of the economy, later taken up and perfected by Soviet

[10] Nicolas Werth, 'Rumeurs défaitistes et apocalyptiques dans l'URSS des années 1920 et 1930', *Vingtième Siècle*, 71 (July–September 2001), 25–35.

[11] Jan T. Gross, 'Themes for a Social History of War Experience and Collaboration', in István Deák et al., eds., *The Politics of Retribution in Europe* (Princeton: Princeton University Press, 2000), 15–35.

[12] Tony Judt, 'The Past Is Another Country: Myth and Memory in Postwar Europe', in Deák et al., *The Politics of Retribution*, 302–3.

communism.[13] The war experience in eastern Europe was a powerful stimulus for economic growth, and the most dynamic growth during the war occurred arguably in the production of raw materials such as the extraction of hard and brown coal and natural gas. Hungary, for instance, benefited from German capital and experienced a boom in industrialisation. The intended future integration of these territories into the German Reich made it plausible for the Germans to promote agricultural production at the expense of consumer goods or industry. The war economy imposed by the Germans led to a growing autarky of these economies and their gradual disconnection from international trade. The expropriation of Jewish property, the acquisition of capital in Nazi-occupied eastern Europe formerly held by companies from Western countries, and the organisation of the labour force to serve the imperial ambitions of the Third Reich thus prefigured – unintentionally – patterns of post-war communist economies.

The establishment of communist rule in eastern Europe

Although the concrete modalities of the establishment of communist power in eastern Europe after 1945 varied widely, with the exception of Yugoslavia and Czechoslovakia they followed quite similar mechanisms.[14] Internationally, the Soviet Union had not only earned high prestige due to the victory against Hitler but also achieved substantial territorial gains. Domestically, the institutionalisation of communist rule in eastern Europe occurred in an atmosphere of swelling mistrust, repression, and dissemination of fear. Stalin's transition from the ravages of war to 'peace' was conducted on the basis of brutal, hate-filled campaigns that made the last eight years before his death the most horrific of his quarter-century rule.[15] Faced with the general exhaustion of the populace in the last years of the war, Stalin reacted with inhuman treatment of Soviet ex-prisoners of war, the deportation of whole populations, and the intensification of the gulag system. At the same time, however, the need for legitimisation of the Soviet regime in the newly established people's democracies but also in the materially devastated Soviet Union required urgent attention to the practical business of economic and social reconstruction. Under the pressure of the Soviet military presence, domestic

---

[13] Gross, 'Themes for a Social History', 16–20.
[14] Joseph Rothschild, *Return to Diversity: A Political History of East Central Europe Since World War II*, 2nd edn (New York and Oxford: Oxford University Press, 1993), 76–123.
[15] Nina Tumarkin, *The Living and the Dead: The Rise and Fall of the Cult of World War II in Russia* (New York: Basic Books, 1994), 102.

political parties in eastern Europe either aligned themselves with the communist parties or had to subordinate themselves to the latter's hegemony. Along with the deployment of Soviet troops, they experienced the monopolisation of the political space by communist parties and the nationalisation of the economy, culture, and education.[16]

Hatred and victimisation

In many places, the aftermath of Nazi occupation entailed social convulsions of revolutionary scope resulting in domestic unrest or mass expulsions. This social revolution had perhaps the greatest impact on the western territories of the Soviet Union.[17] With approximately every fifth inhabitant killed under the occupation, Belarus suffered the highest relative death toll. Ukraine had endured the biggest losses in human lives in absolute terms, as the number of inhabitants dropped from 41 million in 1941 to 32 million in July 1946. In addition, Ukraine had been in a *de facto* state of emergency for about twenty years, from the end of the 1920s up to the end of the 1940s. With entry into the war on 17 September 1939, the Soviet Union occupied western Ukraine, crushing old institutions, nationalising the economy, collectivising, and installing a terror regime. When Soviet troops again occupied Ukrainian territory by ousting the German army in 1944, the devastation of the war in the urban centres had caused a mixture of anarchy and ruthless terror by the Soviet secret police, the NKVD, mass deportations, and high crime rates. Recruitment for the Red Army and mass deportations of women to Germany brought about an important change in the structure of the population in the countryside. The new phase of liberation promised not only rebuilding and repatriation of prisoners of war but also 'filtration', i.e. the checking of presumed collaborators.

Post-war border changes between Poland and Ukraine entailed mass expulsions and had a strong impact on the attitudes of individuals and communities. In both 1945 and 1946 approximately 800,000 people resettled from central Poland to the Western territories. In addition, from January to December 1946 some 400,000 people arrived in Poland (750,000 people in 1945) coming from former eastern Poland, which had been incorporated by the Soviet Union.[18] On the eve of the

---

[16] Andrzej Paczkowski, *Od sfałszowanego zwycięstwa do prawdziwej klęski. Szkice do portretu PRL* (Krakow: Wydawnictwo Literackie, 1999).

[17] Dieter Pohl, 'Schlachtfeld zweier totalitärer Diktaturen – die Ukraine im Zweiten Weltkrieg', *Österreichische Osthefte*, 42, 3–4 (2000), 361.

[18] Krystyna Kersten, *The Establishment of Communist Rule in Poland 1943–1948* (Berkeley: University of California Press, 1991), 306–7.

1946 elections, approximately one-quarter of Polish society consisted of people who were starting a new life in circumstances more or less different from those to which they had been accustomed. The massive resettlement of the Ukrainian population from the new Polish territory (which had been moved westwards) was in reality an expulsion. Preceded by the conflicts between a nationalising Polish state and the Ukrainian borderlands before the war, the terror by the Ukrainian Liberation Army (Ukrains'ka Povstans'ka Armija) against the population and the invading Soviets grew into a civil war after 1945. In the course of a massive resettlement, mostly supported by Poles, up to the middle of 1946 almost half a million Ukrainians had left Poland moving eastwards. As a consequence, the specific Polish–Ukrainian borderland culture was destroyed, and the brutal methods of mass forced resettlement designed to solve the 'Ukrainian problem' had a harmful influence on the consciousness not only of the displaced Ukrainians but also of the Poles.

While Czechoslovakia celebrated 1945 as 'the first year of peace and freedom', this year provided the unique opportunity of fulfilling the centuries-old desire to 'cleanse' the Czech lands of Germans. Though it concerned first of all the Germans as representatives of three centuries of a ruling class of foreigners, it was also directed against Hungarians.[19] In the words of Prime Minister Zdeněk Fierlinger, the cleansing (očista) of the land of Germans would express the united will of all the people and resolve once and for all a problem that had burdened them for a whole millennium. The forced expulsion of an estimated 3 million Germans from Czechoslovakia (odsun) was equivalent to a considerable demographic bloodletting, depriving the Czech lands of between a third and a quarter of its population.[20]

The tumultuous war years left a profound legacy for the imagining of the Czech nation, as the expulsion of Germans and the attempted liquidation of Jews provided for the first time an experiential identity of národ (nation), vlast (power), and lid (people) and their coincidence with the political boundaries of the state, notwithstanding the Slovak minority. This totality became an important ideological carrier for the communists'

---

[19] Sayer, *The Coasts of Bohemia*, 241.
[20] Beneš's decrees put the property of 'Germans, Hungarians, traitors, and collaborators' under state control, deprived them of Czechoslovak citizenship, expropriated their lands and movables, and dissolved all German institutions of higher education, among them the German university of Prague. While in the census of 1930 29.5 per cent of the population of the Czech lands had declared their national identity as German, in the 1950 census it was only 1.8 per cent. The self-declared Hungarian population of Slovakia fell from 17.6 to 10.3 per cent over the same period (Sayer, *The Coasts of Bohemia*, 242–3).

project of erasing all boundaries between the personal and the political, between the society and the state. As the expulsion of national minorities corresponded to the desire to establish a homogeneous community, it negated more than 300 years of personal ties, economic relations, and cultural diversity.

While hatred of Nazi occupation was one major motive force, it would be wrong to interpret the social consequences of the war as animated exclusively by an opposition to the fascist enemy or the ethnic populations associated with it. Besides the enemy outside, the acts of violence and retribution committed from 1945 onwards in post-war eastern Europe also included different kinds of enemies within. All over the territories occupied by the Red Army, the NKVD operated brutally against nationalist activists, enemies of the people, and spies. In Ukraine alone between February 1944 and October 1945, the NKVD killed 98,000 people. The Ukrainian Liberation Army in East Galicia fought the Germans but also – partly collaborating with them – was engaged in a struggle against NKVD troops. Although the partisan movement in Ukraine was not as strong as the Soviet myth of a powerful liberation army with a strong popular support would have it, serious estimates speak of between 150,000 and 220,000 partisans.[21]

Anti-Semitism was a further salient feature of the conflict between national majorities and minorities, although its concrete expression varied widely. Jews suffered most during the Second World War – if not always in absolute numbers, then undoubtedly in terms of existential annihilation. Approximately 3 million Jewish and 3 million non-Jewish citizens of Poland were killed during the war; this amounted to the loss of one-tenth of non-Jewish citizens, while the Jewish community was practically exterminated in its entirety. Between 1945 and 1947, approximately 1,500 Jews lost their lives and the panic after the Kielce pogrom caused some 150,000 Jews to flee the country.[22] In other parts of eastern Europe during the war, strong endogenous motivations for the persecution of Jews supported the extermination policies pursued by the Nazis. In Hungary, for instance, the anti-Jewish laws of 1938, 1939, and 1941 had the approval of a large portion of the Hungarian bourgeoisie and were largely responsible for the death of over half a million Hungarian Jews. The positive reception of the anti-Jewish laws in Hungary was only seemingly due to the important position occupied by Jews in the capitalist

---

[21] Pohl, 'Schlachtfeld zweier totalitärer Diktaturen', 354–6.
[22] Piotr Wróbel, 'Double Memory: Poles and Jews After the Holocaust', *East European Politics and Societies*, 11, 3 (1997), 572–4.

system.[23] The main reason is more likely to be found in the backwardness of the masses and identity problems of the bourgeoisie. The anti-Jewish laws allowed the Hungarian middle classes to ensure their careers and a higher standard of life at the expense of Jewish citizens.

In Yugoslavia, by contrast, the Second World War was fought primarily as a civil war between Croats and Serbs. Here, the definitions of enemies were not clearly those between a foreign invader and a domestic partisan organisation. They varied according to the significance attached to events by participants in the conflict. After the German army failed to take Moscow in December 1941, Tito's partisans, for instance, ceased to consider Nazi Germany as the main enemy, shifting their struggle to the ideological target of Yugoslav 'rightist elements'.[24] They reckoned that the war was entering the second proletarian stage, in which the struggle against the fascists had become secondary to the class struggle against the domestic counter-revolution.

Confusion between victory and defeat

Besides social devastation, the war bequeathed deep moral confusion, leaving many of these societies in an in-between condition between victory and defeat, or 'victory in defeat'.[25] When Bulgaria declared war on Germany in 1944, the Soviet Union had already declared war on Bulgaria itself. Thus, Bulgaria was simultaneously at war with the United States, Great Britain, the Soviet Union, and Nazi Germany. This sentiment of confusion was perhaps strongest in countries like Poland, where self-sustained, society-wide, but ultimately unsuccessful resistance movements failed to fulfil hopes for a self-determined post-war order. Polish society was conscious of a double failure of its elites, first, to protect Poles from a German attack in 1939 and, second, to prove capable of resisting the Soviet assault on Polish independence after 1944. In a spirit of defeat, the new communist authorities failed to live up to society's expectations of supplying basic necessities and of giving a clear perspective for post-war life. In the defeat of all methods of struggle against Soviet domination, Poles developed several models in coping with the past, often manipulated by the authorities. Aiming at national revival, they felt a pressing need to construct history as a narrative of active heroism against the humiliating and guilt-ridden memory of

---

[23] Bibò, *Misère des petits états d'Europe de l'Est*, 205–378.
[24] Ivo Banac, *With Stalin Against Tito: Cominformist Splits in Yugoslav Communism* (Ithaca and London: Cornell University Press, 1988), 82.
[25] Lendvai, *Die Ungarn*, 511.

defeat.[26] It portrayed the Pole as a heroic soldier, fighting on all the barricades and battlefields of the world; the Pole suffered the most, shed the most blood, and was systematically betrayed by his allies. Although the romantic folly of the Poles is often contrasted with the realism of the Czechs, it is forgotten that the realism represented by Hácha or by Beneš failed, just as did Polish romanticism.[27]

On top of the powerlessness against the Nazis and Soviets, a Polish feeling of undeserved injury of a nation abandoned by its Western allies grew into exasperation. The underground state and the Homeland Army (Armia Krajowa) had been animated by the will to have Poland liberated by *Polish* resistance. Encouraged by Soviet aircraft and American supplies, the initial high sprits and optimism of the Warsaw uprising in summer 1944 ended in massive bloodshed, striking a decisive blow against the morale of the Polish people. After five years of unrelenting hope, the heavy losses in the wake of the failed uprising and the impotence of the Polish government left Poles demoralised and with almost no spirit of resistance in 1945. There is good reason to summarise the history of Poland and of the Poles between 1943 and 1948 in a single sentence; 'everyone suffered defeat and, at the same time, everyone was victorious'.[28]

From 1945, 'People's Courts' in Hungary and Romania, but especially the Fatherland Front in Bulgaria, settled post-war scores with thousands of real or potential political rivals on the grounds of crimes of sabotage and conspiracy. No distinction was made between pro-German, pro-Western, and anti-communist candidates for punishment, all in the name of the nation and its wartime sufferings.[29] The sentiment of being victims of fascism accompanied a strong tendency towards maintaining spaces of national independence against a seemingly inevitable Soviet domination. Rather than being a novelty, this maintenance of independence had characterised the attempts of political leadership in these countries from the belated process of nation-building at the end of the nineteenth century up to the interwar period.[30] Those regimes that were allied to Germany, such as Slovakia, Hungary, Croatia, and Bulgaria, carefully manoeuvred between drawing the maximum benefit from the German alliance and preserving a minimum of independence as

[26] Amir Weiner, *Making Sense of War: The Second World War and the Fate of the Bolshevik Revolution* (Princeton: Princeton University Press, 2002), 232.
[27] Kersten, *The Establishment of Communist Rule*, 469–70.
[28] Kersten, *The Establishment of Communist Rule*, 469.
[29] Judt, 'The Past Is Another Country', 300.
[30] Bulgaria being a notable exception, as it had considerably profited from Russia's help in gaining large parts of Macedonia in 1878.

an assurance for the future in case of a German defeat.[31] Countries with either a direct link to Nazism or a coalition during the war such as Tiso's Slovak state or Horthy's Hungary had to uphold the myth of the necessity of pacts with Hitler in order to maintain or restore essential goals of national interest.[32] The communist practice of manipulating history by organised forgetting, for instance, maintained the confusion about the activities of the communist party or of the wartime Slovak state.

The confusion between victory and defeat failed to produce a 'new start' (*Stunde Null*), which was significant for post-war West Germany, symbolically separating wartime from peacetime. The Second World War petered out in a string of ever more contentious and unproductive meetings of foreign ministers.[33] With the exception of a series of imposed agreements with minor belligerents, signed in Paris in 1946, the Allies never resolved their post-war dealings with former enemy states by any final peace treaty. This confusion about defeat and victory was expressed in the widespread perception of a menacing imminent third world war. Playing on this perceived threat, Stalin enforced the 'weeding out' of the enemies of the people.[34] Outside Russia, rumours of war also circulated, for instance, in the lead-up to the Polish elections of autumn 1946. Perhaps the most obvious symbol of this fear of annihilation is the huge number of pillboxes that Hoxha's regime in Albania placed all over the country. They were meant to protect society from the menace by potential enemies who were presumably ubiquitous. Estimates of the number of such pillboxes vary between 600,000 and 1 million. That these pillboxes were not only a fad becomes clear when one considers that for the cost of two of them one could have built a two-bedroom apartment.[35]

Physically and economically exhausted by the war effort, the Soviet Union nevertheless achieved an impressive territorial expansion into eastern Europe. In comparison, the economic and political success of the United States was far from certain. As the United States failed to ensure what had been central foreign policy objectives since 1939 – democracy, freedom from fear and want, and the integrity of small nations – the post-1945 scenario resembled surrender barely less complete than might have been expected from a military victory of the Soviet Union over its two chief allies. National glory and international prestige

---

[31] István Deák, 'Introduction', in Deák et al., *The Politics of Retribution*, 8–9.
[32] Shari J. Cohen, *Politics Without a Past: The Absence of History in Postcommunist Nationalism* (Durham and London: Duke University Press, 1997), 85–117.
[33] Judt, 'The Past Is Another Country', 293–302.
[34] Richard Overy, *Russia's War* (London: Penguin Books, 1997), 317.
[35] Slavenka Drakulić, *Café Europa* (London: Abacus, 1996), 54.

for the Soviet Union, however, came at the huge price of the death of an estimated 25 million Soviet citizens and material devastation on an unprecedented scale. Moreover, the military expansion into eastern Europe concealed the dearth of moral purpose in Soviet-type societies after the Second World War. Domestically, the great victory of the Soviet Union entailed the fiercest persecution of enemies of the people, deportation of whole peoples, and the swelling of the gulag, plunging the Soviet people into a second Dark Age.[36] Never since the termination of the civil war had the emotional detachment of the mass of the Russian people from the doctrines of the communist party been so drastic. Although the party had become a great and highly successful apparatus of dictatorial administration, it had ceased to be a source of emotional inspiration. Despite the human suffering and material damage inflicted upon the Soviet Union, the sense of victimisation among Russians was arguably highest not during but right after the victory against fascism. Far from aiming at a social consensus, Stalin's post-war objectives were characterised by the suppression of the intelligentsia through purges and by subjugating workers and the peasantry through economic pressure and criminal law.[37]

Purges (the enemy inside)

Internationally, the communist 'bloc' formed when the governments of Poland and Czechoslovakia, who had previously agreed to participate in the Paris conference about the Marshall Plan on 12 July 1947, were forced by the Soviets to withdraw. Internally, however, the massive political purges in new people's democracies between 1948 and 1952 were not only limited to power struggles in leading party circles. Rather, they proliferated until they terrorised whole societies. The modalities of repression and the scope of the purges differed from country to country.[38] For Poland, for instance, the Second World War entailed not only the annihilation of its state and a ruthless occupation regime but also the extermination of approximately 2 million members of the professional and intellectual elites. By contrast, Hungary did not experience such heavy losses among elites. Moreover, it lived through a short democratic interlude that followed the war and allowed non-communist forces to organise. This relative initial advantage of a lower degree of social disruption translated into more intense repression during the establishment

---

[36] Overy, *Russia's War*, 290.
[37] Donald Filtzer, *Soviet Workers and Late Stalinism: Labour and the Restoration of the Stalinist System After World War II* (Cambridge: Cambridge University Press, 2002), 264.
[38] Rothschild, *Return to Diversity*, 132–40.

of Stalinist rule as of 1948. The physical presence of middle and professional classes in Hungary was taken as a justification for an extension of
'class struggle' against 'reactionary elements' and 'foreign agents'.
Political repression in the early 1950s in Hungary, for instance, entailed
the imprisonment of some 150,000 people (of a total population of 10
million) and the execution of at least 2,000. Between 1952 and 1955,
more than 10 per cent of the Hungarian population were subject to police
action, while more communists were executed than under the Horthy
regime.[39]
   Conversely, the Soviet takeover of the Baltic countries occurred before
the devastation of war and met an intact society with elites ready to pursue
an existential fight for physical survival. Its 'pacification' was achieved
through mass deportations, the eradication of traditional village life,
and large-scale repression. The numbers involved in and intensity of
armed resistance in the guerrilla wars waged against the Soviet army
between 1944 and 1950 indicate the strong national spirit underlying
the struggle for independence.[40] Although different in scope, armed
resistance in Lithuania, Estonia, and Latvia relied crucially on a decentralised movement of local communities, which provided the rebels with
all their supplies and information.[41] Consequently, the Sovietisation of
politics and culture provoked the emergence of quasi-parallel structures
of societal and public life, separating ethnic Baltic people from ethnic
Russians. Strikingly enough, the value systems of Latvians, Estonians,
and Lithuanians in the early 1990s were much closer to that of western
Europeans than to those of other east European countries.[42]
   In eastern Europe, Sovietisation started with the campaign against
Yugoslavia in 1948, when the Cominform declared the Yugoslav communist party to be in the hands of fascists. Although Yugoslav communism
was established without the direct intervention of the Red Army and
resisted the infiltration by Bolsheviks, Tito's methods of securing his rule

---

[39] Ferenc Vali, *Rift and Revolt in Hungary: Nationalism Versus Communism* (Cambridge, MA: Harvard University Press, 1961), 64.
[40] See Overy, *Russia's War*, 311–12. Resistance in western Ukraine caused an estimated 14,400 'terrorist raids' between 1944 and 1953, and the deportation of approximately 300,000–400,000 people. In Lithuania, Soviet sources admitted the loss of 20,000 men, fighting a nationalist army estimated at 30,000. According to data from the Soviet Ministry of Interior, in 1947 and 1948 some 25,000 Lithuanian guerrillas were killed. On the whole, between 1944 and 1953 between 200,000 and 250,000 Balts were deported and another 150,000 sent to the gulag.
[41] Roger D. Petersen, *Resistance and Rebellion: Lessons from Eastern Europe* (Cambridge: Cambridge University Press, 2001), 205–9.
[42] Arpad Szakolczai and László Füstös, 'Value Systems in Axial Moments: A Comparative Analysis of 24 European Countries', *European Sociological Review*, 14, 3 (1998), 211–29.

were very much Stalinist in their nature. As early as the late 1930s, Tito had purged the Yugoslav communist party in order to establish a fully centralised party on the Soviet model. With the possible exception of Romania, no other regime followed the Soviet model more intimately in the institutionalisation of politics, economy, and domestic security. The proclaimed internationalist orientation of communist countries credited Tito's Yugoslavia with avoiding a bloody civil war along ethnic lines, which was seen as inevitable had Tito's rival, the Četnik leader Draža Mihajlović, come into power.[43] His early split with Stalin in 1947–8 allowed him to gain a reputation as a liberal pluralist in the socialist camp. Between 1945 and 1946, however, some 250,000 people were killed in political persecutions and concentration camps.[44] After the split from Stalin, Tito took the opportunity to stage a massive anti-Cominformist purge to cleanse the land of all potential troublemakers, which led to a widening purge against real and imaginary followers of the Cominform (*ibeovci*).[45]

While Tito's success vindicated his methods with the partisan-led struggle for Yugoslav independence from Stalin's Soviet Union, the initially insignificant Romanian communist party gained influence as a result of the seizure of northern Transylvania by the Red Army in 1944 and the subsequent Soviet pressure on domestic Romanian policy. Externally, Romania's late shift of war alliances in August 1944 led to the involvement of the Romanian army on the side of the Allies. Internally, the Soviets supported the National Democratic Front and, in late February 1945, forced King Michael to dismiss the Radescu government. He had to nominate the government of Petru Groza, in which the communists controlled only three ministries but which would be altogether subservient to the Soviet Union and responsive to communist pressure. Once in power, the Romanian communist party turned its underground conspiratorial experience of the inter-war period into a deliberate perpetuation of a climate of fear and suspicion.[46]

Purges all over eastern Europe affected not only obscure figures but also prominent party leaders such as Koçi Xoxe in Albania (May–June 1949), László Rajk (September 1949) in Hungary, Traicho Kostov (June 1949) in Bulgaria, Lucreţiu Pătrăşcanu (February 1948) in Romania, or Rudolf Slánský, Bedrich Geminder, and Vladimir Clementis (November 1952) in Czechoslovakia. Commonly, the purges are seen as the major

---

[43] Hugh Seton-Watson, *Nationalism and Communism: Essays 1946–1963* (London: Methuen, 1964), 90.

[44] Noel Malcolm, *Bosnia: A Short History* (Basingstoke: Macmillan, 1994), 193.

[45] Banac, *With Stalin Against Tito*, 154.

[46] Vladimir Tismaneanu, *Stalinism for All Seasons: A Political History of Romanian Communism* (Berkeley: University of California Press, 2003), 37–84.

move to implement Moscow-steered power in eastern Europe by eliminating domestic communist party elites. Yet these trials and the radical
purging of party cadres were not the symbol of strength or a moral
purpose defending a communist ethos. Not unlike 1917 in Russia, the
violence unleashed under the Second World War regimes of occupation
was the necessary background for Bolshevik techniques of power.[47] The
main targets of purge trials were those communist leaders who had not
passed an initiation in party matters in the Soviet Union. They readily
admitted that they were not good communists, and that, by these trials,
by admitting sins they did not commit, they were able to rectify their
errors. With the possible exception of Pătrăşcanu in Romania, none of the
communists stepped out of their role during the public trials, remaining
faithful communists by confessing to all the charges. We may blame
Stalin's paranoia for their execution or assume the sheer desire for
Soviet domination to be at the root of establishing leaderships dependent
on Moscow. The trickster nature of Bolshevik leadership, however, suggests that it was entirely rational to purge politicians with an ideal of
communism as a consolidated system aimed at domestic peace and
stability. Communists without the experiential background of civil war
and the permanent late civil war in the Soviet Union were indeed not
good communists in a truly objective sense. By their sincere belief in the
superiority of communism, by their genuine efforts to fight the 'real'
enemies and consolidate the system, they represented a fundamental
threat to the power, even the survival, of the party.[48] They lacked the
initiating experience in the Soviet Union that would have taught them the
fundamental secret of the communist party: that it was an impotent
trickster. In other words, the intentions behind the purges were not
primarily directed at the consolidation of leadership dependent on the
Soviet Union but, very much in the spirit of the permanent revolution in
one country, deliberately maintained countries in a condition of fear,
insecurity, and confusion.

The division of two worlds

The establishment of communist rule was supported by social disintegration and the dissolution of political identities, i.e. liminal conditions that
lent themselves well to the pursuit of Bolshevik-type practices of power.

[47] Gross, 'Themes for a Social History', 22–3.
[48] Agnes Horváth, 'The Nature of the Trickster's Game: An Interpretive Understanding of
Communism', Ph.D dissertation (Florence: European University Institute, 2000),
200–1.

The end of the Second World War did not inaugurate a period of peace or a new start. Although the wartime experience varied from country to country, one may rightly assume that it bequeathed to the post-war era not only physical exhaustion and material destruction but also moral confusion and contested memories. 'One could not hope to understand the period without the realisation that the wartime experience of spiritual crisis, crisis of values, and normative disorganisation profoundly affected notions of commonweal, collective good, and group interests in the societies of the region. The old operative definitions of legality, justice, legitimacy, common purpose, national interest, or *raison d'état* were put in doubt, shattered.'[49]

Despite the deep crisis of the interwar years and the failure to gain national sovereignty and achieve nation-building in large parts of eastern Europe, however, the European civil war from 1917 to 1945 reinstated the moral value of having lived through an – albeit precarious – time of independence. Amidst despair and hopelessness, different political forces focused primarily not on social or economic reform but on preserving the physical existence of the nation and a sense of identity.[50] Beyond attempts by the Nazis and the Soviets to obliterate this taste for independence, this symbolisation was significant for later versions of national communism.[51] Even under conditions of extreme repression and mass murder, such as in the failed Polish resistance movement, people maintained hopes for a miraculous change and a belief in the messianic role of the West. In the desperate situation of foreign manipulation of elections, they ceased to believe that anything could be achieved through their own action – change had to come from external sources.[52]

The anti-fascist myth (the enemy outside)

Besides the identification of enemies within, the anti-fascist myth was the major symbol for giving meaning and stability to new people's democracies. Communist regimes dealt very selectively with the history of the Second World War, leaving out any mention of the fate of Jews. The public defence by a strongly centralised state against – essentially undefined – fascist enemies became the foremost content defining new popular democracies after 1945. Leaders in such democracies attempted to bolster their political legitimacy by conveying the historical continuity

---

[49] Gross, 'Themes for a Social History', 23.
[50] Kersten, *The Establishment of Communist Rule*, 469.
[51] Rothschild, *Return to Diversity*, 22–6.
[52] Kersten, *The Establishment of Communist Rule*, 314.

of fascism and, at the same time, stressing the democratic credentials of the anti-fascist resistance by communist regimes.

Although the anti-fascist myth followed the communist logic of the identification of the enemy, two dramatic events at the very end of the war reinforced Stalin's fear and suspicion.[53] The death of Roosevelt and Churchill's failure to be re-elected in 1945 deprived Stalin of the warm personal relationships he had entertained with the Western leaders, especially the US president. The sudden shift from classic trilateral diplomacy into a hopeless international morass swept aside expectations and opened up uncertainty. Perhaps more crucially, the atomic bombardment of Japan in August 1945 not only caught Stalin by surprise but also demonstrated the vulnerability of the Soviet Union in the not-so-distant future. Furthermore, Stalin's communist expansion had to face not only the task of consolidating power in people's democracies but also of containing the centrifugal trends in world communism. Andrei Zhdanov was the driving force behind the secret meeting in Szklarska Poręba in September 1947, which ushered in the creation of the Information Bureau of the Communist and Workers' Parties (Cominform) in Belgrade.[54] Zhdanov's two-camps theory declared that the world had split into an imperialist, anti-democratic camp represented by the Western Allies and a democratic, anti-imperialist camp led by the Soviet Union, which sought to consolidate democracy by eradicating the remnants of fascism.

The appearance of an anti-fascist class enemy in the wake of 1945 had social foundations in the publicly approved and discursively incited radicalisation of desires for revenge, which large parts of the populations associated with concrete experiences of liberation. In establishing puppet regimes in eastern Europe, Soviet communism would have probably faced a more arduous task had it not been for the exhaustion of the population, the uprooted social situation, the desire to stop fighting after years of war, and the new wave of hatred and victimisation. In Poland, for instance, Stalin was quite aware of the weakness of Polish communists, an important reason why he ruthlessly prevented the reconstruction of the provisional government as foreseen by the Yalta accords.[55]

---

[53] Vladislav Zubok and Constantine Pleshakov, *Inside the Kremlin's Cold War* (Cambridge, MA: Harvard University Press, 1996), 39–46.
[54] Vladimir Tismaneanu, *Reinventing Politics: Eastern Europe from Stalin to Havel* (New York: Free Press, 1992), 24.
[55] Kersten, *The Establishment of Communist Rule*, 146.

Both in the Soviet Union and in many parts of eastern Europe, communist myths of the war represented a historical narrative full of inconsistencies, inventions, and lies.[56] In the Soviet Union, Stalin resumed the goal of building a communist society in the course of the next twenty to thirty years. Simultaneously, the mythic construction of Stalin's heroic deeds came along with a new wave of weeding out enemies.[57] The Great Fatherland War was to suit the needs of the regime, serving as a stirring but safely distant reminder of the success of the socialist system and its supreme leader. Unlike the communist patriotism in the wake of the civil war in the early 1920s, the cult of the Great Fatherland War exuded a profound falseness, as it had been purposefully manipulated and twisted to serve political needs.[58] Stalin's priority was the pragmatic rebuilding of society by freezing the memory of the Second World War in an officially commanded version of history. He tried to curb the memory of the war and of its heroes such as Marshal Zhukov or those involved in the Leningrad resistance, reserving a central position for himself. Although he could not place a taboo on the war as he had done with the terror of the 1930s, he avoided popular commemoration by demoting Victory Day from a state holiday to a regular working day in 1947.

The watchword of the day in people's democracies was state vigilance against possible reversals operated by remnants of pre-1945 state structures. In the words of the Romanian first secretary of the communist party, Gheorghiu-Dej, state vigilance required the purging and purification of ideology, science, literature, art, and music – of all aspects of culture.[59] Masterminded by the communist party, the sentence in the trial in Kunmadaras in May 1946 equated this Hungarian anti-Jewish pogrom with an assault on the new system, and defined the purpose of the new democracy as being an anti-fascist bulwark.[60] Suggesting historical continuity between Nazism and the anti-Jewish riot of Kunmadaras, the people's tribunal interpreted anti-Jewish actions as attacks on the democratic tradition of the country. Such a representation of a continuity of fascism allowed post-war rulers to present themselves as the heirs of an anti-fascist past. The emergence of new people's democracies in eastern Europe after the Second World War, therefore, was explained not as the result of the collapse of the pre-war regime, but as a constant and continuing anti-fascist struggle. In the case of the German Democratic

[56] Cohen, *Politics Without a Past*, 97.   [57] Weiner, *Making Sense of War*, 33–5.
[58] Tumarkin, *The Living and the Dead*, 155.   [59] See Banac, *With Stalin Against Tito*, 132.
[60] Péter Apor, 'The Creative Fear: Fascism, Anti-Semitism, Democracy and the Foundation of the People's Democracy in Hungary', in Bo Strath, ed., *Myth and Memory in the Construction of Community* (Brussels: Peter Lang, 2000), 263–79.

Republic, a clear distinction had to be made between the anti-fascist
present and the fascist past, as well as between the current socialist
regime and the newly established – and capitalist – Federal Republic of
Germany.[61] The anti-fascist foundation myth radically severed East
Germany's destiny from that of West Germany and, at the same time,
harked back to the good socialist traditions of Germany such as the
peasants' wars in the sixteenth century.

Similarly, in Yugoslavia, cultural politics and political discourse reconstructed the war on an anti-fascist and, later, anti-Soviet basis. The
Cominformist movement in Yugoslavia showed that the cleavage lines
between supporters of Stalin and of Tito reflected to a great degree those
of the civil war between the different nationalities.[62] Conversely, the split
between Tito and Stalin was not a move towards political pluralism, but
rather a necessary step for Tito's endeavour to consolidate his regime.
Similarly, the double mythologisation of both a fascist enemy and a
Stalinist one reflected how the civil war was instrumentalised for purposes
of national independence. It aimed to suppress historical memory of a
civil war and its devastating consequences. Yugoslavia had been patched
together by numerous wars, an unfortunate experiment in the interwar
period, and a cruel civil war between 1941 and 1945. Communism was
crucial to the establishment of a post-war Yugoslav state that was held
together by the skilful use of fear: the fear of Great Serbian restoration,
the fear of a return to the wartime massacres, and (after 1948) the fear
of the Soviet Union.[63] One of the effects of fear was that the war was
de-ethnicised and predominantly seen from a class perspective. Tito and
the communist party leadership concealed the enmities underlying the
civil war by emphasising the internationalist brotherhood of the Yugoslav
nations. Despite this appeal to brotherhood and unity, cultural politics
in the Yugoslav republics developed intolerance against minorities and
political conflict with other republics. The ideological programme to
fabricate the heroic struggle of the anti-fascist struggle by 'organised
forgetting' bracketed the experiential reality of the Second World War
in order to provide people's democracies with popular legitimacy. Official
memory did not reflect plurality, but restricted itself to a fragmented and
selective version that, particularly in the educational system, deliberately
recalled only those memories that affirmed the political supremacy of

[61] Herfried Münkler, 'Antifaschismus und antifaschistischer Widerstand als politischer
Gründungsmythos der DDR', *Aus Politik und Zeitgeschichte*, B 45/98, 16–29.
[62] Banac, *With Stalin Against Tito*, 151.
[63] Ivo Banac, 'The Fearful Asymmetry of War: The Causes and Consequences of
Yugoslavia's Demise', *Daedalus*, 121, 2 (1992), 168.

its ruling party. Most importantly, the war's inter-ethnic dimension was silenced.

Containment

The Cold War was often portrayed as historically inevitable, since the ideology and practice of totalitarianism left no option other than to confront the communist threat firmly. Any claim about the inevitability of the Cold War as an outgrowth of a contest between the United States and the Soviet Union would mean following an outcome-logic. The situational logic of warfare but also of the uncertainty in the immediate postwar period suggests caution in judgements. During the Second World War, the general nature of the Allied response to Stalin's wartime objectives was one of deep-felt emotion and solidarity with the fate of Soviet Russia. Why were the Allies not tougher on Stalin, who just two years before had sealed a pact with Hitler? The answer should take into account the experiential basis of the desperate and solitary British fight for mere survival, under tremendous strain and anxiety, with the outbreak of war between Germany and the Soviet Union presenting 'the first ray of hope Englishmen had seen in this war'.[64] Churchill identified Hitler's attack on the Soviet Union with the existential threat for Britain, arguing that the fight of every Russian for his homeland is the fight of all free humans and free peoples in all parts of the world.[65] Forged in the desperate war situation of 1940 and 1941, the relationships between the democratically elected American leadership and Stalin were emotionally close.[66] This emotional closeness was reflected in how Roosevelt at times gave preferential treatment to Stalin at the expense of Churchill but also in the often very tense relations between senior commanders in the camp of the Western Allies.

Assessments of the early post-war period were much more sensitive to the global contingency of history. It was seen as absurd to consider the accidental constellation of the Cold War as being potentially more durable than the international constellation of the outset of the twentieth century.[67] In the immediate aftermath of the war, for instance, an armed conflict between the United States and the Soviet Union seemed improbable. A good indicator for this was the business class's attitude, which – despite some anti-Soviet rhetoric – placed priority on the prospective

[64] George F. Kennan, *Russia and the West Under Lenin and Stalin* (Boston and Toronto: Little, Brown and Company, 1961), 354.
[65] Winston Churchill, *The Second World War*, vol. III, *The Grand Alliance* (Boston: Houghton Mifflin, 1950), 372–3.
[66] Overy, *Russia's War*, 291.
[67] Raymond Aron, *Les guerres en chaîne*, 12th edn (Paris: Gallimard, 1951), 132–3.

business to be done with a very big customer. This initially positive attitude in business and political circles, however, changed quite abruptly in early 1946. The acceptance of Kennan's strategic advice in his long cable of 22 February 1946 quite unexpectedly struck a chord of emotion at just the right moment, while it might have been neglected six months earlier and regarded as redundant preaching to the converted had it arrived, say, six months later.[68] Seriously doubtful about the Soviet leadership's grip on the reality of international politics, Kennan advised the US administration to be realistic rather than hysterical or aggressive. His article 'The Sources of Soviet Conduct' published in the July 1947 issue of *Foreign Affairs* under the pseudonym 'X' was a call to apply a vigilant and effective application of counter-force against the threat of Soviet expansion. If the strategy of 'containment' was exposed to haphazard use and growing confusion about the ideas and concrete aims involved, this also held true for Kennan's original definition of the doctrine. By his own account, it was based on careless and indiscriminate language, leading him to emphatically deny the paternity of the concept twenty years later.[69]

The roots of the Cold War were not confined to a contest over material goods, economic wealth, territory, technological competition, or revenge for historical defeats.[70] The turn of events in the wake of 1945 produced not only a shift in military alliances by dissolving the war coalition, but also generated a Manichaean split between a free society and the evil empire of totalitarianism.[71] Totalitarian Nazi Germany was replaced with the 'evil' Soviet empire. When President Truman in a speech to a joint session of Congress on 12 March 1947 called for the United States to engage in the Greek civil war, he acknowledged the division of the world into two hostile blocs. He made it clear that the United States would oppose any attempt to alter that dividing line with all its economic and military might. Truman personally and his administration cared very much about the usage of the term 'totalitarianism'. This notion and the struggle against it in the American political lexicon mobilised public support and produced a striking increase in Truman's popularity.

---

[68] George F. Kennan and John Lukacs, *George F. Kennan and the Origins of Containment 1944–1946: The Kennan–Lukacs Correspondence* (Columbia: University of Missouri Press, 1997), 24–5.

[69] John Lewis Gaddis, 'The Strategy of Containment', in Thomas H. Etzold and John Lewis Gaddis, *Containment: Documents on American Policy and Strategy, 1945–1950* (New York: Columbia University Press, 1978), 25.

[70] Stefan Rossbach, *Gnostic Wars: The Cold War in the Context of a History of Western Spirituality* (Edinburgh: Edinburgh University Press, 1999).

[71] Abbot Gleason, *Totalitarianism: The Inner History of the Cold War* (Oxford: Oxford University Press, 1995), 72–88.

The deep uncertainty about political and economic choices in immediate post-war Europe crystallised in a Manichean conflict between good
and evil, which confirmed how the power of Gnostic spirituality with a
drive to world-immanent eschatology symbolised institutionalised conflict patterns. From an experiential perspective, the immediate post-war
period shaped the order of individual souls and society. According to
Kennan, the conflict's spiritual aspect in a certain way actually defined
the Cold War as the 'total externalisation of evil'.[72] Generated in the
confusion between victory and defeat, the total externalisation of evil was
a crucial means of symbolising the beginning of the post-war era of
normalisation. The main threat to Western democracy was not an imminent Soviet attack but the poor condition of European post-war economies and the social and political instability that resulted. The split into
two worlds was not supposed to close all doors but rather to keep open the
possibility of reconciliation. The declaration of the 'Truman doctrine'
maintained that 'the seeds of totalitarian regimes are nurtured by misery
and want. They spread and grow in the soil of poverty and strife. They
reach their full growth when the hope of a people for a better life has died.
We must keep that hope alive.'[73] The policy of containment was an
attempt to avoid the contagion of Western economies with the socially
impoverishing but politically explosive communist economic models.
The foundations of the Marshall plan as a pillar of the containment policy
highlighted the need not for US military assistance but for economic
aid, trying to counteract political passions by the creation of economic
interests.[74]

While people in West Germany equated Nazi Germany with Eastern
totalitarianism, East Germans associated fascism with capitalism. The
externalisation of evil against the totalitarian enemy was perhaps of greatest importance in the effort of democratising the western part of divided
Germany. For the American high commissioner in Germany, General
Clay, the ideological contest between East and West Germany was perhaps more efficient than all American efforts of democratisation of post-
war Germany.[75] In the United States, the incipient Cold War entailed an
almost schizophrenic state of mind. Feeling besieged and threatened by

[72] Rossbach, *Gnostic Wars*, 187.   [73] Quoted in Gleason, *Totalitarianism*, 73.
[74] A paper prepared by the Kennan group defined the critical state of western European
economies and social attitudes resulting from this, not a possible Soviet military attack, as
the main threat to the European balance of power; see Kersten, *The Establishment of
Communist Rule*, 401.
[75] Barbara Mettler, *Demokratisierung und Kalter Krieg. Berlin: Zur amerikanischen Informations-
und Rundfunkpolitik in Westdeutschland 1945–1949* (Berlin: Verlag Volker Spiess, 1975),
85–6.

external insecurity, the United States did not really question its own
moral and material superiority.[76] In a strategic reassessment, drafted by
a special State and Defence Department study group in early 1950, a
successful conduct of the policy of containment was seen as equivalent to
avoiding a diplomatic freeze. A freeze would inhibit economic initiatives
by the United States and deprive it of opportunities for maintaining a
moral ascendancy in its struggle with the Soviet system.[77]

Although the Cold War must be divided into different phases, there is
an overwhelming continuity not only of policies but also of a central
conception. The symbolisation of good and evil peaked in the moral
crusade of the Reagan era.[78] Taking the broader meaning of containment
as close to one of the central meanings of the classical notion of *arete*, to a
balanced existence, a taking care of oneself, one could argue that post-war
containment in many aspects was an attempt to recognise and impose
limits on the limitless existence of Western life.[79] Whereas in Kennan's
opinion containment in the context of American–Soviet relations was
supposed 'to tide us over a difficult period' of an estimated ten or fifteen
years, containment was transformed into a doctrine, into an 'indestruc-
tible myth'.[80]

As any mythological construction, it has not only a conceptual but also
a perceptual structure. As the veritable war panic in the Soviet Union of
the early 1950s intimates, this perception sustained the mythologisation
of the enemy. The Marshall plan as the principal piece of containment
policy was supposed to constitute a beginning, the foundation of a new
sense of purpose in Western society, on the grounds of avoiding contagion with the virus of totalitarianism.[81] In this sense, containment was not
only meant to protect democracy, welfare, and justice against an outside
threat but also to reinforce the primacy Western civilisation as a universal
value despite the existence of international communism.

The meanings of the Second World War

The Second World War bequeathed an ambivalent heritage. It left east
European societies powerless but also produced symbols, meanings, and
memories that would sustain hopes for their national self-affirmation.

---

[76] Stanley Hoffmann, *Primacy or World Order: American Foreign Policy Since the Cold War*
(New York: McGraw-Hill, 1980), 7–8.
[77] NSC 68 of 14 April 1950, in Etzold and Gaddis, *Containment*, 402.
[78] Gleason, *Totalitarianism*, 190–210.
[79] Kennan mentions 'environmental destructiveness' and the 'tendency to live beyond our
means' as two examples.
[80] See Rossbach, *Gnostic Wars*, 213.   [81] Rossbach, *Gnostic Wars*, 211–12.

Material destruction, physical extermination, genocide, and forced migration could also generate genuine solidarity and community, shared in the equality of miserable conditions. The expulsion of minorities and the redrawing of their territorial boundaries brought about a national homogenisation in countries such as Poland, Czechoslovakia, and Hungary. In the Soviet case, a genuine sense of liberation emerged in the aftermath of the German attack, which made repressive political control by secret police crumble and freed many Soviet officials, managers, and soldiers from an atmosphere of passivity and fear of responsibility.[82] Paradoxically, the first phase of the war was the exception to the rule. The military successes and the great improvement in Soviet fighting power from the late autumn of 1942 relate directly to the demotion of the military commissars in the Soviet army. The heightened sense of subjectivity and individual responsibility at the war conjuncture proved significant for the genuine acceptance of and identification with the Soviet regime. Patriotism during the war was not a political artefact created by Stalin's propaganda but was primarily experienced from below, endowing people in existential crisis with a greater sense of initiative and responsibility. The first two years of the Second World War caused a paradoxical sense of freedom and moral strength. It was 'a period of spontaneous de-Stalinisation. We were in full crisis ... People suddenly were forced to make their own decisions, to take responsibility for themselves. Events pressed us into becoming truly independent human beings ... Strange as it may sound, 1941 was more of a liberation than was 1945.'[83] The Great Fatherland War also stimulated free thought and autonomy that accompanied the activities of masses of people together risking or sacrificing their lives in defence of their country and its state.[84]

The anti-fascist myth and the policy of containment sealed what the devastation of the Second World War and the advance of communism into eastern Europe had prefigured. Each camp drew meaning and legitimacy from the fact that the 'Other' (the enemy) represented the missing link to achieve full identity, something that was arguably lost once the anti-Hitler coalition had broken apart. This symbolisation of war experiences as a dichotomy between good and evil, however, must not be confined to the confrontation between two blocs in what came to be called the Cold War. The growing reciprocity in the ongoing competition

[82] Overy, *Russia's War*, 329–30.
[83] Mikhail Gefter as quoted in Tumarkin, *The Living and the Dead*, 65.
[84] Michael Urban et al., *The Rebirth of Politics in Russia* (Cambridge: Cambridge University Press, 1997), 30.

led to an increasing similarity of competitors' attitudes in a bipolar world, which was counterbalanced by the fear of annihilation. Mutual opposition not only eased the adjustment of their relations, but kept them in a mimetic relationship of *frères ennemis* and adversary partners.[85]

The ideological divide between the 'liberal democracies' and the 'people's democracies' operated with culturally determinist views according to which Western democracy was individualist and free, while communism was collectivist and totalitarian. The conceptual determinism of the postwar period concealed the manifold meanings of the war. Thus, the split into a bipolar world was not so much an 'inevitable' confrontation of two political systems. Rather, the experiential basis of uncertainty and threat propelled the search for a moral purpose for society. The symbolisation of the Cold War rested on the definition of enemies and on a number of regional conflicts, of which the Korean war between 1950 and 1953 was the most significant.

The division of two worlds was in both camps a process of meaning-formation under situational premises of existential uncertainty. The major assault by communist ideology on public discourse, the streamlining of education, and the restrictions of the freedom of the press and historiography came along with the streamlining of public discourse and rising political radicalism in the West. Politically, the Cold War constructed a deliberative filter that established the antagonism of political systems based on the incompatibility of values, procedures, and behaviour. Yet, seen from the situational logic of action and the meanings attached to representations, memories, and images, the Cold War made incompatible what was actually incomparable.[86] While the problem was similarly pressing for each side, symbols, meanings, and representations were not based on a common ground of references. Any reported act of repression or toleration was judged on the grounds of radically different situational premises.

---

[85] William Zimmerman, *Soviet Perspectives on International Relations 1956–1967* (Princeton: Princeton University Press, 1969), 135 and 282.
[86] Arne Naess et al., *Democracy, Ideology, and Objectivity: Studies in the Semantics and Cognitive Analysis of Ideological Controversy* (Oxford: Blackwell, 1956), 259.

7 The articulation of dissidence

In a time of universal deceit, telling the truth is a revolutionary act.

Attributed to George Orwell

Challenges to communist power

The late Stalin era made the Soviet Union into the military and technological superpower for which industrialisation and the victory in the Second World War had laid the foundations. While the territorial expansion of the Soviet Union into eastern Europe, the success of communist movements worldwide from China in 1949 to Vietnam and Cuba in the 1950s, and military and technological successes such as the H-bomb and the launch of Sputnik in 1957 testified to growing strength, communist power was challenged by an impressive return to diversity, especially in eastern Europe.[1] This chapter argues that despite the failure to overcome communist power, the revolutionary events in Hungary in 1956, in Czechoslovakia in 1968, and in Poland in 1980 produced authority vacuums that entailed new symbolisations as markers of certainty, which became the spiritual foundations of democracy.

Explanations of communism's collapse that are sensitive to the past have argued that all regimes that ended peacefully were fully integrated into the Soviet bloc.[2] Due to the centralised control of domestic militaries by the Soviet centre, Gorbachev's policy of non-intervention at the end of the 1980s prevented power incumbents from using military force in defence of their power. By contrast, all the countries that experienced violence during the collapse of communist party hegemony were either completely outside the bloc (Albania), associated with it but not a full member (Yugoslavia), or a member in 'poor standing' (Romania). The latter, for example, refused to participate in many Warsaw Pact exercises

---

[1] Joseph Rothschild, *Return to Diversity: A Political History of East Central Europe Since World War II*, 2nd edn (New York and Oxford: Oxford University Press, 1993).

[2] Valerie Bunce, *Subversive Institutions: The Design and the Destruction of Socialism and the State* (Cambridge: Cambridge University Press, 1999), 70–1 and 134.

and had no Soviet troops stationed within its borders. While these arguments are consistent with a perspective on communist rule as being
centred on Soviet domination over its satellites, an experiential perspective needs to challenge not only the idea that the cornerstone of
communist power was military force but also the very idea of a bloc. At
a relatively early stage, the Soviet Union had lost much of its capacity to
control the domestic affairs of its allies by power alliances, authority,
or informal channels mastered by Stalin.[3] With the control options of
the Soviet Union reduced to economic pressure, political disapproval,
and isolation, communist power from 1956 at the latest could be maintained only by preventing its east European satellites from drifting away
to the 'imperialist' camp. Despite the real differences between, say,
Czechoslovakia after 1969, Ceauşescu's Romania or Kádár's Hungary,
it is therefore possible to talk about a continuing legitimation crisis of
communist power.[4] This legitimation crisis was not an objective force
due to the progress of which communism was doomed to fail, and
democracy of a Western type was bound to impose itself. Rather, it
indicated that the ideology and practices that sustained communist
power in the first place would generate the sources of anti-totalitarian
revolt. If, according to Hannah Arendt, fear, loneliness, and despair make
modern tyranny possible in the shape of a totalitarian system, then this
fear, loneliness, and despair bear the seeds of the self-destruction of the
totalitarian system.[5] No ideological universalism can annihilate man's
capacity for new beginnings and political freedom that is generated by
the human need for autonomy, community, and self-assertion.

Despite this inherent weakness of communism, its collapse was not an
inevitable consequence of subversive institutions. Rather, traumatic
experiences of revolution and defeat were important forces from 'below'
that transformed meanings and consciousness among the citizenry in
some parts of the 'Soviet bloc'. Rather than being simply 'symbolic' in
the popular understanding of inefficient, these challenges to communist
power were quests for meaning, where freedom was not an imported good
or an idea of values and institutions but was generated at these conjunctures. Dissidence was not a specific type of political subjectivity that could
be learnt in textbooks or developed in the enlightened minds of isolated

---

[3] Zbigniew Brzezinski, *The Soviet Bloc: Unity and Conflict* (Cambridge, MA: Harvard University Press, 1967).
[4] Leslie Holmes, *The End of Communist Power: Anti-Corruption Campaigns and Legitimation Crisis* (Cambridge and Oxford: Polity Press, 1993), 22–3.
[5] Hannah Arendt, *The Origins of Totalitarianism* (London: George Allen, 1951), 478.

individuals. Rather, it emerged as an existential response to dramatic social experiences often involving violence, humiliation, and despair. The primary goal was not to topple communist power but to disclose its artificiality and falseness, a process that started with de-Stalinisation. Such experiences were radically political, as they were lived as concrete experiences of solidarity and community.

De-Stalinisation

The beginning of de-Stalinisation is commonly associated with Khrushchev's speech 'On the Cult of Personality and Its Consequences' at a closed session of the Twentieth Party Congress of the Communist Party of the Soviet Union (CPSU) on 25 February 1956. The need to formalise such a criticism in an initially closed speech, however, may have been a function of the ongoing power struggle between Mikoyan, Malenkov, and Khrushchev for ascendancy. The death of Joseph Stalin on 5 March 1953 had provoked a deeply emotional reaction of grief and despair not only in the Soviet Union but also in many parts of eastern Europe. This sudden loss of an absolute authority that had dominated the destinies of more than one generation of Russian people filled Stalin's successors with fear and indecision.[6] During the 'silent de-Stalinisation' that followed, revisions of Stalin's repressive politics were carried out in a secretive and ad hoc fashion.[7] This silent de-Stalinisation essentially shattered the Soviet claim to total power, bringing about the self-deconstruction of the fundamental principle of Stalinist rule.

Moreover, the dramatic intensity of de-Stalinisation must be seen against a largely de-dramatised setting on the eve of Stalin's death, when Soviet society was characterised by a pervasive atmosphere of immobility.[8] Stalin's attempt to streamline society was faced with an unwelcome but increasing emotional detachment of the people from the country's supreme political purpose and, simultaneously, the growing rigidity of caste stratification in Soviet society. With the disappearance of the age cohorts that had a personal recollection of pre-revolutionary times, a spiritual breach between the rulers and the ruled opened up. Criticism of Stalin's methods and fundamental opposition to his rule had

---

[6] Michael Urban et al., *The Rebirth of Politics in Russia* (Cambridge: Cambridge University Press, 1997), 32.
[7] See Kathleen E. Smith, *Remembering Stalin's Victims: Popular Memory and the End of the USSR* (Ithaca and London: Cornell University Press, 1996), 23.
[8] George F. Kennan, *Sketches from a Life* (New York: Pantheon Books, 1989), 153–6.

preceded his death, as the first de-Stalinisation in the Second World War or the resistance movements in the Baltic countries indicate. The anti-Semitic campaign in the 'Doctors' Plot' of the late Stalin era was another turning point, a first stage in the regime's progressive and ultimately fatal loss of legitimacy in the eyes of the educated elite.[9] Stalin's death made the ruling class aware that it was no longer able to claim even to itself that the end justifies the means.[10] As Stalin's successors dispensed with Stalin's methods, the ruling class was not able to preserve the dogmatic character of communism.[11] The reluctant abandonment of the ideology and dogma crucial for the consolidation of communism would yield to a stronger power: fear of the effect public opinion in the world would have on its absolute power.

Khrushchev's critique of the Stalin cult occurred in the context of a major structural transformation that had been going on since Stalin's death and reflected tendencies in society that had started much earlier. The short three months of Lavrenti Beria's rise to power between March and July 1953 indicated a clear shift towards a more pragmatic approach to politics. The Baltic countries were given serious prospects of national autonomy.[12] Moreover, Beria initiated the wave of liberations from gulag camps and installed Imre Nagy as first party secretary in Hungary. Most importantly, the workers' protests on 17 June 1953 in the German Democratic Republic were directly linked to Stalin's death and to Beria's short-term liberalisation policies. The production of consumer goods was stepped up, leading to a situation where their growth outstripped the growth of industrial production. In early 1953, the communist regime in East Germany appeared to be further weakened by a steady flight of citizens into West Germany and by growing food shortages.[13] As the new Soviet leadership was not willing to continue the extraordinary economic and financial support for the East German regime, the politburo of the Socialist United Party (SED) implemented a new line by imposing a general increase of 10 per cent in all work quotas and threatening wage reductions.[14] Although the ensuing mass demonstrations of

[9] Sheila Fitzpatrick, 'I Sailed away with a Mighty Push, Never to Return', *London Review of Books*, 27, 6 (17 March 2005), 6.
[10] Nikita S. Khrushchev, *Khrushchev Remembers*, trans. and ed. Strobe Talbot (New York: Bantam, 1970), 372.
[11] Seweryn Bialer, *Stalin's Successors* (Cambridge: Cambridge University Press, 1982).
[12] Leonard Schapiro, *The Origin of the Communist Autocracy* (London: G. Bell and Sons, 1955), 247.
[13] In the first half of 1953 alone an estimated 225,000 people left the GDR.
[14] Arnulf Baring, *Uprising in East Germany: June 17, 1953*, trans. from the German by Gerald Onn (Ithaca and London: Cornell University Press, 1972).

17 June 1953 involved up to 300,000 people, they failed to entail a popular uprising, as the centres were industrial work units and rarely involved the wider population. The utterly spontaneous wave of demonstrations lacked any strategic or practical objectives and had ebbed away before Soviet troops intervened.

While these attempts at liberalisation were soon overshadowed by the power struggle in the Kremlin, the second experience of de-Stalinisation after 1956 brought about real spaces of freedom. Under Khrushchev's rule, social unrest considerably increased, and the authorities had to repress eleven uprisings of more than 300 people.[15] De-Stalinisation revived the category 'democracy' in Soviet society.[16] One central aspect of Gorbachev's rise to power in 1985 is that he and his major allies such as Ligachev and Yakovlev were part of the generation of the 1960s (*shestidesiatki*), whose perceptions of social and political reality were largely shaped in the aftermath of 1956. This group of leaders not only joined the party after the Second World War and had become professional politicians during the Khrushchev era. They had also experienced significant personal mobility and, in the case of Yakovlev, exchange programmes with the United States. Arguably, the letter of the Soviet dissident movement to the Soviet leaders on 19 March 1970 prefigured the intellectual thrust of Gorbachev's *perestroika* and his discourse on democratisation.[17] Much of its specific vocabulary – such as 'stagnation', the urgent need to accelerate 'scientific and technical progress', or 'democratisation' that should strengthen and maintain the leading role of the party, through the introduction of 'multi-candidate elections' and 'measures directed toward increasing public discussion in the work of governing bodies' – would become a prominent part of the regime's reform discourse in the *perestroika* period. In parts of eastern Europe, this process of detachment from and suspicion of communism was reinforced by aspirations to national independence.

Varieties of revolution

Apart from the 'great events' that marked deep notches in the history of humanity in the twentieth century, other, 'second-class' revolutions are

---

[15] Vladimir A. Kozlov et al., *Massovye besporiadki v SSSR pri Khrushcheve i Brezhneve (1953–nachalo 1980-x gg.)* (Novosibirsk: Siobirskii Khronograf. 1999).
[16] Urban et al., *The Rebirth of Politics in Russia*, 36.
[17] See the text in Richard Sakwa, ed., *The Rise and Fall of the Soviet Union 1917–1991* (London and New York: Routledge, 1999), 374–9; for an analysis, see Urban et al., *The Rebirth of Politics in Russia*, 60–4.

crucial for the evolution of individual nations.[18] The revolutions in Hungary in 1956, in Czechoslovakia in 1968, or in Poland in 1980 have been perceived mostly as failed revolts by the populace against the all-mighty Soviet military machine.[19] They varied considerably as regards the scope of collective action, the reform objectives, the geopolitical setting, and the responses of power incumbents. As they did not enforce substantial discontinuities in power structures – despite prompting some modifications of the ideological and practical course of communist regimes – they are classified as either preludes or aftermaths of a particular subphase of communist political evolution. In the aftermath of the thaw period, the Soviet Union entered the period of stagnation, Hungary after 1956 developed Kadarism, Czechoslovakia after 1968 took on the path of repressive normalisation, and martial law in Poland in late 1981 entailed a precarious rebalancing of the status quo.

The Hungarian revolution was often described as a genuine attempt to discontinue Soviet-type rule and to replace it with a national government based on workers' councils. In Czechoslovakia, the impetus for change came from within the regime, essentially propelled by ideological disillu-sionment with Stalinism and aiming at 'socialism with a human face'. In the aftermath of the Hungarian revolution in 1956, a short period of mass terror was followed by an extended search for compromise. In post-1968 Czechoslovakia, a short-term search for compromise was followed by a long-term repressive policy in the normalisation regime. Repression in Czechoslovakia continued because of the absence of broad societal resist-ance, of centres of independent political activity, and of significant pop-ular mobilisation. Such tendencies prevailed in Hungary and Poland where the cleavage between state and society was much stronger.

The deep impact of Stalinist repression in Hungary bore the seeds of challenges to communist power. The reburial in summer 1956 of László Rajk, a rehabilitated victim of a 1949 show trial, proved to be a dress rehearsal for solidarity from below as it brought thousands of people together in a symbolic manifestation against Stalinist rule.[20] From the beginning to the end of the Hungarian revolution of 1956, the demands of the various revolutionary committees and workers' councils for national independence and democratic freedom were not couched in terms of

---

[18] Milan Kundera, *Ignorance: A Novel*, trans. Linda Asher (New York: Harper Perennial, 2002), 11–12. Kundera also mentions 1948 as the moment when Yugoslav citizens rose up against Stalin.
[19] Grzegorz Ekiert, *The State Against Society: Political Crises and Their Aftermath in East Central Europe* (Princeton: Princeton University Press, 1996), 207.
[20] George Schöpflin, *Politics in Eastern Europe 1945–1992* (Oxford and Cambridge: Blackwell, 1993), 125–6.

claims for material welfare or of philosophic justifications, as in Kossuth's declaration of independence of 1849, but placed spiritual values over economic and social aspects.[21] The cleansing of public places of symbols of power such as the red star, Stalin statues, and Soviet war memorials signified spiritual liberation.[22]

Although a specifically Hungarian event, October 1956 was ignited by the 'spark' provided by the Polish October.[23] The triumphant speech of Władysław Gomułka, the reinstated first secretary of the Polish communist party, before an enthusiastic Polish public on 20 October 1956 was published in full in a Hungarian newspaper three days later. This very day the first student demonstration in Hungary assembled up to 10,000 demonstrators and took over the streets of Budapest in a few hours.[24] The slogans chanted in front of the statue of the Polish general József Bem – the hero of the Hungarian revolution of 1848–9 – included 'Independence based on freedom and equality!', 'Poland shows us the way; let's follow the Hungarian way!', and 'Long live the Polish nation!'[25] Starting from 23 October, there was a virtual explosion in public debate, exchanges of points of view that took the form of resolutions, manifestos, handbills, and brief tracts. Broadcasting at very short intervals, the Hungarian revolutionaries indulged themselves in the sheer pleasure of speech.[26] The Yugoslav press and diplomatic corps had an extraordinary influence in disseminating the news of the events of October 1956 in Poland and in Hungary to all satellite states, in a perspective radically different from the official Soviet accounts. One important impulse for Yugoslavia's role in informing Poles about Hungarian events and vice versa was the animosity against Mátyás Rákosi, who had conducted the 1948 anti-Titoist campaign more zealously than other communist leaders.[27]

The sudden success of previously cautious opposition intellectuals without any purposeful strategic vision in Hungary in 1956 would have been impossible without the previous moral collapse of authority.[28] In a

[21] Ferenc Vali, *Rift and Revolt in Hungary: Nationalism Versus Communism* (Cambridge, MA: Harvard University Press, 1961), 332–5.
[22] György Litvan, ed., *The Hungarian Revolution of 1956* (New York: Longman, 1996), 66.
[23] Johanna Granville, 'Satellites or Prime Movers? Polish and Hungarian Reactions to the 1956 Events: New Archival Evidence', *East European Quarterly*, 35, 4 (2002), 443.
[24] George Gömöri, 'From the Diary of an Eye-Witness: Notes on the Hungarian Revolution', in Leopold Tyrmand, ed., *Kultura Essays* (New York: Free Press, 1970), 137–50.
[25] Granville, 'Satellites or Prime Movers?', 449.
[26] See Ekiert, *The State Against Society*, 59.
[27] Granville, 'Satellites or Prime Movers?', 444.
[28] György Konrád, *Antipolitics: An Essay*, trans. from the Hungarian by Richard E. Allen (San Diego/New York/London: Harcourt Brace Jovanovich, 1984), 70.

state of deep confusion and lacking orders from the government authorities, Hungarian coercive forces were reluctant to act decisively against
the popular demonstrations during the first days of the revolution. The
political leadership did not intervene between 23 and 28 October nor did
the well-equipped Hungarian army implement the martial law decree that
the government eventually proclaimed. The virtual collapse of the communist party gave rise to rapid establishment of new institutions such as
independent workers' councils, revolutionary committees, and political
parties.[29]
    The Soviet intervention crushed this movement of national independ-
ence, prompting more than 200,000 Hungarians to flee the country.
During and immediately after the revolution, tens of thousands were
imprisoned and more than 2,000 people were executed. Leaving
Hungarian society initially powerless, the restoration under Janoś Kádár
soon opened up spaces of economic freedom and also a partial deconstruction of the political symbolism of communism.[30] In 1962, the reha-
bilitation of the victims of show trials in the early 1950s was followed by a
general amnesty for political prisoners jailed after 1956. In the same year,
Janoś Kádár struck a blow at the search for enemies as an institutionalised
pattern of fear when he declared, 'Whoever is not against us is with us.' In
April 1963, the political committee of the party abolished the exclusion of
class aliens from university entrance. Hungarian society responded to this
repressive paternalism with different strategies. While some withdrew
into indifference and apathy, others became massively involved in the
second economy. Thus, the socialisation from below of mass organisations and state agencies partly preserved intellectual traditions and independent life-styles.[31] This interaction between the state and society could
be seen as 'the silent revolution from below', in which initially scattered
social groups forced concessions from their bureaucratic rulers and
prompted others to argue about 'the advantage of being atomised'.[32]
    A movement based on spontaneous and quickly accelerating rhythms of
mass demonstrations is more vulnerable to being destroyed than slowly
built up networks of political resistance. Whereas the Hungarian revolution

---

[29] Whereas on the eve of the revolution the Hungarian Workers' Party had 811,135
    members and 42,406 candidates for membership, in the course of autumn 1956 the
    membership dramatically dropped to 37,818 in December 1956, before rising to around
    500,000 by January 1962; see Ekiert, *The State Against Society*, 50 and 85.
[30] Ivan T. Berend, *The Hungarian Economic Reforms 1953–1988* (Cambridge: Cambridge
    University Press, 1988), 134–6.
[31] Elemer Hankiss, 'Demobilization, Self-Mobilization and Quasi-Mobilization 1948–1987',
    East European Politics and Societies, 3, 1 (1989), 122–31.
[32] Quoted in Ekiert, *The State Against Society*, 104.

occurred in a short fourteen-day explosion, the Prague spring in 1968 lasted several months. Initially, the Czechoslovak reform process was largely confined to the official institutions of the party-state and kept these institutional structures relatively intact. As no serious independent organisational bases emerged within society to challenge the authority of the party-state, the political stability of the regime never seemed to be seriously threatened during the whole period of the Czechoslovak reform movement.[33] While the Czech party-state survived the intra-elite conflict almost intact, in Hungary in 1956 the communist party was literally crushed and paralysed.

Unlike the Hungarian revolution in 1956 and the Polish revolution in 1980, which had national solidarity and spiritual revival at their centre, the Prague spring is usually not considered as a 'revolution', although its comprehensive social dimension would suggest such a description to be appropriate.[34] Objectively, the Prague spring can be embedded in a regularity of cycles of crisis that span eight decades (1918, 1938–9, 1945, 1948, 1968, 1968–9, 1989–90, and 1992) of 'uninterrupted revolution'. Each date seems to constitute a brutal rupture with the past, but nevertheless maintains crucial continuities with it. Czechoslovak politics can be characterised in terms of an extraordinary toing and froing of political and social lives that generally took on a revolutionary character.[35] Subjectively, the Prague spring was the result of a gradual awakening of society, a sort of creeping opening of the hidden sphere. In a specific way, the Prague spring was not the beginning but the 'final act of a long drama originally played out chiefly in the theatre of the spirit and the conscience of society. And that somewhere at the beginning of this drama, there were individuals who were willing to live within the truth, even when things were at their worst ... One thing, however, seems clear: the attempt at political reform was not the cause of society's reawakening, but rather the final outcome of that reawakening.'[36]

Indeed, the creeping discontent had an important influence on the regime-initiated outbreak of the crisis. When Alexander Dubček replaced Antonín Novotný as the leader of the communist party in January 1968, Czechoslovak society remained apathetic.[37] Despite a significant

---

[33] Ekiert, *The State Against Society*, 158.

[34] François Fejtö and Jacques Rupnik, eds., *Le printemps tchécoslovaque 1968* (Paris: Editions Complexes, 1999), 127–34.

[35] Gordon Skilling, '1968. Une révolution interrompue', in Fejtö and Rupnik, *Le printemps tchécoslovaque 1968*, 285–8.

[36] Václav Havel, 'The Power of the Powerless', in John Keane, ed., *The Power of the Powerless: Citizens Against the State in Eastern Europe* (London: Hutchinson, 1985), 43.

[37] Ekiert, *The State Against Society*, 138–44.

opening in the political opportunity structure and the emergence of
relatively unconstrained public space, the institutional structure of the
Czechoslovak regime remained almost intact and the reform movement
was channelled through existing institutional structures. Yet, after the
abolition of censorship in May 1968, Czechoslovakia experienced an
explosion of information, and the press played a major role as a voice of
social criticism, stimulating political debates and establishing freedom of
opinion. As would become clear after the Soviet intervention, it was
primarily the cultural realm where spaces of freedom survived beyond
the military invasion and could be reframed as an integral part of the
European cultural tradition. The Soviet intervention in Czechoslovakia
on 21 August 1968 produced a strong resistance movement underpinned
by a spontaneous and deep solidarity of the overwhelming majority of the
population.[38] Although the existence of a broad resistance movement was
not a foregone conclusion until the end of 21 August, small-scale events
such as the failure to disseminate intervention propaganda and the proclamation of the Presidium of the Communist Party critical of the intervention helped to shape initial public perceptions. The Presidium
proclamation, which declared the illegitimacy of the Soviet invasion,
gained political importance only through the spontaneous emergence of
a broad resistance movement. If much of the spontaneous popular mobilisation between 21 and 27 August was symbolic, the bonding effect of
manifestations of solidarity invigorated personal responsibility and
friendly relationships in society where the absence of dissenters brought
pride and satisfaction in a common enterprise. Thus, the capitulation of
the reform movement before the military repression gave rise to the
strongest formulation of an alternative and meaningful way of living.
The symbol of protest against humiliation by Soviet power became Jan
Palach's self-immolation in Václav Square in January 1969. Although
Palach's example could not be followed, nor had he exactly been a victim
of communist repression, this great ethical act of martyrdom would be
commemorated in massive spontaneous demonstrations in January
1989.[39] Despite the marginalisation of Charter 77, for many people the
symbolic markers of national protest against humiliation were crucial for
making 1989 the fulfilment of the Prague spring.

[38] F. H. Eidlin, *The Logic of 'Normalization': The Soviet Intervention in Czechoslovakia of 21 August 1968 and the Czechoslovak Response* (New York: Columbia University Press, 1980), 93–156.
[39] Padraic Kenney, *A Carnival of Revolution: Central Europe 1989* (Princeton: Princeton University Press, 2002), 244–9.

The Polish self-limiting revolution began in the strike movement in July and August 1980 and finished with the proclamation of martial law in December 1981.[40] It was both the culmination point of a previous cycle of crises and the prelude to the round-table negotiations between the Polish communist party and the Solidarność trade union in early 1989. A complex cycle of crises since at least 1956 had resulted in a gradual but far from inevitable convergence of different forces in society, united in dissidence and solidarity against the communist state.[41] Initially, the Polish intelligentsia had not opposed communism but had supported communist authorities – more for patriotic than ideological reasons – in an effort to rebuild a devastated country. Even though the cycle of political crises of 1956, 1968, 1970, and 1976 did not create authority vacuums such as in Hungary in 1956 or in Poland itself in 1980, they had an 'after-life', which nurtured oppositional activity and resistance with a powerful symbolic repertoire.[42] The emergence of the Solidarność trade union enlarged an already existing counter-public. The massive drop in party membership and the membership of nearly 10 million Poles in Solidarność intimated a situation of dual sovereignty.[43] The power of symbols against communism owed its emergence not to an anarchical mentality but to the cautious and unpredictable forging of an alliance between originally diverging sectors of society such as leftist intellectuals, the Catholic Church, and the workers. Still, the initiation of an important strike movement in Gdańsk and Szczecziń in July 1980 was not inevitable. Although the election of Karol Wojtyła as Pope John Paul II in October 1978 was not the source of the broad movement that brought Solidarność into being, his first pilgrimage to Poland in June 1979 became the dress rehearsal in terms of spiritual mobilisation of Polish society. Organising this visit without the help of the authorities, some 10 million Poles attended outdoor celebrations, reclaiming individual dignity and spiritual liberty, but also experiencing a collective spirit of mobilisation and empowerment.

The Polish revolution was not primarily a matter of setting the 'micro' level of society against the 'macro' dimension of the state. Solidarność's

---

[40] Jadwiga Staniszkis, *Poland's Self-Limiting Revolution* (Princeton: Princeton University Press, 1984).

[41] Neil Ascherson, *The Polish August: The Self-Limiting Revolution* (London: Penguin, 1981); Timothy Garton Ash, *The Polish Revolution: Solidarity* (London: Granta Books, 1991).

[42] See Jane Curry and Luba Fajfer, *Poland's Permanent Revolution* (Washington, DC: American University Press, 1996).

[43] In Poland, the number of party members declined from nearly 3.1 million in 1980 to approximately 2.7 million in 1981 and to some 2.1 million in 1984, then remaining relatively stable up to 1988; see Ekiert, *The State Against Society*, 50, 85, and 318.

emergence bridged the gap between 'micro' and 'macro', being the moment 'when individuals, brought up in the totalitarian situation, were able to overcome their own moral indifference to society and to themselves'.[44] The spirit of collective action was continued in the 'long march' between 1982 and 1988 through the underground under conditions of illegality and social atomisation. The link between individual destiny and collective identity was expressed by the dissident Adam Michnik in a letter to the minister of interior, General Kiszczak, who had been responsible for the proclamation of martial law. 'For me, General, prison is not such a painful punishment. On that December night it was not I who was condemned but freedom: it is not I who is being held prisoner but Poland.'[45]

The articulation of dissidence

The different symbolisations of revolutionary experiences converged on various forms of resistance, which can be seen as the experiential basis of dissidence. It is difficult to 'measure' dissidence comparatively according to the kind and degree of political freedom and the specific forms of dissidence achieved. Rather, it has to be appreciated with regard to the sociopolitical background against which it arose. What could be an astoundingly free act in Romania's ethnocentric and paranoid dictatorship could be seen as insignificant in the enlightened despotism of Kádár. The Prague spring caused much excitement in the Baltic republics, where the incidence of individual acts of defiance such as raising the national flag increased.[46] Along with the relative openness of Yugoslavia and its citizens' interest in the West came exchanges with central Europe, which both reinforced a sense of Yugoslavia's material superiority over central Europe and strengthened patriotic feelings domestically. By contrast, Soviet citizens, Albanians, Czechs, and East Germans were far less mobile, to the point of being prevented from any contact with the West. Based on geography, geopolitical factors, and the practical absence of an intellectual emigration, for instance, Bulgaria's objective isolation was intensified by feelings of being overlooked and forsaken. In this context, even the illusion of the Hungarian writer György Konrád's appeal to the

[44] Jadwiga Staniszkis, *The Dynamics of the Breakthrough in Eastern Europe: The Polish Experience* (Berkeley: University of California Press, 1991), 237.
[45] Adam Michnik, *Polnischer Frieden. Aufsätze zur Konzeption des Widerstandes*, ed. Helga Hirsch (Berlin: Rotbuch Verlag, 1985), 68.
[46] Stanley Vardys and Judith Sedaitis, *Lithuania: The Rebel Nation* (Boulder: Westview Press, 1997), 85.

'international intellectual aristocracy' of Europe and the West seems pretentious and inconceivable.[47]

Although images from the 'West' were influential in shaping perceptions of often idealised images of democracy as 'total' freedom, the emergence of dissidence was not predetermined by enlightened individuals who espoused systemic alternatives such as liberal democracy or market capitalism but was forged in performative dramatic action. A comparison between the death of Tito in spring of 1980 and the rise of Solidarność in the summer of 1980 indicates the dramatic conjuncture that would foster the unity of the nation in Poland and accelerate the fragmentation of the Yugoslav federation. While Poland was ethnically the most homogeneous country in the Eastern bloc, Yugoslavia was a multi-ethnic federation composed of six federal regions, one of which (Serbia) contained two autonomous provinces (Vojvodina and Kosovo) as of 1974. Moreover, the establishment of communist rule in each country had followed two entirely different paths. Not only were Polish–Russian relations historically very conflict-ridden, but also the war in 1920 and the non-aggression pact between Germany and the Soviet Union in August 1939, with the ensuing occupation of eastern Poland by Soviet forces, had already presaged Stalin's post-war Soviet policy. Aiming for a completely dependent communist party-regime in a country that had been exhausted by a particularly devastating occupation, Stalin neither supported the Warsaw uprising nor did he want simply a friendly government in Poland as he used to declare. The imposition of Soviet rule in Poland allowed for hardly any manifestation of national independence or self-affirmation.

Conversely, the seeds of dissidence in the communist bloc can be seen in the wide-reaching political impact of the split between Stalin and Tito, when Yugoslavia was excluded from the Cominform in 1948. Under the impression of the emerging totalitarian paradigm, many Western observers judged Tito's conflict with Stalin as a sign of emerging political pluralism in Yugoslavia and Stalin's reaction as an act of aggression against Tito. However, this was to underestimate the degree to which Tito's administrative centralisation, the monopolisation of party leadership, and the domestic form of revolutionary terror had been very Stalinist in nature.[48] The strong presence of pro-Stalin Cominformists

---

[47] Maria Todorova, 'Improbable Maverick or Typical Conformist? Seven Thoughts on the New Bulgaria', in Ivo Banac, ed., *Eastern Europe in Revolution* (Ithaca and London: Cornell University Press, 1992), 161.

[48] Ivo Banac, *With Stalin Against Tito: Cominformist Splits in Yugoslav Communism* (Ithaca and London: Cornell University Press, 1988), 257.

in Yugoslavia was also a sign of Serbian resistance against Tito's leader-ship. As this first case of 'national communism' suggests, dissidence relied upon a sense of patriotism and the concern for balancing power relations between different nationalities by reinforcing Stalinism as an image of the 'enemy outside'.

Tito's death not only left a void of political authority but also symbol-ised the loss of meaning of the post-war Yugoslav order. Shortly after his death on 4 May 1980, a funeral ritual was arranged that was intended to guarantee the transferral of symbolic power from Tito's dead body to the symbol of the Yugoslav flag.[49] This funeral was significant in so far as it externalised the great emotion in large parts of the population.[50] Yet such emotions also allowed rival memories about the civil war between 1941 and 1945 to resurface. The Balkans had been the stage of a recurrent tragic 'play' of minorities and majorities, of victims and perpetrators. The roles of minority and majority were reshuffled anew in endless combina-tions and coalitions, creating an atmosphere of insecurity in which every-body could become a victim. During the ceremonies, many national, not Yugoslav, folksongs were sung, while too many wreaths carried inscrip-tions that read 'Croatian' or 'Serbian' and not 'Yugoslav'. The issue of the flag, however, seems crucial. The efforts to substitute the Yugoslav flag for Tito's body as the symbol of continuity backfired. Rather than divorce the physical from the symbolical body, the two were not only in proximity but in direct contact. On the coffin's last journey, with the Yugoslav flag draped over it, tens of thousands at the funeral and millions of television spectators had the impression that it was not a body but the Yugoslav flag as the symbol of the country that was slowly going towards its tomb. Tito's funeral as a symbolic event strongly weakened the internationalist mythology embodied by Tito and reinforced the latent resurgence of nationalist aspirations.

Solidarność in Poland generated a mentality of eschatological relativ-ism that did not refer to the current state or present-day concerns but anticipated a condition of full freedom. It connected the spiritual revival of individuals and their self-realisation with romantic myths of a collective revival of the nation, identical with the recovery of independence and, consequently, with the reconstruction of society.[51] The intensity of

---

[49] Maja Brkljacic, 'A Case of a Very Difficult Transition: The Ritual of the Funeral of Josip Broz Tito', *Limen* No.1, http://limen.mmc.hr/limen1-2001/maja_brkljacic.html, 1–7.
[50] It is reported that from Kragujevac – a middle-sized city in Serbia which experienced a Nazi pogrom in the Second World War – alone an estimated 120,000 letters arrived which were sent to Ljubljana (Brkljacic, 'A Case of a Very Difficult Transition', 2).
[51] Sergiusz Kowalski, *Krytyka solidarnosciowego rozumu* (Warsaw: Wydawnictwo PEN, 1990), 76.

emotions in the months between August 1980 and December 1981 translated into the generation of new symbols. The primary symbol created in the Polish summer of 1980 was the red slogan 'Solidarność'. The spirit of Poland's self-limiting revolution in 1980 and 1981 was not 'How can the system of power be reformed?', but 'How can one defend oneself from the system?'[52] This convergence of Polish society against and outside the communist state came down to breaching the humiliation imposed by communist rule.

The proclamation of martial law in December 1981 reinforced the perception of victimhood and humiliation, as society was turned again into an object of power politics. Although organisationally bruised and illegal after 1981, Solidarność maintained an overwhelming symbolic presence in terms of flags, slogans, plaques, and flower crosses which maintained the memory of suffering and promised the expected resurrection of the trade union. Despite martial law and the imprisonment of its leadership, Solidarność as a 'monolithic collective subject'[53] was maintained through individual life-conduct on a social scale, which was committed to pursuing the meanings and aspirations of the trade union movement.

The we-image of Solidarność as a collective subject survived the period of martial law because it was preserved through the individual I-images of the leaders of Solidarność and the Polish people. Despite being held accountable for the bad economic situation, Solidarność continued to enjoy a high moral reputation, which was maintained through regular decentralised gatherings in the multiplicity of secret communities in the hidden sphere, under the shelter of the Catholic Church. Although Polish society was largely demobilised in early 1989, the symbols of Solidarność were decisive for bringing about the round-table negotiations. As a *communitas* experience, these talks reversed the antagonism between 'us' and 'them' that was so vital for the emergence of Solidarność in 1980.

As the previous discussion has shown, dissidence was not coterminous with national revolutions. The constitution of subjectivity was not simply about replacing communist ideology with national symbols or the rhetoric of Western democracy. In East Germany, for instance, an elaborate set of anti-fascist mythologies could not make up for the country's lack of a national identity. The formalisation of national Stalinism in Romania was a complex process where political opportunities merged with cultural specificities. State power in Romania united Bolshevik practices with an

---

[52] Quoted in Harald Wydra, *Continuities in Poland's Permanent Transition* (Basingstoke: Macmillan, 2001), 34.
[53] This term was coined by Jerzy Szacki.

already existing state-centred nationalism and a strongly bureaucratised state. Based on an increased concentration of national values and symbols, the monolithic party-state produced a monolithic nation.[54] The initially marginalised communist party had relied, perhaps more than any other party, on Stalinist help in its Bolshevisation and in assuming power.[55] The result was a monolithic bureaucratic nationalism, where manifestations of national sentiments against Soviet communism would be absorbed in the specifically Romanian form of Marxism-Leninism. While the new Soviet leadership tolerated and promoted new directions in the politics of its satellites, Romania embarked upon National Stalinism, culminating in the political trial of Lucreţiu Pătrăşcanu in 1954. Severely confused, traumatised, and outraged after the Twentieth Congress of the CPSU, the Romanian communist leaders reacted with deep distrust towards Khrushchev. The low degree of resistance to the Ceauşescu regime during the communist period was largely due to the fact that the regime successfully integrated national identity into the very foundation of communist rule.

Although the social transformations after 1953 increased levels of education, changed patterns of social mobility, and led to growing urbanisation and thus transformed modest cleavages under Stalin into substantial ones in the early 1980s, the magnitude of value changes should not cause us to underestimate the thrust for reform even in the late Stalin years.[56] In the Soviet Union, the desire for change in this period was not dissimilar to that at the end of the Brezhnev era. Similarly, the reconstruction of the cult of the Great Fatherland War was a ritualised symbol of national pride during the time of stagnation.[57] Simultaneously, from 1956 onwards a transformation in the communicative context – although vague, limited, or contradictory – took place, which was mediated by the focus on democracy and socialist legality as virtues to be recaptured in their proposed return to 'Leninist principles'.[58]

Soviet dissent had a tragic history, as it remained scattered and its immediate demands were frustrated, whereas the Poles could claim that

---

[54] Katherine Verdery, *National Ideology Under Socialism: Identity and Cultural Politics in Ceausescu's Romania* (Berkeley: University of California Press, 1991), 314–15.
[55] Vladimir Tismaneanu, *Stalinism for All Seasons: A Political History of Romanian Communism* (Berkeley: University of California Press, 2003), 144.
[56] Donna Bahry, 'Society Transformed? Rethinking the Social Roots of Perestroika', *Slavic Review*, 52, 3 (1993), 512–54.
[57] Nina Tumarkin, *The Living and the Dead: The Rise and Fall of the Cult of World War II in Russia* (New York: Basic Books, 1994), 133.
[58] Urban et al., *The Rebirth of Politics in Russia*, 36.

dissidence was the normality rather than the exception.[59] Apart from the early ideologically motivated dissidence of party leaders fallen into disgrace such as Trotsky, poets and writers such as Osip Mandelstam, Isaak Babel, and Anna Akhmatova but also Mikhail Bulgakov and Boris Pasternak remained consistent voices of liberty, often calculating the risk of being deported or killed. In Mandelstam's words, poetry is respected only in Russia, as there is no other place where more people are killed for it.[60] Bolsheviks such as Bukharin warned Stalin that poets are always right because history is on their side.[61] Rare attempts at speaking the truth during the Great Terror occurred even in the regional top hierarchy. At a meeting of the Central Committee in October 1937, the first secretary of the Kursk regional committee of the communist party, Peskarev, criticised in the presence of Stalin the condemnation of some 87,000 innocent people within three years on the grounds of unlawful acts.[62]

The extermination of a large part of the peasantry and intellectual elite in Ukraine entailed the division of each individual's personality because, although the struggle had to be waged in the outer world, it also 'destroyed the human soul'.[63] Similarly, communist practices of discipline and surveillance provoked a peculiar game of self-stigmatisation, where individuals would respond to pressure by dissimulation and self-censorship. Testimony from show trials in eastern Europe such as in Brno in 1952 suggested the experience of the 'doubling of the self'.[64] While the post-totalitarian system renounced Stalin's terror, the new trend towards socialist legality maintained the principle of identification of the enemy as the authorities replaced strategies of despotism with those of penetration. The creation of spaces of freedom made life and choices about existence easier but also blurred the distinction between compromises that had to be accepted.[65] Ideologically, the original source of political discourse

[59] Ludmilla Alexeyeva, *Soviet Dissent: Contemporary Movements for National, Religious, and Human Rights* (Middletown, CT: Wesleyan University Press, 1987), 449; Jacek Kuroń and Jacek Żakowski, *PRL dla początkujących* (Wrocław: Wydawnictwo dolnośląskie, 1995), 147.

[60] Nadezhda Mandelstam, *Hope Against Hope: A Memoir* (New York: Atheneum, 1970), 159.

[61] Vitaly Shentalinsky, *The KGB's Literary Archive* (London: Harvill Press, 1997), 183.

[62] Peskarev was arrested in September 1938 and shot in March 1939; see *Izvestiya*, 8 February 2001, 9.

[63] Jurij Lawrynenko, 'The Literature of Borderline Situations', in Tyrmand, *Kultura Essays*, 198–210.

[64] Karel Bartosek, 'Europe centrale et du Sud-Est', in Stéphane Courtois et al., eds., *Le livre noir du communisme* (Paris: Robert Laffont, 1997), 448.

[65] Agnes Horváth and Arpad Szakolczai, *The Dissolution of Communist Power: The Case of Hungary* (London: Routledge, 1992), 217.

dissenting from the correct line was not based on a theoretical model of a class of intellectuals or an underlying 'civil society'. Rather, it was articulated in the frame of the dominant state ideology, Marxism. Marxism was not only dominant as the official state ideology but, as a radical critique, also became the only possible language in which to articulate critical intellectual discourse. This combination entailed the paradoxical consequence that, to be considered seriously, reform attempts had to be formulated in a Marxist idiom. In this logic, Stalinism appeared as a distortion of the 'good' Lenin and the 'modest' Marx. Only a few others – such as Leszek Kołakowski in Poland or Milovan Djilas in Yugoslavia – succeeded in shaping their dissent in terms of a 'creative Marxism', which would be lucid about Marxism's ideological shortcomings.[66]

The restructuring of Soviet society intensified the ritualisation of political life as well as the consolidation of practices of social control.[67] Although concrete daily repression in the Soviet Union subsided after the 1950s, the KGB remained a major symbol of intimidation and terror with a considerable impact on social control.[68] The post-Stalin era brought about a further dissimulative split in the behaviour of typical Soviet citizens, making the switching of faces a ritualised skill. One could sit at a Komsomol meeting and raise one's arm in a ritualised vote without reflection, while being immersed in reading Alexander Solzhenitsyn.[69] This is why the most lasting and dangerous impact of communism is to be expected at the level of the depth of personality.[70] Although one might argue that quite soon a new generation of individuals will come into politics with no personal experience of the Soviet regime, the momentous task is one of a social and cultural dimension. Dissimulation became a major mechanism for people in Soviet-type states, who had to cope with the pressure of an omnipresent party-state on private and social life. Dissimulation became a strategy for interaction with the regime, aiming to respond to fear and subordination but also to develop spaces for privacy. The sphere of Soviet privacy originated in dissimulation, unlike its counterpart in the West. Therefore, the meaning of statements that use the phrase *chastnaia zhizn* (a rough equivalent of

[66] Milovan Djilas, *Fall of the New Class: A History of Communism's Self-Destruction* (New York: Alfred A. Knopf, 1998), 260.
[67] Oleg Kharkhordin, *The Collective and the Individual in Russia: A Study of Practices* (Berkeley: University of California Press, 1999), 279–82.
[68] Donna Bahry and Brian Silver, 'Intimidation and the Symbolic Uses of Terror in the USSR', *American Political Science Review*, 81, 4 (1987), 1067.
[69] Kharkhordin, *The Collective and the Individual*, 278.
[70] Horváth and Szakolczai, *The Dissolution of Communist Power*, 217.

180

'private life' in English) in Russian may be radically different from those in English or French.[71]

The key role of Marxism as a language of regime criticism made radical dissent within the political arena almost impossible. The dividing line in communist societies ran not between state and society but right through individual subjects who practised dissimulation, self-stigmatisation, and self-censorship. While the ritualisation of life under communism replaced open resistance with informal networks, subcultures, and friendships, it also promoted acquiescence and the silent complicity of regime critics with the official externality. Inclusion and exclusion denoted specific techniques applied by communist authorities in order to sanction non-compliance, or to achieve compliance and support legitimacy.[72] The practices of dissimulation and the strong interpenetration of communist party logic made intellectuals barely distinct from the state bureaucracy.

Western perceptions of resistance to communism oscillated between open fascination and disbelief. They exalted the resistance movements in the revolutionary upheavals for their courage but also criticised them for their politically naïve stance and the absence of a clear political programme for an alternative to communist power. The deliberate choice to withdraw from politics and not to seek political opportunities would keep dissident literature more charming than politically efficient and make of 'civil society' a 'private society'. Its ethical individualism failed to propose an alternative political model and to rally scattered individuals around a forceful idea for political reform.[73]

Dissidence was a way of circumventing the strategy applied by communist authorities. Going beyond a stereotypical distinction between 'us' and 'them', the important step was to recognise that dissident intellectuals themselves had assimilated behaviour patterns and attitudes they identified in the communists. Dissidents excluded themselves from the process of carrots and sticks in order to achieve the integration of subjectivity, personality, and human dignity. Dissidence implied detachment and extrication from oppression with a view to totalising tendencies in any area of human activity. At the same time, however, the discourse of 'ethical civil society' was not a hermetically isolated self-referential discourse in a 'society against the state' scenario. Rather, it was nurtured by the idea of the self-constitution of subjects on the basis of constitutive

[71] Kharkhordin, The Collective and the Individual, 357–8.
[72] Ken Jowitt, 'An Organizational Approach to the Study of Political Culture in Marxist-Leninist Systems', American Political Science Review, 68, 3 (1974), 1183–4.
[73] G. M. Tamás, 'The Legacy of Dissent', in Vladimir Tismaneanu, ed., The Revolutions of 1989 (London and New York: Routledge, 1999), 196–7.

principles that were beyond the immanence of the world of really existing socialism.[74] The revolutionary Polish Solidarność movement, for instance, was guided by a deliberate non-engagement in political reform, aiming instead at the subjectivisation (*podmiotowość*) of Polish society. In the economically more 'liberal' Hungary, dissidents did not want to reform the system politically but responded to an existential threat with a 'total' existential strategy. In the words of György Konrád, the Hungarian writer and dissident, the relationship between anti-politics and politics corresponded to that between two mountains. The absolute detachment between these two spheres would continue even if sympathetic individuals or friends were to form a new government.[75] In Havel's definition, 'living within the lie can constitute the system only if it is universal. The principle must embrace and permeate everything. There are no terms whatsoever on which it can coexist with living within the truth, and therefore everyone who steps out of line denies it in principle and threatens it in its entirety.'[76]

The power of the powerless

The suppression of the revolutions in 1956, in 1968, and in 1981 showed the impossibility of altering the Yalta system from inside east central Europe by means of dynamic, uncontrolled mass movements.[77] In György Konrád's view, the re-establishment of freedom required the moral force of an ethics of non-violence that could overcome this power only if it renounced any arrangement with it, i.e. also dispensed with the physical guarantees of power.[78] The particular strength of east Europeans consisted in handling internal paradoxes more flexibly, in taking pleasure in diversity, in knowing how to convert differences into creative tension, and in understanding and loving other cultures. The new way of life envisaged by the ethics of non-violence was not drawn by a beautiful alternative political model but generated from the socially experienced existential tension of coping with the constant assault on the basics of human coexistence.

The continuous humiliation and the tediousness of daily life could be overcome only by developing a dignified and meaningful life-conduct in the second, 'hidden sphere'. Dissidence implied a choice of an option alternative to the ritualised distortion of reality practices imposed by

[74] Jeffrey C. Isaac, *Democracy in Dark Times* (Ithaca and London: Cornell University Press, 1998).
[75] Konrád, *Antipolitics*, 231.   [76] Havel, 'The Power of the Powerless', 40.
[77] Konrád, *Antipolitics*, 70.   [78] Konrád, *Antipolitics*, 92–113.

communism. 'Under the orderly surface of the life of lies ... there slumbers the hidden sphere of life in its real aims ... The singular, explosive, incalculable political power of living within the truth resides in the fact that living openly within the truth has an ally, invisible to be sure, but omnipresent: this hidden sphere.'[79] Yet, the hidden sphere as a spiritual area for the constitution of subjectivity did not originate from an innate tendency towards informality but had its roots in a particularly severe social control such as in Czechoslovakia. Havel's truth-teller is there to disclose the central feature of communism, which was to deny existing reality and to trade the imaginary for the real. If a greengrocer hangs a sign in his shop window calling for the workers of the world to unite, the meaning of the action is ritualistic. The greengrocer shows through his slogan that he adheres to the rules of the system out of fear, showing the illusion of an identity.

Dissidence was not systemic 'democratic opposition', where a well-defined group or class in society would pursue well-established policy goals.[80] It was an existential option for detachment from practices of Soviet power, which aimed to disclose the confusion of power, the humiliation of human beings, and the atomisation of social life. According to Václav Havel, even the most beautiful alternative political model could not inspire political instincts. Rather, the real sphere of potential politics in the post-totalitarian system was in the 'continuing and cruel tension between the complex demands of that system and the aims of life, that is, the elementary need of human beings to live, to a certain extent at least, in harmony with themselves, that is, to live in a bearable way, not to be humiliated by the superiors and officials, not to be continually watched by the police, to be able to express themselves freely, to find an outlet for their creativity, to enjoy legal security, and so on.'[81]

The bureaucratic repression had not only shown that the emperor had no clothes but also made clear that the true endeavour to be accomplished was a life in truth, an attempt to save the dignity and identity of the subject in the absurd world of post-totalitarianism. The articulation of dissidence, therefore, must not be mistaken for a political culture of accommodation based on an inherent rationality with a view to the outcome of 'liberal democracy'. One must not confuse the undoubtedly influential image of democracy as an urgent hope that permeated politics of dissidence with the yardstick of liberal democracy as an institutionalised logic.

[79] Havel, 'The Power of the Powerless', 57.
[80] Aviezer Tucker, *The Philosophy and Politics of Czech Dissidence from Patocka to Havel* (Pittsburgh: University of Pittsburgh Press, 2000), 115–17.
[81] Havel, 'The Power of the Powerless', 51–2.

In a similar vein, the opposition between state and 'civil society' does not seem entirely appropriate. The social significance of dissidence does not rest upon the numbers of people involved. In the categories of an open political system, the confrontation between 1,000 Chartists dedicated to life in truth and the impressive Soviet military machine would have appeared hopeless politically. In the situation of the existential resistance in the post-totalitarian system, this confrontation appears in a fundamentally different light.[82]

Dissidence should be seen primarily as an existential answer of denouncing the violent nature of the existing system. The 'power of the powerless' was not an ideology, even less a utopia, but a form of life-conduct detached from the official sphere and relying upon informal networks of emotional community that remained relatively resistant to communist manipulation. In the phase of late communism, dissidence became synonymous with groups of persons forming pockets of society that actively or passively resisted communist rules. Dissidence embodied an attempt at existential representation of the people without the claim to represent them in a system of constituted power. In terms of 'method', it is a movement of detachment from the workings and the rationale of a political reality that permeates all spheres of public and private life. Dissidence modelled political reality in so far as it promoted a new consciousness with the goal of moral regeneration, claiming to create a new way of life.

The 'return to Europe' was undoubtedly one of the central symbolic markers of the *annus mirabilis* 1989. The penetration of images of Western modes of life and values and their acceptance in eastern Europe played an important role in disengaging citizens from the contagion of communist symbolism. The long-term habit in many countries of seeing themselves not in the category of eastern Europe but in that of the West was reinforced by the availability of commodities and the recognition of anything from the West as infinitely better than something from the East. Yet the feeling of being abandoned by the West gave rise to symbolisations of cultural spaces. Reflecting a long-standing tradition of self-inclusion in the Western type of civilisation, Milan Kundera claimed in 1984 that central Europe as a cultural space had been kidnapped by the barbaric and uncivilised Russian East.[83] Thus, the symbolism of the West was not simply a value equivalent to liberal democracy or market capitalism. Quite the opposite: Western life-styles come also to be of pragmatic

---

[82] Havel, 'The Power of the Powerless', 44.
[83] Milan Kundera, 'The Tragedy of Central Europe', *New York Review of Books*, 26 April 1984.

significance not only for regime critics but also for communist authorities attempting to restore their own legitimacy. The millions of Yugoslavs who went abroad in the 1970s, 1980s, and 1990s were not economic or political emigrants but instead simply wanted to spend their money there.[84] For many Poles, the real moments of freedom dated back to Gierek's economic miracle on credits, when a short-term consumer boom in the early 1970s brought many commodities from the West into the country and partly free travel became available. This influx of Western goods led dissidents to feel that the communists had effectively bought the Poles.

A critic might well argue against the political relevance of dissidence, as it was not directed at political reform, let alone revolution. According to Albert Hirschman's well-known paradigm of exit and voice, realistic options for physical exit from a system of organisation such as a state reduce the articulation of voice. From this perspective, the year 1989 in the German Democratic Republic saw a fruitful synergy between exit and voice.[85] The failure to voice political reforms in 1956, in 1968, or in the cycles of crises in Poland's permanent revolution altered the character of the original option. Dissidence presupposed renouncing physical exit but demanded that one combine voice with spiritual exit from society. In other words, it voiced exit as an existential choice to abandon the tangled web of communist social order through individual life-conduct and defiance at the personal level. Rather than formulating alternatives in abstract terms of an antagonism between Western liberalism and collectivist communism, the politics of anti-politics was an existential response to life realities and power structures in specific countries. By separating 'us' from 'them', the actors of anti-politics did not seek to prescribe their ideology for the purpose of political reform but claimed a self-conscious exclusion from the moral corruption of communism. During the 1960s and 1970s, the number of non-conformist associations and dissident groups increased considerably, opening up spaces of liberty from state authorities in some areas of individual, social, and cultural life. The dynamic growth of dissident movements materialised in counter-publics, 'second' economies, or 'second' societies.[86] If the foundation of communist power was based on the surveillance of the individual by the collective, overcoming this double bind meant to exclude oneself from the collective.

---

[84] Slavenka Drakulić, *Café Europa* (London: Abacus, 1996), 16.
[85] Albert O. Hirschman, 'Exit, Voice, and the Fate of the German Democratic Republic: An Essay in Conceptual History', *World Politics*, 45 (1993), 173–202.
[86] Gordon Skilling, *Samizdat and an Independent Society in Central and Eastern Europe* (Columbus: Ohio State University Press, 1989).

While the presence of Soviet military power stifled the voice of dissidence, this very military power and its violence were at the roots of non-violent strategies. Gorbachev's commitment to non-violence (*nye streliat*) was not simply the guiding idea of a policy of non-intervention by the Soviet Union, but had its very social foundations in the lessons of de-Stalinisation and the violent invasions of Hungary and Czechoslovakia.

If the articulation of voice is limited to the public arena, one under-emphasises the role of the hidden sphere for inspiring changes in life-conduct. Although people were deprived of a public arena for political voice, nevertheless the power of voice was articulated through infra-politics in the hidden sphere. As James Scott has suggested, politics is not just about openly declared dominance and revolt, but also about the 'disguised, low-profile, undeclared' resistance of subordinate groups.[87] Between quiescence and revolt, there is a complex reality of infrapolitics, i.e. negotiations and interplay between the public and the hidden tran-script.[88] The public transcript reflects existing relations between domi-nant elites and subordinates. Out of prudence or fear, the latter's public performance will usually be – with rare exceptions – aimed at complying with the expectations of the powerful. The hidden transcript, by contrast, consists of speeches, gestures, and practices that occur offstage and defy the consensus of existing power relations established in the public tran-script, thus contradicting or inflecting it. Produced for a different audi-ence and under different constraints of power from the public transcript, the hidden transcript assumes the form of political struggle when frontal assaults are impossible or highly unlikely to succeed. From this perspec-tive, it seems more accurate to see the realities of power not as straightfor-ward division between state and society, between the powerful and the subordinate, but rather to acknowledge a tension between compliance and the potential of acts of resistance. Thus, the deference and consent to domination may only be a preliminary form of subversion. Breaking the silence by the publication of a hidden transcript is not only a psycholog-ical release for the one who speaks on behalf of others; it is also a moment of political electricity.

The compulsory emigration of Solzhenitsyn, for instance, was not due to this power position but rested on his writings that were a 'dreadful well-spring of truth' with the risk of 'incalculable transformations in social consciousness', which in turn might one day produce political debacles

[87] James Scott, *Domination and the Art of Resistance* (New Haven and London: Yale University Press, 1990), 198–9.
[88] Scott, *Domination and the Art of Resistance*, 2–5.

unpredictable in their consequences.[89] What the Soviet authorities feared was the potentially explosive situation if the hidden transcripts became public. Since the authorised publication of *One Day in the Life of Ivan Denisovich* in 1962 as a way of discrediting the Stalin era, Solzhenitsyn's daring and clairvoyant criticism of the wretched history and inherent instability of the Soviet system had been supported by hundreds of letters, a fact that was important in drafting the manuscript of *The Gulag Archipelago*.[90] After the manuscript had been smuggled to the West, the Politburo recognised the potentially subversive and politically dangerous dimensions even outside the Soviet Union and decided to deport him from the country without his consent. Similarly, Havel's essay 'The Power of the Powerless' was not a treatise destined to gather dust, but had considerable impact on activists in other countries, making it politically more significant in Poland than in Czechoslovakia. For Zbigniew Bujak, later a prominent Solidarność activist, the ultimate victories of Solidarność and of Charter 77 were an astonishing fulfilment of the prophecies and knowledge contained in Havel's essay, which reached Polish workers in the Ursus factory in 1979 at a point when they felt they were at the end of the road. 'Reading it gave us the theoretical underpinnings for our activity. It maintained our spirits; we did not give up, and a year later, in August 1980 – it became clear that the party apparatus and the factory management were afraid of us. We mattered. And the rank and file saw us as leaders of the movement.'[91]

The option for a peaceful resistance even in countries such as Czechoslovakia or the Soviet Union must have seemed utopian or hopelessly irrational. The demands of Solidarność in August 1980 must have seemed absurd when judged with knowledge of the bloody suppression of the workers' revolt in Gdańsk in late 1970. A 'realist' perspective would assume that non-violence is a strategy doomed to failure because it would not threaten a system firmly rooted in repressive terror, military power, and political ruthlessness. Yet, whereas Stalin's rationale could be summarised in his question about how many divisions the pope had, its logic of totalising power prompted non-violent resistance as a 'rational' response. Non-violence was not based on autonomous preferences but was a symbol in its own right, generated in the experiences of humiliation, despair, and powerlessness. The communities of fate that had endured,

[89] Havel, 'The Power of the Powerless', 42.
[90] David Remnick, *Resurrection: The Struggle for a New Russia* (New York: Random House, 1997), 116–19.
[91] Quoted in Abbot Gleason, *Totalitarianism: The Inner History of the Cold War* (Oxford: Oxford University Press, 1995), 187–8.

however, would face a diminished and corrupted communist power with an attitude that had gained strength from the challenges; they felt empowered to face the future undaunted.

The moral perfectionism of ethical individualism was criticised as a retreat into the private realm, allied with irresponsibility to the social cause. Yet dissidence appeared in different forms dependent on the shape and penetration of society by communist power. While under Husak's normalisation regime individual moral codes prevailed over more socially oriented 'collective' ideas of a parallel polis, in Poland the strongly political meaning of society (*społeczeństwo*) made the socially inclusive idea of the nation the focus of dissidence. Alexander Solzhenitsyn was writing from a religious and Slavophile perspective when he exposed the cruelties of systematic terror and the gulag concentration camps, while the eminent scientist and human rights activist Andrei Sakharov became the symbol of a more secular and Westernising critique of the Soviet system.[92]

Russian dissidence was heralded by some figures who constituted the modern equivalent of the truth-telling holy fool. The Russian word for truth has the double meaning of both scientific verity (*pravda-istina*) and moral justice (*pravda-spravedlivost*). Dmitri Likhachev was an outstanding and less well known *pravednik* (truth-teller) who emerged in the mid-1980s when he became a part-time tutor on Russian cultural history to Gorbachev and his wife Raisa. As a survivor of the gulag on Solovetsky island, his suffering gave him moral authority, which he invested in advocating the comprehensive recovery of the Russian cultural heritage and opening up to the outside world. His urge to speak the truth to power was obvious in his prominent role in the fight against the putsch of August 1991 as well as in his critique of Yeltsin's war in Chechnya or in his appeal to the Russian Orthodox Church to publicly acknowledge its complicity with Soviet repression. Throughout the Soviet period, the face of a truth-seeker was often hidden, as in a *matryoshka*, inside the outer face of power that pursued presumably objective, scientific truth in the name of communist propaganda.

Ethical individualism as a search for meaning in metaphysical truth did not 'cause' the collapse of communism. Dissident thought and action attacked the dehumanising basis of Soviet power not primarily on the grounds of an innate moral urgency based on democratic individualism or the rational insight in the universality of human dignity. Rather, this self-declared anti-political defensive movement was highly political, as it aimed to reconstitute the basics of genuine human life, searching for a

---

[92] James Billington, *Russia in Search of Itself* (Washington, DC: Woodrow Wilson Center, 2004), 60–5.

ground upon which to build a meaningful existence. The vision of a Soviet bloc that would release those under its domination underemphasises the truly political character of dissidence, which aimed to engage the public in a display of civic spirit. Rejecting the Jacobin–Bolshevik insurrectionist version of revolution, the articulation of dissidence and subjectivisation of society can be seen as a civilising effort characterised by an engaged citizenry.[93] If communist rule was the existentially wholesale invasion of the individual, the first and fundamental answer had to be existential and individual as well. If the attack on the basis of human life and dignity is total, then the reconstruction of life, dignity, and ethics must be total as well.

To base a strategy of resistance against a powerful state apparatus on the subjectivity of pursuing a truthful life was a risky enterprise. This deliberate totality of the existential option to combat communism in the 'hidden' sphere was going against one's own self-interest. The immense investment of time in underground pursuits went at the expense of developing professional careers or benefiting from some liberties such as occasional travel to the West. Many dissidents served long prison sentences, had to work in menial jobs, and/or were exposed to public denigration and abuse in the official media. Most of all, there was pervasive uncertainty about the possible absurdity of one's own resistance with no guarantee whatsoever about a possible 'success'. The complete unpredictability of 'success' in terms of specific political changes, however, is part of the existential solution of living within the truth. Firmly grounded in their own identity, some people consider it worth risking the game of change where the stakes are all or nothing.[94] Its logic was not sacrificial but rather self-sacrificial. Communicative interaction and performative symbolism uncovered the sacrificial 'inhuman' logic of the collective symbolism of communism. Although communism was perceived as the 'enemy', the aim was not the enemy's annihilation but the creation of a way of living that would set an example for others to follow.

[93] Barbara Falk, *The Dilemmas of Dissidence in East-Central Europe: Citizen Intellectuals and Philosopher Kings* (Budapest: Central European University Press, 2003).
[94] Havel, 'The Power of the Powerless', 44.

8   The collapse of communism

Among democratic nations, men easily attain a certain equality of conditions: they can never attain the equality they desire. It perpetually retires from before them, yet without hiding itself from their sight, and in retiring draws them on.
                                                        Alexis de Tocqueville

Between past and future

The collapse of communism was so surprising and consequential that it made a profound impression even on the critical observer. Cautious predictions about a potential collapse of the Soviet Union forecast not a sudden and complete disintegration of the country, but a stable pattern of decay.[1] The Cold War was so deeply rooted in the life-worlds of contemporaries that it is difficult to resist the impression that 1989 was a decisive rupture point. For some, the end of communism was tantamount to the event that marked the 'end of the short twentieth century', if not 'the end of history'.[2] For others, Soviet communism arguably could be qualified as a historical chapter with a clearly definable beginning, a 'middle', and an end.[3] Unlike what the French Revolution or Napoleon's empire bequeathed to posterity in terms of symbols, institutions, ideas, and memories, however, the Soviet empire's collapse left nothing behind but a *tabula rasa*, as its principles, codes, institutions, and history became superseded.[4]

---

[1] Ken Jowitt, 'The New World Disorder', in Larry Diamond and Marc Plattner, eds., *The Global Resurgence of Democracy* (Baltimore and London: Johns Hopkins University Press, 1996), 26–35.

[2] Eric Hobsbawm, *The Age of Extremes: A History of the World, 1914–1991* (London: Vintage, 1996); Francis Fukuyama, *The End of History and the Last Man* (New York: Avon, 1993).

[3] Martin Malia, *The Soviet Tragedy: A History of Socialism in Russia, 1917–1991* (New York: Free Press, 1991).

[4] François Furet, *The Passing of an Illusion* (Chicago and London: University of Chicago Press, 1999).

While there has been serious disagreement about the degree to which political organisation after communism would be influenced by legacies of the past, there has been tacit agreement about analytically disconnecting the old order from the new for two central reasons. Organisationally, the pluralisation of political competition became visible in the existence of multiple parties, free elections, the rule of law, and freedom of the press. The dissolution of communist parties replaced the total claim on power by limiting political authority on the grounds of constitutional guarantees of basic human and civil rights (*glasnost*). Similarly, transformations of economic and property order and the orderly political management of pressing production and distribution problems (*perestroika*) became central. Symbolically, rejecting communism occurred in the tension between retraditionalisation and an uncertain future, in a condition in between past and future. The revolutions of 1989 showed the conspicuous absence of charismatic actors, eschatological recipes, or teleological intentions.[5] No new utopia of progress shone at the horizon of expectation; the overall feeling was of a conservative 'return to normality'. Contrary to the class of 1945 or to the class of 1968, who had a certain set of ideals and a certain vision of society, the class of 1989 is nowhere to be found.[6] Whereas ten years on from 1917 there was already a rich literature on the actors, methods, and motivations of the October Revolution, a decade after 1989 accounts of the events of that year and their aftermath were relatively scarce, often reducing actors to objects of History as a reified actor.[7] In this conspicuous absence of charismatic leaders with an elaborate ideological agenda for future political order, the 'actors' have become historical forces such as 'modernisation', 'democratisation', and 'globalisation'.

A practical consequence of this reification of history was to classify regime transformations according to outcome-logic where the reform period 'from below' would be disconnected from the transformation period 'from above'. Conceptually, the breakdown of the old order was disconnected from the emergence of the new order because behaviour patterns under the rules of communism were not considered to be appropriate to democratic government. With only a minor risk of oversimplification, there have been two approaches. On the one hand, there is the idea that the structural preconditions of authoritarian political culture

---

[5] Shmuel N. Eisenstadt, 'The Breakdown of Communist Regimes', in Vladimir Tismaneanu, ed., *The Revolutions of 1989* (London and New York: Routledge, 1999), 89–107.

[6] Timothy Garton Ash, 'Conclusions', in Sorin Antohi and Vladimir Tismaneanu, eds., *Between Past and Future* (Budapest: Central European University Press, 2000), 402.

[7] Padraic Kenney, 'What Is the History of 1989? New Scholarship from East-Central Europe', *East European Politics and Societies*, 13, 2 (1999), 419–31.

and the lack of democratic experience would constrain the options of successful transitions and consolidations of democracy. This logic of causality has perhaps been most prominent in the paradigm of 'post-communism', which relied on the rejection of the communist past, both in terms of Marxist-Leninist ideology and regarding the political practice in formerly communist countries. The leftovers of communism were compared to a 'kind of desertification' that swept away ideas, values, institutions, solidarities, and people.[8] Beyond its application to the twenty-seven formerly communist countries in Eurasia, in a more 'universal' meaning it also applies to the global post-socialist epoch after 1989/91, thus including not only the countries concerned but everywhere else, reflecting the irruption of uncertainty in the West.[9]

On the other hand, the 'transition-to-democracy' approach focused on elite pacts and democratic dispositions of key actors. While post-communism has largely been a negative concept evaluating the present outcomes of the breakdown of communism by stressing legacies of the past, the transition-to-democracy literature has focused on the institutional choice in the autonomous moment of the political. The concept of transition has suffered from multiple and indiscriminate use because it was seen as an interval, which would be demarcated by an outcome associated with a specific form of liberal democratic government. The labelling of transitions as 'successful', 'halting', or 'failed' has been common. This use of the notion of transition is reasonable as far as it is a descriptive category for the purpose of classifying phases of development. Yet, if transitions are qualified as successful or failed, then their meaning is transformed from a process category of an interval in time into a systemic variable. How can a transition fail, halt, or be considered stable, however, if the very parameters of transitology have defined it as the phase of uncertainty? Moreover, in much of the literature on democratic transition, uncertainty is still regarded as a means to an end. According to a classical formulation, 'the process of establishing a democracy is a process of institutionalising uncertainty, of subjecting all interests to uncertainty'.[10] From such a perspective, uncertainty remains an independent variable to a constitutional form, democracy. If transitions are to be understood in terms of a theory of abnormality, however, can they be 'measured' by the degree of congruity with a developmental goal? One

[8] George Schöpflin, *Politics in Eastern Europe 1945–1992* (Oxford and Cambridge: Blackwell, 1993), 256.
[9] Richard Sakwa, *Postcommunism* (Buckingham: Open University Press, 1999), 125.
[10] Adam Przeworski, 'Problems in the Study of Transition to Democracy', in Guillermo O'Donnell et al., *Transitions from Authoritarian Rule: Comparative Perspective* (Baltimore and London: Johns Hopkins University Press, 1988), 58.

possible reason for this may be that the transition paradigm paid little attention to the experiential basis of history. It has reified 'transition' as an outcome of historical development. The relative success of political democracy in some countries such as Poland, Slovenia, Hungary, or the Baltic countries, for instance, would suggest that mass mobilisation reduced the uncertainty of the transition. It would then be concluded that because uncertainty was lower, the transition in these cases produced a sharp break with the communist past.[11]

Perhaps the most authoritative account of institutional choice in deep uncertainty defined the situation after communism's collapse by three criteria.[12] First, no constituted authority survived the old regime, which left a *tabula rasa* after its demise. Second, there is a lack of crystallised political agency, as the hopes for a strengthened civil society and the applicability of Western models are deceived. Third, structural predispositions and a reasonably unified will to create new centres of authority are missing. In such reasoning, 1989 abruptly throws eastern Europe into a situation void of authority, agency, and normative rules, where non-contingent givens are missing. From this perspective of methodological exceptionalism, individual dispositions of leaders are separated from attitudes and dispositions of collective groups or 'forces from below'. Individual experience is attributed a quality of mere passivity, as the people of state socialist societies had not 'made' the breakdown of the old regime but had just 'experienced' it with the same degree of surprise and amazement as outside observers. Hence, they had remained 'the same' while the institutional shell of their society was crumbling. This vision postulates the coincidence of macro-change with micro-continuity on the individual level, together with a sense of panic, urgency, and uncertainty resulting from the former. Such a distinction between micro-continuity and macro-change limits the impact of social experiences on the transformation of individual cognitive frames.

Following this logic further, the constitution of political authority is located at the level of strategic interaction among elites, more precisely between four separate groups. These are hard-liners and reformers within the regime as well as moderates and radicals in the opposition.[13] This idea of strategic choice and bargaining is couched in a logic of heroism that identifies enlightened elites who act in accordance with systemic

[11] Valerie Bunce, 'Rethinking Recent Democratisation: Lessons from the Postcommunist Experience', *World Politics*, 55, 2 (2003), 188–9.

[12] This paragraph is based on Jon Elster et al., *Institutional Design in Post-Communist Societies* (Cambridge: Cambridge University Press, 1998), 25–6.

[13] Adam Przeworski, *Democracy and the Market* (Cambridge: Cambridge University Press, 1991).

requirements set from outside the domestic context. In other words, the success of 'democratic consolidation' in east central Europe has led scholars to assume the democratic dispositions of key actors. Following this outcome-logic, the deep uncertainty about future political options that surrounded the round-table scenarios in Poland, Hungary, and Bulgaria would not really constitute a threat for democratisers. Some authors then conclude that the unequal distribution of power produced the quickest and most stable transitions from communist rule.[14] In countries where democrats enjoyed a decisive power advantage, democracy emerged. In countries in which dictators maintained a decisive power advantage, dictatorship emerged.

Such elite-focused accounts of transition take non-elites into account only in so far as their potential for protest or rejection may thwart the success of pacts. Because national traditions, records of resistance, and modalities of the breakdown of communism varied from country to country, generalisations require extreme caution. However, it is safe to say that dispositions of actors who decide upon institutional choices in the empty space of power are not disconnected from pressures from below, from the images and memories that symbolise a nation's history, and thus that identify them with past occurrences. Did the breakdown of communism mean the end of the old order and the reconstruction of a new one on the basis of heroic individuals with democratic dispositions? Were the people mere passive onlookers who only experienced it? If communism becomes reified as a 'legacy', how does this square with the overall impression that the revolutions or transitions themselves did not produce new ideas or forms of government? Can one exclude the people's participation in regime changes on the assumption that transitions were negotiated in pacts between elites and politicians, and rarely induced by mass mobilisations? While such questions are immensely difficult to address, a tentative interpretive assessment may be ventured.

The politics of enchantment

The vast literature on transitions and democratisation has shown a clear leaning towards a bifurcation of analysis. Can meanings of democracy prior to the breakdown of communism legitimately be discarded from the thinking about democratisation? Did the processes of de-Stalinisation

---

[14] For instance, see Michael McFaul, 'The Fourth Wave of Democracy and Dictatorship: Noncooperative Transitions in the Postcommunist World', in Michael McFaul and Kathryn Stoner-Weiss, eds., *After the Collapse of Communism* (Cambridge: Cambridge University Press, 2004), 58–95.

and the revolutionary uprisings in eastern Europe contribute nothing to democratisation, only because they were not animated by liberal conceptions of rule of law or a realistic policy orientation? The oblivion to which the east European revolutions before 1989, or Gorbachev's *perestroika*, have been consigned seems to suggest that these socialised aspects of democratic symbolism were not appropriate for a liberal revolution. If the symbols of democracy disintegrated shortly after the collapse of communism, does it mean that they should be excluded from the democratic revolution? This bifurcation of analysis has underemphasised the fact that the dissolution of the symbols of democracy does not mean that they were ineffective in blazing the trail for democracy. Quite the opposite: the unified symbolism was vital for a total resistance against communist power. The processes of overthrowing these symbols were transformative in their own right, and replaced 'old' meanings of democracy with 'new' ones.

From 1989 onwards, not only did communist parties crumble like houses of cards but practically all determining political and social markers of certainty were destroyed, renamed, or sold out. As much as the emergence of communism brought about a new way of life with a new terminology such as 'the dictatorship of the proletariat', the 'vanguard party', the 'correct line', and 'democratic centralism', the politics of enchantment generated a variety of dynamic potentials for the appearance of genuinely new ways of life, epitomised in the aspirations of *glasnost* and *perestroika*. New symbols such as round tables, the velvet revolution, the market, and the return to Europe represented the winds of change, the spring of peoples marching towards liberty. The discourses of democratic consolidation have largely neglected the importance of meanings of democracy for the articulation of political authority. The complex tasks of simultaneous transitions in the political, economic, social, and legal spheres required doing away with the past by disarticulating Leninist legacies. At the level of meaning-formation, however, the experience of the dissolution of communism shaped identifications, beliefs, dispositions, and preferences. It recaptured some of the excitement to start anew, which had characterised the articulation of Bolshevik power in 1917, the establishment of communist rule in eastern Europe after 1945, or the small revolutions in eastern Europe. The liberalisation under *perestroika* and *glasnost* dramatically produced an unprecedented proliferation of symbols and counter-symbols, which undermined the party's monopoly on power, knowledge, and the 'truthful' path for society.

In practically all countries, the pervasive desire to forget about communism was matched by an equally enormous desire to return to different 'pasts' by restoring independent statehood or national identity, or, as in Russia, to resolve the nagging question of whether it should understand itself as an empire or a nation-state. The democratic moment, therefore, not only required the formalisation of political authority as achieved in different political processes between 1989 and 1991, such as round-table negotiations, founding elections, or popular mobilisation and broad coalition alliances. It also included enchanted participation and the search for meaning. Whereas an outcome-logic considers the Hungarian revolution, the Prague spring, Gorbachev's *perestroika*, Solidarność, or Charter 77 as legacies of the old order, the symbolisation of such 'legacies' cannot be frozen in the past. The experiences associated with these symbols are not simply the dead letter of the past but, in existential uncertainty, can have a transformative potential that can determine the choices of people and leaders.

Beyond the determination of leaders or an abstract allegiance to a model of liberal democracy, the catalyst to dialogue was the broad social unrest on dozens of stages. Both in central Europe and in the Soviet Union, people in the late 1980s broke down borders of all kinds, suspending acquired social roles and questioning political hierarchies. Because of the broad impact of grassroots movements, we can speak of a 'carnival of revolution' in eastern Europe or a 'carnival of *perestroika*' in the Soviet Union.[15] The performative power of resistance went beyond the large cities to places such as Międzyrzecz, Teplice, and Nagymaros, and included workers as much as retirees or high school students.[16] The carnivalesque opposition in large parts of eastern Europe preceded Gorbachev's pluralism of opinions by some years. Gorbachev's cultural revolution touched upon almost every field in public and private everyday life and extended the opportunities that had been already seized by boycotts of elections or of sterile party congresses. Although the monopoly of the CPSU was lifted only in 1990, the communicative dynamic released by Gorbachev's reform gave full opportunity to the radical forces of the cultural intelligentsia to go beyond the boundaries set by the party secretary. Where Gorbachev's *glasnost* allowed criticism of Stalin, of corruption inside the communist party, and of censorship, radicals would attack Lenin, the single-party rule as such, or demand absolute commitment to free speech.

It is an irony of history that the arguably two foremost actors of regime change in eastern Europe and Russia, the Polish Solidarność movement

---

[15] Padraic Kenney, *A Carnival of Revolution* (Princeton: Princeton University Press, 2002).
[16] Kenney, *A Carnival of Revolution*, 300–1.

and the general secretary of the CPSU Mikhail Gorbachev, were not intent to debunking communism as an institutional structure. Gorbachev's programme of democratisation had at its core a bid for a renewal of the representative nature of the party. Influenced by a vision of a reformed Soviet socialist society that remained faithful to traditional Marxist socialism and romantic Leninism, but that broke with the dictatorial features of the system, he went well beyond previous doctrinal limits.[17] *Perestroika* was presented as a continuation of earlier efforts of progressive forces within the party back in 1953, 1956, and 1965. Although the disintegration of the Soviet Union occurred at the end of 1991, there is good reason to assume that 1989 was also the cardinal year in the disarticulation of communist power there.[18] In that year, comprehensive political reforms would come into effect that included the introduction of competitive elections for regional soviets and the reorganisation of the party secretariat, which before long would substantially reduce its control over state institutions in the republics. The revival of local soviets by means of contested elections and the establishment of a new all-union body, the Congress of People's Deputies, meant an assault on the monopoly of power and the myth that the party was in possession of knowledge about the correct line. While both Gorbachev and Yeltsin endorsed 'democratisation', the dividing issue was their position on the leading role of the party. At the televised First Congress of People's Deputies on 31 May, Gorbachev defined the CPSU as the guarantor of democracy, whereas Yeltsin characterised the party as the main obstacle to democratisation.[19]

The introduction of new mechanisms of intra-party democracy and, simultaneously, of official electoral accountability was sociologically, not legally, at odds with the fundamental principle of communist power. The reorganisation of the party secretariat introduced labour-intensive party commissions and made the supervisory functions of union-wide party committees practically impossible due to time constraints.[20] The growing number of civic movements and politically oriented associations in late communism practised a very high degree of internal democracy. These movements emphasised non-hierarchical relations, of a

[17] George W. Breslauer, *Gorbachev and Yeltsin as Leaders* (Cambridge: Cambridge University Press, 2002), 63.
[18] Michael Waller, *The End of the Communist Power Monopoly* (Manchester and New York: Manchester University Press, 1993), 234.
[19] Breslauer, *Gorbachev and Yeltsin as Leaders*, 135.
[20] Stephen Kotkin, *Armageddon Averted: The Soviet Collapse 1970–2000* (Oxford: Oxford University Press, 2001), 77.

highly decentralised and participatory character, while political parties
practised community, equality, and non-hierarchy.[21]

Gorbachev's emphasis on a law-based state (*pravovoe gosudarstvo*)
ignored the fact that the true basis of communist power was not in the
constitutionally enshrined regulations but in the permanent control of
state institutions by the party apparatus. While state management and
party apparatus were legally separated, in practice the apparently expert
and 'non-political' bodies of professional managers took the most 'political' of all decisions in the state. There was a virtual overlap between party
and state, as the same group of people on all possible levels of state
administration would meet, with only minor adjustments, first in the
capacity of a party body, then in the capacity of an industrial board.[22]
Soviet-type institutions collapsed not because they were too rigid but
because they were too flexible. *Perestroika* was less a sudden relaxation
of comprehensive control, and more a massive increase in the already
wide discretion of groups and associations at the non-state level.[23] The
new autonomy given to local soviets reinforced claims by national elites
and their bids for political career opportunities. In the strongly ethnicised
framework of Soviet nationality policy, and with increasing economic
problems and public criticism raised against the CPSU, the political
reforms supported state disintegration. While the institutionalisation of
ethnicity as a basis for Soviet nationalism had been a guarantee for the
central role of the communist party in the Soviet Union, the strengthening of the soviets in the republics and the idea of a nascent parliamentar-
ism largely supported ideas of national independent statehood. After
Lithuania and the Russian Republic declared their sovereignty in spring
1990, Gorbachev announced plans for a new union treaty with a view to
safeguarding the statehood of the Soviet Union. While the tides of
nationalist mobilisation in the late Soviet Union were impossible to
imagine in 1985, they became inevitable four years later.[24] In the tidal
waves of state breakdown, the confusion of political leadership and the
uncertainties about the country's identity and future became manifest.
Gorbachev's zigzag policies in 1990 and 1991 included radical shifts to

[21] Steven M. Fish, *Democracy from Scratch* (Stanford: Stanford University Press, 1995), 113–18.
[22] Zygmunt Bauman, 'The Second Generation Socialism', in Leonard Schapiro, ed., *Political Opposition in One-Party States* (London: Macmillan, 1972), 235.
[23] Steven L. Solnick, *Stealing the State: Control and Collapse in Soviet Institutions* (Cambridge, MA, and London: Harvard University Press, 1998), 22–3.
[24] Mark Beissinger, *Nationalist Mobilization and the Collapse of the Soviet State* (Cambridge: Cambridge University Press, 2002).

the left such as the 500-day programme for a transition to the market, which he dropped in mid-September in order to ask for special emergency powers for the sake of saving the integrity of the Soviet Union. In December 1990, Gorbachev responded to a question about whether he was going to the 'right': 'Actually, I'm going round in circles.'[25] In spring 1991, within reach of a new draft of a union treaty with the right to secession, Gorbachev opened direct negotiations with the nine republics still willing to consider a relationship with Moscow. Yet the attachment to the Union was superseded by new forms of enchantment in a rapid process of fragmentation of power, identities, and meanings.

Transitional uncertainty: enemies, cleansing and purity

People are not only citizens of a state or members of a party but also emotional beings, whose lives are affected by existential crises, which in turn, shape their memories, desires, and beliefs. What prevailed in eastern Europe after 1989 was fragmentation, characterising the region as 'brittle'.[26] While individual contexts took different shapes, the revolutions of 1989 were, to a large extent, modelled with binary oppositions, where the separation of 'we' from 'them' or the opposition between good and evil appeared as symbolisations of uncertainty. Politically, the rejection of communism was more of a 'double rejection' rather than the positive adoption of a well-defined alternative. The first rejection concerned the external domination to which non-Soviet members of the formerly communist bloc had been subjected, whereas the second rejection was that of communism as a system of power.[27] This double rejection reflected the centrality of the unified symbolism against the communist enemy as underlying the crisis of legitimacy as the central feature of communism's weakness.[28] The convergence of the delegalised Solidarność and the crisis-ridden communist party at the Polish roundtable in early 1989, for instance, turned the radical separation between 'us' and 'them', so crucial for the Polish self-limiting revolution in 1980 and 1981, into an understanding among 'elites'. This pact, however, was not so much the outcome of articulated strategies. Rather, it was facilitated by a spontaneous community of mutual forgiving and understanding among former enemies under the situational premises of

[25] Kotkin, *Armageddon Averted*, 91–2.
[26] Ken Jowitt, *The New World Disorder* (Berkeley: University of California Press, 1992), 218.
[27] Leslie Holmes, *Post-Communism* (Durham, NC: Duke University Press, 1997), 14.
[28] Leslie Holmes, *The End of Communist Power: Anti-Corruption Campaigns and Legitimation Crisis* (Cambridge and Oxford: Polity Press, 1993).

the negotiations in the Warsaw Magdalenka Palace in early 1989. In this vein, it was highly influenced by the spirit of non-violence of the Polish self-limiting revolution nearly a decade earlier.[29] When the Polish Solidarność opposition unexpectedly won a triumphal victory in the semi-free elections of June 1989, its leaders were completely disconcerted, lacking any strategy, and overwhelmed by the symbolic victory which would bring them power effectively. This is all the more important as the Solidarność opposition was considered the only real, coherent, and viable counter-elite in eastern Europe.

Events in Czechoslovakia followed a different course. In the aftermath of the brutal crackdown by the police on 17 November 1989, the Czechoslovak mass demonstrations essentially symbolised the radical separation of the pure community of 'us' from the dangerous and pollut-ing elements of 'them'. The rhetoric of the velvet revolution maintained popular perceptions of clear-cut categories, helping to establish concepts such as democracy, freedom, humanity, and non-violence as synony-mous for the Czechoslovak people as against the regime.[30]

In Russian politics, a Manichean division of the political world into binary forms of representation came to portray the political conflict in terms of 'us'–'them' distinctions that repeatedly rule out 'them' from the political community.[31] While Marxism-Leninism identified a 'Soviet people' by banishing all enemies of the people to the category 'anti-Soviet', the period of *glasnost* propagated a host of 'democratic' political identities, which soon came to equate 'democratic' with 'anti-communist'. As the political community was polarised over the question of national identity, there was a tendency to preclude a mutual recognition of the particular identities advanced by political subjects. As a conse-quence, political communities such as democrats, advocates of a strong state (*gosudarstvenniki*), patriots, and communists were symbolically mediated. Moreover, the lack of free and open parliamentary elections at the federal level in Russia until the end of 1993 prevented parties from developing identities by means of the articulation of interests and the programmatic focus of political discourse in a competitive political environment. Rather, political subjects remained quite self-referential,

---

[29] See Harald Wydra, *Continuities in Poland's Permanent Transition* (Basingstoke: Macmillan, 2001), 50–4.

[30] James Krapfl, 'The Rhetoric of the Velvet Revolution', *Center for Slavic and East European Studies Newsletter*, 19, 3 (2002), 3–7 and 16–19.

[31] Michael Urban, 'Stages of Political Identity Formation in Late Soviet and Post-Soviet Russia', in Victoria Bonnell, ed., *Identities in Transition: Eastern Europe and Russia After the Collapse of Communism* (Berkeley: University of California, 1996), 147.

and the growing gap between state institutions and society entailed the formation of 'phantom identities'.

The manifold attempts at decommunisation or lustration in different countries have symbolised the need to purify the political scene, expelling people associated with the former communist regime. Although the availability of reliable knowledge in files from the secret service and the intensity of screening, retribution, or disqualification varied widely, the ritual aspect of 'ceremonial purification as a means of removing blood-guiltiness and cleansing a house' has been crucial for breaking the distrust towards many aspects of the public sphere by establishing an enemy group within society.[32]

Economic reforms have been slow in providing social markers of certainty after communism destroyed classes, definite social groups, or political identities. It was in this sense – rather than in the sense of material equality – that communist societies had become 'classless'.[33] After communism, the differences between rich and poor increased rapidly, but they are defined by levels of consumption rather than by social style. Although this weakness of social markers conditions social and political conflict, it is remarkably devoid of class-oriented discourse or clear-cut identities. Those who possess are envied and often loathed. But they are loathed as individuals or as social abstractions – wily *apparatchiki*, *mafiosi*, or cheating businessmen – loathings that are not as easy to politicise as the highly visible and stylised existence of the old aristocracies or gentrified professionals and bureaucrats.

The spell of liberalism as one of the crucial concepts representing an all-encompassing alternative to communism has been subject to confusion, distortion, and disillusionment. Liberalism in post-communist countries has been characterised more by a lack of substantive rationality and images than by knowledge or expertise.[34] The success of political liberalism in post-communist Russia has been substantially hampered by a threefold crisis. Deprived of a normal situation, the development of state–society relations on the basis of the liberal model supported by the middle class and liberal political parties seems to be precluded. Despite the momentous changes in political practice, political legitimacy, and social organisation, there seems to be a pervasive lack of endogenously

---

[32] Natalia Letki, 'Lustration and Democratisation in East-Central Europe', *Europe–Asia Studies*, 54, 4 (2002), 529–52.
[33] Andrew Janos, *East Central Europe in the Modern World: The Politics of the Borderlands from Pre- to Postcommunism* (Stanford: Stanford University Press, 2000), 405.
[34] Jerzy Szacki, *Liberalism After Communism* (Budapest: Central European University Press, 1995); Marcia A. Weigle, 'Political Liberalism in Postcommunist Russia', *Review of Politics*, 58, 3 (1996), 469–503.

created political formulas, ideologies, or classes.[35] Often, mythologisa-
tions of the past underpin economic issues such as post-communist
liberalism.[36] Linking the Czech economic transformation after 1989 to
national revival in the late eighteenth and early nineteenth centuries is to
portray liberalism as fundamental to the constitution of Czech identity,
to a return to what is 'natural.' Such a vision presents the Czech nation as
Europeans naturally inclined to democracy, commerce, and self-reliance.
It thus erases awkward facts such as the times when Czechs were inclined
to pan-Slavism and looked away from western Europe, or acquiesced to
authoritarian rule, either by foreigners or compatriots.

The renaissance of Kantian and Hegelian legacies reflected the optimism for a new peaceful world order after the end of the Cold War.[37] The
surprisingly non-violent end of communism has made political scientists
blinkered with regard to the psychological truism that the perception of
being a victim does not require a war or large-scale violence. Self-perceptions
of ethnic groups or nationalities as victims of existential annihilation
or humiliation abound in the region. The real issue for Serbs, for example, was a collective fear of disintegration and formlessness, as expressed
in the Memorandum published by the Serbian Academy of Science in
1986. Claiming the restoration of national and cultural integrity of the
Serbian people as a historical and democratic right, it denounced
repeated attempts at the physical annihilation of Serbs.[38] There is perhaps no better illustration of how heroisation in post-1989 stands for
fragmentation than the battlefields of ex-Yugoslavia, where warlords have
come to play an important part in establishing collective identity-
patterns. Even in countries without a long-standing ethnic conflict, the
1980s saw waves of hatred and victimisation. Thus, in the winter of
1984/5, the Bulgarian regime launched a massive campaign against
Turkish Muslims, with the aim of changing their names to Slavic
Bulgarian ones. The accompanying brutal measures against Islamic rituals and customs, as well as against the use of the Turkish language,
mobilised resistance and instigated the panic-stricken mass exodus of
more than 320,000 Turks in spring 1989, of which approximately

---

[35] Elemer Hankiss, 'Our Recent Past: Recent Developments in East Central Europe in the
Light of Various Social Philosophies', *East European Politics and Societies*, 8, 3 (1994),
535–41.
[36] Kieran Williams, 'National Myths in the New Czech Liberalism', in Geoffrey Hosking
and George Schöpflin, eds., *Myths and Nationhood* (London: Hurst, 1997), 132–40.
[37] Pierre Hassner, *Violence and Peace: From the Atomic Bomb to Ethnic Cleansing* (Budapest/
London/New York: Central European University Press, 1996), 29–32.
[38] Mirko Grmek et al., *Le nettoyage ethnique. Documents historiques sur une idéologie serbe*
(Paris: Fayard, 1993), 265–6.

160,000 had come back by the second half of 1990.[39] After the forced assimilation policies in communist Bulgaria, the National Education Act in 1991 reintroduced Turkish language instruction in public schools. Although this was met by some opposition from Bulgarian nationalists as well as practical problems, such as lack of teaching materials and irregular school lessons, the Turkish minority has been progressively integrated.

In the second half of the 1990s, symbolisations of a heroic leader have become important for collective identity-formation. In the void of post-communist uncertainty, monarchical discourse rose in Bulgarian politics and led to the election of former king Simeon II as prime minister.[40] Numerous exculpatory mythologies, such as narratives of mass national resistance to communism, tend to heroise national history and, simultaneously, minimise the heroic meaning of the efforts of former dissidents. Public reburials of national heroes evoke personal losses and the identification with specific aspects of the dead person's biography.[41] Experiencing death's 'ultimate questions' such as fear and awe in public settings – for example, in mass reburials like those of Imre Nagy or the Yugoslav skeletons from the Second World War – enhances their emotional significance.

The gap between the 'objective' presence of the targets and 'subjective' perception appears to be particularly acute. Even in countries with a high degree of ethnic homogeneity and an extremely low number of Jews, anti-Semitism has become the language of nostalgia, resentment, and self-victimisation. Although it did not rise as a consequence of the collapse of communism but had been there for a long time, anti-Semitism in the 1990s has become the most persistent, enduring, and tragically effective mythology of scapegoating. The Russians' own movement for the protection of the environment and historical monuments (Pamyat) was soon hijacked by those eager to blame the Jews for all the wrongs suffered.[42] Paradoxically, anti-Semitism in post-communist eastern Europe serves primarily a symbolic function in that it identifies the Jews – though there

[39] Maria Todorova, 'Improbable Maverick or Typical Conformist? Seven Thoughts on the New Bulgaria', in Ivo Banac, ed., *Eastern Europe in Revolution* (Ithaca and London: Cornell University Press, 1992), 154–7.
[40] Ivalyo Znepolski, 'Le retour du discours monarchique. La fluctuation postcommuniste de la souveraineté', paper delivered at the Colloque international 'La reinvention de l'état', 5 and 6 April 2002, Paris.
[41] Katherine Verdery, *The Political Lives of Dead Bodies: Reburial and Postsocialist Change* (New York: Columbia University Press, 1999), 33.
[42] Geoffrey Hosking, *A History of the Soviet Union, 1917–1991* (London: Fontana, 1992), 486.

were few left, especially in eastern Europe – with the causes of national disaster from communism to the effects of economic liberalism.[43]

While the Serbs identified with both the Serbian and Yugoslav states in a positive manner and their sense of victimisation was ethnic, in the late Soviet Union the sense of victimisation was political, leading to the country's breakdown through nationalist mobilisation.[44] While in the late Gorbachev era the myth of a historical mission of the Soviet people was progressively deconstructed, political discourse in nascent Russia soon turned towards the re-establishment of a patriotic myth of a Russian mission.[45] It is therefore not surprising that the attempts to remythologise the Russian state draw heavily on the inspiration of state patriotism linked with a mixture of Soviet symbolism and traditional religious symbolism. In this respect, one can point to the controversy about the burial of Lenin's mummy, an initiative already taken by Yeltsin and by patriarch Alexei II (though as yet without success). In December 2000, the Russian Duma by an overwhelming majority (381 votes to 51) restored the Soviet anthem at the request of President Putin. Similarly, the tsarist flag and eagle were adopted as the country's state symbols.[46] The symbolic significance of the second war in Chechnya is in line with the most elementary aspects of preserving territorial integrity and the monopoly of violence. The disorder and lawlessness in Chechnya are presented as an extreme case, but as also existing in Russia, as epitomised by a widely circulated aphorism of President Putin: 'We've got Chechnya wherever you look.'[47]

Beyond perception, therefore, one must not forget that, for large parts of the population, the feeling of victimisation in almost any country in the region is real. War-torn regions paid the highest price in terms of death tolls and mass migration. The wars in ex-Yugoslavia between 1991 and 1999 may have caused the death of approximately 220,000 people, including 160,000 Bosnians, 30,000 Croats, and 25,000 Serbs. Of a total of more than 2 million expelled people, by the year 2000, 1.2 million Bosnians still had not returned home.[48] Self-victimisation also bears

---

[43] Vladimir Tismaneanu, *Fantasies of Salvation* (Princeton: Princeton University Press, 1998), 96–7.
[44] Veljko Vujacic, 'Historical Legacies, Nationalist Mobilization, and Political Outcomes in Russia and Serbia: A Weberian View', *Theory and Society*, 25 (1996), 765–801.
[45] Michael Urban, 'Remythologizing the Russian State', *Europe–Asia Studies*, 50, 6 (1998), 969–92.
[46] See *Moscow Times*, 9 December 2000.
[47] Quoted in Sergey Prozorov, 'Russian Postcommunism and Questions of Democracy: Postcommunist Constitution of State–Society Relations as a Moment of the Political', paper presented at the European Consortium for Political Research conference, 6–8 September 2001, Canterbury, 25.
[48] *Exit Milošević*, supplement to *Le Monde*, 8–9 October 2000.

heavily on the economy, social structure, and demography. The situation in 1989 in many respects threw the region back to levels of development of pre-1914 or pre-1945. For the population, expectations for the future were very low, in many cases much lower than during the 1970s or 1980s, when the economic situation was more desperate but hope for political reform was much higher. The primary factor for the region's backwardness was inherently psychological, based on an endemic sense of relative deprivation generated by images of the material progress of the advanced West.[49] In particular, the awareness of being doomed to continue to live on 'starvation wages' perpetuates a collective feeling of remaining second-rate Europeans. In this vein, the level of backwardness in Russia and eastern Europe with regard to the Western world at the beginning of the 1990s was much higher than, say, at the outbreak of the Second World War.[50] Crime rates increased drastically between 1989 and 1995.[51] The demographic collapse in the aftermath of communism throughout the entire region was reflected in the net natural decrease of the population with the exception of Poland, the Czech Republic, and Slovakia.[52] With the highest per capita alcohol consumption in the world, Russia also shows a wider gap in life expectancy between men (fifty-nine) and women (seventy-three) than any other country. The mortality rate of 15.1 deaths per 1,000 people puts Russia ahead of only Afghanistan among the countries of Europe, Asia, and America; the death rate among working-age Russians today is higher than a century ago.[53]

The demise of symbols of democracy

In an environment of uncertainty and epistemological anarchy, the very symbols of the revolutions in 1989 or 1991 have all but eroded.[54] For many analysts, these symbols of democracy did not match the

---

[49] Janos, *East Central Europe in the Modern World*, 414–17.

[50] Ivan T. Berend, *Central and Eastern Europe, 1944–1993: Detour from the Periphery to the Periphery* (Cambridge: Cambridge University Press, 1996).

[51] A subregional summary shows rates of increase in central Europe of 108.9 per cent, in south-eastern Europe of 269.3 per cent, in the Baltic states of 84.0 per cent, and in the former Soviet Union (excluding the Caucasus) of 59.2 per cent. Homicide rates in central Europe went up by 78.0 per cent, in the Baltic states by 174.4 per cent, and in the former Soviet Union (excluding the Caucasus) by 92.3 per cent; see UNICEF, *Children at Risk in Central and Eastern Europe: Perils and Promises*, Regional Report No. 4 (1997), Florence, 10.

[52] Crude birth rates fell steadily between 1980 and 1986, in some countries (Czech Republic, Poland, and Romania) by almost 50 per cent; see UNICEF, *Public Policy and Social Conditions*, Regional Monitoring Report No. 3 (1993), Florence, 94.

[53] See *International Herald Tribune*, 9 June 1997.

[54] Tismaneanu, *Fantasies of Salvation*, 153.

requirements of institutional democratic arrangements for effective government. It has been a central claim of the literature on democratic
transitions that anti-politics or 'living in truth' are dispositions that are
not adapted to institutionalising a new political order or to conducting
public policy.[55] The politics of enchantment and its symbolic compre-
hensiveness cannot be appropriate for the institutionalised democratic
government with its focus on policies, rule of law, and accountability.
They are not appropriate to a democratic 'outcome', which makes their
failure to survive a proof of their inadequacy.

The harsh criticism of dissident politics in many countries seemed to
confirm this perspective. Domestically, the heritage of dissidence was met
largely with embarrassment, if not open scorn and contempt, by post-
1989 political elites. As after communism everybody tended to present
himself as an anti-communist with hindsight, former dissidents were not
considered to be moral examples but could indeed have been neurotic
self-absorbed individuals manipulated by Western intelligence services.[56]
As the proudest symbols of this 'non-heroic' resistance such as Wałęsa,
Havel, or Konrád were 'deconstructed', it became increasingly clear that
demagogues, priests, and colonels, more than democrats and capitalists,
would shape eastern Europe's general institutional identity.[57]

Before Gorbachev's accession to power, Solidarność in Poland was
incontestably the most powerful symbol of liberty in the communist
world. Its emergence in 1980 was followed by almost a decade of existing
underground, where the movement was decisively weakened. Solidarność
lost its legal status, its widespread support in the factories, and also
open support in public opinion. However, the symbolic appeal of Lech
Wałęsa as the trade union's leading figure was decisive for the re-emergence
as a negotiation partner for the communist regime. It was the badge of
Solidarność that was on the front page of the first officially legalised
opposition newspaper in a communist country, the *Gazeta Wyborcza*. The
overwhelming success in the June elections of 1989 for the Solidarność
camp was largely attributed to the familiar Solidarność logo and the person
of Lech Wałęsa. The internecine conflict in the post-Solidarność camp and
its institutional differentiation in several 'wars at the top' between 1989 and
1993 shifted the focus to the economic and material conditions of transition, thus replacing political symbols of the Polish revolution such as the

---

[55] Claus Offe, *Varieties of Transition: The East European and East German Experience*
(Cambridge, MA: MIT Press, 1997), 187.
[56] G. M. Tamás, 'The Legacy of Dissent', in Vladimir Tismaneanu, ed., *The Revolutions of
1989* (London and New York: Routledge, 1999), 181–2.
[57] Jowitt, *The New World Disorder*.

Solidarność badge or the person of Lech Wałęsa with a plan for economic reform, the Balcerowicz plan.[58]

A similar kind of symbolic disarticulation applies to the velvet revolution in Czechoslovakia, which stands for the peaceful mass gatherings that toppled the Czechoslovak government in November 1989. While the notions 'velvet revolution' (*nezná revoluce*) or 'soft revolution' (*hebká revoluce*) referred only to the mass protests in November, they soon came to signify the whole process of the demise of communism. The velvet symbol was applied to other historical periods and even to mean a specific Czechoslovak 'velvet know-how', which could be exported to other countries. The experience of November 1989 was likened to the events of 1918: the birth of the Czechoslovak state was referred to as a 'velvet revolution of 1918', while Czechoslovak normalisation from 1968 onwards was termed 'velvet totality'.[59] The velvet symbol was also used to highlight a sense of Czech exceptionalism (*nejsme jako oni*), which played on the idea of a Czech civil society and democratic tradition. As time went by, however, the velvet symbol was subject to a transformation in meaning, turning it gradually into a sign of weakness, of 'alibiism', and of the half-heartedness of the Czech November, which failed to achieve a catharsis. Thus, the velvet symbol became double-edged, standing for the alleged political passivity of Czech leadership usually prone to avoiding conflicts and choosing the 'realist' option, such as in 1938, 1948, or 1968. Consequently, the attribute 'velvet' could even be applied to the neo-liberal politics as pursued by the Klaus government and implying 'velvet corruption'.[60]

In Hungary, the democratic breakthrough between March and June 1989 consisted in a considerable shift from a dichotomy between official-dom and the opposition towards a growing self-inclusion of party hard-liners into the opposition.[61] Following demands by the opposition, the Hungarian parliament had declared 15 March a public holiday, the day for the commemoration of the revolution of 1848. Although they were opposing a celebration organised by the authorities in preference to an alternative ceremony of more than 100,000 participants, it was never-theless a unique opportunity for the opposition to shape the modalities of the negotiations proposed by the communist party. Three months later,

[58] Jan T. Gross, 'Polen nach der Revolution. Die Marginalisierung des Politischen', *Transit*, 3 (1991), 69–78.

[59] Vladimír Macura, 'Samtene Revolution – samtene Scheidung', in Walter Koschmal et al., eds., *Deutsche und Tschechen. Geschichte-Kultur-Politik* (Munich: Beck, 2001), 549.

[60] Aviezer Tucker, *The Philosophy and Politics of Czech Dissidence from Patočka to Havel* (Pittsburgh: University of Pittsburgh Press, 2000), 209–41.

[61] Kenney, *A Carnival of Revolution*, 261–5.

the reburial of Imre Nagy on 16 June 1989 did not prove to be an unambiguous demarcation between 'us' and 'them'. The authorities carefully orchestrated this mass event. The officially authorised speech by Fidesz representative Viktor Orbán articulated the spirit of the times, criticising the party's sudden shift to reappropriate a heritage they had been despising for more than thirty years. This reburial as a performative act before 250,000 people was the climatic moment that, on its own, symbolised Hungary's negotiated revolution.

In Romania, the violent overthrow of Ceauşescu in December 1989 produced various rituals and symbolisations of resistance and anti-communism.[62] Although the myth of a spontaneous revolution has been disavowed, the broadcast revolution spawned numerous slogans, indicating the rejection of communism (*jos comunismul*) as the central intention of the popular revolt. Not only have specific symbols and rituals become obsolete quite soon after 1989, but also, although many Romanians seem to be conscious of having lived through a revolution, frequent references to a 'stolen', 'confiscated', or 'unfinished' revolution suggest that the perception of no change at all prevails. Thus, the country that experienced the most radical break with the former system has arguably been most affected by the 'permanence of the past'.

The popular mass mobilisation in East Germany, such as in the gatherings of an estimated 80,000 people in Leipzig during Gorbachev's visit in early October 1989, appropriated the notion of the *Volk* (the people) – used by the East German regime to create a national identity – as a central rallying cry by stating 'Wir sind das Volk' (we are the people).[63] A significant change occurred when this re-identification changed to the slogan 'Wir sind ein Volk' (we are one people/nation). It is practically impossible to track down who used it first but 'at the very latest' it was used at the beginning of December 1989 during demonstrations in Saxony, especially in Leipzig. This symbolisation of 'one people' has not welded together what should belong together in Germany, despite huge material and administrative efforts. As Christian Meier argued, the experiential basis of West Germans and that of East Germans were radically different. Although affected by the prospect of reunification, most West Germans were more concerned with not disrupting their own lives. East Germans, by contrast, were excited and confused, seeing

---

[62] Anneli Ute Gabanyi, 'Rumänien. Die inszenierte Revolution', *Südosteuropa*, 47, 3–4 (1998), 168–83.
[63] Fred L. Casmir, '"Wir sind ein Volk": Illusions and Reality of German Unification', in Fred L. Casmir, ed., *Communication in Eastern Europe: The Role of History, Culture, and Media in Contemporary Conflicts* (Mahwah, NJ: Lawrence Erlbaum, 1995), 31–56.

totally new possibilities and a new playing field when unification became a possibility; in many cases, though, they needed assistance and help, even basic explanations.

Yeltsin's direct election as Russian president on 12 June 1991 was the symbolic rebirth of democratic Russia, but also was highly ambiguous in the context of the constitutional arrangement of the late Soviet era.[64] When amending the Soviet constitution in April 1991, the idea was to place the presidency in a position subordinate to the legislature, consisting of the Congress of People's Deputies and the Supreme Soviet. The ambiguity about which institution was finally supreme and the sheer power of Yeltsin's popular election only two months later developed into a deep polarisation inside the central state institutions. The style of politics turned towards Bonapartism, which aimed at preventing particularistic interests from emerging.

Practically, the option for constitutional government was characterised by the democratic movement of anti-communism championed by Yeltsin on the one hand, and by the replication of the core features of communist doctrine on the other. After the putsch attempt in August 1991, Yeltsin dissolved the Russian communist party but did not opt for democratic elections or a constituent assembly. At the height of the democratic euphoria, he did not fully exploit his charisma and reputation. Faced with rapid state disintegration and the collapse of political authority, the Yeltsin administration not only failed to defend Russia's state assets; in addition, the radical shift towards economic shock therapy facilitated the appropriation of these assets by an economic oligarchy emerging from former political and administrative elites.[65] During the democratic moment, Yeltsin pursued policies that were clearly driven by binary oppositions. Rather, in place of the monolithic party, he developed a unified executive and an unqualified endorsement of monetarism as the economic philosophy that represented the polar opposite of political economy under communism.[66] Yeltsin's administration elevated not only the myth of market economy but also the cult of a strong leader to absolute status in the months after 1991. Moreover, the Russian experience exemplifies the political moment of the exception, where the struggle over sovereignty cannot be mediated. The contest for power in a political moment does not differentiate between 'naturally inclined'

---

[64] Graeme Gill and Roger D. Markwick, *Russia's Stillborn Democracy? From Gorbachev to Yeltsin* (Oxford: Oxford University Press, 2000), 122–4.

[65] Solnick, *Stealing the State*.

[66] Michael Urban et al., *The Rebirth of Politics in Russia* (Cambridge: Cambridge University Press, 1997), 261–3.

democrats or communists but follows the situational logic of annihilating the enemy. The standoff between the Supreme Soviet and President Yeltsin in autumn 1993 pointed to the absence of a national mythology that would have attenuated the extreme polarisation of two institutions that had signified the turn for democratisation in 1989 and 1991.

In many ways, the dissolution of the unified political symbolism of communist power and its 'correct line' has coincided with the ascendancy of the alternative symbolic universes expressed in Western values of democracy. The loss of faith in the communist authorities was accompanied by the institution of an internationally sustained infrastructure for democratic values. The international context in the 1970s and 1980s created an accumulated force of international public opinion. Institutions such as the European Union, NATO, and the Conference on (later Organization for) Security and Co-operation in Europe and growing financial support for political parties in eastern Europe were not designed to bring down the Iron Curtain but in fact created an evident 'infrastructure for democratic values'.

In quite a few ways, the dissolution of democratic symbolism suggests another humiliating example when eastern Europe's liberation largely depended on the mercy of the Soviets. After the collapse of communism, governments in much of eastern Europe and Russia were forced to do the same as they had done over decades and centuries, namely to control, inspire, and accelerate reform in society. The inability to create sustainable political formulas and a rather poor set of viable alternative models from national histories has led east Europeans to focus on political strategies and ideological kits that were largely imported from the West. What matters most, perhaps, is that the share of dissidence in the destruction of communism was hardly recognised by domestic and international publics. Western public perceptions attributed it either to the Gorbachev factor or to the magic of the symbol 'democracy'. If symbolisation is about the symbol's power to evoke feelings or attitudes, then the plurality of symbolisations of 1989 and 1991 has obfuscated any clear constitutive foundation in a concrete event. Attempts to draw a line under or to break with the communist past have often been the result of officially authorised policy rather than a symbolic watershed. The year 1989 faded quickly in people's memories because it had failed to become a cathartic moment.[67] Unlike the fall of the Berlin wall on 9 November and the revolution of 17 November in Czechoslovakia, the negotiated revolutions such as in Hungary and Poland have not become events to be commemorated.

[67] Kenney, *A Carnival of Revolution*, 304.

The sudden end of communism was followed by the quick obliteration of 1989 in post-1989 political discourse. In many ways, the very events of 1989 have entered into the no-man's land of mythical pasts. The dissolution of the symbols of democracy and the disenchantment with the new order has arguably put post-communism on historical sands at least as unstable as those on which the post-war edifice was mounted.[68] The events of 1989 but also of 1990 and 1991 have not become the models for new national holidays (which in most cases hark back to other events in national histories). A previous legitimising event such as the declaration of Russian state sovereignty on 12 June 1990 is no longer celebrated as 'independence day' but, in an amorphous fashion, as a 'Russia day', while for many it is coterminous with the destruction of the Soviet state.[69] The events of the August putsch in 1991, originally standing for the manifestation of an active and independent citizenry in the defence of the White House, have been overshadowed by the unconstitutional shelling of the same White House by its former defender, President Yeltsin.

Symbols such as Europe, democracy, or market that were actively used by dissidents to undermine the legitimacy of communism lost their unified 'total' meaning. As Slavenka Drakulić put it, Europe 'describes only one part of it, the western part, in a geographical, cultural, historical, and political sense. Now, it looks as if all of the ex-communist east European countries have the same almost palpable wish to push that dividing line as far to the east as possible, so that eventually Europe will be a whole undivided continent. Yet it is this desire itself that forms the current dividing line. The West does not feel the need to belong (it just is) or to allow the countries standing at its threshold to enter.'[70]

The 'return to Europe' after 1989 bequeathed to western Europe the task of representing the whole of Europe. This Europe has, despite concrete steps towards unification, remained an ideal image that seems to retreat further the closer Easterners approach. In a similar vein, 'central Europe' as one of the primary symbols of democratisation in the former Eastern bloc has remained an inherently liminal category. Lacking clearcut boundaries and identities, central Europe has remained subject to fluidity, uncertainty, and reversals of status.[71] In the 1990s, the 'return to Europe' lost its quasi-magical attraction and became associated with a

---

[68] Tony Judt, 'The Past Is Another Country: Myth and Memory in Postwar Europe', in István Deák et al., eds., *The Politics of Retribution in Europe* (Princeton: Princeton University Press, 2000), 315–17.

[69] Richard Sakwa, 'Subjectivity and Citizenship in Post-Communist Russia' (unpublished typescript, 2005).

[70] Slavenka Drakulić, *Café Europa* (London: Abacus, 1996), 12.

[71] György Konrád, *Identität und Hysterie* (Frankfurt am Main: Suhrkamp, 1995), 141–2.

matter of technical feasibility, normative adaptability, and political com-
patibility. In this process, east European countries have been focused
on their individual trajectories and interested in their neighbours only
to the extent that they perceive them as competitors for the limited
resources of the West.[72] Hence, the incipient co-operation between
central European countries, such as in the Visegrad four, failed to reconcile their Western culture, their Eastern politics, and their in-between
geographical situation.[73]

Moreover, the eastern enlargement of the European Union has concealed that Western countries were far from enthusiastic about eastern
Europe's liberation, as its belonging to the Soviet bloc had the double
virtue of keeping it away from the prosperous West while at the same time
allowing the latter the luxury of lamenting the very circumstances from
which it was benefiting. In essence, the West itself abounds with a whole
set of mythologies about pre-1989 and about the experiences of 1989.

The democratic moment destroyed the democratisers but it confirmed
the commitment of the people to democratic elections, change in government, and accountability. Although lack of political choice before the
overarching paradigms of procedural liberal democracy and market
economy revealed the absence of alternatives in terms of constitutional
acts, the democratic moment introduced the 'people' in their role both
as the source of power and as the source of government for the people.
While *perestroika* generated intra-party democracy in the Soviet communist party and the round-table pacts in Hungary or Poland allowed for a
non-violent transition, the mass mobilisations such as in Czechoslovakia
and the GDR resembled most popular revolutions. The orange revolution in late 2004 in Ukraine rearticulated the bonds between citizens and
the state. Here, democracy was effectively refounded, as the presumed
fraud in the presidential elections was followed by a civic upsurge in the
defence of substantive political rights.[74]

The 'democratisation' of meanings of democracy

The collapse of communism came down not only to the rejection of
communist ideology and institutions, but also of any type of unified

---

[72] Sorin Antohi, 'Habits of the Mind: Europe's Post-1989 Symbolic Geographies', in
Antohi and Tismaneanu, *Between Past and Future*, 69.
[73] Jacques Rupnik, 'Europe centrale. Les atouts et les limites de la coopération régionale',
Pouvoirs, 74 (1995), 183–9.
[74] Sakwa, 'Subjectivity and Citizenship'.

collective symbolism. Paradoxically, the dissolution of the symbols that stood for active citizenship and represented democratic hopes by resisting communist power was a crucial precondition for freedom and independence, but also for interest-based party politics and representation. An analysis of post-communist discourses on democracy in thirteen different countries in the region has elaborated the wide and diverse set of different discourses of democracy in different countries.[75] It has distilled out four democratisation roads: the liberal, the republican, the participatory, and the statist. These roads do not preclude the possibilities of other trajectories, nor are they mutually exclusive. Liberal discourses define democracy in terms of the aggregation and reconciliation of given interests emanating from the private realm and represented by parties and interest groups under relatively neutral constitutional rules that specify a range of individual rights. The state remains limited as it is constrained by the separation of powers and individual pursuit of material interests. With certain caveats, liberal democratic discourses are found in countries such as Yugoslavia in the late 1990s (i.e. Serbia and Montenegro – though it is limited in its toleration of perceived extremists), Georgia (with a moralistic view of politics), Slovakia (with a commitment to the common good), and Bulgaria (with a denial of the need for checks on the power of an active citizenry). Conversely, discourses of civic republicanism in Poland and civic enthusiasm in the Czech Republic point to the importance of active, public-spirited citizenship. While the republican view shares the liberal emphasis on the separation of powers and the rule of law, it is quite critical of sectional interests of career politicians and favours formal and informal opportunities for the exercise of active citizenship. Some discourses integrate a moralistic commitment to a politics of the common good, such as Democratic Enthusiasm in Georgia or Developing Pluralism in Slovakia, while others, such as Civil Fundamentalism in Romania, treat political truth in unitary terms as something existing and not something to be discovered in dialogue. The third type, the participatory road, has not become political reality in any country, but some discourses in countries such as Bulgaria, Poland, the Czech Republic, and Yugoslavia suggest that it takes the shape of a radicalised republicanism, where the potential of an active citizenry should be maximised. Especially in Yugoslavia, the discourse of participatory self-management reminds the observer of the self-management

---

[75] John Dryzek and Leslie Holmes, *Post-Communist Democratization* (Cambridge: Cambridge University Press, 2002).

model practised under Tito. This participatory road Yugoslav-style is detached from a liberal model, which many Yugoslavs still associate with Western enemies of their country, and it cuts across political divisions in a deeply torn society. The fourth road, the statist one, involves a strong state with effective leadership committed to uncorrupted and constitutional government. Such a version is especially attractive where civil society is weak, society is deeply divided, and corruption and organised crime are rampant. Indeed, under the conditions of the disintegration of the Soviet Union and the weakness of the Russian state in sensitive areas such as tax collection or law enforcement, the only way to match politics to the centuries-old liberal project for Russia seems to be state liberalism.[76] While such discourses largely reflect historical traditions before 1989 and experiences thereafter, they not only are seemingly realistic but also carry aspirations and hopes.

Different understandings of democratisation have been reflected in interpretive accounts of the democratic credentials of a state. In the Russian case, the choice of super-presidentialism is seen as the single institutional choice that degraded Russian democracy as it established 'democratic politics' almost without accountability.[77] In this view, Yeltsin's choices were not influenced by structural, cultural, or historical conditions but should be reconstructed from autonomy of the political moment. The pernicious effects of super-presidentialism are seen in the concentration of power, in the option for a radical privatisation programme whose second phase of loans-for-shares facilitated the emergence of a powerful caste of oligarchs, and in a lack of law enforcement. Yet, democratic development can also be assessed not from the central national perspective but from the regional one, which gives priority to the dramatic rise in local cultural identity, regional myths, and symbols. As Nicolai Petro's study of Novgorod suggests, economic growth, associational life, and the priority of self-government can thrive in the absence of a party system.[78] Occupying a unique place in the nation's historical memory, Novgorod has drawn on its symbolic heritage, its ethnic diversity, its religious tolerance, and the tradition of a confederated system of administration since the fifteenth century. The ability to elect independent

[76] Marcia A. Weigle, *Russia's Liberal Project* (University Park, PA: Penn State University Press, 2000).
[77] Steven M. Fish, 'Conclusion: Democracy and Russian Politics', in Zoltan Barany and Robert G. Moser, eds., *Russian Politics* (Cambridge: Cambridge University Press, 2001), 215–51.
[78] Nicolai Petro, *Crafting Democracy: How Novgorod Has Coped with Rapid Social Change* (Ithaca and London: Cornell University Press, 2004).

heads of local municipalities to the regional legislature strengthens rather than weakens the legislature's independence from the governor and produces an unprecedented degree of local autonomy.

The experiential basis of the 'constitutional moment'

Highlighting history and culture makes a case for the symbolic foundations of democracy. The institutional design of democratic polities has required constitutionalism to be based on deliberation and discursive processes rather than on a search for tradition. There is good reason to assume that rights are a product of critical reflection, suitably disciplined and constrained in the way a legal system requires.[79] If the demise of the monopoly of the communist party and the beginning of the new order on the basis of sovereignty, law, and democratic individualism are separated into two analytical units, the influential impact of transformative experiences under communism is overlooked. Any reference to legacy becomes by definition preservative, while future orientation is seen as transformative. This is reflected in what constitutionalist thought has defined as the distinction between preservative and transformative constitutions. Preservative constitutions tend to protect long-standing traditions, often an idealised past from which constitutional rights are derived. Transformative constitutions such as in South Africa, in contrast, broke radically with the past. While east European constitutions have a strongly preservative character, as they resort to national, pre-communist traditions, such a classification omits the fact that the historical evolution of communism has consisted of a sequence of transformative processes, where meanings were shaped, dissolved, and reshaped. In political terms, many countries have either attempted to draw a line under the past, by a kind of democratic organised forgetting, or, as in Russia, by embarking upon a painful process of reconstituting a complex heritage from pre- and post-revolutionary Russia, which are all part of a nation's identity. From an experiential perspective, however, what appears as preservative in east European constitutionalism can be seen as fundamentally transformative, as it has been shaped by active attempts to transform communism.

Hence, there is good reason to understand the constitutional moment and the disarticulation of communism not as two separate entities, but as one movement. If the constitutional moment is only about regulating the relations between the state and other states, between the parts of the state with each other, between the state and the citizen, and among citizens,

[79] Cass Sunstein, *Designing Democracy: What Constitutions Do* (Oxford: Oxford University Press, 2001).

then the outcome sidelines the situational premises. The systemic understanding of the constitutive act as regulating relations between specific
subjects presupposes the existence of constituted identities such as states
or citizens. Under communist rule, however, the absence of a shared
public identity as citizens not only prevented truthful discourse between
rulers and the ruled; it also isolated individuals in privatised and indifferent spaces, which obstructed any disinterested public discussion of
national issues.[80] Repressed communication and highly restricted political opportunities prevented the circulation of individual and collective
representations of identity, making interaction among politically constituted subjects qua subjects very difficult. This lack of interaction left just
the presence of manifest differences or varieties towards which each
subject would remain indifferent.[81] If the specificity of the constitution
as a constitutive act is to regulate the relations among citizens and
between citizens and the state, the constitutional articulation in constituent power contributes to the emergence and self-identification of subjects. In many ways, the participants in a constituent assembly or the
competing alternatives laid out in the constitution have not been at all
clear at the beginning of the process. Rather they become articulated as a
part of the struggle itself.[82] As a Solidarność member in the Polish Sejm
declared in September 1989: 'I represent subjects that do not yet exist.'[83]

   Before constitutions become legal acts, the politics of enchantment
in its existential dimension underpins the constitutional moment. The
transformations after 1989 and 1991 are arguably much bigger than
scholars have realised, acquiring a cosmic dimension, where the reordering of people's entire meaningful worlds is at stake.[84] The dissolution of
communist political authority was preceded by the dissolution of existing
structures, boundaries, and values. Pasts and futures were redefined,
meanings became vacuous and identities uncertain. The unprecedented
political transformations came along with the emotional dimension of
enchantment and enlivening. These emotional outbursts, the irrationality, and violence in political action must not be taken as pathological or
dysfunctional. Political transformations comprise more than the technical design of institutions. This 'something more' includes meaning, feelings, the sacred, ideas of morality, and the 'non-rational' as ingredients of
political legitimacy and authority.

[80] Jowitt, The New World Disorder, 211.
[81] Urban et al., The Rebirth of Politics in Russia, 18.
[82] Keith Banting and Richard Simeon, Redesigning the State: The Politics of Constitutional
   Change in Industrial Nations (Toronto: University of Toronto Press, 1985), 19.
[83] Wydra, Continuities, 93.   [84] Verdery, The Political Lives of Dead Bodies, 25–35.

It is problematic to isolate the democratic moment of 1989 from the experiential basis of its social foundations with a view to the logic of appropriateness with a constituted system of power. Democratisation was also the effect of a host of memories of people's experiences, which joined images of popular sovereignty and democratic rights as forming the existential basis for the constitution of new political authority. More than just symbols of the end of communism, Solidarność, *perestroika*, *glasnost*, and the velvet revolution harboured the emancipatory meanings of democracy based on decades of attempts to reconstruct public life. Constituent power has to integrate the idea of a long-drawn-out rebirth where the creative, civic side of politics emancipates itself from the destructive side of communist power. In this vein, the years 1989 and 1991 also suggest a new deep source of hope, whose basis is not the inevitability of progress but the reversibility of destruction.[85] How can it be explained that the three countries with the best democratic credentials in the former Soviet hemisphere, Poland, Hungary, and Czechoslovakia, opted for radical continuity in the constitutional order? In all three, democrats used the former communist constitutions as a point of departure for institutionalising democracy.[86] From a liberal perspective, the failure to radically discontinue the communist constitution in these countries came down to missing the constitutional moment. From an experiential perspective, however, the constitutional moment is not equivalent to a voluntary consent to the rules of the game. Rather, the reconstitution of democratic politics needs to take into account the symbolism of non-violent and principled resistance that made the round-tables of 1989 and the velvet revolution possible. On the one hand, the unconstitutionality of communism appeared to be at odds with the democratic legitimacy of the new order. On the other, however, without this unconstitutionality, the existential option to challenge communism by means of symbols and life-conduct would not have been possible. The method of radical continuity, therefore, is consistent with the spirit of dissidence as existentially representative, which appeared to be a more radical political solution than revolutionary change.

---

[85] Karol Soltan, '1989 as Rebirth', in Antohi and Tismaneanu, *Between Past and Future*, 34.
[86] Allison Stanger, 'Leninist Legacies and Legacies of State Socialism in Postcommunist Eastern Europe's Constitutional Development', in Grzegorz Ekiert and Stephen Hanson, eds., *Capitalism and Democracy in Central and Eastern Europe* (Cambridge: Cambridge University Press, 2003), 182–209.

Part III

Democracy as a process of meaning-formation

9   The power of memory

> The struggle of man against power is the struggle of memory against
> forgetting.   Milan Kundera

The breakdown of communism revealed the momentous task of trying to make sense of several decades of falsification of history and distortion of memory. 'It's as if the regime were guilty of two crimes on a massive scale: murder and the unending assault against memory. In making a secret of history, the Kremlin made its subjects just a little more insane, a little more desperate.'[1] A growing body of literature, responding to the repressive nature of communism but primarily interested in the practical side of reshaping public policies and returning to 'normal politics', has drawn attention to how transitional justice and the politics of memory can contribute to reworking the past.[2] Post-communist societies faced the difficult choice between public policies of retribution, disqualification, or reconciliation; in addition, in many countries, the breakdown of communism did not appear as a decisive breakthrough at all. Much of the post-communist predicament seems to consist in an apparent contradiction between simultaneous claims about the extinction of historical consciousness and persistent influence of too much memory.[3] This dilemma calls for reassessing the temporality applied to studies of communism,

---

[1] David Remnick, *Lenin's Tomb: The Last Days of the Soviet Empire* (New York: Vintage Books, 1993), 101.

[2] Barbara Misztal, 'How Not to Deal with the Past: Lustration in Poland', *Archives Européennes de Sociologie*, 40, 1 (1999), 31–55; Alexandra Barahona de Brito, et al., *The Politics of Memory and Democratization: Transitional Justice in Democratizing Societies* (Oxford: Oxford University Press, 2001); Kathleen E. Smith, *Mythmaking in the New Russia: Politics and Memory in the Yeltsin Era* (Ithaca and London: Cornell University Press, 2002); Jon Elster, *Closing the Books: Transitional Justice in Historical Perspective* (Cambridge: Cambridge University Press, 2004).

[3] Jean-François Gossiaux, 'Les deux passés du Kosovo', *Socio-Anthropologie*, 4, 2 (1998), 43–53; Jerzy Szacki, 'Dwie historie', in Piotr Wandycz, ed., *Spór o PRL* (Krakow: Wydawnictwo Znak, 1996), 68–74; Christoph Reinprecht, *Nostalgie und Amnesie. Bewertungen von Vergangenheit in der Tschechischen Republik und Ungarn* (Vienna: Verlag für Gesellschaftskritik, 1996); Wojciech Roszkowski, 'Wygłuszanie pamięci', *Rzeczpospolita*, 25 October 1999.

democratisation, and post-communism. The recovery of the primacy of historical events as experiences of meaning-formation as pursued in the preceding chapters necessitates three considerations.

First, it would be an oversimplification to reduce communism to a legacy of repression.[4] While it has been common to refer to political transformations in eastern Europe and Russia by distinguishing stages of development such as pre-communist, communist, and post-communist pasts, such tendencies to package the past are as misdirected as are assumptions about timeless antagonisms or the continuity of a political culture of authoritarianism. Against such trends of classifying history into blocs and phases, social inquiry requires revisiting dyadic schemes that separate the 'communist legacy' from the 'present' on the assumption of the continuity of an ontology of tradition. Beyond generalised assertions about 'history matters' or a 'revenge of the past', much of the best research on the consequences of the collapse of communism has stressed how contentious meanings of critical junctures influenced transformative periods of reconstruction.[5]

Second, political memory is not only the officially imposed collective memory in a given system; it is also available for implementation against such official memory. The malleability of historical memory by voluntarism is conditioned by what broad layers of society consider as relevant. Therefore, political memory is attuned to the responsiveness of popular masses, more particularly to the communicative and cultural interpenetration with society. As the articulation of dissidence suggests, the cultural creativity and the political symbolism of memory can turn meanings of history against power incumbents and their strategies of organised forgetting.

Third, the political evolution of communism has been tightly intertwined with the emergence of democratic consciousness. While the practices of communist power aimed at annihilating the past, the challenges to communist power and growing mental and social resistance supported the emergence of contested memories and a counter-symbolism that would undermine the sacrificial logic of communist power. Next to a red book of the communist utopia and a black book of communist crimes, there is the need for a grey book of the history of central European countries under communism. These societies were both victims and

[4] David Joravsky, 'Communism in Historical Perspective', *American Historical Review*, 99, 3 (1994), 837–57.
[5] László Bruszt and David Stark, *Post-Socialist Pathways: Transforming Politics and Property in East Central Europe* (Cambridge: Cambridge University Press, 1998).

accomplices, wavering at different times between resistance and adaptation.[6] Similarly, the strong desire to write and rewrite biographies and autobiographies all over the formerly communist east central and south-eastern Europe presents a good opportunity to highlight zones of light and zones of darkness.

Critical events such as the Russian Revolution, the Second World War, and the revolutions in eastern Europe constituted the social context in which communist rule organised forgetting and introduced mythic time-dimensions into politics. Their 'revolutionary memory' is unlikely to be streamlined by the totalising attempt at organised forgetting. Taking the specific blend of their generative structure and their ambivalent associative dimension, memories of revolutions and the Second World War were crucial in providing communist rule with legitimacy but also harboured considerable potential for dissidence. As a manifestation of individual consciousness, memory can be truly subversive, essentially anti-totalitarian, and 'democratising'. The democratic power of memory is in its manifestation against communicative silencing of injustice, genocide, and the official production of organised forgetting.[7] Subsequently, I shall argue that memories of such events are key elements for challenging official doctrine, organised forgetting, and the freezing of the past. Taking my departure from an account of communist techniques of the production of history, I shall then deal with the fragmentation, the mobilisation, and the political uses of memory.

Memory as representing multiple pasts

The key obstacle to theorising memory is arguably that it is a manifestation of individual consciousness, which is circumstantial and unique for different cases of historical evolution. Tainted with subjectivity, the multiplicity of past events further limits the possibility of generalisable claims and seems to be in opposition to much of concept-building in the social sciences. However, memory cannot be disconnected from the social and 'objective' background conditions of its coming into existence through action. If memory has remained a vital factor in identity politics, then the 'past' needs to be integrated in the understanding of the emergence of the new order. Unlike history, it cannot be reduced to an object of inquiry with regard to its adaptability to types of regimes or goals of development.

[6] Jacques Rupnik, 'Was tun mit der kommunistischen Vergangenheit? Tschechische Republik', *Transit*, 22 (Winter 2001–2), 124.

[7] Jan-Werner Müller, *Memory and Power in Post-War Europe* (Cambridge: Cambridge University Press, 2002), 33–4.

Similarly, memory cannot be limited to possible structural constraints, which 'communist legacies' have on post-communist politics in terms of retribution, reconciliation, trials, or purges. Rather, it remains culturally present and potentially politically 'available'.[8] While history is something that definitely belongs to the past, memory is generated in history but remains alive in representations, beliefs, and attitudes of future generations. In other words, the 'material' for memory is shaped by multiple lines of meaning, which generate different forms of social and cultural memory. These become influential in terms of discursive patterns, political symbolism, and performative ritual action.[9] The point is not to make a judgement about 'good' or 'bad' memories but to acknowledge the ambivalence of memory that can be mobilised for political purposes.

To link critical events under communism to memory is consistent with the central characteristic of recent attention to memory in the social sciences. The main reason why memory has acquired a dynamic force is the fact that the past is no longer a guarantee for the future. In this view, the end of the twentieth century seems to be characterised by pervasive uncertainty about what the future could be. The demise of any form of teleology of history burdens the present with the 'duty to remember'. This insight is valuable as a starting point for the understanding of the predicament of memory in post-communist eastern Europe. The aftermath of communism made it possible for large parts of eastern Europe to overcome their historical and geographical situation by securing accession to NATO and to the European Union. While this acceleration of history has been a leading idea in assessments of post-communism, the articulation of memory under communism has to include a whole sequence of accelerations, where the situational logic of action produced multiple representations of the events.

In Russia, the October Revolution fundamentally restructured political institutions and social structures but also time perceptions, historical consciousness, and memory. The Second World War was not only a military conflict between states but also entailed an unprecedented socialisation of warfare that witnessed massive expulsions, systematic extermination, and reshaping of boundaries, thus stamping perceptions of citizens and official politics of commemoration.[10] The memories of the revolutions in Hungary in 1956, in Czechoslovakia in 1968, and the

---

[8] Pierre Nora, ed., *Realms of Memory: Rethinking the French Past* (New York: Columbia University Press, 1996).
[9] Paul Connerton, *How Societies Remember* (Cambridge: Cambridge University Press, 1989).
[10] Amir Weiner, *Making Sense of War: The Second World War and the Fate of the Bolshevik Revolution* (Princeton: Princeton University Press, 2001).

cycles of contention in Poland in 1956, 1968, 1970, 1976, and 1980 played an important role for the rejection of communist rule in 1989.[11] Memory is the socially relevant representation of transformations of consciousness in events-that-model. While recollections and traditions are shaped in such periods, their 'content' in terms of symbolisation of experiences is malleable as they are fabricated in an ongoing process of interpretation and contention. There is often a considerable discrepancy between what political history has made of an event and what the lived experience of this event meant to many people at the time. It is striking, for instance, how three years after the attacks on the Twin Towers in New York and the Pentagon in Washington the emotional complexity and crushing immediacy of 11 September 2001 had been squeezed out of the memories people harbour of this day.[12] Although its historical complexity has been growing ever since, '9/11' was turned into a symbol, a motive, a problem of intelligence and finance, and, above all, a political rallying cry concerning what the United States stands for and where it stands now.

Whereas political memory is by no means exclusively 'generated' in socially dense and dramatic contexts, revolutionary periods, wars, and political crises leave an extraordinary impact both on the self-definition of the regime and on the social memory of citizens. The task of a genealogy of political memory is to integrate the emotional intensity of the lived-through experiences with their symbolic representations. What is at stake is to combine the generative dimension of memory with its associative dimension as it keeps pasts available for the future. Although for the outside observer past revolutions and wars are only one version of reality, for the participants the lived-through uncertainty and self-resolution of crisis acquire the status of totality.[13] They generate a social microcosm of the lived-in world, which in its totality is relatively autonomous from the complex reality of 'normal times'. While smaller events also generate memories, they often lack the critical mass that is necessary for becoming constitutive of a memory regime.[14]

[11] Jan Kubik, *The Power of Symbols Against the Symbols of Power: The Rise of Solidarity and the Fall of State Socialism in Poland* (University Park: Penn State University Press, 1994); Heino Nyyssönen, *The Presence of the Past in Politics: '1956' after 1956 in Hungary* (Jyväskylä: SoPhi. University of Jyväskylä, 1999).
[12] *International Herald Tribune*, 11–12 September 2004, 6.
[13] Don Handelman, *Models and Mirrors: Towards an Anthropology of Public Events* (Cambridge: Cambridge University Press, 1990), 27–8.
[14] This concept was elaborated with regard to the political uses of the Holocaust in Germany; see Eric Langenbacher, 'Memory Regimes in Contemporary Germany', paper presented at the Joint Sessions of the European Consortium for Political Research in Edinburgh, April 2003.

In other words, memory is the effect of historical ruptures but itself has effects on the further evolution of history. Essentially, memory merges different meanings and cultural patterns under the situational premises of uncertainty.[15] Such events are characterised by a high degree of anticipation, in terms of both hopes and fears about the hypothetical future of the community. Thus memory comprises two 'functions'. On the one hand, it represents lived experiences such as communities of fate in a revolution, a war, or a national emergency. On the other hand, these communities of fate remain available as the symbolic reference that emerged in order to make sense of this experience. Hence, transformative experiences both constrain and enable the creation of symbolic meaning. While power incumbents use social experiences for the creation of official collective memory through organised forgetting, such experiences also generate social and cultural forms of memory, which remain largely beyond the control of centralised power. Symbols of critical events can remain available for political uses in the present not because they were integrated into collective national memory by political power, but because their influence persists in alternative symbolism, multiple memories, and a tension between forgetfulness and remembering. If the individuality of memory allows the different pasts to remain available, communities of memory can mobilise such counter-memories in order to challenge symbols of power. The first period of de-Stalinisation became a source of meaning for many citizens, even providing them with a genuine sense of identification with the Soviet system.[16] The devastation of the Second World War not only was a national disaster but also offered identification, morality, and meaning. This was largely due to the fact that the sheer suffering and endurance during the war for many people was their experience that could not be distorted by an officially imposed memory.

The availability of different and sometimes contradicting memories suggests that cultural references are not logically coherent or assigned identical meaning by different individuals or groups. Remembering and forgetting are by definition contentious issues, an observation that speaks against a conception of memory as standing for collective identity.

[15] Marshall Sahlins, *Islands of History* (Chicago: University of Chicago Press, 1987); William Sewell jnr, 'Historical Events as Transformations of Structures: Inventing Revolution at the Bastille', *Theory and Society*, 25 (1996), 861; Tony Judt, 'The Past Is Another Country: Myth and Memory in Postwar Europe', in István Deák et al., eds., *The Politics of Retribution in Europe* (Princeton: Princeton University Press, 2000), 293–323; Bo Strath, ed., *Myth and Memory in the Construction of Community* (Brussels: Peter Lang, 2000).

[16] Michael Urban, et al., *The Rebirth of Politics in Russia* (Cambridge: Cambridge University Press, 1997), 30.

Moreover, the engineering of history by a political regime is contingent upon other unexpected events, of very minor or even invisible scope to the public or to recorded history. There is ample evidence for how the power of history and culture can generate action without elite engineering.[17] In Lithuania, the meaning of the clash between the crowds – commemorating the dead in the struggle for independence – and Soviet militia in Kaunas on All Souls' Day in 1940 needed no definition by Lithuanian elites to become a symbol for national identification and for the value of resistance. Czechs gathered on Václav Square in November 1989 without direction, and East Germans had showed up to the Monday demonstrations some weeks earlier. The eruption of 'unofficial' or 'independent' symbols, principles, and traditions during the Solidarność period in Poland strongly suggests that there was no need to define the meaning of an independent society. Drawing on other experiences in the 'cycles of crises' such as the workers' unrest in Gdańsk in December 1970, Polish workers knew that they had to stay inside their factories rather than go outside in order to present their strike demands. In Hungary, the power of the social memory of the 1956 revolution extended the period of the 'long 1950s' in Hungarian history up to the late 1980s and became crucial for the disarticulation of communist power. Deprived of channels of political articulation and resources for collective protest and resistance, Hungarian society maintained silent pressure and stood as a reminder of what might happen if the Stalinist methods and practices were to be repeated.[18] Such communicative memory can undermine the mythical quality of officially engineered history. On these grounds, and despite the manufacturing of political memory by elites, it is important not to overstress the construction of memory for present political purposes. As a comparative study of the politics of commemoration of 1848 in different countries such as Slovakia, Hungary, and Romania has argued, the nature and structure of 'available pasts' constrains opportunities of commemoration.[19]

The ambivalence of memory

The stability of nation-states in western Europe has largely been based on a politically fabricated and culturally sustained pool of symbols associated

[17] Roger D. Petersen, *Resistance and Rebellion: Lessons from Eastern Europe* (Cambridge: Cambridge University Press, 2001), 299.
[18] Grzegorz Ekiert, *The State Against Society: Political Crises and Their Aftermath in East Central Europe* (Princeton: Princeton University Press, 1996), 103.
[19] Rogers Brubaker and Margit Feischmidt, '1848 in 1998: The Politics of Commemoration in Hungary, Romania, and Slovakia', *Comparative Studies in Society and History*, 44, 4 (2002), 700–44.

with revolutionary events, the consequences of wars, or the founding events of constitutions. The history of state-formation has bequeathed upon political societies in eastern Europe a myriad of contested memories to deal with. The non-congruity of national consciousness with the territorial frame of the state in eastern Europe was a major driving force of nationalism in its irredentist form of claiming lost territory and in its aggressive form of discriminating against ethnic minorities. Frequent border changes, forced migrations, and recurrent wars produced myths of victimisation, vengeance, and retribution.[20] The reluctance to confront oneself with a complex, painful, and thus-far untouched past must be seen in the context of traumatic experiences. A crucial precondition for starting anew in western Europe after the Second World War was a 'blessed act of oblivion', as advocated by Winston Churchill in his famous Zurich speech on 19 September 1946.[21] Following liberal approaches to history, such acts are crucial elements for establishing constitutive beginnings and forging collective identities.[22] While these acts stress the dissociative character of memory, the social memory of traumatic experiences harbours a distinctively associative dimension, which bestows upon memory a representative function, as it represents that past for the present.[23] Blessed acts of oblivion do not erase social memory, but they quite successfully draw a line under the past with the purpose of identity-formation. Building up new identities is inherently linked to the capacity for forgetting a certain part of our past. To put it provocatively, we are not only the past that we (can) remember (as the historicists have always argued), but we are also the past that we can forget.[24] Forgetting may be divided into four types of experiences.[25] For my purpose, the third and fourth types are especially interesting. The third refers to events that put too much of a strain on collective consciousness, causing pain or trauma. The outstanding event of that type in the twentieth century is the

---

[20] Maria Todorova, 'The Course and Discourses of Bulgarian Nationalism', in Peter F. Sugar, ed., *Eastern European Nationalism in the Twentieth Century* (Washington, DC: American University Press, 1995), 55–102.

[21] W. W. Rostow, *The Division of Europe After World War II: 1946* (Aldershot: Gower, 1982), 152.

[22] Deliberate forgetting and historical error are seen as crucial to successful nation-building; see Ernest Renan, 'What Is a Nation', in Geoff Eley and Ronald G. Suny, eds., *Becoming National: A Reader* (New York: Oxford University Press, 1996), 45.

[23] Paul Ricoeur, *La mémoire, l'histoire, l'oubli* (Paris: Seuil, 2000), 106.

[24] F. R. Ankersmit, 'The Sublime Dissociation of the Past: Or How to Be(come) What One Is No Longer', *History and Theory*, 40, 3 (2001), 308.

[25] Ankersmit, 'The Sublime Dissociation of the Past', 300. The first type of forgetting refers to those aspects of the past that are devoid of any relevance for our present or future identity. The second type concerns forgetting something that is truly relevant to our identity and our actions, though we were unaware of this importance.

Holocaust, which was 'forgotten' both in Germany and elsewhere over approximately two decades. In the fourth type, this forgetting of a trauma is arguably not possible. One may think of the great transformations such as the French Revolution or the industrial revolution that changed the life of western Europeans profoundly.

What is relevant here is the distinction between the third and the fourth types of forgetting as to the quality of the trauma and the possibility of creating a new identity. Events such as the Holocaust may entail the worst-case scenario of the coexistence of two identities (the former one and a new identity, crystallising around the traumatic experience). In the fourth type, historical transformations cause feelings of a profound and irreparable loss, of cultural despair, and of hopeless disorientation. Here, the traumatic experience is more dramatic, since a former identity is irrevocably lost forever and superseded by a new historical or cultural identity. Consequently, the new identity is constituted by a trauma for which no cure is to be found and which leads to a permanent loss of the former identity. Summing up, it might be possible to distinguish two kinds of trauma: whereas the third type of forgetting, however dramatic, will leave identity intact, the kind of trauma related to the fourth type of forgetting involves the transition from a former to a new identity which may imply the loss of one's former self. Social revolutions and socialised warfare imply the destruction and reconstitution of identity.

In this vein, much of the politics of memory in eastern Europe and Russia has been characterised not by remembering in order not to forget but rather by the difficulty of forgetting. Communist manipulation of history could organise forgetting for the purpose of distorting historical truth, but it did not produce blessed acts of forgetting. In contrast to the memory of Auschwitz in Germany, for instance, even the memory of the Great Fatherland War in Russia is anything but unequivocal.[26] The double heritage of Nazism and Bolshevik communism in many parts of the region remains difficult to balance without indulging in the exorcising of one through the other.

If the sentiment of loss is a crucial condition for the memory boom, then eastern Europe is of interest precisely because there has been a multiplicity of traumatic experiences. Unlike the 'new start' of the American and French Revolutions, or of post-war Germany, revolutionary ruptures in eastern Europe and Russia were characterised by recurrent loss of identity without the acquisition of a new one. The permanent

---

[26] Andreas Langenohl, *Erinnerung und Modernisierung. Die öffentliche Rekonstruktion politischer Kollektivität am Beispiel des neuen Rußland* (Göttingen: Vandenhoeck & Ruprecht, 2001), 314.

revolution of communism is illustrative here. Whenever the Bolsheviks initiated a radical turn, observers focused on the possible results or consequences of this policy (such as the New Economic Policy or de-Stalinisation). Thus, they attached less importance to movement itself, which in the 'permanent revolution in one country' was of utmost significance as it maintained social disruption and confusion. As Solzhenitsyn put it, 'We forget everything. What we remember is not what actually happened, not history, but merely that hackneyed dotted line they have chosen to drive into our memories by incessant hammering . . . It makes us an easy prey for liars.'[27] The rise of Soviet communism was accompanied by civil war, large-scale social engineering, massive repression, famines, and a considerable demographic loss. The Great Terror in 1936–8 or the Soviet Union's victory in the Second World War only increased Stalin's fear of enemies, leading to massive deportation of entire populations into the gulag or resettlement.

The production of history

Communist regimes used organised forgetting to obfuscate such traumatic experiences. This political technique of imposing a politically 'correct line' consisted essentially of three pillars. First, the destruction of memory aimed to invalidate any uncontrolled references to historical time before the advent of Soviet communism. Similarly, the claim to infallibility required constant adjustments of historical reality to the needs of communist parties. Second, totalitarian language came along with a 'culture of lies' preventing groups with alternative visions about their identity from emerging. Organised forgetting was based on a tissue of lies, inventions, and fantasies that was unconsciously sustained by dissimulation and had a disastrous effect on group identity and historical consciousness. Finally, the public space was characterised by 'communicative silencing', by a dearth of open historical debate, of critical discussion, and of exchange of memories to which the public acquiesced for fear of losing social opportunities and social mobility.

While organised forgetting of past occurrences had a stabilising effect on communist power, it also contained the seeds for a process of dismembering the capacity for perceptions of history. As suggested in a study of Czechoslovakia, the communist production of history streamlined national history according to the expectation of a successful struggle

---

[27] Alexander Solzhenitsyn, *The Gulag Archipelago 1918–1956: An Experiment in Literary Investigation*, vols. I and II, trans. from the Russian by Thomas P. Whitney (Boulder: Westview Press, 1998), 299.

against man's exploitation by capitalists.[28] The transformation of man's nature into the new socialist man relied heavily upon the institutionalisation of utopian time regimes, which would turn upside down orientations in time and thus alter personal identities.[29] The Romanian state, for instance, introduced new time-perceptions seeking to create the background expectancies upon which citizens' sense of the 'normal' is erected. The aim was to keep people permanently off balance, to undermine the sense of a 'normal' order, and to institute uncertainty as the rule. This practice of 'etatisation' of time entailed a yawning gap between elites and the populace. While the party elites lived by promised images of a radiant future, the populace lived under the impression of flattened time and endless repetition. This production of history by politically crafting time-perceptions 'reinterpreted' elements of national tradition in order to accommodate communist rule. Nicolae Ceaușescu's *History of Romania*, a collection of texts from speeches in which he mentions historical events, is organised into five sections, the first containing observations about the necessary relation of historiography to politics and the remaining four covering antiquity and the middle ages, the fourteenth to nineteenth centuries, 1821–1918, and 1919–48.

The organisation of forgetting reinforced mythic time-dimensions. The selective creation of pasts and their instrumentality for the future justified contemporary interests, as mythic time-dimensions are an essential part of the metaphorical political world.[30] Unlike historical time, mythical time-perceptions conceived of the past as absolute, dispensing with the question of 'why' something happened. History was stripped of its eventfulness by regressing ever further back into a never-ending sequence of becoming.[31] The recourse to mythic time-dimensions under communism was consistent with the communist party's zeal to produce its own law and history by the manipulation of history and the destruction of memory. The resurgence of foundation myths is quite typical of crises of legitimacy, when political formulas and models for the future are often missing. The history of the Second World War was dealt with selectively, leaving out any mention of the fate of the Jews or the building-up of myths of enemies which would maintain the confusion about the activities of the

[28] Derek Sayer, *The Coasts of Bohemia: A Czech History* (Princeton: Princeton University Press, 1997), 283–4.
[29] Katherine Verdery, *What Was Socialism and What Comes Next?* (Princeton: Princeton University Press, 1996), 54–7.
[30] Murray Edelman, *The Symbolic Uses of Politics* (Urbana: University of Illinois Press, 1985), 187.
[31] Ernst Cassirer, *The Philosophy of Symbolic Forms*, vol. II, *Mythical Thought* (New Haven and London: Yale University Press, 1985), 105–6.

communist party or the actual conflict lines in the war. Fear of victimisation has been one, if not the most important, element in many national
historiographies. In the case of Kosovo, for instance, both the Serbs and
the Albanians rooted arguments about their own distinctiveness in history
and religion in claims of their temporal ancestry in this region.[32] Both
Serbs and Albanians appeared to share legitimacy-patterns anchored in a
remote and timeless past. Serbs claimed the status of an elected people
based on the legend of Prince Lazar, whose defeat by the Turks in 1389
was a sacrifice bound to be redeemed. Albanians tended to go further
back in time to the sixth and seventh centuries, claiming an Illyrian–
Albanian continuity and superiority over Slavic people. When Slobodan
Milošević unleashed nationalist aggression against the Albanian ethnic
majority in Kosovo, he could draw on the mythical consciousness in
popular memory of 1389, which was commemorated in a unique gathering of some 2 million people on Kosovo polje in July 1989.

The fragmentation of memory

History under communism became an object of forgetfulness rather than
a source of historiographic inquiry and search for truth. On the one hand,
cynicism and mistrust pervaded many social, cultural, and even personal
exchanges. On the other hand, the capacity of communist states to
produce history was checked by private and unofficial versions of countless occurrences that would form powerful counter-histories of a mutually
antagonistic and divisive nature.[33] Rather than maintaining a unitary
communist identity, the production of history by organised forgetting
entailed the fragmentation of memories.

Fragmentation of memories concerns not only the object of memory,
i.e. the factual content of a given event, but also the social carriers, i.e.
actors who do the remembering. As can be demonstrated by looking at
the politics of memory in post-war Germany, one can differentiate between
communicative, collective, and cultural memory.[34] Communicative memory is mainly individual memory that grows in milieus of spatial proximity,
regular interaction, common forms of life, and shared experiences. Beyond
the common experience in a social milieu, communicative memory is
specific for generations. Explicitly subjective memories are bound up in
an implicit generational memory. For collective memory to become an
important factor in constructing and reconstructing events, the existence of

---

[32] Gossiaux, 'Les deux passés', 43–53.   [33] Judt, 'The Past Is Another Country', 308.
[34] Aleida Assmann and Ute Frevert, *Geschichtsvergessenheit, Geschichtsversessenheit. Vom
Umgang mit deutschen Vergangenheiten nach 1945* (Stuttgart: DVA, 1999), 41–50.

a self-conscious political community is required. Collective memory is political memory, shaped by institutional control over the availability of memory; it has a strong tendency towards unification, and is quite resistant to decay or oblivion. It is characterised by minimal content and by symbolic reductionism that may be centred on one single event. The memories of both victors and losers tend towards a strongly affect-oriented interpretation of historical data and are therefore prone to becoming immune to alternative versions of history. The differentiation into memories of victors, memories of victims, and memories of perpetrators is characteristic for most collective memories in modern societies. Beyond both forms of memory, a third realm opens up, which can be termed cultural memory. Cultural memory proper requires 'translation' by external media to make complex symbolic forms available to everybody. Media of cultural memory comprise artefacts such as texts, pictures, and sculpture as well as spatial compositions such as monuments, architecture, landscape, and temporal orders such as feasts, customs, or rituals. While collective memory expresses a common experience and a common will, by cultural memory members of a political society communicate beyond the individual lifetime in a long-term historical perspective. Their aim is to become aware of an identity, forged through belonging to broad historical experiences beyond generational boundaries.

The discrepancy between different forms of memory is thus not a particularity of post-communist eastern Europe. Coming to terms with the past in Germany has been a laborious and politically contested enterprise that has produced a whole terminology of its own and, far from subsiding, has been prolific in the second half of the 1990s and beyond.[35] For the immediate German post-war history, the split between communicative memory and collective memory has been significant. In the Federal Republic of Germany of the 1950s one could identify two cultures: one public culture characterised by the paradigm of guilt, with another, hidden culture of silence guided by the paradigm of shame.[36]

Beyond repressive methods designed to streamline historical consciousness, memory in eastern Europe has had the transformative power of generating counter-narratives and alternative social memory. This fragmentation of memories was perhaps most intense where political societies were subject at separate times to the domination of both Nazism and

---

[35] The German terms 'Vergangenheitsbewältigung' or 'Geschichtsaufarbeitung', for instance, cannot be translated in one word, e.g., in English; Robert G. Moeller, 'What Has "Coming to Terms with the Past" Meant in Post-World War II Germany? From History to Memory to the "History of Memory"', *Central European History*, 35, 2 (2001), 223–56.

[36] Assmann and Frevert, *Geschichtsvergessenheit*, 111.

232 Democracy as a process of meaning-formation

communism. Following upon an entirely different perception of enemies in the experiences of non-Jewish Poles and Jewish Poles during the Second World War, the memories in its aftermath were divided.[37] Catholic Poles and Jewish Poles, for instance, relied upon selective perceptions of the past, mutually ignoring the other's history by presenting themselves as unique victims. This double memory looked for reward for their suffering as a basis for the claim of their moral superiority. Recently, the role of non-Jewish Poles in the massacre of Jews in the village of Jedwabne during the Second World War became the single most important public debate about Poland's past.[38] The permanence of fragmented memories about the communist past, radicalised by the relatively clear-cut antagonism between communist authorities and the Solidarność opposition, led to particularly contested assessments of Poland's post-war history.[39]

In ethnically divided societies such as Yugoslavia, cultural politics and political discourse in separate republics deepened the fragmentation of memories. Tito subordinated memories of the civil war to the dominant collective memory of the anti-fascist myth, which was supported by the myth of the unifying partisan experience and the heroic figure of Tito himself. The initially stabilising imposition of organised forgetting reinforced geographically and nationally specific memories, which sustained mythologies of victimisation that became crucial to Yugoslavia's bloody disintegration. In 1946, Yugoslav state propaganda fixed the total number of Yugoslav dead in the Second World War at 1.7 million, a number that remained basically uncontested in handbooks, schoolbooks, and official state doctrine for forty years, before recent historical scholarship established the number at an estimated 1 million. Whereas this mythical construction initially reinforced the impression of a particularly great number of victims in the anti-fascist struggle for a united Yugoslavia, the Serbian leadership used it in the 1980s in order to prove the huge number of Serbs killed by Croatian Ustaše. The freezing of numbers of the dead could have completely different consequences, however, depending on the changing circumstances. Whereas the artificially elevated numbers of Yugoslav war victims contributed to radicalising Serbian nationalist feelings, the numbers of dead used by the anti-fascist myth in East Germany provoked the opposite reaction. The East German Socialist United Party (SED) drew much of its legitimacy from the

[37] Piotr Wróbel, 'Double Memory: Poles and Jews After the Holocaust', *East European Politics and Societies*, 11, 3 (1997), 560–74.
[38] Jan T. Gross, *Neighbors: The Destruction of the Jewish Community in Jedwabne, Poland* (London: Penguin Books, 2002).
[39] Krystyna Kersten, 'Bilans zamknięcia', in *Spór o PRL* (Kraków: Znak, 1996), 17–27.

reference to its dead in the anti-fascist fight against Hitler between 1933 and 1945. It appears to be this focus on the dead which contributed to the freezing and ritualisation of a cult of the dead that kept a whole population as prisoners of those dead, a dead-end that contributed to a process of indifference.[40]

The fragmentation of memories in Russia has consisted in a contest of rival versions of Russian history making use of tsarist, pre-revolutionary, Soviet, and post-Soviet Russian heritage.[41] There, political discourse has largely turned around the opposition between democrats-Westernisers and patriots-communists. The state breakdown of the Soviet Union filled communists with a profound grief over the loss of territory and disintegration of values, provoking a strongly patriotic reaction.[42] The leader of the Communist Party of the Russian Federation, Gennadi Zyuganov, interpreted history as a dramatic narrative, portraying the Russian nation as torn between being a hero-victim and being exposed to enemies from the West. History is seen as taking its departure from the inevitable Russian Revolution, rising in the periods of Lenin and Stalin before entering decay through de-Stalinisation and reducing Russia to a victim after the end of the Soviet Union. Next to the hero-victim, the maleficent West becomes the symbol of evil, which is represented by an interior fifth column that adopted a liberal democratic ideology in order to destroy Russian spirituality and culture.

The mobilisation of memory

The fragmentation of memories under communism has been central to the political symbolism of democratisation. The fragmentation of memories was a necessary condition for democratisation in so far as it uncovered the artificiality and falseness of the totality suggested by the People-as-One or the anti-fascist myth. On the one hand, coercive practices of organised forgetting under communist rule were mainly directed against communicative memory for the purpose of modelling a unitary collective memory. In the aftermath of the Second World War, for instance, this happened via the construction of fascist conspiracies, through the linkage of national history with communist/Stalinist ideology, through an amalgam of socialist internationalism and open nationalism and through the

[40] Herfried Münkler, 'Antifaschismus und antifaschistischer Widerstand als politischer Gründungsmythos der DDR', *Aus Politik und Zeitgeschichte*, 45 (1998), 16–29.
[41] Jutta Scherrer, 'Russia – In Search of a Useful Past', in Attila Pok, et al., *European History: Challenge for a Common Future* (Hamburg: Körber-Stiftung, 2002), 90–108.
[42] Michael Urban, 'Remythologizing the Russian State', *Europe–Asia Studies*, 50, 6 (1998), 969–92.

silencing of open ethnic conflict by calling on the people to feel brother-hood and unity. Communist regimes tended to establish a uniformity of national history by which the history of communism and the nation in one country was presented as a predestined historical outcome attuned to the ideological claims of Marxist-Leninist theory. On the other hand, com-municative memory took on an important role in the reconstruction of historical events and the shaping of symbolic politics. Much of the rising counter-public, parallel society, or second polity in eastern Europe would not have come into existence without the mobilisation of communicative memory.

Keeping dissident versions of memorable acts available, powerful counter-narratives resist a collective logic of one truth or one meaning. They consist in different truths that are subject to contested and ongoing interpretations, thus articulating society's continuing quest for meaning. Symbolism is not about one specific memory but about something absent, which the longing for commemoration represents. Evidently, as George Orwell's remark 'he who controls the past controls the future' suggests, communist regimes were masters in implementing the fragmen-tation of memories. Yet, while representations of the past could be frozen in official discourse and collective memory, communist rule failed to manipulate individual consciousness and communities of remembering that resisted the dominant versions of organised forgetting. Historical experiences hidden in communicative memory are mobilised for the purpose of reconstitution of identity when political societies are con-fronted with a sudden loss, leading to an existential crisis. After the attacks on the Twin Towers on 11 September 2001, for instance, the United States reacted with a wave of patriotism, reproducing national symbols such as the flag in huge quantities, evoking the republican ideals of nation-building. Yet, there was also an upsurge of comparisons with other traumatic events, in particular with the Japanese attack on Pearl Harbor in December 1941. The notion 'ground zero' was instantly used by the media to symbolise the area where the Twin Towers once stood. The spontaneous naming of this space 'ground zero' recalled the place where an atomic bomb had exploded on US territory on 16 July 1945.[43]

In Russia, the October Revolution has been codified as the birth of modern Russian society in an essentialist way. Some argue that the

---

[43] This was at Alamogordo in New Mexico. The reference to the atomic bomb is of great interest when seen in context with Bin Laden's claim that one of his principal objectives is to combat the Americans because they started by dropping atomic bombs on Hiroshima and Nagasaki; see Jean-Pierre Dupuy, *Avions-nous oublié le mal?* (Paris: Bayard, 2002), 48–9.

revolution is to be interpreted as a typical social conflict in Russian history with the contrast of the alienated masses and detached elites. A different type of interpretation conceives of the revolution as a modernising enterprise in the tradition of the tsarist empire, thus legitimately establishing a spirit of imperial modernisation. Finally, some view the revolution as a grand crime against the Russian nation and the Russian spirit.[44] Similarly, one can speak about what are coming to be seen as the two lives of the Russian Revolution, the first life being considered as part of the present, inseparable from contemporary politics, the second life as being detached from the present and moving into history and national legend.[45]

The inexpressible suffering during the Second World War in the Soviet Union was also felt to be a liberation from repression and an identification with the nation. As far as the social texture of everyday life is concerned, this period of havoc, devastation, national suffering, and death has brought not only spaces of freedom but even the genuine acceptance of, and identification with, the Soviet system. In Hungary, Czechoslovakia, and Poland, memories of the revolutions were harboured in the communicative memory of dissident structures. It is true that, some years down the line from the Prague spring, people could hardly remember the events of 1968 as real because change was so dramatic following the arrival of Soviet troops and because official accounts of the events were so pervasive and so different from their own experiences.[46] Yet, it became a milestone for the transformation of consciousness, as power-lessness before a military invasion mobilised the 'powers of the powerless' consisting in an opposition in a hidden sphere and united by living in truth.

This realm of the hidden sphere lived on the merger of communicative with cultural memory. In pre-1989 Hungary, the memory of Imre Nagy and the 1956 revolution had survived in counter-narratives defying the system of organised forgetting. The 1956 revolution prefigured the recent democratic changes in Hungary, as the memory of thirty-year-old events and the chance that demands of that time might be satisfied have acted as a considerable integrating force. Imre Poszgay's official acknowledgement that the 1956 events were not a counter-revolution but a popular uprising undercut the legitimacy of the communist regime and offered a powerful symbolic resource to emerging political opposition. The

---

[44] See Langenohl, *Erinnerung und Modernisierung*, 265–8.
[45] See Sheila Fitzpatrick, *The Russian Revolution*, 2nd edn (Oxford: Oxford University Press, 2001), 171.
[46] Milan Šimečka, *The Restoration of Order: The Normalization of Czechoslovakia, 1969–1976* (London: Verso, 1984), 15–16.

convergence of different and often opposed traditions in Poland's permanent revolution was largely sustained by the memories of 1956, 1968,
1970, and 1976. A series of violent explosions (October 1956, March
1968, December 1970, June 1976) was remembered in communicative
memory but also became part of cultural memory, thus creating a spirit of
silent, daily, and obstinate resistance. As Adam Michnik remarked, this
was the reason why Poles could breathe a cleaner air than elsewhere, an
air of spirituality which was renewed every day, invisible but essential for
culture and national consciousness. In post-martial law Poland after
1981, the memory of the Solidarność experience was kept alive in informal structures under the shelter of the Catholic Church and depending
on individual life-conduct.[47]

Educational politics and public discourse in Yugoslavia were efficient
in organising the forgetting about the civil war between 1941 and 1945,
but could not undo the power of communicative memory. Although the
disintegration of Yugoslavia from the late 1980s onwards was due to a
complex blend of political, economic, and military factors, the fragmentation of memories in Yugoslavian politics played a paramount role for
the identification of different ethnic communities with myths of victimisation and vengeance of the interethnic civil war between 1941 and
1945. Yugoslavia remains the primary example where the production of
history after 1945 shifted from the emphasis on salient national identity to
a divided identity.[48] Despite Tito's slogan of 'brotherhood and unity',
Yugoslav society was marked by fragmented memories, by a freezing of
constructed historical evidence into abstract time, and by a subordination
of history to the legitimacy of the regime.[49] The memories of the civil war
were not bad memories as such. Tito's Moscow-independent seizure
of power was formative for identities in the post-war generation in
Yugoslavia, where the war was not seen as futile and senseless bloodletting, but on the contrary as a heroic and meaningful experience that
was worth more than its 1 million victims.[50] Whereas organised forgetting
about war memories was central for establishing a mythical cult suggesting solidarity, brotherhood, or a founding event for a national revolution,

---

[47] Harald Wydra, *Continuities in Poland's Permanent Transition* (Basingstoke: Macmillan,
2001), 144–6.
[48] Andrew B. Wachtel, *Making a Nation, Breaking a Nation: Literature and Cultural Politics in
Yugoslavia* (Stanford: Stanford University Press, 1998), 187.
[49] Wolfgang Höpken, 'War, Memory, and Education in a Fragmented Society: The Case of
Yugoslavia', *East European Politics and Societies*, 13, 1 (1999), 190–227.
[50] Slavenka Drakulić, *The Balkan Express: Fragments from the Other Side of the War* (New
York and London: W. W. Norton, 1993), 12.

Tito's death and funeral in May 1980 formed a critical moment that represented the fragmentation of communicative memory.

The mobilisation of memory after 1989 has often 'rationalised' backwardness or national humiliation by setting a new horizon of expectation. Memories of the domestic 'small revolutions' were sidelined from official collective memory. With regard to 1968, shame looms large as the source of the lack of interest professed by the Czechs for their recent past.[51] This shame or even cynicism might stem from the irreconcilability of two histories or truths that were inherent to 1968: on the one hand, the account of a civic, human, and spontaneous Prague spring; on the other, the representation of 1968 as a failure rooted in the political naivety of Czechoslovaks. As the notorious 'hyphen debate' in Czechoslovakia indicated, contested memories about the balance of power in the federal state considerably contributed to the velvet divorce. Slovak representatives in the Federal Assembly resisted the idea of Czech representatives to name the new republic the Czechoslovak Republic, reminiscent of the earlier states, when the Czech part had been dominant. Insisting upon their national distinctiveness, the proposal by Czechs to adopt the neologism Czecho-slovak Republic under the condition that slovak remains in the lower case sparked off demonstrations in Bratislava demanding a Slovak state of their own. This unhappy compromise produced demonstrations in Bratislava the very next day, demanding a Slovak state, and within three weeks the Federal Assembly was forced to come up with a new compromise, 'The Czech and Slovak Federal Republic'.[52]

This tension between the dissociation from the past and the production of the past for political needs in the present has been particularly acute in Russia. Civic initiatives such as Memorial focused on the factual elucidation of the victims of Stalinism, disclosing crimes in tens of thousands of cases in the late 1980s. Although in October 1992 the Duma passed a comprehensive law rehabilitating victims of political repressions since 7 November 1917, the Russian leadership has recently embraced patriotic discourse, which restores the memory of historical events and emblematic leading figures of both pre- and post-revolutionary Russian history.[53]

[51] Petr Pithart, 'La dualité du Printemps tchéchoslovaque. Société civile et communistes réformateurs', in François Fejtö and Jacques Rupnik, eds., *Le Printemps tchécoslovaque 1968* (Paris: Editions Complexes), 85–6.
[52] Tony Judt, 'Metamorphosis: The Democratic Revolution in Czechoslovakia', in Ivo Banac, ed., *Eastern Europe in Revolution* (Ithaca and London: Cornell University Press, 1992), 105.
[53] Kathleen Smith, *Remembering Stalin's Victims: Popular Memory and the End of the USSR* (Ithaca and London: Cornell University Press, 1996), 78–173.

In search of a structuring principle of Russian history, Yeltsin's and Putin's leadership has focused identity-formation on the reaffirmation of the imperial legacy such as in the reburial of the last tsar in late 1998 or the re-establishment of the melody of the Soviet national anthem.[54] Among a great variety of possible nationally significant events, the day of the victory in the Great Fatherland War (9 May) stands out as embodying Russia's patriotic sentiment. In this vein, Putin's project of rejecting any myth of Russia's path as permanently deviant from the normal course of development associated with the West is compensated for by his attempt to turn Russia into a 'normal' country. This return to normality in itself is a mythical construct, as it needs to retrieve a variety of national symbols, whose mythologisation is essential to attenuate Russia's permanent contradiction with itself.[55] Similarly, the multiple symbols of Russian political culture that are condensed on Red Square represent the ongoing search for truth and meaning in the face of the availability of conflicting memories. Each element present is reminiscent of different forms of political domination and phases in national history, often sharply in contradiction with each other. On this unique spot Saint Basil's cathedral evokes the Great Russia of Ivan the Terrible. The Kremlin walls and the red stars on the towers recall the tsarist regime and the revolution but also symbolise post-communist presidential power. Lenin's mausoleum indicates the omnipresence of ideology and the cult of personality. The crosses of the cathedrals emphasise the religious essence of the square.[56]

The democratic uses of memory

Connecting the generative context of memory in events-that-model to the associative dimension of available pasts does not provide a comprehensive view of how post-communist countries can or should come to terms with the past. Rather, I have suggested that the study of communism and post-communism should be 'released' from the logically constructed opposition between a legacy and the present. The multiplicity of memories does not indicate a pathological condition of a brittle region that is detrimental to democratic identity. Thus, transiting between past and future has not been the pathological condition of formerly communist

[54] *Kommersant*, 9 December 2000.
[55] See Richard Sakwa, 'Myth and Political Identity in Russia', paper presented at the conference Myth and Democracy in Eastern Europe, 26–28 October 2002, University of Regensburg.
[56] Claire Petrouchine, *Il faut qu'une place soit ouverte ou fermée. La place Rouge, Moscou, printemps 1999* (Mémoire de DEA Université Lumière Lyon II, 1999), 119.

societies but is consistent with a central pattern of identity-formation in modern nation-states.

As a comparison with post-war West Germany and post-war France indicates, the permanence of the past has not been an east European pathology. West German post-war history of memory can be divided into three phases.[57] A first phase, which can be called 'politics of the past', stretched from 1945 to 1957. It was characterised by an unremitting defence against memory and a strategy of 'communicative silencing', necessary for providing a sense of community in the early post-war years. It was informed by the victim-syndrome, which sustained a clear separation between the Nazi regime and the German people, attributing the role of perpetrator to the former, that of the victim to the latter. A second phase can be conjectured as spanning from 1958 to 1984, when critiques of coming to terms with the past increased. On the one hand, it consisted of a rising number of trials against Nazi perpetrators; on the other hand, it saw an increasing self-criticism about the forms of coming to terms – or not – with the past. A third phase, starting from 1985, saw an increasing importance of memory, strengthening official commemoration and symbols. This classification shows interesting parallels with the four phases that were proposed as a parallel history of the Vichy regime in France.[58] The first phase was the 'mourning phase' (1944–54) that highlighted pain and grief, thus preventing society from working on the pain. External signs of this phase were the purges and the subsequent amnesty. Vichy was silenced, while the resistance movement was focused upon. The second phase (1954–71) was the phase of repressed memories, when 'resistancialism' was established as the dominant myth of an anti-fascist France. It sought to minimise the importance of the Vichy regime and turned the 'Résistance' into an object of memory, identifying it with the French nation as a whole. The third phase (1971–4) witnessed the shattering of the societal consensus on the myth and the return of repression. Finally, the phase of obsessive memory (from 1974 continuing to today) has been marked by the reawakening of Jewish memory through memoirs of victims, research on the Holocaust, and trials of its perpetrators, and the growing importance of reminiscences of the occupation in the French political debate.

As the German and French cases suggest, memory is both a preservative, 'backward-looking', and a transformative, 'forward-looking' power. The fragmentation and mobilisation of memories become symbolic

---

[57] This account also relies on Assmann and Frevert, *Geschichtsvergessenheit*, 144–5.
[58] Henry Rousso, *The Vichy Syndrome: History and Memory in France Since 1944*, trans. Arthur Goldhammer (Cambridge, MA: Harvard University Press, 1991).

markers of certainty by representing a nation's controversial history for the present. The return to different 'pasts' in post-communist Europe amounted to a *bricolage* of recovering national identity, a sense of pride but also of healing wounds in individual and collective memory. The collapse of communism has reinforced an important mobilisation of nationally unique and historically specific events from the 'pre-communist' period at the expense of the inquiry into the Stalinist past in Russia, or the small revolutions in Hungary, Czechoslovakia, and Poland. Despite the establishment of national institutes of memory practically everywhere in the region, the systematic elucidation of crimes has kept a rather low profile.[59] The politics of identity-formation instead included symbolisations representing moves 'back to the truth', 'back to the nation', 'back to normality', 'back to Europe', or 'back to the present'.[60] For much of non-Russian eastern Europe, the Second World War cut off their ties with Western democracy, a major reason why these countries wanted to return to the starting point of 1945–6.[61] In Romania, since 1989, due to the failed rupture in its 'stolen' or 'confiscated' revolution of 1989, the perception of a 'permanence of the past' has prevailed.[62] Russians came to write the 'white pages of the past', trying to reconstruct a brave and safe pre-revolutionary society that was toppled overnight by a small group of Bolshevik rogues. Coming to terms with the past has been replaced by a mythologised representation of an intact world of pre-revolutionary Russia.[63]

Contested memories indicate how communicative and cultural memory can be generative of existential representation of a people. The desire to overcome the backward condition of one's own country or the oppression of communist rule often tallied with reaching the shores of Western civilisation. Since the nineteenth century, domestic political discourse among the Russian and east European intelligentsia focused on the self-perception of one's own nation as being an island cut off from progress, modernity, and the 'normal' course of history, associated with the West. Much of the history of Westernisation in Russia has been the story of tsarism representing itself as a mirror of European courts but also of an

[59] Carmen González Enríquez, 'De-communization and Political Justice in Central and Eastern Europe', in Barahona de Brito et al., *Politics of Memory*, 218–47.
[60] Mikko Lagerspetz, 'Postsocialism as a Return: Notes on a Discursive Strategy', *East European Politics and Societies*, 13, 2 (1999), 377–90.
[61] Timothy Garton Ash, *The Uses of Adversity* (New York: Random House, 1989), 258.
[62] Hans-Christian Maner, 'Die andauernde Vergangenheit', *Osteuropa*, 48, 10 (1998), 1024–40.
[63] Jutta Scherrer, *Requiem für den Roten Oktober. Rußlands Intelligenzija im Umbruch 1986–1996* (Leipzig: Leipziger Universitätsverlag, 1996), 127–8.

intelligentsia under the spell of Western civilisation.[64] The unachieved social progress, the denied recognition, and the failed political reform became objects of political strife, nationalist rhetoric, and historiographical contention. In Romania, for instance, the nationalist European discourse, with the aim of reintegration into Western civilisation, has considered the country as a 'Latin island' in the Slavic sea.[65] For many people, especially in east central Europe, the establishment of communist regimes after 1945 came down to being cut off from 'natural' ties with the West. In the perception of opposition elites, Poland under communism had itself become an 'island' isolated from the mainstream course of progress and development, where the transmission of ideas had been completely blocked and many things had to be (re)invented anew.[66] The reconstruction of the notion of central Europe in the 1980s, for instance, was underpinned by the self-perception of dissidents in countries such as Czechoslovakia, Poland, and Hungary as having being kidnapped by the 'barbarian East' and thus isolated from European civilisation.

Facing the paradox of how Czechoslovakia as the economically most developed democratic country in central Europe could produce the most rigid, deepest-rooted, and long-living communism in the region, it is safe to argue that in Prague and in other parts of central Europe the Vichy syndrome has just begun.[67] It is hardly surprising that post-communism has been characterised by similar tendencies to appropriate the spontaneity of communicative memory for state-induced patriotism and the symbolic reductionism of collective memory. The new political leadership defined the epoch of communist rule as a 'dark age' or a past that must be clearly delimited as separate from the present.[68] In the wake of Imre Nagy's reburial, Hungarian official politics reappropriated this memory by substituting civic informality, spontaneity, and solidarity with state-induced patriotic legalisation and the symbolic reductionism of collective memory.[69] In the Baltic countries, Soviet official historiography had presented the years 1918–40 as an interlude, so that, for

---

[64] See Richard Wortman, *Scenarios of Power: Myth and Ceremony in Russian Monarchy*, 2 vols. (Princeton: Princeton University Press, 1995/2000).
[65] Lucien Boia, 'The Romanian Consciousness Faced with National Ideology and European Sentiment', in Pok, et al., *European History*, 133–44.
[66] Wydra, *Continuities*, 103.
[67] Rupnik, 'Was tun mit der kommunistischen Vergangenheit?', 127.
[68] See the initial policy of the first post-communist government in Poland or the Czech Republic's Law on the Illegal Character of the Communist Regime of 1991.
[69] Mate Szabo, 'Rituale der Vergangenheitsbewältigung', in Andreas Pribersky and Berthold Unfried, eds., *Symbole und Rituale des Politischen. Ost- und Westeuropa im Vergleich* (Frankfurt am Main: Peter Lang, 1999), 154.

example, the annexation of Estonia into the Soviet Union was seen as the legitimate re-establishment of Soviet power. Conversely, the reconstruction of memory in these countries reflects the heritage of independent statehood after 1918 and the annexation by the Red Army in 1940. In the new, post-communist interpretation of history, the pre-war independence period is, on the contrary, of great importance. It is no longer the pre-war era, but the period of Soviet rule, that is viewed as an unnatural interlude that delayed the natural development of the country.[70]

Two propositions can be made with a view to integrating the power of memory into a reflection on the emergence of democracy. A first proposition claims to rethink the temporality of political evolution in the study of communism and post-communism. The multiplicity of individual and collective memories in eastern Europe suggests that the differentiation between pre-communist, communist, or post-communist pasts is artificial at best. Accelerations of history cannot be readily appropriated for historicist accounts of democratisation. Communism not only destroyed memories but also produced the counter-memories that contributed decisively to its own dismantling. If processes such as de-Stalinisation, the Hungarian and Polish revolutions in 1956 and 1980, or the Prague spring in 1968 did not bring about democratic transitions as a new constitutional form of government, their afterlife in terms of political symbolism was a powerful element in the political spirituality of democratisation.

A second proposition suggests that communism was not only a power system based on repressive institutions that constrained freedom by means of a totalitarian drive to control the minds of people. Against the repressive character of organised forgetting, the mobilisation of multiple pasts at the level of communicative memory was an essential element in the evolution of an alternative consciousness, an attempt to ground existence in historicity, truthfulness, and subjectivity. Against communicative silencing, the democratic credentials of memory have been based on truth-telling, historiographical inquiry, drawing history lessons, confessions, and acknowledgement of shame or accountability. This claim is consistent with the central precondition for the memory boom in recent years, which was identified in the social tendency to the democratisation of history. Important waves of decolonisation such as of the Third World, of minorities, and of the countries under totalitarian rule have fostered an unprecedented development of 'minority memory' as a means to regain the past as an element of identity-formation. Challenging the ready-made

[70] Lagerspetz, 'Postsocialism', 383.

and doctrinal interpretation of history by communists, the struggle of memory against forgetting was crucial in the struggle against oppression.[71] The communist legacy has often been associated with 'bad' memories as separate from or opposed to 'good' memories relating to national traditions or pre-communist pasts. As far as the power of memory represents the past with an elaborate symbolisation, the 'communist past' is not only a legacy of totalitarian repression but also an expression of a democratic consciousness against communist collectivism.

[71] Milan Kundera, *The Book of Laughter and Forgetting* (New York: Penguin, 1981), 3.

10　The future that failed

The belief that there is only one reality is the most dangerous self-deception.
Paul Watzlawick

The preceding chapter has argued that memory has been a democratising force by making consciousness the centre of resistance to attempts to maintain total power over people. Communicative and cultural memory maintained national traditions, developed civic informality, and prefigured public opinion. In other words, the memory representing traumatic experiences in one's country's past could become a source of freedom and identity. Whereas democratisation can be linked to truthfulness and existential representation in the past, one needs to bear in mind that, since the age of the democratic revolutions in the late eighteenth century, the emergence of democratic politics has been associated with a utopian bent and expectations of a better future. The communist experiment rooted identities in an alternative form of 'second' reality, which would see popular sovereignty in the abolition of oppression. It attempted to legitimise political domination not by security, property, or liberty but by the promise of salvation and total freedom, which could be attained by the transformation of human nature and the advent of a new society. This chapter argues that democratic consciousness under communism was not generated primarily by preferences of enlightened democrats; rather, it was a reaction against communism's ideological prescription of totality. Rejecting the utopian and teleological project of the second reality required grounding existence in concrete life, not in fantasies of salvation.

The authority of second reality

Identity-formation has been one of the most encompassing and inconclusive endeavours in the fragmentation of the post-communist world. Nationality changes in the wake of territorial reshuffles, abrupt reversals in the conditions of economic and public life, and the collapse of political authority in their aftermath shattered previously existing individual and collective identities.[1] In analytical terms, identities are often considered as 'dependent variables' with a view to explaining 'independent variables' such as the integration of a political system or democratic institution-building.[2] It has been common to highlight the integrative aspect of 'European identity', 'democratic identity', or 'capitalist identity'. Identity is taken as one of many inputs into a political system, as a delineated set of attributes of political culture. Identity-based conflicts are seen as responsible for fragmentation, distrust, or ethnic separatism and thus as obstacles to successful democratic institution-building. Some caution is needed, however, when identity-formation is opposed to the interest-based working of the systemic logic of political economy or political regimes. Political identities in communist eastern Europe are, with hindsight, assumed to have been coherent and unified due to repression and military force.[3] Like claims about identification with 'democracy' or 'Europe', however, any claim about 'socialist identities' in communist countries must be taken with caution.

While identities in a political or social system in relative equilibrium are comparatively stable and thus prior to intentions, in situations of existential uncertainty identifications are contingent upon the contextual intentions of the agents that do the identifying. Consistent with recent research, a political anthropology of transformative experiences must go 'beyond identity'.[4] Identification – of oneself and of others – as intrinsic to social life and reality will not necessarily result in the internal sameness and coherent, bounded groupness that political leaders may seek to achieve. Under communism, identification was essentially provided by developmental goals in the pursuit of a utopia, which involved the creation of a new man and the eschatological expectation of an end stage of human development. The institutionalisation of utopia concerned not only the material capacity to monopolise the state and economic institutions but also the control of consciousness, language, and identity.

These patterns of identity-formation reflected the lack of a sense of reality as a central feature of communism. The identity of the People-as-One was supported by the identification of 'enemies of the people' and the promise of a paradise after the transition to 'communism'. Identities

---

[1] Michael Burawoy and Katherine Verdery, eds., *Uncertain Transition: Ethnographies of Change in the Postsocialist World* (Lanham, MD: Rowman & Littlefield, 1999).
[2] Jon Elster et al., *Institutional Design in Post-Communist Societies* (Cambridge: Cambridge University Press, 1998), 247–70.
[3] Claus Offe, *Varieties of Transition: The East European and East German Experience* (Cambridge, MA: MIT Press, 1997), 73.
[4] Rogers Brubaker and Frederick Cooper, 'Beyond "Identity"', *Theory and Society*, 29, 1 (2000), 1–47.

under communism were not stable, as patterns of representation and political projects were inherently 'defined' by a dream world, where the daily life of shortage, delusion, and victimisation was opposed to the eschatological vision of a better world. The political authority of communism relied heavily on compensating for uncertainty with promises of a radiant future. Communism as a political religion ideologically prescribed an eschatological vision of engineering the future. The end of politics implied by Lenin's *State and Revolution* was consistent with the monopolisation of political life, the control of knowledge, and the creation of history and law. Revolutionary messianism entailed states of consciousness where a split between a first and a second reality can be characterised as a deliberate desire not to understand, as an alienation from a true meaningful life in order.[5] Taking examples from literature such as Thomas More's *Utopia*, Cervantes's *Don Quixote*, and Robert Musil's *Man Without Qualities*, Eric Voegelin argued that the emergence of second reality is tightly linked to how man's consciousness is transformed in response to a crisis situation. People start to refuse the perception of reality, projecting fantasies and imaginary realities on to their everyday existence. This selective consciousness may become socially relevant once it attracts the attention of more or less important social groups. Under specific circumstances a minority group may impose selective consciousness by force in order to establish a second reality as the authoritative frame of political existence. The influence of second realities in politics can hardly be proved empirically by measuring the activities of objective givens such as, say, an election, a parliament, or a constitution. The 'test' can be attempted only by sensing the spell that images, beliefs, and fantasies cast on philosophers, political leaders, and ordinary people.

Marx's vision of a classless society was related to the uprootedness of the economic process and the social conditions of his time. Based on the general claim that all transformations in human arrangements rely upon material force, he claimed that new modes of production and wage-earning led to relationships of oppression in which the workers were inevitably alienated and enslaved. The state as a compound of bureaucracy, police, and military structures crushes the people it pretends to represent. The fantasy aspect of second reality constructed by Marx is

---

[5] The concept 'second reality' was, to my knowledge, introduced by Eric Voegelin. Like Girard, Voegelin took Cervantes's Don Quixote as the paradigm of living in a second reality; see Eric Voegelin, *Hitler and the Germans*, trans., ed., and intro. Detlev Clemens and Brendan Purcell (Columbia and London: University of Missouri Press, 1999), 239–56.

less based on how the mechanisms of oppression can be overcome and more on the formidable prediction that overthrowing the old class will abolish not only classes but domination as such.

Analytical psychology has argued that there are two kinds of thinking.[6] On the one hand, there is the modern acquisition of a directed thinking that boasts mobility and disposability of psychic energy, which is guided by the logical pursuit of an initial idea and is structured by language. This thinking is 'reality-thinking', by means of which we imitate the successiveness of objectively real things. Directed thinking is the principal means by which we manage the laborious achievement of adaptation to reality, as the images inside our mind follow one another in the same strictly causal sequence as the events taking place outside it. Conversely, there is a type of thinking that lacks any leading ideas and the sense of direction emanating from them. In this second kind of thinking, intense images and feelings develop a tendency to suspend coherence in language and project a dream reality on to life. The distinction between these two types of thinking separates a pre-modern from a modern type of thinking. While routine politics tends to be characterised by directed thinking, liminal situations are more likely to generate fantasy-thinking, which oscillates between hazy but powerful visions of the future and a dogmatic, often mythologised version of history. The denial of reality draws on archetypical memory images, which come to the fore in the impulses and passions released in critical events. They suspend 'normal', goal-oriented, rational 'directed thinking' and let 'fantasy-thinking' come to the fore. In moments of war, social revolutions, or the disintegration of political structures, directed thinking is weakened, as rational language and strategic thinking is difficult to articulate.

The fascination with Lenin's will power has somehow concealed the logic of fanatic revolutionary messianism. Its strategic and practical implications were at odds not only with Russian social reality but also with rational analysis. Mirroring Pisarev's commitment to fantasy-thinking, Lenin subscribed to the necessity of dreaming, a claim he remained faithful to even later in his life.[7] In 1921, he acknowledged that his logic of messianism had been animated by unconscious dream-like fantasies rather than any intentional consciousness. 'It was a fantastic idea for a Communist to dream that in three years you could drastically change the economic structure of our country . . . let us confess our sins: there were many such fantasy-makers in our midst. But how can you begin a

[6] Carl G. Jung, *The Basic Writings of C. G. Jung*, ed. and intro. Violet Staub de Laszlo (New York: Modern Library, 1959), 10–22.
[7] Vladimir I. Lenin, *What Is to Be Done?* (London: Penguin, 1989), 229–30.

Socialist revolution in our country without fantasy-makers?'[8] To argue that Lenin's *State and Revolution* was utopian and not appropriate to the needs of consolidating Bolshevik power bars insight into the seriousness of his revolutionary messianism. Salvationism was not only an integral part of Marxism but was fully embraced by the Bolshevik revolutionaries who declared the construction of a new man, a new society, the withering away of the state, and/or Trotsky's 'red paradise'.[9]

Second realities may command authority not despite their haziness but precisely because of it. The disastrous state of the Soviet economy and its inefficiency induced many analysts to predict its non-viability as a political power system. However, as John Maynard Keynes remarked after a short visit to Russia, conventional criticism committed two mistakes. We hate communism so much, he said, because we regard it as a religion and thus exaggerate its economic inefficiency. Yet, being so impressed by its economic inefficiency, we underestimate it as a religion.[10]

The political uses of second reality

Much political thought has affirmed human autonomy from dependence on mythical or metaphysical references. The complex story of the break with a transcendental source of political authority at the end of the Middle Ages and thereafter, however, did not discontinue the need for quasi-divine and invisible sources of power. The overthrow of God as a source of legitimate authority came along with the redivinisation of politics with society as the collective or 'mortal' god. The theoretical foundations of modern politics testify to the importance of arresting existential uncertainty by the authority of an invisible power. This invisible power is of a higher authority, emanating from natural law that precedes and may suspend positive law. Rather than commanding reason, its authority lies in the spell exerted on the collective imagination by myths and symbols.

The symbolic sources of political authority rest upon the recognition of the superiority of those setting the yardstick but also on individuals' yearning for confirmation of their own worth. An etymological inquiry

---

[8] Quoted in John Dunn, *Modern Revolutions* (Cambridge: Cambridge University Press, 1972), 46.

[9] Andrew Janos, *East Central Europe in the Modern World: The Politics of the Borderlands from Pre- to Postcommunism* (Stanford: Stanford University Press, 2000), 158.

[10] John Maynard Keynes, 'A Short View of Russia', in *Essays in Persuasion: The Collected Writings of John M. Keynes*, vol. IX (New York: Macmillan/Cambridge University Press, 1984), 267.

confirms the magical-religious source of the term 'authority'.[11] The Roman source *auctoritas* refers to the basis of Augustus' power, which emanated from his efficient prestige as separated from his *potestas*, the legal power. *Auctor* or *auctoritas* are derived from *augeo*, which means increase, originate, or promote. In Indo-Iranian the root *aug-* means force; in Sanskrit *ojas-* means the force of gods. However, *augeo* has another meaning in addition to 'increase' in terms of building upon something that already exists: *augeo*, precisely, means to produce something beyond one's own being, to bring about something beyond one's own capacity. This is the privilege of the gods and nature who promote, who create, and who constitute. In Roman times, authority referred to a sacred force, the word for which, due to the mystical reality of *augeo*, implied the capacity to originate life in nature and to create laws. Thus, the bearer of authority is less characterised by force in terms of assuring compliance with rules than by his capacity of creating something, making something happen. In a similar vein, Max Weber made a plea for the efficiency of the spiritual influence of a god that is worshipped from afar. In his account, it is this 'effective influence from afar' (*Fernwirkung*) which presumably was a factor that participated in the evolution of the concept of Yahweh as the universal and omnipotent God.[12]

The founders of modern political thought could not do without mythical categories. Machiavelli's conception of modern politics highlighted the need for human action to counteract necessity and contingency by political virtue. Confronted with the puzzle of how to account for contingency in politics, which threatens to frustrate the hopes, expectations, and outcomes of our actions, he secularised the half-mythical power of fortune that had to be counteracted by human virtue.[13] Hobbes's 'individualist' foundation of political order in the interest of self-preservation works on the premise of a non-human authority. To explain how a social contract could establish a sovereign power in conditions of the absence of civil law in the state of nature, Hobbes refers to a sacred oath as the expression of the fear of that invisible power, which is the worship of God.[14] Rousseau's solution for taming the self-destructive force of self-love (*amour propre*) resorts to patriotism by the worship of the collective

[11] For a concise summary, see Dominique Colas, *Sociologie politique* (Paris: PUF, 2002), 105–6.
[12] Max Weber, *Wirtschaft und Gesellschaft*, ed. Johannes Winckelmann, 5th edn (Tübingen: Mohr, 1980), 254.
[13] Ernst Cassirer, *The Myth of the State* (New Haven and London: Yale University Press, 1946), 157–60.
[14] Thomas Hobbes, *Leviathan*, ed. Richard Tuck (Cambridge: Cambridge University Press, 1991), 99.

god of the nation.[15] The legitimacy of the social contract and the popular basis of democracy consist in the ritual participation in the vote and the counting of each vote. Rousseau's general will is a myth, which is nonetheless necessary to vindicate the acceptance of a majoritarian vote. Marxism posits the proletariat as the carrier of salvation. The class becomes a collective redeemer class with an eschatological expectation of the end of oppression. Lenin's professional revolutionaries dedicate their lives to the pursuit of revolutionary messianism, dreaming about the end of politics.[16] The heroism of collectives such as the nation and the class but also the individual *virtù* or the 'will to power' are mythical representations that reflect archetypical beliefs in humanity. In principle, there is not much difference between the supreme sacrifice required for a cause such as the Bolshevik party or the nation, as in both cases it is the most effective mobilising force in a situation of despair.

The modern nation-state largely relies on symbols of heroic victory, imperial expansions, and phases of economic growth but also on the narrative impact of the mythical quality of the nation as an imagined community.[17] Historically, the nation as the collective body of the people represented in the state has drawn much of its legitimacy from the identification of and military competition with enemy nations. The stability of nation-states in western Europe has largely relied on a politically fabricated and culturally sustained pool of symbols associated with revolutionary events, the consequences of wars (such as liberation or traumatic war losses), or the founding events of constitutions.[18] Following liberal approaches to history, blessed acts of oblivion are crucial elements for establishing constitutive beginnings and forging collective identities. Deliberate forgetting and historical error are seen as crucial to successful nation-building.[19] As the *Stunde Null* in post-Second World War West Germany suggests, they may boost the democratic credentials of countries by drawing a clear line over the legacy of the past and set out for a new start.

Myths about nationhood, for instance, need not be specific to ethnocultural types of communities that were held together by tradition, language, or literature. The rise of nationalism anywhere requires the

---

[15] Jean-Jacques Rousseau, *The Social Contract and Discourses*, trans. and intro. G. D. H. Cole (London: Dent, 1993), 142.
[16] A. J. Polan, *Lenin and the End of Politics* (London: Methuen, 1984).
[17] See Benedict Anderson, *Imagined Communities: Reflections on the Origin and Spread of Nationalism* revised edn (London: Verso, 1991).
[18] Pierre Nora, ed., *Realms of Memory: Rethinking the French Past* (New York: Columbia University Press, 1996).
[19] Ernest Renan, 'What Is a Nation', in *Becoming National: A Reader*, ed. Geoff Eley and Ronald G. Suny (New York: Oxford University Press, 1996), 45.

ascendancy of the idea of a chosen people, when all individual or collec-tive desire or demands must be subordinated to a national interest. The French Revolution has perhaps been the paradigmatic example of a mythological reality that projected a potential future based on an urgent hope for equality and liberty. Beyond the formalisation of political prin-ciples and structures, the truly intriguing point about the French Revolution is not so much what kind of future it headed for but that it has been constructed by many commentators in terms of a myth of identity and of origin.[20] Since this decisive break with the principles of the *ancien régime*, modern political societies have been confronted by the challenge of establishing constitutive principles.

Comparing aspects of myth in the origins of Western civilisation, Franz Borkenau postulated two patterns of myth-making. First, he argued that myth arose where primitives were pushed out of the timelessness of eternal repetition by a unique historic happening, a consequential break with tradition and a profound shock to an established order. It does not arise where primitive communities become mere passive objects of inte-gration in the high culture, but where primitives invade a decaying high culture as conquerors. Myth belongs to the type 'indirect affiliation'; it emerges where a 'dark age' intervenes between the older and the younger culture, i.e. between that of antiquity and that of the rising western Europe.[21] In the early Middle Ages the most important myth-production happened neither among the primitives nor in the domain of the old high culture but at the crossroads of the contact of two contrasting forms of life, in the border zone.[22] If some analogy with eastern Europe is claimed, it is by no means to suggest that this region should be considered as a less developed form of political culture. It is rather to suggest that key actors may abide by the second reality as they are drawn by the superiority of an acknowledged high culture and the search for recognition. The self-sustained perception of belated domestic development combined with the strength of the mythic concept of 'the West' shaped the thought of 'Third World' revolutionaries such as Sun Yat-Sen or Lenin.[23]

---

[20] See François Furet, *Interpreting the French Revolution* (Cambridge: Cambridge University Press, 1981).

[21] Franz Borkenau, *End and Beginning: On the Generations of Cultures and the Origins of the West*, ed. and intro. Richard Loewenthal (New York: Columbia University Press, 1981), 206.

[22] In the case of the West, this was along the Danube and the Rhine, while in southern Europe the intensive Germanisation turned Lombardy and Friaul into 'barbaric terri-tory' and thus into a main focus of myth-formation; see Borkenau, *End and Beginning*, 207.

[23] David Joravsky, 'Communism in Historical Perspective', *American Historical Review*, 99, 3 (1994), 851.

Revolutionary communism in Russia was not primarily a product of Marx's utopia, but distinctively engaged with images of European modernity. In an economically backward society, the state's strategy of development embraced the idea of progress and modernisation by acknowledging that Europe was superior technically and economically. Thus, communism emanated not only from domestic revolutionary desires but also from a longstanding engagement with the West, which entered the consciousness of Soviet and of east European citizens as a culturally imperative empire of the mind. Rather than emancipating the individual, however, communism sidelined individual responsibility and elevated the collective to the status of the real moral subject. It imposed belief in a historical goal of communist society emerging from a progressive pattern of phases of history.

The psychological appeal of the 'West' as a second reality, however, must not be mistaken for a determinate ideological belief-system. Prior to the Bolshevik experiment, tsarist authority presented itself as 'European'. It credited itself with the secularisation of the Russian state through the introduction of legal and administrative reforms based on European models. Similarly, the Russian intelligentsia was under the spell of what was perceived as the superior civilisation of the West. Belated efforts at modernisation invoked the need for the magic of 'proclaimed reality' in order to divert from 'existing reality'. In Russia, one thinks of how Grigori Potemkin in 1787 decorated the route of the Polish king and the Austrian emperor with fake prosperous and well-off villages.[24]

For the idea of progress to materialise, revolutionaries were obliged to break with all previous experience and to open the horizon of expectation as a second reality. The growing gap between spaces of experiences and horizons of expectations can be seen as a central feature of modernity.[25] Experience and expectation are not simply mirroring past and future. Each category is of a different substance, as experience is concentrated, while expectations are scattered, uncertain. Moreover, in politics, prior experience is not simply translated into expectations. The crucial point is that political change based on mobilisation of power and technology is driven by the dissolution of former experience and meanings, and is based on insecurity and the formulation of new expectations. Big events such as the Crusades, colonial expansion, and the Reformation – but also the French Revolution – testify to the discrepancy between spaces of

[24] Cecile Vaissie, *Pour votre liberté et pour la notre. Le combat des dissidents de Russie* (Paris: Robert Laffont, 1999), 89.
[25] Reinhart Koselleck, *Futures Past: On the Semantics of Historical Time* (Cambridge, MA: MIT Press, 1985), 270–88.

experiences and newly discovered and attainable horizons of expectations. While the French Revolution was preceded by enlightened aspirations for human emancipation, it was the disruptive experience of the
event that opened up new horizons of expectation that were either discredited or simply inexpressible before it. In the political realm, Kant
invented 'republicanism' to express the urgent need of humanity to arrive at
the best possible state of political organisation. As a concept of movement,
'republicanism' did for political action what 'progress' promised to do for
the whole of history. While 'republic' before the French Revolution indicated a political condition, 'republicanism' assumed a teleological quality
of expectation, a hypothetical future political reality to be anticipated.

In the twentieth century, however, the material destruction and moral
catastrophe of the First World War brought about deep disillusionment
with technological prowess and republican forms of democracy. The
German case shows how second reality could gain political ascendency
with a return to mythological representations of the past, even in open
antagonism to the dominant materialist and technological spirit of the
times. During the first half of the twentieth century, the encounter of
rationality-driven, progress-oriented science and mythology-driven,
backward-oriented politics reached an extreme.[26] The mythologisation
of scientific terms and their application to a political project tinged with
world-immanent eschatology was crucial to how the Nazis applied the
term 'race' to politics. The use of biological terms such as 'race' in a
largely mythical and magical sense is one important example of how
scientific approaches to nature can be subject to a magical–mythical
perspective on society and how scientific terms can be transformed into
mythical terms in a different context.[27] Modern man has overcome
beliefs in natural magic but has by no means given up the belief in a sort
of 'social magic'.[28] Social magic must not be reduced to irrationality,
however, but manifests a rationality of its own, as it is the background
condition for mobilising beliefs and establishing authority. Such an influence must not be confined to the consolidation of totalitarian movements
in the first half of the twentieth century. The rise of democratic politics in
nineteenth-century Britain, for instance, was tightly linked to the compelling magnetism of demagogues in their pursuit of power.[29] Even in
modern conditions, social magic remains potentially strong, because in

[26] Cassirer, *The Myth of the State*.
[27] Norbert Elias, *The Germans: Power Struggles and the Development of Habitus in the
Nineteenth and Twentieth Centuries*, trans. from the German and with a preface by Eric
Dunning and Stephen Mennell (Cambridge: Polity Press, 1996), 389–90.
[28] Cassirer, *The Myth of the State*, 279–85.
[29] Peter Gay, *The Cultivation of Hatred* (New York and London: W. W. Norton, 1993), 283.

desperate situations man will always have recourse to desperate means. If reason has failed us, there remains always the *ultima ratio*, the power of the miraculous and mysterious.

Beliefs in social magic are manifest in the admiration for 'great criminals', which does not result so much from their repellent actions, but rather from the violence to which it bears witness. Acts of violence and crimes acquire heroic or meritorious effects with happy and beneficial consequences for fellow-citizens because citizens consecrate as great men those who liberate a community of its enemies by violence.[30] Although dictators in totalitarian states are among the most despised great criminals of recorded history, leaders such as Lenin and Stalin, but also Hitler and Milošević exerted a considerable spell on the public and the leadership in democratic societies.[31] Hitler was a 'witch doctor' or 'shaman' who ruled the Germans not only by external constraint but because their emotional attachment to him served as a defence mechanism against their powerlessness before events.[32]

In a different but quite related fashion, Stalin's revolution was not only based on material and economic engineering. Social realism in the 1930s was largely based on the messianic idea of engineering souls, which espoused the extremely suggestive and powerful potentiality of incipient mass propaganda by Soviet cinema in the 1930s. Films were not supposed to show how life really is but how it should be. Images were highly standardised as plots included three paradigmatic types of personality: the Bolshevik party functionary, completely dedicated to his cause; the Soviet worker trying to fulfil or overfulfil the achievements proposed by the plan; and the enemy who wants to sabotage the working process. As Marxist-Leninist discourse could claim to make sense only by retreating into the mythic dimension of language, the pronounced element of 'magic' appeared in Soviet parlance, attributing exceptional heroic capacity to Soviet leaders. Thus, leading Soviet and Russian politicians made frequent recourse to magical words so as to construct their community and the

---

[30] Georges Sorel, *Reflections on Violence* (New York and London: Collier Books, 1967), 58.

[31] After the Munich Accord of September 1938, Hitler's international reputation was at its height. Roosevelt's appreciation of Stalin was based on the assumption that Stalin's difficult qualities – his aloofness, suspiciousness, wariness, and disinclination for collaboration with others – could be overcome by making him actively participate in the creation of a new post-war Europe; see George F. Kennan and John Lukacs, *George F. Kennan and the Origins of Containment 1944–1946: The Kennan–Lukacs Correspondence* (Columbia: University of Missouri Press, 1997), 33. In 1995, Slobodan Milošević was still appreciated by international mediators almost without exception as intelligent and witty; see Laura Silber and Alan Little, *The Death of Yugoslavia*, revised edn (London: Penguin Books, 1996), 386.

[32] Elias, *The Germans*, 387–9.

outsiders. One can see a basic equivalence between, say, Leonid Brezhnev's 'plans of the Communist Party' and Gorbachev's 'the constitution', and between either of the foregoing and Boris Yeltsin's 'reform'. Each of these terms has served 'to draw a magic circle around the leader and his supporters, to define that group as a community of the righteous, and to declare others unworthy of membership in it, excising and excommunicating them in the process'.[33]

Second reality and identity-formation

The victory of democracy in former communist countries has often been associated with the sheer power of Western values and the efficiency of democratic institutions. Though it may sound plausible, however, the idealisation of democracy should not be confused with a deliberate 'rational' choice based on stable individual preferences for a well-articulated model of 'liberal democracy'. The identification with democracy cannot be confined to the psychological attraction of one entity (the East) to a superimposed model (the West). Rather, it needs to be related to the meaning-formation in the situational logic of action. Detachment from normal behaviour in a social environment has been a long-term practice in human societies, where the potential of a different reality is furthered by attempts to acquire role distance. Any strongly coercive situation will produce a phenomenon called 'role distance', or 'ecstasy'.[34]

The existence of a sphere of welfare, peace, and liberty behind the Iron Curtain would provide a model of identification for people in eastern Europe. Consistent with mimetic theory, however, the desire for identification is not determined by a pre-existing outside model; rather, this desire creates models. The democratic age of the masses at the beginning of the twentieth century had the positive effect of endowing Europe with an unprecedented vitality, mainly based on the rise of equality in different aspects of social, political, and juridical life. This 'Americanisation of Europe' happened as a subconscious process of imitation and rising psychological appeal.[35] As Tocqueville had already recognised, the conflict between rich and poor reveals that social distance intensifies the longing for identification and recognition. 'The heart of man is not so

[33] Michael Urban, 'Stages of Political Identity Formation in Late Soviet and Post-Soviet Russia', in Victoria E. Bonnell, ed., *Identities in Transition: Eastern Europe and Russia After the Collapse of Communism* (Berkeley: University of California at Berkeley, Center for Slavic and East European Studies, 1996), 148.

[34] Peter L. Berger, *Invitation to Sociology: A Humanistic Perspective* (New York and London: Penguin Books, 1991), 156–60.

[35] José Ortega y Gasset, *La rebelión de las masas* (Madrid: Castalia, 1998), 142–4.

much caught by the undisturbed possession of anything valuable as by the desire, as yet imperfectly satisfied, of possessing it, and by the incessant dread of losing it ... In communities of this kind, the imagination of the poor is driven to seek another world; the desire of acquiring the comforts of the world haunts the imagination of the poor and the dread of losing them that of the rich.'[36]

Collective identities must be conceived in a triadic structure, where between inside and outside lies the boundary, between left and right is the centre, between past and future is the present.[37] Modern nation-states produced an inherent double bind as they asked their citizens to follow a twofold code of norms, divided into the moral code of egalitarianism with the human individual as the highest value and the inegalitarian Machiavellian code of princes, which sets the nation and the state as the highest value.[38] Different communities such as Croats or Serbs felt increasingly attached to and represented by the category 'nation', a second reality that became almost the sole content of their identity as opposed to the second reality built up by the antagonist. In the Croatian–Serbian conflict, nationalising states such as Croatia were perceived as existential threats by the Serbian national minority on Croatian territory. Their support by Serbia as the external homeland, however, reinforced Croatia's perception of nationalist aggression and contributed to the outbreak of the war.[39] Similarly, communist leaders were in a constant tension between the fear of victimisation as experienced in their personal history and the utopian goal of abolishing the state and universalising communism. Different regimes in central Europe crossed the threshold of modern times amidst newly developing 'east European' conditions, but with defective 'Western-like' structures. East central Europe was a region that lay between those two models.[40] Precisely because of that duality, the imperial growth of Russia and the formation of the modern state in the West produced in this middle region a number of variant models instead of one unified one, as if all the permutations and possible combinations were being experimented with.

---

[36] Alexis de Tocqueville, *Democracy in America: The Complete and Unabridged*, 2 vols., trans. Henry Reeve (New York: Bantam Classic, 2000), 653–4.
[37] Shmuel N. Eisenstadt and Bernhard Giesen, 'The Construction of Collective Identity', *European Journal of Sociology*, 36 (1995), 72–102.
[38] Elias, *The Germans*, 154–6.
[39] Rogers Brubaker, *Nationalism Reframed* (Cambridge: Cambridge University Press, 1996).
[40] Jeno Szücs, 'Three Historical Regions of Europe', in John Keane, ed., *Civil Society and the State* (London: Verso, 1988), 322.

Although a dominant version of modernisation theory has portrayed the success of democracy in post-communist Europe as the victory of Western liberal capitalism, the influence of Western ideas in Russia, for instance, was rather ambivalent. If the Decembrist movement after 1812 is considered to be the carrier of liberal and 'democratic' ideas, it was largely inspired by a rediscovery of truly Russian values and beliefs. The aristocratic elite in the military reclaimed the renewal of Russian nationhood by partial rejection of the achievements of European Russia as represented by autocratic tsarism and the St Petersburg court.[41] Paradoxical as it may appear, Siberia – with the youthful energy of its unbridled peasants – was seen as the land of democratic hope and potential.

The conditions of isolation, poverty, and claustrophobia under Soviet communism could not but intensify the spell of the West or Europe as second reality. East Europeans and Russians saw themselves increasingly in the categories of equals with the West due to the belief that the West would be the future both in terms of commodities and in terms of liberty. After the Second World War, Polish intellectuals were thrown into a double bind between a feeling of being Russia's victim and their unrequited love for the West.[42] Baltic countries such as Lithuania, for instance, seem also to have two relevant Others, Soviet Russia and the West.[43] Similarly, Central Europeans learnt to refuse the post-totalitarian condition by trying to embrace a distant 'elsewhere' reality.[44] The chronically overburdened network of horizontal surveillance enacted under communist rule opened up pockets of freedom and spheres of reality that allowed spaces of parallel societies, second economies, or second polities.[45] Despite the deliberate distortion of reality, the attack on human dignity, and the falsification of history, social pressure under communism produced a new type of counter-symbolisation, as communist authorities recognised that they needed to leave certain outlets for the population in order to attenuate the drawn-out legitimacy crisis. The power of the authorities relied upon the desire of the governed to leave the social community temporarily, and upon the principle of doing nothing that would counteract the fulfilment of this desire.

---

[41] Orlando Figes, *Natasha's Dance: A Cultural History of Russia* (London: Penguin Books, 2003), 72–146.
[42] Czesław Miłosz, *Zniewolony umysł* (Krakow: Krajowa Agencja Wydawnicza, 1989), 66.
[43] Roger D. Petersen, *Resistance and Rebellion: Lessons from Eastern Europe* (Cambridge: Cambridge University Press, 2001), 286–7.
[44] Milan Kundera, *Life Is Elsewhere*, trans. from the Czech by Peter Kussi (New York and London: Penguin Books, 1986), 176.
[45] Gordon Skilling, *Samizdat and an Independent Society in Central and Eastern Europe* (Columbus: Ohio State University Press, 1989), 157–218.

Cultural representations between East and West reflected the power of second realities by establishing two dominant paradigms.[46] When the communist regimes took power, they dismantled established institutions, social networks, identities, dignity, and self-esteem, developing the 'paradigm of the prisoner'. For Easterners, Western freedom and prosperity was not only a goal to emulate but also invincible proof that life was worth living. Despite the oppression and humiliating compromises, their life was not devoid of value and meaning. At the same time, the existence of communism helped people living in the West to develop the 'paradigm of the missionary'. The fate of the 'prisoners' behind the Iron Curtain was an indispensable source of meaning for Western identity, reinforcing its missionary zeal towards the East. Eastern Europe's desire to become the West's or Europe's equal has perhaps been the most pervasive, albeit most vague, realm of second reality. At bottom, the deep disillusionment with revolutionary messianism was replaced by a pervasive perception of a different hypothetical ideal world that kept alive a double imagination in which the future was imagined in terms of paradise.[47] In the early 1970s, the short-term influx of Western goods and the possibility of free travel to the West in Poland's economic miracle in the mid-1970s created a mirage of a 'second Poland' that temporarily marginalised opposition movements. However, the 'second society' failed to develop into an autonomous sphere of social existence, as it remained essentially indeterminate, blurred, an in-between of unfulfilled and deceived beliefs and desires. 'It was a no-man's land, where the governing principles and the rules of play of the first society did not work, but the principles and rules of a different type of social existence had hardly emerged.'[48]

The popular representation of communist power as the enemy of the people was reinforced by images of alternative realities such as the West. The West was admired for its superiority but also expected to recognise the dissidents' effort of self-extrication. As a consequence, people in the East did not pursue clear-cut models or institutionalised logics but wanted to belong to the 'West', the reality that was most withheld but most ardently desired. 'People yearned for Western political institutions, a Western standard of living, Western freedom ... but not for capitalism.'[49] The West appeared to be a set of hazy images rather than a rationally

---

[46] Elemer Hankiss, 'European Paradigms: East and West, 1945–1994', *Daedalus*, 123, 3 (1994), 115–26.

[47] Josef Skvorecky, *Talkin' Moscow Blues* (London and Boston: Faber and Faber, 1988), 136–8.

[48] Hankiss, 'East European Alternatives', 107–8.

[49] Jerzy Szacki, *Liberalism After Communism* (Budapest: Central European University Press, 1995), 120.

constructed policy directed at outcomes. Terms such 'market', 'democracy', 'capitalism', and 'Europe' were characterised by the dissolution of
any possible substantive or semantic meaning and tinged with an explosive mix of eschatological hope and vagueness. As Adam Michnik put
it: 'I think that we know precisely what we do not want, but none of us
knows precisely what we do want. There is no language which could
correctly describe our aspirations ... The values whose presence we
sense intuitively – and to which we want to be faithful – are values existing
at the meeting point of different spheres of our human condition, and
hence the language in which they could be described cannot be internally
homogeneous. Hence we are looking for another language that would
pinpoint the inexpressible.'[50]
    The political energies deployed in the enterprise of democratisation
before 1989 or in joining the European Union in eastern Europe were
driven by a collective imagination, including utopian expectations and
'thoughtful wishing' about what lies ahead.[51] While different movements
of dissidence in Europe grounded subjectivity in community experiences
intent on recovering life in truth, the spirit of the nation, or human
dignity, second realities were influential markers of certainty. The evolution of subjectivity took different shapes, often influenced by romantic
myths, but also by victimisation and collective fear. Many of these processes produced powerful second realities dependent on traumatic experiences in the past and cultural memory. For Adam Michnik, for instance,
his Polishness and the identification with the Polish nation, i.e. with the
weak, beaten, and humiliated, was the core of his identity.[52] In small
countries such as Latvia, national survival was strongly related to an
existential fear of a substantial Russian minority. After 1990, the need
for self-affirmation made the government opt for an ethnic rather than a
republican definition of citizenship, based on proficiency in the Latvian
language.[53]
    Another type of imagination was at play in Yugoslavia. The outbreak of
war between Serbia and Croatia owed a great deal to perceptions of
existential threat generated in a media war throughout the 1980s, where

[50] Adam Michnik, *Polskie pytania* (Paris: Zeszyty Literackie, 1987), 42–4 (my translation).
[51] Laurence Whitehead, *Democratisation: Theory and Experience* (Oxford: Oxford University
    Press, 2002), 239.
[52] Adam Michnik, *Diabeł naszego czasu. Publicystyka z lat 1985–1994* (Warsaw: Niezależna
    oficyna wydawnicza, 1995), 393.
[53] Nils Muiznieks, 'Latvia: Origins, Evolution, and Triumph', in Ian Brenner and Ray
    Taras, eds., *Nations and Politics in the Soviet Successor States* (Cambridge: Cambridge
    University Press, 1993), 182.

intellectuals and public discourse engaged in the social construction of imaginary enemies.[54] Emir Kusturica's film epic 'Underground' captured how in the perceptions of Yugoslavs the Second World War had not ended and how the potential of being threatened existentially by ethnic enemies prefigured the wars in the early 1990s. This film has as its protagonists two Serbian friends who fight the German occupation from their base in an underground bunker in town. One of the two friends leaves their hideout and realises that the war has ended. However, he keeps on suggesting to the other one – who remained in the bunker with a bunch of partisans – that the war has not yet finished. For two decades or so, this group of anti-fascist fighters for the freedom of Yugoslavia keeps adhering to the illusion of living in war-like conditions. Setting the war experiences of the early 1990s in Croatia and Bosnia in the wider perspective of Yugoslavia's history in the twentieth century, Kusturica's film is a powerful allegory about how the consolidation of Yugoslav communism relied upon the second reality of encirclement by enemies.

The detachment from second reality under communism shows two divergent trends.[55] The Great Fatherland War had features of a national revolution as far as it reinitiated the focus on the imperial legacy and further led to a retraditionalisation and pragmatism, causing the closure of its historical horizon. The domestic closure coincided with increasing exposure abroad, as the global competition demanded more complex and innovative strategies in a period when stagnation and internal contradictions in the power structure intensified. Rather than an objective force of political evolution, retraditionalisation was strongly tinged with mythological constructions of reality. Both the political leadership and a considerable part of the population were aroused by the attraction of commodities and the magic of capitalism, which cast a spell over east European societies.

The social diffusion of democratic consciousness

The political antagonism in the Cold War largely concealed the fact that the non-attainability of the commodities and political liberties of the West exerted symbolic power as a marker of certainty. In the language of social anthropology, for substantial parts of people in the East, the 'West' was

---

[54] Slavenka Drakulić, 'Intellectuals as Bad Guys', *East European Politics and Societies*, 13, 2 (1999), 271–7.
[55] Johan Arnason, *The Future that Failed: Origins and Destinies of the Soviet Model* (London: Routledge, 1993), 212–15.

associated with the sacred; it was seen as a kind of paradise, but was also marked by prohibition as it embodied the 'class enemy'. Marked disparities strike the observer not when conditions are very unequal but rather when everything is nearly on the same level. Thus, the desire for equality tends to become more insatiable in proportion to the completeness of equality.[56] Tocqueville's remarks on growing equality can also be applied to the ardent quest of Easterners for being equal with the West. The return to Europe was anchored in the West's role as an empire of the mind in the Eastern perception, based on genuinely heartfelt emotions and deeply held ideals. Second realities were also created through exchanges of goods, through a communicative and emotional engagement with the Western world. In terms of consumption, capitalism renders desire concrete and specific by offering specific – if ever-changing – goods to satisfy it. By contrast, socialism aroused desire without focalising it, and kept it alive by deprivation.[57]

The emergence of democratic consciousness under communism can be seen in the context of prohibition and non-communication. The intense desire of 'becoming like the West' was reinforced by the central aspect of prohibition, which itself was a direct consequence of ideological and social control as well as of non-communication. Reminiscent of Emile Durkheim's distinction between the profane and the sacred world, the two worlds are not only different; they are also closed for each other.[58] The production of an ideal coincides with the definition of the sacred out of a moment of effervescence. Above the real world of the profane there becomes superimposed another world that, although only existing in the mind, is attributed a higher dignity and becomes an ideal world.[59] This complete Otherness requires isolation and non-attainability as the sacred is characterised by an extraordinary contagion. It should be stressed that East and West here are not to be understood as different geographical places. Soviet communism saw itself as competing with the model of Western modernity for superiority. Although Westerners considered east central Europe to be outside Europe, Poles, Czechs, Slovaks, or Hungarians would see themselves as being between 'East' and 'West'. Having been forced to become part of the Eastern bloc due to unfortunate historical circumstances, they had a strong desire to belong to and be recognised by the 'West'.

[56] Tocqueville, *Democracy in America*, 664.
[57] Katherine Verdery, *What Was Socialism and What Comes Next?* (Princeton: Princeton University Press, 1996), 28.
[58] Emile Durkheim, *Les formes élémentaires de la vie religieuse* (Paris: Quadrige/PUF, 1990), 453–9.
[59] Durkheim, *Les formes élémentaires de la vie religieuse*, 602–3.

In the Durkheimian tradition, the representation of the sacred does not tolerate profane thoughts and makes the antagonism between sacred and profane a psychological and social fact. While democratisation in eastern Europe undoubtedly owes something to the sheer power of the West as a realm of freedom, it would be an oversimplification to speak about the West as a 'social fact'. It is important to recall that personhood in communist societies rested primarily on their embeddedness in social relations, not on their autonomy. Reality for a socialist 'person' was very different from the autonomous, self-actualising, possessive individual characteristic of capitalism, as not only socialist production and property relations but also all facets of daily life were dependent on an individual's ability to mobilise contacts.[60] In this vein, dissident action was much less driven by a collectively sustained social fact, but rather composed resistance as individual acts of defiance which were diffused among citizens by example and imitation. In a widely neglected but recently rediscovered sociological tradition, Gabriel Tarde argued that imitation relies upon the collective spiritual disposition of otherwise individually centred monads.[61] In other words, the spatial dispersion of a public is combined with spiritual proximity. As transformations in the domains of science, law, art, economy, or politics suggest, transformation of consciousness can be generated at spatial and temporal distance.

An anti-totalitarian consciousness cannot be imposed through a collective entity such as the state or a 'civil society', but requires specific individuals that give expression to what some have recognised. In this view, events and the experiences of monads are the existential ground to the social world. 'If we look at the [human] social world, the only one we know from the inside, we see the agents, the humans, much more differentiated, much more individually characterised, much richer in continuous variations, than the governmental apparatus, the system of laws and beliefs, even the dictionaries and the grammars which are maintained through their activities.'[62] Any social activity must be linked to the psychological and bodily activities, to the co-operation of a great many other individuals. Far from mere psychologism, the study of social facts can only concern acts that testify to the interconnection of mental attitudes and actions by 'inter-mental psychology'. The connectivity of mind, imitation, and action in 'inter-mental psychology' must be to 'the

---

[60] Katherine Verdery, 'Privatization as Transforming Persons', in Sorin Antohi and Vladimir Tismaneanu, eds., *Between Past and Future* (Budapest: Central European University Press, 2000), 188.

[61] See Gabriel Tarde, *Les lois de l'imitation* (Paris: Seuil, 1993).

[62] Quoted in Bruno Latour, 'Gabriel Tarde and the End of the Social', in Patrick Joyce, ed., *The Social and Its Problems* (London: Routledge, 2001), 122.

social sciences what the study of the cell is to the biological sciences'.[63] Great scientific theories such as those of Newton or Darwin were prepared by the accumulation of countless tiny facts, which constitute in some sense the organisms of which those geniuses are the souls. Left to itself, a monad can do nothing.[64] A cinematographic allegory by the Russian film director Andrei Tarkovsky illustrates how individually experienced images make up the whole of the picture. 'One has to work out a principle which allows for film to affect people individually. The "total" images must become something private ... The basic principle – as it were, the mainspring – is, I think, that as little as possible has actually to be shown, and from that little the audience has to build up an idea of the rest, of the whole ... And if one looks at it from the point of view of symbols, then the symbol in cinema is a symbol of nature, of reality. Of course it isn't a question of details, but of what is hidden.'[65] Tarkovsky here rejects the idea that images shown are unequivocal and restricted to one objective interpretation. One must allow for the possibility that an image affects people individually by deliberately reducing the explicit parts, the objects that are shown, thus giving the audience a maximum range for acquiring the truthful side of reality.

For the Russian intelligentsia, the images of Western modernity and its potential benefits for Russia constituted a moral purpose that supported their practical action of struggle against the tsarist regime. In the complex processes of de-Stalinisation and the small revolutions in eastern Europe, notions of the enemy were recast, generating a dividing line between growing dissidence and communist authorities. Democratisation depended on a complex and contingent process of deconstruction and reconstruction of the political symbolism of communism, which was intertwined with the utopian urge for 'democracy' as representing a state of full freedom. Much as the articulation of communist power relied upon the experiential basis of 'symbolic structures' such as the People-as-One, the anti-fascist myth, or dissidence, an inquiry into the emergence of democracy needs to trace the modalities of the disengagement from this collective symbolism.

In this sense, the myth of an originally 'humanist Marxism', supposedly betrayed by Lenin and Stalin, helped the critical Marxists of east central

---

[63] Gabriel Tarde, *On Communication and Social Influence*, ed. Terry N. Clark (Chicago: University of Chicago Press, 1969), 138.
[64] Quoted in Latour, 'The End of the Social', 127.
[65] Andrei Tarkovsky, *Time Within Time: The Diaries 1970–1986* (London and Boston: Faber and Faber, 1994), 65.

Europe – the 'revisionists' – formulate their rejection of communism.[66] Solidarność's fundamentalist mentality in 1980 and 1981 may seem indeed inconsequential for bringing down the communist regime. The once acclaimed identity of Solidarność soon disintegrated and became a myth. After the collapse of the communist enemy, the second reality of the myth of Solidarność became the centre of 'wars at the top', where contention about the appropriation of Solidarność's 'heritage' was essential to the disintegration of the movement. Yet it was not the unity of the myth as an artefact, but the persistent hope voiced and practised by the individual life-conduct of countless individuals in the underground, which was crucial for the survival of Solidarność's spirit.[67]

Individualism in Russia has emerged as a reaction to strongly collectivist, and thus clearly illiberal, forms of organisation. Practices of dissimulation in the Soviet Union did not create a private, let alone 'democratic', individual. In order to achieve individual freedom, practices of dissimulation or adaptation were driven by external constraints, not by internal forces. The spirit of togetherness was embodied in family ties and the integrity of the *narod*, which drew on *sobornost* as perhaps the major distinctive element of Russian civilisation. *Sobornost* derives from *sobor*, meaning different things such as 'cathedral', 'council', and 'the gathering of people previously scattered'. *Sobornost* as communitarian predisposition emerged strongly in patterns of representation in *perestroika* and marked much of the political discourse in the Congress of People's Deputies and Supreme Soviet both in the late Soviet Union and the Russian Congress of People's Deputies.[68] From the perspective of liberal democracy as an institutionalised system of power, the communal *sobornost* tradition can be seen as potentially impeding democracy as an institutionalised conflict of interests.

The articulation of the 'power of the powerless' can appear as a process of inter-mental psychology, where an individual ethics of rejecting the contagion of a systemic logic is diffused in the infrapolitics of the hidden sphere. Although the hidden is concealed from the public, it can be existentially representative of a people's reality. Solzhenitsyn's political influence, for instance, was not rooted in some exclusive political power he possessed as an individual but 'in the experience of those millions of

[66] Vladimir Tismaneanu, *Fantasies of Salvation: Democracy, Nationalism, and Myth in Post-Communist Europe* (Princeton: Princeton University Press, 1998), 26.

[67] Jan Kubik, *The Power of Symbols Against the Symbols of Power: The Rise of Solidarity and the Fall of State Socialism in Poland* (University Park: Penn State University Press, 1994), 257.

[68] Marcia A. Weigle, *Russia's Liberal Project: State–Society Relations in the Transition from Communism* (University Park, PA: Penn State University Press, 2000), 424–5.

gulag victims which he simply amplified and communicated to millions of other people of good will'.[69] The project of rejecting second reality was based on the countless accounts of truth by scattered individuals and was taken up, reflected upon, and articulated by outstanding individuals.

Without experiencing the absurdity of post-totalitarianism, no ethics of a life in truth could have been developed in order to overcome the domination of the absurd. The 'individualism' of dissidence was a direct response to the ritualistic logic created by the second-reality regime of communist power. It was an attempt to overcome contagion with its own absurdity. The only possible way to do this was to spiritually unite in a community of the shattered and in a truthful life in the hidden sphere. Driven by moral perfectionism and ethical individualism, dissidence tried to mobilise people not at the level of collective imagination about one definite goal for society, but instead hoped to inspire the individual's care of the soul. Havel, for instance, put the importance of national belonging at the same level as the belonging to humanity. 'To me, my Czechness is a given, along with the fact that I am a man, or that I have fair hair, or that I live in the twentieth century.'[70] Czechoslovak communism did not collapse as a result of pressure from civil society because there was practically no civil society. It did not collapse as a result of dissident activity, either.[71] Rather, the diffusion of an alternative consciousness reinjected indeterminacy in the social body of communist societies.

The very nature of vague, potentially all-encompassing, and dream-like images of the communist utopia contained the possibility of their dissolution and the radical change of meaning. Hermann Broch captured very well that democracy as a civilising force can be identified in its negative, anti-tyrannical function. Writing in 1947, he argued that, as long as democratic consciousness is alive, it appears as an attempt to breach the atomisation of individuals under totalitarianism, to overcome the passivity created by tyrannical rule, and to create the indeterminacy of action. Thus, even if democracy did not exist, it would be opposite to totalitarian rule.[72] Since the modern type of totalitarian rule is not just a political regime but in its claim for totality becomes a social force, the

[69] Václav Havel, 'The Power of the Powerless', in John Keane, ed., *The Power of the Powerless: Citizens Against the State in Eastern Europe* (London: Hutchinson and Co., 1985), 60.
[70] Quoted in Aviezer Tucker, *The Philosophy and Politics of Czech Dissidence from Patočka to Havel* (Pittsburgh: University of Pittsburgh Press, 2000), 255.
[71] Tucker, *Czech Dissidence*, 170.
[72] Hermann Broch, *Kommentierte Werkausgabe*, ed. Paul Michael Lützeler, vol. XI, *Politische Schriften* (Frankfurt am Main: Suhrkamp, 1978), 278.

re-establishment of democracy might require its totalisation in terms of re-educating society with a view to constitutive principles.

Democratisation, therefore, has to acknowledge the power of countless individuals who denounce the sacrificial logic of communist power. Whereas Bolshevik communism bestowed a catastrophic rupture upon society, followed by permanent revolution, the process of democratic resistance set out to overcome the sacrificial logic of violence by denouncing doublethink, the ritualistic elimination of enemies, and the fantasies of revolutionary messianism. Alternative visions of society based on the appeal to moral justice, human dignity and a life in truth were criticised for the lack of realistic options for reform. The visionary logic of ultimate ends that appears inappropriate to the logic of the modern state must be seen as utterly unrealistic. Following Patočka's devastating assessment of Czech elites, Havel manifested his profound disdain for the provincial political tradition of 'Czech realism' that did not further Czech independence but rather produced national humiliation such as in 1938, 1948, and 1968.[73]

Democratic preferences are not generated in the enlightened mind whose prudence and ethics of responsibility reflect the insight into objective forces such as modernisation or a 'civil society' tradition. The formation of democratic consciousness has to take into account the second reality of mythological constructions, in so far as this is an emotive standard to judge a changing reality and provide markers of certainty.[74] If democratisation is reduced to an exogenous model deriving from Western models of individualism and liberal values, the significance of values created under different cultural conditions gains ascendancy over the meanings attached to experiences. Such meanings of democracy, however, under communism drew on idealised expectations, tinged with eschatological visions of a state of full freedom. György Konrád saw Solidarność's unexpected vigour and popularity as a confirmation that 'democracy is on our minds: it is what we crave the most because it is what we lack the most, in every sphere of activity, in our economy and culture as much as in politics – and especially in those areas where we meet face to face and can look in the eye the people who make the decisions in our name and order us to carry them out'.[75]

Dispositions of actors largely depend on movements of engagement and detachment. How transformations of consciousness work in maelstrom scenarios can be illustrated by Norbert Elias's reading of Edgar

---

[73] Tucker, *Czech Dissidence*, 101–2.   [74] Tismaneanu, *Fantasies of Salvation*, 26.
[75] Konrád, 'Antipolitcs', 142.

Allan Poe's short story 'Fishermen in the Maelstrom'.[76] In this tale, a fishing boat sailed by two brothers is sucked into the abyss of an enormous whirlpool. The older brother, immobilised by fear, is drawn into the maelstrom. The younger brother, exercising more self-control, observes the objects being drawn into the abyss and notices certain regularities in their process. His strategy of salvation relies on studying carefully how the maelstrom swallows up objects. The decisive link is not between the fisherman and the objects disappearing but in the in-between invisible bond of involvement or detachment. Detachment from the objects in terms of not looking at them is not the right procedure because in this case the observer fails to gain the insight in the workings of the mechanism. Conversely, too long an involvement with the objects would prevent the observer from acting and disengaging from this potentially deadly fascination.

In existential uncertainty and in the absence of genuine elites that can be creative in peaceful conditions, freedom is not given or legally guaranteed. In Jan Patočka's terms, freedom requires true drama to be acted out. Freedom does not begin after dramatic events – only once the struggle is concluded – but has its place precisely within it.[77] Those exposed to extreme situations of force are free in that they understand not by mere observation of facts but by an existential option to overcome demoralisation and despair. The lived experiences of extreme situations such as war, revolution, or other existential disruptions make the solidarity of the shaken appear, the solidarity of those who are capable of understanding what life and death are all about, and so what history is about. The work of subjectivity has been a work of emancipation based on breaking the ritualised logic of responding to violence with violence and on overcoming the collectivist rationality of second realities. What appears to be a futile and powerless attitude before an inalterable political structure at a given moment in time was a rational response in the means-to-end context of the situation.

The haziness of the visions alternative to a dominant political system must not cause them to be discarded as unrealistic. The articulation of dissidence was not only wishful thinking but must be taken as an authoritative form of power that provided for orientation, for markers of certainty. The experiential basis of the politics of dissidence was not a class of intellectuals with dispositions appropriate to party politics or electoral competition. Rather, it was based on the insight that any realistic

[76] Norbert Elias, *Involvement and Detachment* (Oxford: Blackwell, 1987), 48.
[77] Jan Patočka, *Heretical Essays in the Philosophy of History*, ed. James Dodd (Chicago and La Salle: Open Court, 1996), 133–7.

resistance would require dismantling the authority of second reality as the bedrock of communist power. What could be seen as wishful thinking, however, may command authority precisely because of the absence of the political rationality of professional politicians. In the empty space of power, vision and realism are not opposites but tend to coalesce. To discard dissident politics in eastern Europe or the indigenous communitarian ideal of *sobornost* as inadequate to the demands of a working democratic system is to empty democratisation of its historical and anthropological roots.

11 Democracy as a civilising process

> To 'fraternise' with another person did not, however, mean that a certain performance of the contract, contributing to the attainment of some specific object, was reciprocally guaranteed or expected ... The contract rather meant that the person would 'become' something different in quality (or status) from the quality he possessed before ... Each party must thus make a new 'soul' enter his body.   Max Weber

Problems of democratic essentialism

The two preceding chapters have argued that the experience of communism has been crucial for the historical composition of meanings of democracy. Democratic attitudes developed during the resistance of techniques of communist power that subordinated individual freedom to the collectivist logic of total images about the past and the future. This final chapter contrasts such an experiential approach with the popular and widely propagated idea of 'democratic consolidation'. Discourses of democratic consolidation subordinate logics of experiences to logics of outcome. Their epistemological basis rests upon a deliberative filter according to which communism and democracy were logically generated categories, characterised by non-communication and radical antagonism. In this view, the values and the systemic features of communist and democratic regimes seemed incompatible because situational premises were left largely unmentioned.

This chapter puts forward the hypothesis that the situational premises of 'unconsolidated' moments of uncertainty are crucial for understanding the emergence of democracy as a process of meaning-formation. In theories of democratic transition, consolidation is assumed to have failed when violence or incivility endangers the protection of the three things any social order that is embodied in a state is supposed to protect: life, property or other material life chances, and liberty. From an experiential perspective, however, democratisation can be followed through historical events that liberal democratic theory would consider coterminous with

269

the failure of consolidation. While democratic essentialism tries to tame uncertainty and violence through democratically shaped institutions, this chapter argues that the historical foundations of democracy develop under conditions of the absence of constitutional guarantees and of democratic 'values'. Instead, democratisation required a specific type of subjectivity, capable of interpreting the existential condition of people under oppression and of attributing meaning to experiences of violence and incivility.

Responding to the need to define the political distinctiveness of a democratic regime, the historical evolution of the Cold War shaped a consensus over 'what democracy is'.[1] This essentialist temptation has conceived of democracy as a complex set of operative guidelines that rest on rules of prudence, not on deeply ingrained habits of tolerance, moderation, mutual respect, fair play, readiness to compromise, and trust in public authorities. The argument implies that civic institutions and civility have emerged as a result of a long and uninterrupted period of democratic stability. According to this view, democracy institutionalises 'normal', limited political uncertainty. Thus, a civic culture is the product of institutions whose complex sets of rules keep consent contingent, while the prudence of actors keeps uncertainty bounded.

This essentialism advocates closure and dismisses the social processes, cultural foundations, and historical specificity of east European countries for challenging the totalitarian nature of communism. Prescribing 'what democracy is', the liberal consensus denies the possibility of an inquiry into democratisation before the breakdown of communism on two main grounds. On the one hand, the system of communist power prevented people outside the higher echelons of the ruling party from engaging in institutionalised conflict about power. On the other, these countries lacked democratic experience and civic culture because the communist system of power excluded the established democratic game of representative democracy.

Why has the idea of democratic transformations as processes of meaning-formation not been thematised in theories of democratisation? The rise of Soviet communism and its attempt to total subjugation of freedom to a goal of historical development has shifted the interest from the egalitarian impulse of the organisation of popular will towards the promotion of the guarantees of liberty through constitutional government. The 'procedural' approach to democracy criticised approaches

---

[1] Philippe C. Schmitter and Terry Lynn Karl, 'What Democracy Is ... and Is Not', in Larry Diamond and Marc F. Plattner, eds., *The Global Resurgence of Democracy*, 2nd edn (Baltimore: Johns Hopkins University Press, 1996), 49–62

such as Madisonian or populistic democracy as a method, which specifies
a set of goals to be maximised.[2] On the contrary, the polyarchal model of
democracy followed a descriptive method by which democratic nations as
members of a class are compared with a view to the characteristics they
have in common. After the collapse of communism, there is strong
evidence that the procedural approach – despite numerous variations
and nuances – has itself adopted an attitude by which it maximises a set
of goals. This maximisation of goals is not about a specific ideological
tenet such as avoidance of factions or popular sovereignty. Rather, it
subordinates culturally and historically specific meanings of democracy
to logically generated categories.

This spirit of 'maximisation' is reflected in various attempts to apply
a checklist of indices according to which Russia's democracy, for
instance, appears to be incomplete, partial, or derailed.[3] A self-declared
minimalist approach to democracy accepts the diversity of 'starting
points' but still postulates the need for convergence on the electoral
standard and a minimum standard of economic wealth.[4] While it is
minimal in content (the mere possibility of changing governments can
avoid bloodshed), it is 'maximalist' in form, setting goals that are seen as
essential in order to converge on a universally valid democratic standard.
A prominent classification suggested that a consolidated democracy as
the form of governance in a state would require five autonomous, but
interconnected, arenas.[5] Such conditions are a free and lively civil society
as well as a relatively autonomous and valued political society. Moreover,
there should be the rule of law for the sake of ensuring legal guarantees
for citizens' freedoms and independent associational life. Finally, there
must be a state bureaucracy usable by the new democratic government
and an institutionalised economic society. Driven by a belief in the
equilibrium of a constituted political order, this set of arenas and their
interconnection defines democracy as the only game in town by imposing
a logical construction as the starting point of democratisation. Cultural

[2] Robert A. Dahl, *A Preface to Democratic Theory* (Chicago and London: University of Chicago Press), 63.
[3] Stephen White, *Russia's New Politics: The Management of a Postcommunist Society* (Cambridge: Cambridge University Press, 2000), 275–82; Michael McFaul, *Russia's Unfinished Revolution: Political Change from Gorbachev to Putin* (Ithaca and London: Cornell University Press, 2002), 338–71; Steven M. Fish, *Democracy Derailed in Russia: The Failure of Open Politics* (Cambridge: Cambridge University Press, 2005).
[4] Adam Przeworski, 'Minimalist Conceptions of Democracy: A Defense', in Ian Shapiro, ed., *Democracy's Value* (Cambridge: Cambridge University Press, 1999), 23–55.
[5] Juan Linz and Alfred Stepan, *Problems of Democratic Transition and Consolidation: Southern Europe, South America and Post-Communist Europe* (Baltimore and London: Johns Hopkins University Press, 1996), 7–13.

resources such as memory, identity, or symbols are seen as depending on institutional arrangements without anthropological or historical dimensions of their own. Categories such as 'civil society' or the 'state' are made up of a variety of relatively autonomous sectors and fields, whose real differentiation can vary from one society to another. Democracy is emptied of the historically grown web of meanings, memory, psychological attraction, and representations. In such a view, democratic consolidation would require a degree of social unanimity that is quite unrealistic even in the context of established democracies. In another view, the communist legacy as undemocratic government and anti-modern type of rule is considered to be so contradictory to the essentials of democracy that the start of democratisation in 1990 is conceived as 'democratisation backwards'.[6]

There is a temptation to logically construct arenas in a 'pattern-state' as well as to classify political predispositions of states according to 'civil' and 'uncivil' legacies. Culture-oriented approaches to democratic development have claimed that variations in democratic outcomes can be explained by the availability of different degrees of cultural capital. The reification of civil society as causal of democracy is central to Robert Putnam's work on Italy, which traced the conditions of democracy back to civic participation in public affairs and the interaction of citizens as equals, based on mutual trust and respect.[7] While this view defined a civic legacy of northern Italy as the precondition of democratic development, it claimed that southern Italy had been dominated for centuries by a Hobbesian equilibrium of fear, anxiety, and danger, which thwarted co-operative outcomes. In a similar vein, the tendency to dichotomise Russian history between continuity and change has coloured much of the work on authoritarianism and democracy. The idea of claiming a long-standing existence of civil society as an alternative political culture before and after 1917 reifies history in another version of cultural determinism, which discovers democratic credentials in an ideal that is centuries old.[8]

Against this tendency to discover roots of democracy in an essence of culture, explicitly political perspectives downplay historical and cultural factors by highlighting the importance of individual choices of actors in

[6] Richard Rose and Neil Munro, *Elections Without Order: Russia's Challenge to Vladimir Putin* (Cambridge: Cambridge University Press, 2002), 41–60.
[7] Robert Putnam, Robert Leonardi, and Raffaella Nanetti, *Making Democracy Work: Civic Traditions in Modern Italy* (Princeton: Princeton University Press, 1993), 177–8.
[8] Jeffrey W. Hahn, 'Continuity and Change in Russian Political Culture', *British Journal of Political Science*, 21 (1991), 393–421; Nicolai Petro, *The Rebirth of Russian Democracy: An Interpretation of Political Culture* (Cambridge, MA: Harvard University Press, 1995).

the autonomous moment of the political. The complete disappearance of the coercive communist power system leaves a *tabula rasa*, which gives rise to attempts at 'democracy from scratch'.[9] This foundationalist claim about the autonomous moment of the political is problematic, as it presupposes that enlightened elites are endowed with preferences that are in accordance with a dehistoricised Western model of democratic institutions and liberal values.[10] Such institutional choices require being in tune with democracy as an institutional arrangement, i.e. to act appropriately with regard to dominant models and values of representative democracy as well as with their procedural determinants that express such values. If such institutional choices are not appropriate to the expected outcome of the procedural determinant of a democratic 'model', democracy can be regarded as 'derailed'.[11] In this vein, the lack of reciprocal accountability is responsible to a large extent for the poor quality of Russian democracy. While this view assigns much autonomy to individual choices, it essentialises the moment of the political choice in late 1991, while openly discarding cultural, historical, or social influences. While there is a case to argue that Russia could have been Poland but it also could have been Belarus, this juxtaposition implies comparability according to standards of liberal democracy, not with regard to historical articulation of meanings of democracy.

A further, more dynamic, perspective on consolidation looked at political regimes as a composite of partial regimes.[12] Consolidation, therefore, could be seen as a process whereby social relations can become social structures relying on patterns of interaction, which become so regular in their occurrence, so endowed with meaning, so capable of motivating behaviour, that they become autonomous in their internal functioning and resistant to externally induced change. From this perspective, consolidation would not only refer to the stabilisation of a single 'liberal-competitive' political arrangement but would also imply a process of ongoing transformation that would not preclude further political, social, and economic extensions of citizenship. In such a view, consolidation could include a wide variety of potential regime sub-types in a finely tuned way without pretending that everybody will adopt the same rules or norms. Furthermore, one could conceive of consolidation as the expansion of democratic (or, where the term does not fit, of fair,

[9] Steven M. Fish, *Democracy from Scratch* (Stanford: Stanford University Press, 1995).
[10] Giuseppe Di Palma, *To Craft Democracies: An Essay on Democratic Transitions* (Berkeley: University of California Press, 1990), 35.
[11] Fish, *Democracy Derailed in Russia*.
[12] Philippe Schmitter and Nicolas Guilhot, 'From Transition to Consolidation', in Michel Dobry, ed., *Democratic and Capitalist Transitions in Eastern Europe*, 131–46.

bargaining, co-operative, participatory) practices outside the narrow sphere of political parties and legislative–executive relations. In a similar vein, recent propositions suggested a dynamic model of consolidation, which would shift attention from procedural requirements in a given set of constitutionally guaranteed frameworks to the carriers of democratic development. Such a model of consolidation suggests the importance of a determined set of elites, the 'staff', who enforce democratic institutions. Any system of power can become consolidated only as far as this staff ensures that rulers and ruled behave in ways compatible with, and oriented towards, the perpetuation of formal institutional rules.[13]

The historical closure of democratic consolidation threatens to depoliticise politics, as it imposes liberal monism as the meaning of 1989.[14] It assumes a convergence on universally applicable variables such as free elections, economic performance, and reciprocal accountability. In this vein, the claim about the self-enforcing strength of democracy rests upon the assumption that all the relevant political forces find it best to continue to submit their interests and values to the uncertain interplay of the institutions.[15] However, this institutionalisation of democratic 'uncertainty' is connected to a high level of certainty about the enforcement of laws against subversive attempts and uncivil practices. This is precisely what political societies such post-revolutionary Russia after 1917 and post-Second World War eastern Europe, but also some post-communist states such as the Russian Federation, lack. While the criteria of democratic consolidation are in tune with the workings of a constituted system of power, they encase the contingent nature of politics in logically generated and culturally deterministic models of behaviour, values, and procedures. They burden social inquiry with a logic that all but rules out the haphazard and contingent character of a concept's historical articulation.

Theoretically, consolidation postulates different sets of essences that pre-exist historical action and thus deny endogenous sources of democratisation. While the definitions of democracy and their attributes vary, the model of the Western democratic state is established as a totality of thought, which de-democratises the post-communist experience. In a manner reminiscent of former antagonisms in the Cold War, democracies

---

[13] Stephen E. Hanson, 'Defining Democratic Consolidation', in Richard D. Anderson, et al., eds., *Postcommunism and the Theory of Democracy* (Princeton: Princeton University Press, 2001), 141.

[14] Jeffrey C. Isaac, *Democracy in Dark Times* (Ithaca and London: Cornell University Press, 1998).

[15] Adam Przeworski, *Democracy and the Market: Political and Economic Reforms in Eastern Europe and Latin America* (Cambridge: Cambridge University Press, 1991), 26.

are thus separated into 'good' and 'bad'.[16] Such essentialism implies that political transformations are somehow rooted in abstract, ahistorical foundations. These include the constitutionally guaranteed set of rules according to which democracy is the only game in town. Similarly, it presupposes individualism as the source of autonomous, 'democratic' choices. Finally, democracy becomes a goal of development, sustained by the values and procedures proper to liberal form of democracy. Democratic essentialism imposes democratic values generated in a specific historical context at the expense of the subjectivity of meanings of democracy.

This tendency to overdetermination has depoliticised the politics of transformation in a twofold manner. First, it has reduced complex societies to monolithic terms and condemned them to 'non-democracy' because they allegedly had the 'wrong' experiences. Such 'wrong' experiences are presented as a historical causality, which will influence future systemic arrangements in a given political culture. For instance, Czechoslovakia's democratic regime between the two world wars and between 1945 and 1948 was promising for democratic development, while the Russian 'sham constitutionalism' after 1905 and the abortive democracy in 1917 reinforced claims about the continuity of authoritarian political culture in post-communist Russia. Such statements establish causal links between the dispositions of actors in Russia before 1917 and in Czechoslovakia before 1948 not on the grounds of the meanings attached by people to events at the time; rather, the basis for judgements on democratic credentials is the values attached to the unexpected event of the collapse of communism.

A good illustration of why they are untenable is the German case. With hindsight, the success of the Federal Republic after 1949 proved the superiority of post-1949 German democracy as opposed to the negative experience of democracy in the Weimar republic. If the dispositions of elites before and after 1949 in West Germany are compared to that before and after 1989 in East Germany, however, the cultural heritage of Weimar Germany's democratic experiment with its attendant associational life and civic initiatives supported the creation of collective identities after 1945 and thus compensated for the material destruction in the war. While West Germany after 1949 was characterised by a devastated

---

[16] See the special issue: 'The Quality of Democracy in Post-Communist Europe', ed. Derek S. Hutcheson and Elena A. Korosteleva, *Journal of Communist Studies and Transition Politics*, 20 (March 2004), 1; Leonardo Morlino, '"Good" and "Bad" Democracies: How to Conduct Research into the Quality of Democracy', *Journal of Communist Studies and Transition Politics*, 20, 1 (2004), 5–27.

276 Democracy as a process of meaning-formation

economic infrastructure and material poverty, the cultural legacies of a sense of community, social trust, and national identification were crucial in rebuilding a prosperous market economy. On the contrary, the relative material wealth and intact infrastructure in post-communist East Germany after 1989 were accompanied by a lack of social cohesion, distrust, and shattered identities.[17]

Second, quite similar to the empirical theorisation of democracy after the Second World War as a narrow canon of empiricist methods, the doctrine of 'democratic consolidation' has purged political inquiry and the idea of democracy itself of its speculative and visionary impulses.[18] The functional-descriptive features of a constitutional form are reified in a variety of logically derived models that constrain experience to their normative requirements. The victory of liberal democracy has become a totality at the level of thought, granting democratic credentials largely to the external legal-rational exercise of government and thus depriving politics of its existential, symbolic, and anthropological ground. This entails the danger that any deviant forms are regarded as defective, authoritarian, or semi-dictatorships, but the closure of the political space at the level of restricting alternatives also comes down to de-democratisation. The disappointment and nostalgia of post-communist intellectuals are not so much due to their alleged utopianism. Rather, paradigms of transitions and consolidation have encased political development in logical constructions that essentially depoliticise and oppose democratic self-constitution.

The dramatic evolution of communism is at odds with the assumption of the most powerful 'theories' of democracy that fail to satisfactorily explicate the rejection of authoritarianism in Russia.[19] This accounts for Barrington Moore's structural-economic hypothesis 'no bourgeois, no democracy' as well as for economistic theories such as Adam Przeworski's that set a yardstick for the development of democracy in terms of a minimum range of economic growth. If democracy were dependent on the prerequisites of political culture along the lines set out by Gabriel Almond and Sidney Verba, seven hundred years of tsarist autocracy and seventy years of Soviet power would not be favourable preconditions. Finally, arguments stressing civic communities and associationalism in

[17] Claus Offe, *Varieties of Transition: The East European and East German Experience* (Cambridge, MA: MIT Press, 1997).
[18] Isaac, *Democracy in Dark Times*, 38–9.
[19] Philip G. Roeder, 'The Rejection of Authoritarianism', in Anderson, et al., *Postcommunism*, 19–22.

civil society such as those put forward by Robert Putnam are not compatible with the political reality of Soviet society.

The emergence of democracy

While discourses of democratic consolidation presuppose some degree of civility and civic attitudes, this book has argued that democratic aspirations result from the historical creativity of transformative experiences. A civilisational perspective understands 'waves of democratisation' as a sequence of transformative experiences and their symbolisations. From such a perspective, the incivility in revolutions and wars must not be taken as the failure of democratic consolidation, but it is there where the roots of democratic subjectivity are to be looked for. At bottom, the emergence of democracy has been an ongoing and, by definition, potentially endless process of how emotions are mastered as a response to violence. The political evolution of communism can be approached with a focus on situations that effect turns of subjectivity. Such turns of subjectivity are not results of preferences developed through reflection and rationality but arise from reactions of individuals to violent disruptions. Soviet communism as a political enterprise of human emancipation was successful because of its grip on the collective imagination of second reality. However, it failed largely because individual resistance mobilised emotions associated with their own past such as memory, diversity, and solidarity on a social scale. The consequences of such processes of identification were manifold and complex. They involved the grounding of subjective identity in moral perfectionism, in a life in truth but also in the powerful alternative reality of the West or the emotional appeal of national allegiance or cultural traditions.

Furthermore, this shift in individual dispositions requires the diffusion of existential attitudes and an ethic of individual life-conduct, which made people feel represented existentially. Before democratic preferences can be voiced in collective reflection, pressure groups, or acts of voting, the worthiness of individuals as equal and free in a social community must be recognised. Democracy is not based on autonomous preferences but has been a historically complex process where passions are checked by individual behaviour as a response to violence. Before founding elections can be organised, they must be accepted at least by moderates among former power incumbents and the citizenry as a legitimate means of attributing power. Before a civic culture becomes a distinctive element of a democratic system, one needs to look at civilising processes, which usually presuppose pre-political, unconsolidated, and underdetermined situations. Therefore, the civilising process needs to engage with situations that liberal democratic theory and much of comparative politics would consider coterminous with the failure of consolidation. While theories of consolidation impose democracy as a social end and a fixed point in the strategy of modernisation, democratisation in eastern Europe has not been a process of accommodation aimed at 'consolidation'. Rather, it has consisted of a sequence of fluid conjunctures, whose consolidation occurred through processes of symbolisation and meaning-formation. In a similar vein, the challenge of democratisation after communism has been the re-establishment of social bonds between citizens and the state, mutual trust, and civilisational competence.[20]

Waves of democratisation

Momentous political transformations such as the French and October Revolutions and the Second World War deepened the insight into the contagious nature of regime types and gave rise to conceptualisations such as totalitarian democracy.[21] Distinguishing between two types of democracy, liberal and totalitarian, Jacob Talmon located the essential difference between the two schools of democratic thought not in the affirmation of the value of liberty by the former and its denial by the latter. Rather, he suggested that it was in their different attitude to politics. While the liberal approach assumes politics to be a matter of trial and error allowing for conflict, the totalitarian democratic school takes its departure from a sole and exclusive truth in politics. It assumed a law-like linkage between the French and the October Revolutions, where the prospective salvation proclaimed by revolutionaries would forge the universalised faith that lay at the foundations of the totalitarian Soviet democracy. This interpretation rightly identified the moment of the disembodiment of monarchy in the French Revolution as the crossroads of two versions of democracy. This view, however, was still guided by the essentialism of predetermined forms of democracy, liberal or totalitarian, which are the moving forces of history.

Conceptual determinism and outcome-logic have equated notions of a legacy of the past with a dichotomy of a backward and a forward movement. The natural metaphor of waves of democratisation illustrates the sudden, sweeping, and overall character of political change during a

---

[20] Piotr Sztompka, *Trust: A Sociological Theory* (Cambridge: Cambridge University Press, 2000).

[21] Jacob L. Talmon, *The Origins of Totalitarian Democracy* (London: Secker & Warburg, 1952), 535.

determined period of time.[22] This metaphor has remained very popular. Some of the most remarkable works on the end of communism and its aftermath have studied the tidal waves of nationalism as crucial to the disintegration of the Soviet Union or have addressed the project of post-communism as rebuilding the ship on the open sea.[23] In Machiavelli's classical metaphor of *fortuna*, the experiential basis of historical contingency can be likened to 'those ruinous rivers which, when they get angry, flood the plans, ruin the trees and the buildings, take earth from this part and put it elsewhere: everyone flees before them, all yield to the impetus, without being able to bar it anywhere'.[24] Therefore, any substantial analysis of the chances for democracy and market capitalism in eastern Europe must interpret the maelstrom itself, and that means grasping the cultural, political, and economic 'inheritance' of forty years of Leninist rule.[25] Theories of democratic consolidation try to tame or solidify this maelstrom by positing some essential feature such as individual autonomy, democratic preference, or the rationality of a division of labour that remains unaffected by the tidal wave of the maelstrom.

Defining democracy as an institutionalised logic exogenous to communist Europe reifies it as a developmental goal guided by ahistorical forces such as modernisation, state centralisation, or economic liberalisation. The developmental perspective remains faithful to a dichotomic classification of forward-moving waves of democratisation and backward-moving reverse waves. Despite accepting the multiplicity of paths or stages, the goal of a liberal form of democracy subjects action to classificatory schemes of typological models.[26] It is the normative model of full political democracy, generated outside the historical context and artificially separated in logics of causality and outcome, not the historical articulation of democracy as an experience, a work of consciousness, and symbolisation, that remains the axis of analysis. A developmental perspective works on the basis of pre-existing goal values and the assumption that political ideologies such as communism or liberalism travel throughout time and history. From such a perspective, consolidation is obstructed once an electoral regime abuses individual and group rights

---

[22] Joe Foweraker, 'Waves of Democracy', in Paul Barry Clarke and Joe Foweraker, eds., *Encyclopedia of Democratic Thought* (London and New York: Routledge, 2001), 705–9.

[23] Jon Elster, et al., *Institutional Design in Post-Communist Societies* (Cambridge: Cambridge University Press, 1998); Mark Beissinger, *Nationalist Mobilization and the Collapse of the Soviet State* (Cambridge: Cambridge University Press, 2002).

[24] Niccolò Machiavelli, *The Prince*, trans. and ed. Angelo M. Codevilla, et al. (New Haven and London: Yale University Press, 1997), 91.

[25] Jowitt, *The New World Disorder*, 209.

[26] Larry Diamond, *Developing Democracy: Towards Consolidation* (Baltimore: Johns Hopkins University Press, 1999).

and thus fails to deepen legitimacy on a mass level. Consequently, many post-communist countries have been confronted with the gloomy picture of remaining chronically unconsolidated.[27] Finally, democracy may not only be reduced in its political quality over time, it may even effectively disappear, not merely through breakdown or overthrow but also through more insidious processes of decay. From a developmental perspective, such reverse waves are not assessed with regard to the formative power of existential uncertainty, but considered as failures of consolidation.[28]

Conversely, a perspective on democracy as a civilising process is logically distinguished from a developmental perspective on democratisation. Democracy as a process of meaning-formation reflects the substantive meaning of the civilising process, which refers to the elimination of violence from human relations.[29] Waves of democracy cannot be confined to an outcome 'after' communism but have to be problematised with regard to the fluidity of critical junctures, the violent manifestations of incivility, and their symbolisations. Democracy as a process of meaning-formation needs to engage with the boundlessness of action, where incivility threatens and uncertainty thwarts assumptions about outcomes. If there is an 'essence' to democracy, then it can be the question about what makes people denounce claims to total power, resist despotic and unaccountable rule, and submit decision processes about legitimate power to the scrutiny of public opinion and the ensuing act of voting. Before democracy becomes a system in which all players play according to the rules, however, the people in the community need to transform their spirit.

In his theory of the civilising process, Norbert Elias stressed the importance of understanding the part played by networks of interdependence and reciprocity.[30] The growing competition and increasing long-term interdependence with others were favourable to greater control of affects and emotions. The development of self-control and competition for

---

[27] Some authors predicted as the most probable outcome a 'protractedly "unconsolidated democracy"'; see Philippe C. Schmitter and Terry Lynn Karl, 'The Conceptual Travel of Transitologists and Consolidologists: How Far to the East Should They Attempt to Go?', *Slavic Review*, 53, 1 (1994), 185.

[28] Thomas Carothers, 'The End of the Transition Paradigm', *Journal of Democracy*, 13, 1 (2002), 5–21; Michael McFaul, 'The Fourth Wave of Democracy and Dictatorship: Noncooperative Transitions in the Postcommunist World', in Michael McFaul and Kathryn Stoner-Weiss, eds., *After the Collapse of Communism* (Cambridge: Cambridge University Press, 2004), 58–95.

[29] Arpad Szakolczai, 'Civilization and Its Sources', *International Sociology*, 16, 3 (2001), 369–86.

[30] Norbert Elias, *Über den Prozess der Zivilisation*, 2 vols. (Frankfurt am Main: Suhrkamp, 1994).

influence among courtly ruling groups at the outset of modernity was a paradigmatic case of a civilising process. Adopting Elias's work as a methodological approach to social and political reality, it is possible to attune the great divide between totalitarianism and democracy to critical events and their symbolisations. The concept of figuration conveys the notion of a dynamic network of interdependencies between individual or collective actors. A figurational approach to the emergence of democracy should bear in mind the complex emotional involvements of collective identity-formation. It undermines any assumption of division or polarisation between isolated individuals within society. According to Elias, individuals are not *homo clausus* but *homines aperti*. There is no 'I' without a 'you', no 'he' or 'she' without a 'we' or 'you'. Seen in this context, the rationalisation of violence assumes an individual and collective dimension, consisting of a psychological and social reality at the same time. In modern democracies, the rationalisation of emotions is extended and generalised. So is the rational exercise of violence. Monopolies of violence, formerly held by kings, princes, or territorial rulers, become the province of constitutional governments and legal bureaucracies. Relations between master and slave, between kings and subjects, between an imperial power and subordinate satellites, or between a higher and a lower civilisation must not be confined to the antagonism between two closed parts.

The evolution of democracy both as a system of government in Europe and as a political value that held parts of the elite and the populace under its spell should be seen as relying upon the duality of moral codes. While the moral code is egalitarian in character – with 'man', the human individual, as its highest value – the nationalist code derived from the Machiavellian code of princes and feudal power. It is inegalitarian in character, putting the collectivity – state, country, nation – in the position of the highest value.[31] The development of such a dual and inherently contradictory code of norms has been characteristic of transformation of states from aristocratic-dynastic into democratic in the Western world.

Democratisation processes in modern politics were the expression of how symbols for a collectivity became focal points for the emotional bonding of persons to this collectivity. The change in the pattern of people's 'us-and-them feelings', of identification and exclusion, was a primary condition for the development of nationalist sentiments, values, and beliefs.[32] The nation was characterised by shared and collectively

[31] Norbert Elias, *The Germans: Power Struggles and the Development of Habitus in the Nineteenth and Twentieth Centuries* (Cambridge: Polity, 1996), 154–5.
[32] Elias, *The Germans*,144–7.

recognised attitudes such as trust, self-restraint, and mutual respect. While the power politics described by Machiavelli presented the policy of unrestrained self-interest as the principles for rulers of states, self-interest was expanded in modern nation-states. Nevertheless, modern democratic states pursue power politics very much along Machiavelli's lines, though not in the name of princely self-interest but in the name of a nation. While sovereignty in monarchies focused on feelings of interpersonal loyalty and attachment, modern nation-states in the wake of the French Revolution relied to a much higher degree on attachments to symbols of the collectivity. This collectivity itself was endowed with a 'numinous existence of its own outside and above the individuals who formed it – with a kind of holiness formerly associated mainly with superhuman beings'.[33]

Bolshevik power required an unconditional subordination of the individual to the moral code of the collective that was the core of a rationally designed 'new socialist man'. Adapting the English maxim 'my country, right or wrong', Trotsky stressed that history did not provide another way to prove the correct line than to go with and through the party. If the dictatorship of the proletariat claimed the rule of the people as a collective body, the techniques of communist power all but eliminated the influence of the 'people' on political choices. Mass mobilisation in post-revolutionary and Stalinist Russia was intended rather in the conservative sense of keeping the ideological claim on a society without division alive. The absolute loss of individuality is best documented in the confessions of the accused party functionaries in the Moscow show trials. The dictatorship of the proletariat subordinated the moral code of the individual to the idolatry of the collective. The symbolism of identification of the enemy or the anti-fascist myth reinforced the practices of communist power by which the collective was given the capacity to discipline and control the Soviet-type individual.

This 'end of politics' as a practice of totalitarian regimes paradoxically can also be applied to the hegemony of the liberal model of democracy, which came to penetrate the Western world as the symbolic structure that maintained the Cold War. De-Stalinisation dissolved the dogma of communism's proclaimed inevitability and came to focus on the means for creating a social environment with a stronger emphasis on material rewards, social prestige, and upward mobility. Despite its anti-political attitude, dissidence in eastern Europe was realistic, as it reoriented political emotions away from a bias on second reality towards the

[33] Elias, *The Germans*, 146.

memories of individual pasts, from which to draw the solidarity of a nation with the weak and humiliated. The power of memory and the rejection of utopia provided for existential representation that shifted attention from the collective imagination of the 'future to come' or the greatness of a class or nation towards a more individualised and present-oriented approach to the community.

Democracy and subjectivity

Following methodological individualism, democracy as a constitutional form depends on reflective preferences, which occur internally, within each individual's head and not primarily in an interpersonal setting.[34] This view raises the importance of interests as a disciplined, sophisticated, and rational pursuit of advancing one's own power, influence, and wealth. 'Empirical' approaches see representative democracy as institutionalised competition for electoral votes by professional politicians who are guided by individual self-interest and the representation thereof on the aggregate level of party politics. Trying to discriminate between socialism and democracy, Joseph Schumpeter's 'realist' theory of democracy discarded the idea of a public good embodied in a general will. The general will is manufactured not by reason but by appeals to the subconscious, which makes the thinking of normal citizens affective and extra-rational, menacing with ominous consequences such as indulging in dark urges or paving the way for radical groups. Instead, he grounded his vision of democracy as a political method in a specific rationality according to which only the division of labour between the people and its representatives – which presupposes the insulation of governors from fickle public opinion – can promote the long-term interest of the state.[35] This view of empirical democracy as rooted in the political rationality of a division of labour echoes the development of interest as an individually based check to the passions, which was crucial for the expansion of modern capitalism.

The idea of autonomy as the individual's capacity to act on the basis of self-interest in the frame of constitutionally guaranteed claims and rights is at the basis of the workings of representative democracy. The civility and prudence of institutional democracy is based on self-interested politicians whose acceptance of the rules of the game guarantees predictability of institutionalised conflict. Liberal capitalism is largely sustained

---

[34] Robert E. Goodin, *Reflective Democracy* (Oxford: Oxford University Press, 2003), 7.
[35] Joseph A. Schumpeter, *Capitalism, Socialism, and Democracy*, 5th edn (London: George Allen & Unwin, 1976), 257–63.

by individual self-interest, which is a crucial condition for markets to function. According to Albert Hirschman, capitalist behaviour was not only a desperate search for individual salvation, as argued by Max Weber. It also owed much to an equally desperate search for a way of avoiding society's ruin, permanently threatening at the time because of precarious arrangements for internal and external order.[36] In a liberal view, markets are social settings where consumers nurture their *amour propre* (self-love) by a focus on the *amour de soi*, the radical pursuit of genuine self-interest. It is this individual self-interest that avoids the menace of contagion with the possible disintegration of markets in panic and disorder.

A political anthropology of transformative experiences is critical of the ontological stability of human self-interest. Rather, it maintains the primacy of subjectivity in the boundlessness of action, which decides whether people succumb to mimetic violence or whether they are able to avoid reciprocity and achieve reconciliation and peace. Rousseau's important distinction between *amour de soi* in the hypothetical pre-social state of nature and *amour propre* as contaminated by social order and generated out of envy, desires, and passions lacked the anthropological insight that in historical reality the formation of genuine self-interest cannot be detached from the bodily passions and violence. The crucial point is that the autonomy of individuals in institutionalised settings of constituted power is not only constrained, but also actively shaped by social experiences and representations thereof. In such situations, bounded uncertainty can be threatened by the boundlessness of action, and contingent consent can degenerate into the collective logic of forced consent in a persecuting crowd. Democratic institutions themselves can fall prey to contagion with passions. Even established democracies can become prey to this logic of annihilating the enemy by all means when they are existentially threatened. The democratic institutions of Athens condemned Socrates to death. The 'rampant liberalism' characteristic of the McCarthy era showed how democratic institutions can turn into the persecuting crowd, forcing the accused to make confessions of collective guilt, suggesting one great and unique enemy to the people of the United States.[37]

Interpreting democracy as a civilising process does not prescribe a teleology of historical evolution. Rather, the political practices developed throughout the civilising process of modernity can effectively undermine and eventually reverse this very civilising process. The substance that

---

[36] Albert O. Hirschman, *The Passions and the Interests* (Princeton: Princeton University Press, 1977), 130.

[37] Claude Lefort, *La complication. Retour sur le communisme* (Paris: Fayard, 1999), 24–34.

engenders democracy as a civilising force is different from variables
defined by standard accounts of empirical theories of democracy.
Nazism and the Holocaust are both good examples of how the techniques
and essential values of modernity and culture can be mobilised against
the civilising process, once legal and moral constraints break down.[38]
Uncertainty may be bounded in a political system but experiences of
existential uncertainty and projects of second reality can make fantasy
politics the authoritative frame of order and the basis of reality. This is
how the politicisation of life symbolised the identification of enemies on
the basis of 'race' in Nazism and of the 'proletariat' in communism. If
rhythms of the civilising process can be characterised as the balance
between the progressive restriction of violence and the intensification of
the role of conscience in human behaviour, then the process of the breakdown of such civilising results can be seen as a decivilising process.[39]
Democracy as a civilising process, therefore, suggests that the conditions
of the civilising process can turn against themselves.

While the democratic moment in 1989 dissolved the antagonistic distinction between the 'West' as the harbour of democratic rights and
stability and the 'East' as backward and lacking democratic experience,
the victory of Western-style democracy meant not only freedom, stability,
and dignity but also the politicisation of bare life in the eruptions of
unprecedented violence, uncivil war, and ethnic cleansing.[40] Among
the many dramas of post-communism, the Yugoslav wars and especially
the Bosnian catastrophe must be seen as symbolising the dark sides of
democracy. Jeffrey Isaac highlighted four meanings that are symbolised
by the Bosnian catastrophe. Bosnia can be taken as paradigmatic for a
profound crisis challenging international relations and security but also
defying Western democracies. Furthermore, Bosnia is not only a
reproach to democracy but also in some way its future, because massive
expulsion not only from there but also from numerous other places
threatens Western democracies with immigration. Bosnia also stands
for the crisis of democratic humanism, as the knowledge about what
was happening did not enable Westerners to prevent it. Finally, Bosnia
is the symbol of both mass violence and the impossibility of

---

[38] See the two major attempts to account for the social preconditions that facilitated the rise
of Nazi Germany and the Holocaust: Zygmunt Bauman, *Modernity and the Holocaust*
(Ithaca: Cornell University Press, 1989), and Elias, *The Germans*.
[39] Arpad Szakolczai, 'Decivilising Processes and Dissolution of Order with Reference to the
Case of East Europe', paper presented at the Norbert Elias Centenary conference, 1997,
Bielefeld, 7–8.
[40] John Keane, *Reflections on Violence* (London: Verso, 1996); Isaac, *Democracy in Dark
Times*.

compensation. Rather than implying that Bosnia belongs to the non-democratic part of the world, this proves how marginal democracy has remained also in the heart of Europe.

Unlike the outbreak of ethnic violence, the civilising effort in eastern Europe was prior to the institutional guarantees of civility in democratic systems. The politics of dissidence was a crucial factor for the renaissance of the concept of civil society as a trailblazer of the largely non-violent collapse of communist regimes. A related claim suggests that democracy can potentially tame or pre-empt outbreaks of incivility. In John Keane's view, democratic efforts to constitutionalise political power and 'civility politics' are sustained by anti-violence campaigns or peace movements.[41] This attempt to think 'democratically about violence' suggests that violence can be democratised through the public accountability for the means of violence. The civilising features of democracy rest upon the stability of the institutionalised logic of modern liberal democracies where attitudes and behaviour patterns are impervious to the irruption of 'incivility'. Although there is a legitimate case for civil society as the bearer of liberty against the mechanical application of majoritarian politics, the antagonism between institutional democracy and violent incivility is flawed from an experiential perspective. Discussing it at length, Keane misinterprets mimetic violence as a 'natural' and 'deep-seated predisposition' in every individual.[42] The underlying assumption is that democratic constitutionalism with its principle of the rule of law is fundamental for keeping passions and incivility in check. What is 'natural', however, is not the individual predisposition to violence. Rather, mimetic contagion with a propensity to cycles of vengeance and violence threatens when the boundaries of law and civility hold no longer. Human aggressiveness arises as a socially generated relational process and not as an innate attribute of mankind.[43] It is the social magic of violent acts, not the normative imperative of preserving legal ends, that can be considered as the foremost motivation for law's interest in a monopoly of violence.[44]

Democratisation as a process of meaning-formation belies the 'objective' political outcomes of critical events. The preferences and dispositions of dissidents were not inherently democratic in terms of recognising and

---

[41] John Keane, *Violence and Democracy* (Cambridge: Cambridge University Press, 2004), 90.

[42] Keane, *Violence and Democracy*, 8.

[43] Norbert Elias, 'Violence and Civilization: The State Monopoloy of Physical Violence and its Infringement', in John Keane, ed., *Civil Society and the State* (London: Verso, 1988), 177–8.

[44] Walter Benjamin, *Reflections: Essays, Aphorisms, Autobiographical Writings* (New York: Schocken Books, 1986), 280–1.

playing according to the rules of the only game in town. Before the deliberation about constitutional rules and norms and prior to the recognition of a constitutional act, a democratic spirit needs to convey freedom as existentially representative, something that requires experiences of communities of fate and the transformation of consciousness. Historically, the emergence of popular consciousness as being democratic was marked by the performative symbolisation of the people's sacrifice for the attainment of freedom in a community. Since Pericles' speech to the Athenians in 430 BC or Abraham Lincoln's Gettysburg address in 1863, this theatrical dimension of democratisation has been tightly linked to the dramatic setting of war or revolution. Pericles' speech praised the Athenian people for living a form of government that did not emulate the institutions of its neighbours but itself was a model, a paradigm to be imitated. In the Gettysburg address, Lincoln identified the people as the basis, the actor, and the beneficiary of democratic government. The theatricality of oratory performance was not related to legal guarantees but to the socially traumatic experiences of the supreme sacrifice of giving up one's life for one's fellow citizens in the community. Both speeches are eulogies to honour the war dead in either the incipient Peloponnesian war or the battle of Gettysburg in the American Civil War.

These examples of rhetorical affirmations of democratic credentials of a nation came from the official stage from which those in authority speak to those whose public affairs they want to govern. If these famous examples of performative symbolisation of the democratic credentials of a political community related to cases that had democratic practices before they actually named them as such, eastern Europe presents somehow the opposite case. Whereas the people as a political subject is relatively uncontested in the Greek or the American examples, in many east European countries the constitution of the people as a political subject has been a task for political symbolism and myth-making. The theatricality of various dramatic social occurrences in eastern European life was characterised by belated state-formation, wars, and revolutions, mass expulsions, and foreign domination. Territorial boundaries were uncertain and the people as a political subject was more of a project than a reality. Democratisation as a process of meaning-formation must take into account the infrapolitics of the oppressed and downtrodden; the power of the weak or the powerless may threaten the political symbolism that an authoritarian or totalitarian regime has erected.[45]

[45] James Scott, *Domination and the Art of Resistance* (New Haven and London: Yale University Press, 1990); Václav Havel, 'The Power of the Powerless', in John Keane, ed., *The Power of the Powerless: Citizens Against the State in Eastern Europe* (London: Hutchinson and Co., 1985), 23–96.

As Oleg Kharkhordin showed, civil society cannot be confined to Western versions that rest on ethical life in Protestant or Catholic congregations. Rather, there has been a Russian version of civil society that relied on Orthodox Christianity and advocated non-militaristic and civilised life.[46] It aimed at defending individuals from state encroachments on their liberties and its main feature was to strive to entirely supplant the secular state and its use of the means of violence by making church-based means of influence the basis of all sectors of human life. While the Soviet collective, to a certain extent, defended an individual against attacks of his or her immediate bosses, it was unfree in two fundamental aspects. The official collectives were created by decisions from above, and within the organisation the individual had no freedom and hardly any defence against denunciation or terror. In view of an increasingly uncivil post-communist Russian society, where the weak state depends on a large number of semi-public or utterly private entities that use violent methods to keep normal life going, it seems that an idea of civil society based on associational life that opposes or controls the state is difficult to attain. A project of building civil society on the Orthodox model would not favour a strategy of strengthening the state by monopolising violence but rather would promote the diffusion of civil, non-violent ways of life by relying on networks of friendship. While this seems idealistic and dangerous in practice, it acknowledges the endogenous conditions of networks of friendships and the cultural, domestic roots of the civilising process.

Civilising violence

Valuable work on civil society has recognised the connection between a strong civil society and the avoidance of violence.[47] Its fundamental point is that institutionally crafted political democracy generates spaces of civility that account for dual autonomy and independent deliberation. From a liberal perspective, civility under totalitarian rule remains uncultivated. Empirical democratic theory has thus made a case for considering civic culture as a product rather than a producer of democracy.[48] Hence, only a democratic civil culture can potentially tame or pre-empt outbreaks of incivility. Any definition of 'what democracy is', however,

---

[46] Oleg Kharkhordin, *Main Concepts of Russian Politics* (Lanham, MD: University Press of America, 2005), 41–65.
[47] Laurence Whitehead, *Democratisation: Theory and Experience* (Oxford: Oxford University Press, 2002), 81; Keane, *Violence and Democracy*.
[48] Schmitter and Karl, 'What Democracy Is . . . and Is Not', 58.

seems to be flawed if democratic transformations are released from out-
come-oriented logical constructions and attuned to the experiential basis
of their symbolic articulation.

The civilising process is not congruous with the pursuit of a democratic
ideal based on abstract notions of individualism, autonomy, or a pre-
existing civic culture. Individual self-constraint is not a timeless category
by which political behaviour could be modelled, but can be seriously
affected in existential crisis. In a perceptive analysis of the influence of
economic thought on the current political philosophy of liberalism, Jean-
Pierre Dupuy has shown how major exponents of liberal thought systematically avoid confronting the real menace of contagion, disorder, and
sudden breakdowns of capitalist markets such as in mass panics.[49] As he
argued, markets contain the crowd and the potential disintegration into
panic as the autonomy of individual self-interest is menaced by the
contagion in the reciprocity of emotions. Markets endogenously *contain*
the mechanism that threatens them most. Etymologically rich, the double
meaning of 'to contain' is more than just a word game; it simultaneously
connotes inclusion and exclusion. The market contains the contagion of
panic in two ways. While the market impedes panic from breaking out
due to the pursuit of self-interest, the interest-based logic of the market
dissolves in the outbreak of passions such as in panics at stock markets
or rampant inflation. In this vein, Adam Smith's concept of self-love
includes the reciprocity of passions and interests. Concerned with the
'great mob of mankind', i.e. with the behaviour of the average person,
Smith defined self-interest as the craving for honour, dignity, respect, and
recognition.

If the logic of self-interest in markets prevents the uncontrolled outbreak of emotions, the situational premises of existential uncertainty may
cause panic once order dissolves and mimetic passions break loose. From
this perspective, the self-assertiveness of liberal democracy as a system
based on essentials such as individualism and self-interest cannot be
detached from the potential for contagion by critical events or revolutionary situations. The crucial point is that, despite the political antagonism and the military confrontation of the Cold War, democracy has
emerged not against but within communism. Etymologically, emergence
refers to rising from a liquid by virtue of buoyancy. Combining the Latin
roots *ex* (out) and *mergere* (to dip, sink), 'emergence' suggests that the new
has been contained by the old from within which it rose. The related noun
'emergency' with the meaning of 'unforeseen occurrence' suggests its

---

[49] Jean-Pierre Dupuy, *Liberalisme et justice sociale* (Paris: Calmann-Lévy, 1992), 329.

relatedness to uncertainty. Following the symbolisations of critical events and the processes of meaning-formation, it can be argued that threats of contagion with violence have been central to overcoming communism by a specific type of subjectivity.

Ideas about the essence of democracy as a method of changing governments determine 'what democracy is'. During the Cold War, liberal democracy was fundamentally opposed to communism. Essentialist arguments, however, have to face the historical fact that the potential for contagion with communism not only threatened a military confrontation but, at the level of communication and penetration, reinforced the liberal conception of democracy. This is why it can be contended that democracy contained communism in a double sense, both in terms of separation and inclusion. In most straightforward terms, this is the story of the Cold War, throughout which democratic countries provided an effective stronghold against the military expansion of Soviet communism. The primacy of the military confrontation in the Cold War focused so much on the externalisation of the other system as 'evil' that the internal drives were all but overlooked. The main threat to Western democracy was not an imminent Soviet attack but the poor condition of European post-war economies and the social and political instability resulting from this. The policy of containment was largely based on the argument that it served the economic interests of the United States and Europe. Containment policy was a successful attempt to avoid the contagion of Western economies by communism. Democracy contained communism also in the second, inclusive, sense. Any serious assessment of the contest between democracy and communism must face the fact that before monopolising the political space in Russia and eastern Europe, Soviet communism contained a tyrannical impulse that merged with the democratic conditions of mob rule. To the extent that the democratic age was propitious for a totalitarian type of political domination, the reality of communist power menaced Western democracies with contagion. The threat to the 'civilised' Western world during the Cold War consisted in the potential contagion of essentials of democracy. Thus, containment policy not only 'externalised' evil but also was a response to the revolutionary and egalitarian nature of democracy as prone to dissolve self-interest in the panic and disorder characteristic of crowd psychology.

This claim cannot be 'proved' but it might be supported by evidence about how liberal democracy designated itself as an absolute alternative. The Cold War was not only a struggle against totalitarianism, but was also primarily a defence of the liberal model of democracy as a universal value. According to Louis Hartz's study of the liberal tradition in the United States, democratisation in that country emphasised the result of revolution on individual 'freedom'. Tocqueville's central insight – that it was the United States' great advantage that it did not have 'to endure a democratic revolution' – has been all but forgotten.[50] In the absence of the need for a social revolution for the sake of political emancipation, this democratically born country had little sensitivity to social grievances and their political consequences. The psychological heritage of a nation 'born equal' produced liberal absolutism as a frame of mind, which in a war of ideologies would have two automatic effects: it hampers creative action abroad by identifying the alien with the unintelligible, and it inspires hysteria at home by generating the anxiety that unintelligible things produce.

The aggressive anti-communism of the United States in the absence of a concrete military confrontation with the Soviet Union was based on the pervasive fear of contagion with the disease of communism.[51] The fear of contagion became manifest in the hysteria of the 'Red Scare', when McCarthyism made liberal absolutism a totality against the menace of totalitarianism. The fear of the contagion by the 'Other' has been constitutive for the representations of communism in the West as the 'evil empire' as well as for the ascendancy of the West as an empire of the mind in communist countries. When the nation rises to an irrational anti-communist frenzy, it replies to the same instinct, which tends to alienate it from Western democratic governments that are 'socialist'. When it closes down dissent, it answers the same impulse that inspires it to define dubious regimes elsewhere as 'democratic'. This is the peculiar link that a liberal community forges between the world and the domestic picture: its absolute perspective, its 'Americanism'.[52]

Western democracies under the leadership of the United States were engaged not only in a struggle for spheres of political influence or economic and military ascendancy. Democracy was also turned into a prescriptive ideal, standing for a morally superior alternative civilisational truth and source of authority. The ossification of the Cold War confirmed Kennan's intuition that the Americans had failed in their effort to avoid contagion with the virus of totalitarianism. The long post-war struggle against the Soviet Union and its allies would even vindicate the alignment

[50] Louis Hartz, *The Liberal Tradition in America* (New York: Harvest, 1955), 35.
[51] Arnold Toynbee, 'Looking Back Fifty Years', in Royal Institute of International Affairs, ed., *The Impact of the Russian Revolution 1917–1967: The Influence of Bolshevism on the World Outside Russia* (Oxford: Oxford University Press, 1967), 1–31.
[52] Hartz, *The Liberal Tradition in America*, 285.

with the democratic camp of unabashed dictatorships such as those in Indonesia, South Korea, Taiwan, South Vietnam, and Chile. The Cold War was also a struggle over the political ownership of the notion of democracy and accounts for its saliency across the world.[53]

While before 1917 the United States had promoted revolutionary movements of national liberation, after the rise of Bolshevism the majority of Americans regarded anti-Russian attitudes as a badge of respectability. While two world wars against German militarism were followed, in the first case, by American isolationism and, in the second, by West Germany's integration in the Western world, Bolshevism was shunned like an infectious disease. While the fear of contagion between Western democracies and the communist hemisphere was based on hypothetical assumptions, it should not be forgotten that democracy at the end of the Second World War in other parts of Europe was far from being 'consolidated', if any measure of comparison is applied. Given the strong communist parties in France and Italy, for instance, fears of their potential victory in elections were very real.

The threat of contagion with the totalitarian enemy reinforced a universal appeal of the values of liberal democracy. The 'imperial modernisation' of communist power as a practice concealed the absolutism of liberalism at the level of symbolic representation. Consequently, forms of socialist democracy could be reformed only by liberalisation before being institutionally transposed into liberal types of democracy. This is reminiscent of Carl Schmitt's point that waging wars in the name of humanity is not war for the sake of humanity. Rather, a state can usurp the universal concept of humanity for the purpose of self-identification with humanity, peace, justice, progress, or civilisation, thus denying these to the enemy or military opponent.[54]

The potentiality of contagion between the two regimes allows the conjecture that communism contained democracy. Here, the exclusive meaning rests upon the understanding that communism prevented representative parliamentary institutions and a constitutionally guaranteed framework of rule of law from being established as a governmental practice. By dissolving the Constituent Assembly in January 1918 and by thwarting party competition and free elections almost everywhere in eastern Europe, the Bolsheviks contained democracy. Yet, communism also contained democracy in a second, inclusive, meaning. The political

---

[53] John Dunn, Setting the People Free: The Story of Democracy (London: Atlantic Books, 2005), 157–8.

[54] Carl Schmitt, The Concept of the Political (Chicago: University of Chicago Press, 1996), 54.

symbolism of communism imposed a class-based model of totality in the People-as-One, which would appropriate total control over society, set its laws, redefine its past, and predict its future. Communism appeared in 'backward' and 'underdeveloped' countries and lasted for longer than the Nazism and fascism, not least because it espoused democratic values and tended to avoid rather than seek international war. It insisted that the violent recasting of society was the way to achieve genuine liberty, equality, and fraternity while catching up with the world leaders of industrial development. Although the self-assessment of communist regimes as people's democracies was often ridiculed, communism bequeathed symbols such as the dictatorship of the proletariat or the transition to communism as well as an unfulfilled desire for democracy. The absence of political democracy as an institutionalised logic of the liberal type must not be reduced to a general claim about eastern Europe's undemocratic tradition. Communist leaders claimed to embody true democracy: not because of a substantial contribution to political democracy, but because this claim was part of the existential struggle for legitimising power domestically and for achieving international recognition.[55] This self-assessment as true democracy and the simultaneous legitimacy crisis was not simply meaningless but formed the background before which communism's double bind as a ruthless power system and its political symbolism of the People-as-One in a transition to communism coalesce.

The precondition for democratisation under communism was the development of a moral code that reinforced the egalitarian value of the human being and the respect for bare life against the sacrificial and ritualistic logic of communist power. How could individual moral codes overcome the ritualistic communist machinery of violence and vengeance? Anti-politics in eastern Europe pursued a meaningful life by overcoming the distortion of reality through individual acts in everyday reality. The starting point for a divorce from the logic of conformism is the decision to stop lying.[56] The attempt to overcome the corruption of everyday life in communist reality came down to the desire for the 'destatification' of the social reality created by communist power. 'Because politics has flooded nearly every nook and cranny of our lives, I would like to see the flood recede. We ought to depoliticise our lives, free them from politics as from some contagious infection.'[57] This distinction

---

[55] Lefort, *La complication*, 109.   [56] Havel, *The Power of the Powerless*, 43
[57] György Konrád, *Antipolitcs: An Essay*, trans. from the Hungarian by Richard E. Allen (San Diego/New York/London: Harcourt Brace Jovanovich, 1984), 229.

between two different dimensions, two separate spheres, disconnected anti-politics from government. As an act of self-defence, any pressure exerted by anti-politics is confined to its cultural and moral stature alone, renouncing any electoral legitimacy.

Much as the efficiency of the sacrificial rite in pre-modern societies depended on the unanimous participation of everybody in the community, representative democracy works not due to a specific substance, but on the basis of the participation of the public in the ritual of elections. Democracy is a ritual of participation in which substantial issues such as the popular will are symbolically crucial for maintaining popular sovereignty as enabling the division of labour of elites competing for power. However, when this very sovereignty is supposed to manifest itself in the act of voting, the substance of popular will, social solidarities, and civic identities is dissolved. In the uncertainty of the democratic decision, numbers replace substance in the mathematical exercise of counting votes.[58]

Before 'democrats' respect political rights, civil liberties, and constitutional constraints, however, they must overcome the incivility of violence. While the normative prescriptions of democratic essentials are useful to regulate the workings of constituted systems of power, the experiential basis of democratisation as a process of meaning-formation points to how the democratic spirit is asserted through the symbolisation of often traumatic experiences. Before humans institutionalise conflict in order to avoid killing each other, violence and incivility must be overcome by breaking claims to total power and the sacrificial logic of eliminating enemies. The hallmark of dissidence from the communist logic of power was rooted in attitudes and behaviour that were grounded in individual subjectivity, seeking to conduct a life in quest of truth, in a meaningful relation to the world. The underground activities of dissidence by means of the hidden transcript exerted constant pressure, much as a body of water might press against a dam.[59] The amount of pressure varies according to the degree of shared anger and indignation but also the degree to which parts of the hidden transcript leak through and increase the probabilities of a complete rupture. Breaching the ritualistic and sacrificial logic of communism required rejecting the identification of the enemy, and the totalising symbolism of second reality. While these processes of meaning-formation became diffused into the social body, the shaping of the collective psychology of citizens relied upon individual acts. Much as the Christian doctrine demanded truly aristocratic qualities

[58] Claude Lefort, *Essais sur le politique* (Paris: Seuil, 1986), 30.
[59] Scott, *Domination and the Art of Resistance*, 196 and 219.

for salvation, true democracy requires the aristocracy of the mind.[60] Dissidence, truth-telling, and communitarian ways of experiencing democratic attitudes exerted considerable pressure against the dams of repression, breaking these dams and entering the public sphere in peaceful revolutions.

---

[60] Max Weber, *Economy and Society: An Outline of Interpretive Sociology*, ed. by Guenther Roth and Claus Wittich (Berkeley: University of California Press, 1978), 632; Thomas Mann, 'Vom zukünftigen Sieg der Demokratie', in *Essays*, ed. Hermann Kurzke and Stephan Stachorski, vol. IV (Frankfurt am Main: Fischer, 1995), 227.

Index